Even a short list of Bette Davis's most famous films — *Of Human Bondage; Now, Voyager; All About Eve; What Ever Happened to Baby Jane?* — reveals what a major force she was in Hollywood. Her distinctive voice, her remarkable eyes, her range and depth of characterization, all combined to make Bette Davis one of the finest performers in movie history. Drawing on conversations with Davis during the last decade of her life, Charlotte Chandler's biography is a brilliant portrait of an enduring icon from Hollywood's golden age. From her teenage decision to act, through the pressures of fame, failed marriages and the pain of her daughter's betrayal, Davis speaks with candour and comes to life, as forceful a presence in these pages as she is onscreen.

Books by Charlotte Chandler
Published by The House of Ulverscroft:

IT'S ONLY A MOVIE
Alfred Hitchcock, A Personal Biography

CHARLOTTE CHANDLER

THE GIRL WHO WALKED HOME ALONE

Complete and Unabridged

CHARNWOOD
Leicester

First published in Great Britain in 2006 by
Simon & Schuster UK Limited
London

First Charnwood Edition
published 2007
by arrangement with
Simon & Schuster UK Limited
London

British Library CIP Data

Chandler, Charlotte
    The girl who walked home alone: Bette Davis.
    —Large print ed.—Charnwood library series
    1. Davis, Bette, *1908* – 2. Davis, Bette, *1908* –
    —Interviews 3. Motion picture actors and
    actresses—United States—Interviews 4. Motion
    picture actors and actresses—United States—
    Biography 5. Large type books
    I. Title
    791.4′3028′092

    ISBN 978–1–84617–649–4

Published by
ᗡ ᐱ   F. A. Thorpe (Publishing)
Anstey, Leicestershire

Set by Words & Graphics Ltd.
Anstey, Leicestershire
Printed and bound in Great Britain by
T. J. International Ltd., Padstow, Cornwall

This book is printed on acid-free paper

To Bette

Bette Davis

A PERSONAL BIOGRAPHY

'I always take out two women.
I hate to see a girl walk home alone.'

— Groucho Marx, to Charlotte Chandler

Acknowledgments

With special appreciation

Bob Bender, John Springer, Robert Lantz,
and David Rosenthal

With appreciation

Michael Accordino, Chuck Adams, Jan Anderson, Enrica Antonioni, Michelangelo Antonioni, Amelia Antonucci, Dennis Aspland, Linda Ayton, Roy Ward Baker, Marcella Berger, Joan Blondell, Ernest Borgnine, David Brown, Kevin Brownlow, Horst Buchholz, Fred Chase, Larry Cohen, Joan Collins, Joseph Cotten, Joan Crawford, George Cukor, Richard Dalton, Gypsy da Silva, Olivia de Havilland, Mitch Douglas, Lisa Drew, Douglas Fairbanks, Jr., Rudi Fehr, Jean Firstenberg, Geraldine Fitzgerald, Marie Florio, Henry Fonda, Joe Franklin, Steve Friedeman, Roy Furman, Bob Gazzale, Anthony Gentile, Lillian Gish, Milton Goldman, Tracey Guest, Alec Guinness, Dick Guttman, Robert Haller, Marvin Hamlisch, Harry Haun, Edith Head, Paul Henreid, Arthur Hiller, Celeste Holm, Lucy Jarvis, Peter Johnson, Fay

Kanin, Wendy Keys, Alexander Kordonsky, John Landis, Ted Landry, Jerome Lawrence, Christopher Lee, Mervyn LeRoy, Johanna Li, Norman Lloyd, Joshua Logan, Sirio Maccioni, Karl Malden, Joseph Mankiewicz, Groucho Marx, James Mason, Dieter Mueller, Jeremiah Newton, Arthur Novell, Mary Orr, Jerry Pam, Irving Rapper, Debbie Reynolds, Robert Rosen, Ellen R. Sasahara, Sidney Sheldon, Vincent Sherman, Eugene Simion, Joe Sirola, Alberto Sordi, Ann Sothern, Gary Springer, June Springer, Jeff Stafford, James Stewart, Meryl Streep, Richard Todd, Jonah Tully, Brian Ulicky, King Vidor, Emlyn Williams, Tennessee Williams, Will Willoughby, Robert Wise, William Wyler.

The Academy of Motion Picture Arts and Sciences, the American Film Institute, Anthology Film Archives, the British Film Institute, the Cinémathèque Française, the Film Society of Lincoln Center, the Italian Cultural Institute of New York City, the Museum of Modern Art, the New York Public Library for the Performing Arts, the Plaza Athénée Hotel (Paris), the Royal Lancaster Hotel (London), The Savoy Hotel (London), Turner Classic Movies, UCLA Department of Theater, Film, and Television.

Contents

Prologue

Behind those Bette Davis eyes, under the blue eye shadow, beneath the false eyelashes was the private Bette no one, not even Bette herself, really knew. The world knew only her extended self — the image of her as reflected in the parts she played, 'all those bitches I had to take everywhere with me.'

'When I die,' Bette Davis told me, 'they'll probably auction off my false eyelashes.'

And they did.

At the estate auction held at Doyle's Auction House in New York City, Bette's treasured soup tureen, her prized dining room chairs, and a box of her false eyelashes were featured.

The eyelashes brought $600.

★ ★ ★

'On the occasion of Elizabeth Taylor's fiftieth birthday,' agent Robert 'Robby' Lantz told me, 'there was a tremendous party planned at the home of Carole Bayer Sager, who was three doors away from Elizabeth's.'

Lantz was invited to the party, as was Bette Davis, whom he represented for many years, and who was his friend.

'I told Bette that I would take her to the party.

'I'll come by and pick you up at nine o'clock.'

'She said, 'The invitation is for eight o'clock. If I'm invited at eight, I'm coming at eight.'

'I said, 'Bette, I know Elizabeth for a hundred years. I love her dearly, but eight o'clock for Elizabeth means ten. So let's go at nine.'

'She said, 'No. No, no, no!' So, that's all. I do what Bette wishes.

'I picked her up. We arrive at the house, and there's no sign of Elizabeth. There aren't many people there. Gradually, by nine-thirty, maybe a little later, the house had filled with everybody of any consequence in Hollywood; heads of studios, stars, directors, agents.

'The fiftieth birthday of Elizabeth Taylor!

'Bette sat in a big chair in the drawing room, and she didn't look at all pleased. As time went on, she looked even less pleased. She said to me, 'I am not enamored of big parties!'

'I knew we weren't going to get started with dinner until after ten and that Bette was probably going to want to leave early. I made a plan so we could get up and disappear. I arranged with the driver where he should be with the car.

'And that's exactly what happened. Bette had already been there so long, she didn't want to stay until the end of the dinner. We left, and I was hoping we wouldn't be noticed.

'But as we went toward the car, we heard the sound of someone wearing high heels running after us. It was Elizabeth. Running right behind her was Michael Jackson.

'Elizabeth was so out of breath that it took a

moment before she could speak. 'Robby,' she said, 'could you please ask Bette if she wouldn't mind. All Michael wants is, please, could he have his photograph taken with her.'

'Now, Bette was standing right there, but Elizabeth addressed her request to me, rather than to Bette, so I could act as her agent.

'Michael Jackson was at the height of his fame, but that didn't matter to Bette. What mattered to her was that she had been a guest in Elizabeth's house, and it was Elizabeth's birthday.

'Bette reached into her small evening bag and took out her lipstick. It was dark, but she didn't need to look into a mirror as she put it on.

'Bette moved close to Michael, who was trembling slightly, and posed, smiling directly at the camera.

'With Michael's camera, which she had taken from him, it was Elizabeth who took the picture.

''Take one more to be sure,' Bette said, and Elizabeth did.

'Bette Davis was a true star's star.'

★ ★ ★

Princess Diana learned from her hairdresser, Richard Dalton, that he had been invited to meet Bette Davis, who was in London to promote her book *This 'n That*. Thrilled by the opportunity to meet her favorite actress, Diana delegated Dalton to invite Bette to Kensington Palace to have tea with the Princess.

At the television station, Anne Diamond, the show's hostess, introduced her friend, Dalton, to

3

Bette Davis, who was seated on the set.

Dalton was stunned to see how frail the actress was. After numerous serious illnesses, she was skeletal, her face terribly drawn. In one bony hand, she held a cigarette.

Bette relished a long breath of smoke, then slowly looked Dalton up and down as she exhaled. 'Sit down, young man,' she enunciated quite precisely.

Dalton sat down.

Bette was smoking continuously. Occasionally, she reached for a silver goblet. There were whispers that it contained something more than water.

Dalton never found out what the goblet contained, nor did he care. He was amazed that the actress, appearing so ill, was able to carry on at all; but carry on she did, purposefully, astounding everyone present. Everyone there felt that the TV audience would be pleased by their amazing Bette Davis interview.

After the show, Dalton nervously delivered the royal invitation to Bette Davis. He knew how dear to the heart of Diana the invitation was and how much she was looking forward to tea with the great star, and he did his best to convey this. He was anxious to come through for the Princess.

Bette answered without hesitation, but it wasn't the answer Dalton was expecting.

'I have never met royalty,' she replied, 'and it's far too late now.'

Dalton tried to persuade her, to *dissuade* her from her objections. All for naught. He returned to Kensington Palace with his negative report.

He had tried his utmost, but the young and beautiful Princess was not accustomed to hearing the word no. She was dismayed, terribly disappointed, and perplexed.

'What did Bette Davis *mean?*' she asked Dalton. Princess Diana did not live to be old enough to understand.

Introduction

'One must live in the present tense, but I have always lived in the present tensely,' Bette Davis told me.

'I have few regrets, not because I've done everything in my life perfectly, but because my mother, Ruthie, instilled in me the idea that I should never think about what I've missed, only about what I'm missing.'

From the time she was a little girl, Bette felt that life had something exceptional waiting for her, and that it would find her or that she would find *it*.

'None of us knows what our future will be, but you might say I was born with two crystal balls.

'I wanted the lioness's share. I had to be the best. I'm an overachiever. I always had the will to win. I felt it baking cookies. They had to be the *best* cookies anyone ever baked. But there was a price to pay.

'If a man is dedicated to his work, he's more of a man. If a woman feels that way, she's *less* of a woman. Those same qualities that women find so absolutely wonderful in a man, men don't find so wonderful in a woman.

'I'm the one who didn't get the man, which is the more interesting character on the screen, but in real life sometimes I wish I could just have been the girl who got the man, and kept him. I got four husbands and several lovers, but I didn't keep any of them. I was invited to the White House, but no man stayed to share *my* white cottage.'

She enjoyed being Bette Davis but sometimes it was a burden. 'People wished to see the character they saw on the screen, or there were looks of disappointment on their faces.

'They actually expect you to *be* certain characters they saw in the films. They think I'm a difficult person because of the parts I've played. They're disappointed in you if you don't say those lines. They don't want you to be out of character.

'I expect you to tell everyone that I'm not that person. Anyway, I'm not *just* that person.

'I feel your audience, if you are a star, comes to see you with certain preconceptions and expectations. They do not want you so predictable that everything you are going to do is predictable, but they do want you to be at least within fifty percent of the character they are expecting. Speaking loosely, I would estimate about seventy-five percent is generally good. The trick is to go as far as you can, but not too far.

'Of course, I understand that a public person gives up a certain right to privacy, but I never wanted to be in the 'slime light.' 'Press' is all too often made up of two words, 'pry' and 'mess.' They're too busy looking for 'bedlines.'

'No one has been able to get any headlines, or bedlines, from me, thank you very much. I've never been the kiss-and-yell type.

'I've never understood wanting to put public people under the microscope. I do not understand this celebrity culture in which we live. Why are we so fascinated with the private lives of public people?

'Why are we peephole people?

'I've always hated being gossiped about. When I heard that people were talking about me, I consoled myself with what my mother, Ruthie, used to say: 'Birds peck at the best fruit.'

'Sometimes I'm asked, 'Have you ever had a face-lift?' No. Isn't it perfectly obvious? Or, 'Is that your real hair, Miss Davis?' Yes, indeed it is. And these are my real eyes, my real teeth, and my real tits.'

Despite the negative aspects of fame, Bette cherished and enjoyed her own celebrity. She felt she had earned it. 'I'm proud to say that I've paid my dues,' she told me.

'Joe Mankiewicz [writer-director of *All About Eve*] once told me, 'Bette, on your tombstone will be inscribed, 'She did it the hard way.'' When he said that, I took it as a very large compliment. I was totally flattered. Totally. I thought it meant I hadn't slept my way to the top, that I was a *real* actress. I liked that. Of course, I'm not ready for my epitaph, *yet!*

'Then, I rethought what Joe said. Now I think what he meant was that if there *was* a hard way to do something, I'd choose it — for myself and everyone around me. But I had my standard for the film. Excellence. I couldn't let anything get in the way of that. I never made it harder for anyone else than I did for myself. You know, I'm not quite as feisty as people think.

'Someday I mean to call dear Joe and ask him what he meant. Joe is the kind of person who would do crossword puzzles in ink. One thing he was right about. I probably don't really enjoy anything if it's too easy. I enjoy challenges. When something is difficult, it doesn't stop me; it challenges me to go on.

'The one word I'd *never* want on my tombstone is 'quitter.'

'I still pray to God that somebody will send a good script my way. Every phone call, I hope. I wait for the mail. Today, in 1980, you have to be very lucky.

'It used to be that there were so many films, and writers thought about and wrote parts for you, and the studio bought properties for you. Now, you have to fit the part, a part that wasn't created for you that you can do.'

★   ★   ★

On a day in March 1980, in New York City, my phone rang. I picked it up and I heard a distinctive woman's voice saying my name. The voice was one I had been familiar with all my life, though only from movie theaters and on television. It was Bette Davis. She explained that my number had been given to her by our mutual friend, publicist John Springer.

She said that she had read *Hello, I Must Be Going*, my recent book about Groucho Marx, and she wanted to know if I would be free to have lunch with her. She suggested we meet at her apartment, and then go to a restaurant.

The very next day I went to the Lombardy Hotel, on East 56th Street, just off Park Avenue in Manhattan. I took the elevator up to Bette's floor, the fourteenth, where the long hall leading to her apartment, 1404, was dimly lit. There, at the far end, framed in the proscenium arch of the doorway with the light behind her, was Bette Davis, a cinematic vision.

'This way. Here I am.'

She leaned in a graceful pose against the door, her soft shoulder-length hair casually framing her face. Her black dress was not tight, but clinging softly, with a draped effect. Her skirt was knee-length, revealing shapely legs in ultrasheer nylons and black high heels. I had the illusion that I was walking into a 1940s Warner Brothers movie.

'I always like to have the door open and be waiting for the person who's coming so they don't have to arrive and meet a closed door. Don't stand there. Come in.'

My attention was drawn to the slashes of bright red lipstick, but even more striking were her eyes. They were accentuated by blue eye shadow and layers of false lashes with brown, not black, mascara. It was the eyes that dominated.

I was to learn later that Bette customarily took this kind of care with her appearance when meeting someone for the first time. If for no other reason than that she had to put so much effort into a first meeting, she didn't have many of those. She shared with Mae West the belief that the first impression was the one that counted most and always remained. The next time, one met more of a private person and less of a star, someone who had put in fewer hours of preparation. By the third meeting, she could be quite casual, without her false eyelashes, without the carefully coiffed wig, but never without her bright red lips.

She insisted on hanging up my jacket, which I had left on a chair. 'We don't want it to get wrinkled,' she said. 'What a beautiful Hermès scarf you're wearing. Absolutely beautiful.'

Gleefully, she accepted the gift-wrapped box of Swiss chocolates I had brought her, tearing the paper in her haste to open the package, exclaiming, 'I *love* gifts!'

The furnished hotel apartment would have seemed drab had it not been filled with small personal touches — books, flowers, a music box, all of which she had added to create the ambience of a home. 'As a child, I didn't have a secure home and possessions. We were always moving.'

Being 'a homebody,' she immediately had to make a place into her own, wherever she was, even if only for a few days, to make it seem she lived there. 'When I travel, I bring things from my home with me, so I can establish a familiar relationship with my environment.

'Playing house is a childhood game I've never put away. My home has always meant so much to me. It was my kingdom, though it turned out to be my queendom. William Randolph Hearst's San Simeon may have been the most famous house in America, a palace, but when I was invited to dine at San Simeon, there wasn't any soap in the bathroom.

'Wherever I am, I think of the place I'm in as my home, and I can't bear sloppiness or disorganization. I feel sorry for people who waste their time hunting for things. My father could go into his bedroom in pitch darkness and find his socks, always in a pair. I like order, but I'm not crazy-clean like Miss Joan Crawford. Miss Crawford couldn't even use a bathroom unless she'd gotten down on her knees and scrubbed it clean first.

'I like to dust. Have you ever noticed the objects look back at you in a different way after you've dusted them?

'I don't like waste. It's my New England background, of which I'm very proud. I'm a Yankee. Even playing house as a child, I kept a very neat house.

'I'm always collecting things. I don't consider myself materialistic, but things do make me feel good. Reassured. It's easier to know them than people, because objects accept you as you are.'

She introduced me to Sir Rufus, a rabbit music box, wearing a black velvet tailcoat lined with white satin. 'Would you like to meet Sir Rufus? I love music boxes.' She wound him up and played his tune for me.

'He's absolutely ready for a party, at all times,' she said. 'Do you recognize his song? It's Irving Berlin's 'Always,' my favorite. How I miss those sentimental melodies. We live in such an unsentimental time.

'I love the past, but I don't live in it. I have

13

always thought about the ahead.

'The worst thing about the past is to lament the fact that today's so different, whenever it doesn't compare favorably . . .

'It's interesting how memories pop into your head as you get older, the little kind of vignettes that in the midst of washing the dishes come to you, so that they are not really in the past, but in the present, with us.'

She was pleased that I had accepted her invitation so quickly, 'without being coy or playing games.'

Rather than going out for lunch, she proposed we have something in her apartment. She said she wanted a quiet atmosphere for our conversation, and she had prepared our lunch herself rather than having to wait for room service. Then she announced she was 'absolutely starving.'

As she moved toward the kitchen, I asked if I could do anything.

'Absolutely not,' she called back. '*Absolutely not!*' I was later to understand that everything about Bette was absolute.

A few minutes later, she returned with a nicely set tray of bread, crackers, and assorted cold cuts. There were little porcelain dishes of butter, mustard, and mayonnaise. The paper napkins had something written on them.

'Usually, I have my own linen napkins,' she said, 'but for the moment, I only have these paper napkins. They say, 'Happy Hour, five to seven.'' She laughed. 'Imagine scheduling a time to be happy.'

She put the tray down. 'I got all the food at a very nice deli down the street.

'If you're a movie star, people think you're very rich. And they expect you to pay accordingly and to tip accordingly. And you don't even know what tip they're expecting. I understand that, and I try to tip more, so room service isn't something I feel I can afford. Besides, I really would rather prepare our lunch myself.'

The apartment had vases filled with fresh flowers. 'Do you like flowers?' She didn't wait for my answer. 'Of course you do. All of us women do.' A gardenia was floating in a glass bowl. 'I love gardenias. They're so sexy.

'I always liked men who sent me flowers, but I have to admit most of the flowers I've enjoyed in my life, I've bought for myself. A great many of them, I grew. I'm a country mouse, you see.

'I'm rather good at flower arrangement, if I do say so myself. I find flowers very calming. In my professional life, I've enjoyed some complications and challenges. Even chaos. But in my home, there I demand order. It's easy to achieve because the furniture never gets hysterical and seldom moves around on its own. If you have order in your home, it offers a refuge and helps you face disorder in the outside world.'

After lunch, Bette served tea, meticulously prepared by her from loose tea leaves, not bags as she pointed out, with cookies, which she called 'biscuits,' a word she preferred after her several visits to England.

As we were having our tea, she suggested we

15

'get down to business.' Business, as it turned out, was a book she hoped I would write about her as I had written about Groucho and the Marx Brothers. If the idea interested me, which it did, she suggested our making a start on the project while she was in New York and 'totally' available.

'Do you ever have writer's block?' she asked.

'No, never,' I answered. 'Only publishing block.'

She said she envied my being a writer, because as such I was a 'blank page' person and could write on it by myself, while she had to wait for a phone call in order to be able to perform. 'A watched telephone never rings, you know.

'I can tell you I learned it well after my leaving Warner Brothers looked like a debacle instead of a triumph. I detest waiting for the telephone to ring. I still shudder when I think about waiting for Willie to call. That's William Wyler. He was the love of my life in case you don't know.'

She said that she didn't believe in pretending. 'The only limit is to stay within good taste; however, remember this is the '80s, not the '50s. I want to set the record straight. I don't want to seem namby-pamby. I've reached that time in life when I can afford to be more totally frank and forthcoming now that most of me is in the past.'

She wanted a 'summing up' in the manner of Somerset Maugham's *The Summing Up*.

'I read what I could of Maugham before I did *Of Human Bondage*. In those days I was too busy career-building to read much, but I've always liked reading, especially Maugham. Later when I was what you call between jobs, I read *everything* of Maugham. Everything.' She believed that playing Mildred in Maugham's *Of Human Bondage* was 'an absolute turning point' in her career, and that *The Letter* was one of her best films.

'I feel I have something to say that can be of use to other people, especially women, not because I did it right, but because maybe someone can learn something from my mistakes. I think it's possible to learn more from mistakes than from successes, but it's good if anyone can learn from someone else's without having to make them all for yourself.

'Do you want to know the secret of my success? Easy. Brown mascara. I always wear brown mascara.

'Fair actresses should never use black mascara if they want their eyes to show up. It's the opposite of what they think, that black mascara will make them show up more.

'Of course, there's nothing like blue eye shadow to show up blue eyes, but that's obvious. The secret is, if you are fair, black mascara and dark eye shadow will make you look like a clown, or a harlot.

'I feel a woman should write the book about me. No question about it.' She said she wouldn't feel as comfortable speaking to a man. 'No man has ever really understood me. Come to think of it, no man has ever even tried. Well, except maybe for the female impersonators. Physically and vocally, they studied me, outside-in.'

Bette was a great favorite among impersonators who did impressions of the stars because she had such strongly individual characteristics. She considered their attention 'a compliment, highly flattering.' She particularly enjoyed Charles Pierce's Bette Davis, and called him 'supremely talented.'

'For a long time, the impersonators didn't do me. I was worried about it. It meant I didn't have a distinct style.

'People think I don't like those impersonators who do me. Well, they're wrong. I like it very much, as long they are very good. The only time I don't like it is if they aren't good, or worse if they're *better* than I am. I watch them to learn about myself. Until I saw Arthur Blake, I never knew I moved my elbows so much.

'Let me do an impersonation for you of an impersonator doing me.'

She struck a characteristic Bette Davis pose and then spoke as a caricature of herself:

'And now I'd like to do a scene for you — from all of my films.'

Posing, she took a long drag on her cigarette, and then slowly exhaled the smoke.

Then, she turned to me and said, 'So, what do you think?'

It was a rhetorical question.

★   ★   ★

Our many conversations occasionally took place at lunch in a restaurant, but mostly we met in her apartment, her preference because of the privacy it afforded. She felt we could get more work done there.

18

One day, as Bette and I entered the Lombardy, she saw Lew Wasserman, the head of Universal-MCA. Long before he became one of the most powerful men in Hollywood, he had been her agent, and had done much to shape her career. There was a warm greeting, an embrace, and then Wasserman went on his way.

Bette sighed wistfully and said, 'He was such a beautiful boy.'

While we were having lunch, she said, 'I'm going to live a long, long, long, long time.' Bette Davis was in good health, full of energy, though fearing her career was in decline. She was, however, optimistic and hoped that there was another *All About Eve* in her future. She described herself as 'stoically optimistic.'

'I was taught not to wear my heart on my sleeve, to keep a stiff upper lip, all that sort of thing, true to being a New England girl. Letting your emotions show, I was told, is like letting your slip show. I've always felt I had to wear a suit of armor in public, even if the label said Chanel or Orry-Kelly.'

Orry-Kelly was the designer of her costumes at Warner Brothers. After Orry-Kelly, costume designer Edith Head worked on several of her films, including *All About Eve*. As we spoke, Bette arranged her dress carefully, to avoid wrinkling.

'This is one of my favorite dresses. Edith Head told me you owe a responsibility to a wonderful dress. Dear Edith — how I miss her, and Orry-Kelly, too, although when we worked together, I didn't get along all that well with him.

Would you believe Orry-Kelly was his real name? But without the hyphen. Well, why not? Who would make up a name like that? They understood that I was helped to find my character through the right costume. Of course, that wasn't all of it, but it was important to me.

'Edith even had me wearing the right underwear so I'd *feel* the character, though the audience was never going to see my underwear. Most important of all, she understood how I felt about brassieres. I, of course, abhorred them. It's something a man can't fully understand. Edith and Orry understood the art of camouflage. The truth is nobody's perfect. And nobody feels she's perfect. That's the truth. We can all see more faults in our bodies than anyone else can. We can get in closer for inspection and faultfinding.'

From time to time Bette would take a lipstick out of her purse and apply it with three decisive slashes. She rarely used a mirror. 'Even when I'm home alone, I wear my lipstick,' she confided. 'I feel naked without it.'

Frequently she would retouch her lipstick when she finished a cigarette. As soon as she had retouched her lips, she was ready to light another cigarette, and leave her mark on it. Tennessee Williams, who knew her from his play *The Night of the Iguana*, and before, once told me he thought of the color of Bette's lipstick as 'whorehouse red.'

As I spent more time with Bette, and with Bette when she was with other people, I observed that when she showed pleasure she didn't genuinely feel with someone, only her lipstick smiled.

She sometimes changed her mood within a sentence as she relived memories. When the telephone rang a few times, she would answer simply, 'Yes?' She was aware that it was rather abrupt, explaining to me, 'I can't abide wasting time on the phone.

'I am the most notoriously rude person on the telephone among my friends,' she told me. 'Not for years was I ever conscious of it, but I didn't have time to sit and chat for ten hours. So I would answer the phone, 'Yes?' Whatever had to be said was said, then, half the time, I found myself hanging up near the middle of it. 'Good-bye.' Slam! I'm always saying good-bye when they're saying a long good-bye. I say a quick good-bye.'

She was rarely without a cigarette. 'A lot has been made,' she said, 'of the part smoking has played in my roles. There are some who said my cigarette should have received an Oscar. Well, that's an exaggeration. Maybe a best supporting Oscar. I have to admit, I did use smoking to good effect.

'The way I see it, in my films, drinking is the action and smoking is the reaction.'

Bette had celebrity license, and she didn't hesitate to exercise it. 'Being hysterical is like having an orgasm,' she said. 'It's good for you.' There were probably some who didn't feel it was so good for *them*.

Bette said her favorite subject for conversation was work, and her second, men. 'As for the men

21

in my life, I couldn't select my father. That was my mother, Ruthie's, doing. But I could select my husbands, and I was a four-time loser. For this, I received a life sentence, a life of loneliness without possibility of parole.

'In selecting husbands, I confused muscle with strength. They didn't look alike, but in many respects, they were the same man. All my husbands were canaries. Tweet, tweet, tweet!

'I was never the owner of my own feelings. Perhaps it's that little edge of danger that makes passion possible, or anyway more glorious.

'I was a person who couldn't make divorce work. For me, there's nothing lonelier than a turned-down toilet seat.

'Wishful thinking is an important element of happiness. It has to do with looking forward. Part of happiness is being able to look forward to future happiness. It's why men find us so foolish when we women ask them to promise that the passion and bliss we feel now will be mutually shared for years to come.

'The only man who can give you such an assurance would be a romantic who is as much of a fool as you are, or a liar. The latter is easier to find.

'Feelings can't be promised. Actions can be promised, but not emotions.

'At a certain point, after my marriage to Gary [Merrill] ended, I knew I could never marry again. I had to face it. I was over-the-hill, that proverbial hill. I had to face that no man would want me for the reasons I wanted him to want me. I had to recognize a man wouldn't want me

22

for my old body. The greatest turn-on for me, with a man, was *his* desire for me. I always believed it was his desire *only* for me, when I suppose it was just a matter of convenience, and there *I* was, at hand. Men never wanted me, or *seemed* to want me, for my mind. They didn't pay much attention to my mind. That was hard on a person who was as brain-vain as I.

'When they did pay attention to what I said, I wasn't one to mind my p's and q's, whatever those are. We certainly use some strange expressions without questioning them.

'I wasn't rich enough for a man to want me for my money, although there were men poorer than I, and I was assumed to be much richer than I was. Sometimes I myself got confused and assumed I was much richer than I was. And I felt I could always work. I was, after all, a star.

'Certainly a great deal of money has passed through my fingers, but I never counted. For me, money was taking care of my responsibilities, and I had plenty of them. I couldn't afford to be poor.

'I never begrudged the money to any of them. Well, anyway, not too often. The best thing about money is when you have enough of it not to have to think about it, to just take it for granted and have something left over for the people you care about. I would never want to spend my last penny and leave them without anything. Personally, I didn't want bigger houses or fancier dresses, but I like freedom from economic pressure. I've lived as if old age was something for other people. I could never imagine myself being old, never — even after I already was.'

On one occasion, when I arrived at her apartment, Bette greeted me, saying, 'Welcome to the lioness's den!'

'I have been called fearless. Well, I *am* pretty much. I like to think of myself as a lioness, a lioness who couldn't find a lion, as it turned out. I was doomed to live without a real mate in my empty den, though I always was protective of my cubs.

'There are many things in my life of which I am proud, but my greatest joy is in my daughter, B.D. She has grown up to be a wonderful person, beautiful and strong, and honorable. She is the person in the whole world I know I can trust.'

Sometime later, Bette asked me if I'd heard the story about 'Miss Crawford' beating her children with wire coat hangers, and she asked me if I thought it was true. I told her what Douglas Fairbanks, Jr., had told me when he heard this story about his first wife. Referring to Joan Crawford by her real name, he said, 'It couldn't be true. Lucille would never have permitted any wire hangers in her closet. She always insisted on having only covered hangers.'

Fairbanks was Bette's co-star in one of her early films. 'What a handsome boy he was,' she said. 'How could he have married Miss Crawford, even when he was too young to know better?'

The one thing in life she knew, Bette told me, was that her children would *never* write such a hateful book about her.

She believed parents had to be firm, because only through imposing a strict code of values would your child know you loved him or her. 'Until your children hate you, you haven't been a good parent.' She said this to me only a few years before her daughter B.D. wrote *My Mother's Keeper*, a book Bette later referred to as 'a hateful indictment.'

She went on: 'Your children are there but a few short years. They grow up and leave you, but the power they have over you lasts a lifetime.

'From eighteen on, the parent has done most of what they can do. Parents certainly make mistakes. They're human beings. They do the best they can. And if from eighteen on, you're still blaming your parents, it's a complete cop-out. This is ridiculous. You can take over your own life and undo what you think your parents did that was wrong. Of course, we're not talking about horrible extreme abuses. We're talking about the average child growing up today. We're talking about the child who says when I was seven my mother said or did such-and-such to me, or she *didn't* say such-and-such, and it ruined my life.

'I feel today parents aren't saying enough. And I feel strongly there has to be some fear in education. My Latin teacher, Mrs. Greenwood, I never forgot. We were petrified of her, but *we learned Latin.* Constructive fear. Your children, sometimes you have to put the fear of God in them. You must!

'I've always thought every time we finished a film or a play, whatever, it's just like giving birth to a child. 'There it is, ladies and gentlemen. This is my baby. You may like it, and you may not.' And you have to learn to take it, whether they like it or they don't. And everything you do is not going to be liked, and everybody who sees it is not going to like it. As a matter of fact, if everyone said, 'What a good actor!' and there were never any people who hated that actor, you have *nothing*. You have exactly nothing. You don't cause any controversy. You should have more people *for* you than *against* you, but you must have people against you. Or you're not even interesting.

'And this is true socially. If every time you went into a room, everybody smiled and said, 'Oh, my.' *No!* Some of the people are going to say, 'Oh, Lord. What a person!' Always at every party, anyway with me, as a famous woman, there's always one man who decides to get you mad. He's going to get you angry. Number one, he resents you. That you're famous and successful. It's kind of a war.

'The men who do this I wouldn't want. And you can spot them in about ten minutes. Usually across a room looking at you. So they have to get a few more drinks to get brave enough to have the war.

'You know what I think is the best age for a woman? Thirty-five,' she said, changing the subject. 'No question about it. At thirty-five, a woman's old enough to know the score, but still young enough to be in the game. Only I didn't know it when *I* was thirty-five.

'But I must tell you, I was very old at twenty.

Very old. My father handed me my family to support when I was nineteen, the assumption being, I suppose, that I was now old enough to become the man of the house.

'Well, I've never been so complimented in my entire life! A real challenge. Even so, I don't think I'll ever be what I call a very 'mature' person. For my age, I mean. I can't picture myself as the proper grandmother, sitting very peacefully and probably knitting, saying, 'Yes, yes, darling.' But what *is* mature?

'My daughter B.D. once told me she thought I was permanently fourteen. Actually, I liked that.

'Somehow, though, I always ended up as the man of the house. At Christmas, *I* was Santa Claus. Not Mrs. Claus, but Santa himself! As a matter of fact, I was an all-year Santa, a Santa for all seasons. What nobody understood was that inside the grown woman, Bette, even inside Bette grown old, was the wide-eyed child, Ruth Elizabeth, my childhood name, who was herself waiting for Santa Claus.

'What I wanted was a man, and the way life cast me, *I* had to be the man. *I* had to seem strong and tough because I didn't have a man to stand up for me, and I didn't want the world to know I was really soft and vulnerable.

'Men are not allowed to show weakness, and women are not allowed to show strength.

'I never wished I'd been a man. I always felt like a woman and wanted to be a woman. I wanted to be fulfilled professionally and personally, as a woman. There are some who might say I had penis envy, but I only had penis admiration.

'It seems to me that life must be easier for a woman who doesn't really like men, doesn't need them. She can keep her head and connive to get what she wants. Because I've always liked men, my emotions tripped me up. But pretend? That, I never did. Well, except the one time with Willie [William Wyler] when I tried to make him feel I wasn't overanxious when I was. I always had a deep belief that people should know me exactly as I am, especially if someone was going to marry me. I found that men, more than one, pretended to be something they were not — till they got you! I think men pretend more than women. There really is a rude awakening when that wonderful beginning is over, and at some point, a great horror that you didn't see it.

'You know, it's really a joke on all of us — those wonderful beginnings, which of course are wildly involved sexually. It's really a glandular disturbance. That's the Big Masquerade, isn't it?

'Then comes the unmasking. When the sex goes, you look at the person, and suddenly everything is different. You say to yourself, 'I don't believe it! That's what he was *always* like.' Or *she* was always like. You can't begin to imagine what possessed you. Sex *is* the Big Masquerade.

'When I was young, I could see a man who looked beautiful to me, and I could fall in love at first sight. When I met someone, I'd say it was his 'personality,' his 'sense of humor,' but it was always really his looks. I was a fool about men. *Was!* Why do I say 'was'? Before I was thirty-five, I didn't understand about that physical thing. I confused it with love. After that, I understood, but I was still a fool. I would imbue this 'man of my dreams' with every other quality I imagined I wanted in a man. Later, I started to see him the way he *really* was. Suddenly, I could see all of his faults. There he was, the same face and body that had appealed to me, but with none of the other qualities I required. He became like a store dummy, only one that talked and said the wrong things. Or drank too much. Some of them certainly did that.

'I learned this from lines in a film I made called *Mr. Skeffington:* 'When I was young, I believed a woman is beautiful only when she's loved. But I found a woman is beautiful when she goes to the beauty parlor.'

'There are four major reasons marriages fail: money, sex, intellectual incompatibility, and only one bathroom. I think bathrooms, or lack of them, is one of the major causes for divorce. Men are more vain than women. It's not a criticism, just an observation. I mean, if there's only one bathroom, God help you! So, it's everyday annoyances and disagreements — the little things — that cause a bitterness that makes even sex difficult. Or, anyway, *good* sex.

'They talk about friendly divorce. If you're so friendly, why get a divorce? I had three divorces, and none was friendly. I don't believe *any* divorce is *really* friendly. If Farney [Arthur

Farnsworth] hadn't died, perhaps our marriage could have been successful, and I would have been spared two of those divorces. Perhaps not. Probably not. You can live with someone and not really know the other person. You only *think* you do.

'A man only knows that part of you he brings out. He never knows the rest of you, the secret you, the woman you might have been — with another man. And the worst of this is, he doesn't even care! Love is not as necessary to a man's happiness as to a woman's. Women need a man all the time, and men only want a woman some of the time.

'Someone who knew Marilyn Monroe once told me she really didn't like men and sex all that much, because she was tired of men always trying to get her into bed — theirs or hers. Lucky girl. Secretly, I would like to have been a femme fatale.

'My favorite sexual fantasy used to be to make love on a bed covered with gardenias. I told this once to a man I was currently in love with, Johnny Mercer. So, one weekend, he reserved a suite at the Waldorf-Astoria, and when I arrived, the bed was covered with gardenias. I wonder what the maid thought the next morning? All those wilted and crushed gardenias. One thing it accomplished was I never had that fantasy again. There's nothing that finishes a fantasy as surely as its becoming a reality.

'Now, I'm going to tell you something I've never told anyone. For years I've had this other sexual fantasy — unfulfilled, of course. It was to make love to a regiment of men, just like Catherine the Great. I mean one at a time, of course! In *John Paul Jones*, I had the opportunity to be Catherine the Great, at least briefly. So much for *that* sexual fantasy!

'I must admit I absolutely never saw a casting couch, was never invited to lie down on one, and if I had been, I would have left the room without even deeming it worthy of saying no. I could never have imagined being with a man *only* to advance my career.

'Of course, there are some roles that got away, parts I would like to have played. One of the characters I always wanted to play was Helena Rubinstein. She fascinated me because she made a vast fortune in cosmetics and reached hundreds of millions of women. But mostly I identified with her very strongly based on a story I'd heard about her. When she was very old, an armed burglar entered her bedroom and demanded she open her safe and give him her jewels. This was at gunpoint. As he leveled his revolver at her, she said quite calmly, 'Shoot me! What do I care? I'm ninety-four, and *you'll* go to the electric chair.' What a scene!'

A part Bette would have loved was that of Anna in *Anna and the King of Siam*. 'Fox wanted to borrow me in 1945 to play opposite Rex Harrison. What a pair we would have made! I don't know if I liked him more as a man or as an actor. Both equally, I suppose. Unfortunately, I didn't have an intimate experience with him in either way.

'They called him 'sexy Rexy,' you know. I had

31

to content myself with watching him on the screen. Irene Dunne had the part that was *made* for me, Anna. I *did* meet him, of course, a few times, but that's all. He was as great on the stage in *My Fair Lady* as he was in the film, and vice versa. No question about it.'

★ ★ ★

'The reason most people look back on their youth as the best time of life is because a blank page looks better than one that is filled out and not according to our youthful dreams. Personally, I'm proud of the way I've filled out the pages of my life, anyway my professional life. I'm enjoying my life as Bette Davis now, since I won't be around to read about it when it appears in the obituaries. When I am honored at a tribute, I think of it as part of my living obituary. More fun that way.

'When I was born in the early part of the twentieth century, doors were held open *for* women. Now, doors are open *to* women.

'In my day, and less in my mother's day, women were not prepared to have careers and to be able to support themselves. When my father left us and my parents were divorced, my mother had to find her way. Fortunately for our little band of three, she did. She became a brilliant photographer, but when she couldn't support us with her talent, she didn't let pride stand in her way where we were concerned. She took housekeeping jobs. Ruthie had the kind of pride that counts. Even when she was a housekeeper, she always did her best.

'I am a great believer in girls being prepared for life with an education and a way to take care of themselves, just as boys are. If they marry and have children and all goes well, then what they have learned is not wasted because they will have an inner security and independence. Many women will find themselves victims of divorce, as men, ever hunters, find younger women. Some of the fortunate women who do find a partner for life and a happy marriage will outlive their spouse. So say the insurance companies, and they may be left alone or with children, and perhaps parents to support. I reiterate, every girl should be taught as soon as possible skills that will enable her to take care of herself in the world, and of others, too, if need be.

'I think every one of us has something to give, and, man or woman, we should all think about what that is, something in our power to do.

'I'm sick of people who say they're *for* humanity. It's easier to talk about humanity than to do something for one human being. It costs money and effort to give a meal to a starving cat.

'I saw a bag lady in New York City living in the street in the winter. Unimaginable. What would it be like not to have a home? My own home means so much to me. She was going through garbage, but she wouldn't accept charity.

'I thought of her when I played the television part of a bag lady, in *White Mama*, and she helped me feel my character. But more important, the part made me able to feel how a bag lady feels, and really, it could happen to anyone.'

★ ★ ★

When Bette mentioned my book on Groucho, I told her about an occasion when Groucho took both his friend Erin Fleming and me to a party. Someone there asked Groucho, 'How come you bring *two* girls to a party?'

Groucho responded, 'I hate to see a girl walk home alone.'

Bette laughed. 'That's been the story of my adult life. I was always afraid of walking home alone. And it's not only my story, but it's true now for so many women. Many girls and women will walk home alone.'

I asked her if she liked the title *The Girl Who Walked Home Alone* for my book about her. 'Absolutely,' she said. 'I want that title. That's me.'

As we spoke about her life, she said that she wished she had done more self-exploration when she was a young woman, because speaking about her life, thoughts, and feelings helped her to understand herself better. 'Too much of my life has been squandered fighting self-pity, a battle which I should have won easily, but instead lost.

'I've always been put off by people who want a shortcut to knowing you. Questions and answers, rather than conversation. That makes me peevish. I detest it.

'I will have to do a catch-up on my life for you, you know. One can't keep one's memories in an orderly way.'

1

The Early Years

'It was said in my family,' Bette Davis told me, 'that one of my ancestors was a Salem witch.

'Well, I certainly *hope* so! It would explain everything.

'I'm descended from the Pilgrims. The first Davises came to America in 1634. That was my father's side of the family, and they were Puritans. A Puritan worried about getting caught doing something pleasurable. It wasn't a sin if nobody knew.

'My mother's side were English and French. The Keyes family moved here from England in 1688 and married the Favors, who were French Huguenots who'd arrived the same year. Originally, their name was Le Fièvre, the Fever, which may help to explain me. If there was a witch in my family, she was undoubtedly among *them*. When I heard about that witch, I thought, 'I have a lot to live up to. Or down to.'

'In any event, I was at least *born* like a witch: A bolt of lightning hit a tree in front of the house the moment I was born. Mother told me I happened between a flash of lightning and a clap of thunder.'

35

There are some who dispute this story, claiming that there wasn't a storm on that day. 'What do they know? There are always some people around who want to bring you down, who want to deprive you of your storms.

'And I believe I remember that storm.

'You'd think with such a gloriously dramatic entrance I would've been welcome. Not so. Daddy wasn't expecting a child so soon. I was born in the first year of their marriage, and they hadn't planned on a family so quickly. As it turned out, my father hadn't really planned on a family at all. When Mother broke the news, he blamed her for being 'inefficient' and suggested she 'do' something about it, 'it' being me. He was still going to school, and babies would interfere with his academic routine. He regarded the 'it' that was me as being entirely mother's doing. Her fault.'

Ruth Elizabeth Davis was born in Lowell, Massachusetts, on Sunday, April 5, 1908. Her parents, Harlow Morrell Davis and Ruth Favor had been married exactly nine months. Harlow was about to enter Harvard Law School, and Ruthie, as she was called, had shown some interest in the theater, but was prepared to be a housewife and mother. On October 25, 1909, shortly after they had moved to Winchester, Massachusetts, a second child was born, Barbara Harriet Davis.

'When Mother and Father got married in 1907, they were both only twenty-two and no more ready for marriage than they had been when they first met — at the age of seven.

36

According to Mother, I was conceived on their honeymoon night — the Fourth of July. Even there, I came in with a bang.

'There was a water shortage at the hotel, and Mother couldn't take the proper precautions, whatever they were in those days. Father went into an absolute *rage*, raising hell with everybody in the hotel, including Mother. So I was born exactly nine months to the day after the wedding. Nobody could ever say they *had* to get married!

'So now you know I was born in 1908, which makes me a woman of 'a certain age' — a *very* certain age. But I've never been one of those women who won't admit she's forty till she's past seventy.'

Although her birthday was April 5, Bette told me that she liked to celebrate the day of her accidental conception, that Fourth of July, 1907.

'My father never did forgive my mother for her 'carelessness.' Mother should have known what she was getting into when her future mother-in-law warned her that she was making a terrible mistake she would live to regret. 'He will make your life miserable, my dear. You can be certain.' My mother was young and romantic, and didn't listen. It was only later that she remembered the words.

'At the wedding, when some well-wishers threw rice at them, he turned on them and snarled, 'God damn you — I'll *get* you for this!' I've never understood what he meant by that. No one did. I suppose *he* didn't. He was just expressing his irritability.

37

'My father — a very brilliant, disagreeable man. I could not recall one moment of affection between my parents during the early years of my life, when Father was still around.

'When my sister, Bobby, was born, it was undoubtedly an additional blow to my father. He regarded it as adding insult to injury. In his eyes, it was another blunder by my mother. Perhaps if I'd been a son, my father would have felt differently. If Bobby had been a boy, he might have felt differently about two sons.

'I was Ruthie's favorite, and she put much more of her attention into me than into Bobby. I didn't really notice at the time, having been rather self-centered, even at a very early age, so it only seemed natural. I don't like to say I was selfish; perhaps I was self-absorbed, having a sense of self. As for Ruthie, there was only so much of her to go around between Bobby and me, and not much left for herself.

'I admit that Bobby's arrival on the scene wasn't anything I felt I'd been consulted about, and I felt not only should I have been, but if I had been, I most certainly would have said to skip it. I definitely did not see Bobby as a necessary addition to our little family, though once she was there, I got rather used to her.

'My first memory is that of taking my baby sister out of her crib and putting her up on a chair. I was eighteen months old at the time and I thought Bobby was my new doll. When my mother saw what I'd done, she put Bobby back in the crib, but she didn't show great alarm. I said, 'I don't want Dolly there!'

'Mother said, not sharply but firmly, 'That isn't where Bobby belongs.' That was the problem. None of us ever found out where Bobby really belonged — especially Bobby.

'I wasn't punished, and I don't believe I was even strongly rebuked, just told not to do it again. Ruthie explained to me that Bobby was not Dolly, and that I could injure her.

'Well, I certainly didn't want to injure the funny little thing Ruthie had brought home as a surprise, and which she seemed very concerned with. I didn't understand what she saw in it, but above all, I wouldn't have hurt Ruthie for anything. So, after that, I was committed to protecting Bobby.'

In 1910, Harlow graduated from Harvard Law School near the top of his class, an accomplishment Bette viewed with pride. He took a position in the patents department of the United Shoe Machinery Corporation in Boston, moving the Davis family there from Winchester that same year. With his new work, which took him outside the home where he no longer needed to study, Harlow would be spending much less time with his family.

Ruthie, unhappy in her marriage, checked herself briefly into a sanatorium on March 11, 1911. As part of her rehabilitation, she was advised to take up photography, originally meant only to be a hobby. As Bette put it, 'Photography restored my mother's self-image and became her passion, and it provided economic salvation for our family.' Ruthie's favorite photographic subject was Bette.

'There was no real communication of any kind between my father and the rest of us,' Bette said. 'None of us could break through the wall of ice around Harlow Morrell Davis. My sister, Bobby, tried in every way she could to please Daddy, but nothing worked. She was terribly affected by this. I simply stayed out of his way.

'But my father was a very strange man. With all of his irascibility, he loved to play Santa Claus at Christmas, and he could be generous to a fault. When my grandmother lost her money, he helped to support her and her family, and he was very generous with gifts to Ruthie, though in later years, I've learned that this is what guilty husbands do to assuage their consciences. But I believe my father was faithfully unfaithful. One mistress at a time. This is not a criticism. I'd be a fine one to do that! I can understand my father much better now that it is too late to tell him.'

Ruthie suspected Harlow had a mistress. She confronted him with her suspicions, but Bette never knew whether he denied or confirmed her mother's accusations. 'It would have been like him just not to answer,' Bette speculated. They agreed to a divorce.

'I was seven when my parents separated. Daddy said good-bye to us at the railroad station. On the train, my mother told my sister and me that Daddy wouldn't be coming home anymore and that it was going to be just us. Mother thought Bobby and I would be heartbroken.

'Bobby's world was utterly demolished, but I just clapped my hands gleefully and said, 'Oh, goodie! Now we can go on a picnic and have another baby.''

Bobby's reaction was to cry and have an early version of nervous breakdowns to come.

The divorce was finalized in 1918, with Harlow paying $200 a month support to his family. 'This provided meager subsistence for the three of us,' Bette said.

Harlow remarried. Ruthie returned with her daughters to Winchester, where she worked at housekeeping jobs to put Bette and Bobby through school. All the while, she dreamed of a career in photography. Her favorite subjects for portraits were her two daughters, especially the extroverted, theatrical Betty, who had not yet changed her name to Bette.

'Ruthie was a very attractive woman,' Bette told me. 'After Father left us, she received many marriage proposals. But she made the fatal mistake of asking Bobby and me if we would like this or that man as our father. We never did. 'Heavens, no!' we'd say, not understanding how we were wrecking her personal life. It was a terrible responsibility, all the more terrible because we didn't even understand it was a responsibility.

'There are people who give you their unasked-for martyrdom, exacting a price far greater than any you want to pay. They suffer in silence louder than any words. The child goes through life feeling an inexplicable pain. For Bobby and me, it was exactly the opposite. We were carefree because Ruthie made it look easy. She had all the cares, and we were very free.

41

'Thus, Mother had to rear us and put us through school alone. She supported us in whatever ways she could manage, finally settling on photography as a career.' As a photographer, Ruthie was able to put her daughters through high school, for the most part in Newton, Massachusetts. They lived in a small apartment and sometimes visited their father for weekends in Boston.

Among the jobs that Ruthie held while she was studying photography were nursemaid in Manhattan and housemother at a girls school in Millbrook, New York. During Christmas of 1920 in Millbrook, Betty volunteered to dress as the school Santa Claus. She remembered when she and her sister were very young how much they had enjoyed their father dressing up as Santa Claus and giving out their gifts by the tree.

There were candles on the school tree. Her beard caught fire and her face was burned. There was terrible blistering and it was feared there would be scars.

Ruthie was constantly at her daughter's side, and her care was thought to have saved Betty's face from scarring. Bette told me that her skin was never the same again, 'having lost its top layer.' It was paler, thinner, whiter, translucent, and exceedingly sensitive all of her life.

'I was shy. I used to blush easily. On my very white skin, it really showed.' If she caught a glimpse of herself in the mirror without her clothes, 'All by myself in my room, I blushed.'

'When I was a girl developing, I was too modest to look at myself in the mirror without my clothing. I was embarrassed to see my naked breasts as they grew. It was definitely another time.

'Strangely enough, when I was about eleven, I posed nude for a woman sculptor because we needed money. It was for a statue representing springtime, or something like that, for a Boston park. I'd love to see that statue again.'

Bette enjoyed the sun, especially in her gardens, but throughout her life she had to be careful. In her work, her sensitive skin caused her problems with the heavy makeup she sometimes had to wear. She never, however, allowed personal discomfort to stop her from doing what she thought was best for the part.

In 1921, Ruthie moved the family to New York City so that she could attend the Clarence White School of Photography. Among its graduates was Margaret Bourke-White. Betty and Bobby were enrolled in a public high school on the Upper West Side, where they had to find new friends.

'Have you ever had the experience in high school of going to a dance and being the flower against the wall? Only a genuine wallflower knows how it feels. I remember the pain still.' Bette winced as she spoke. 'I was newly arrived, as I was so often in my girlhood. I didn't know much about dancing. I thought people just did it.

'Do you know what corduroy is?' she asked me.

'I do,' I responded. 'It's a great favorite of mine.'

'Well, it wouldn't be if you had been sent to

43

your first dance in a corduroy jumper.

'I was standing there, hoping to disappear, when a kind boy asked me to dance. I thought he'd seen my hidden beauty, but it was what you might call a mercy-dance, and I caught him looking to his buddies to come to the rescue and cut in. When they didn't save him from me, I did. Even then, I had my pride. I made an excuse, and I fled to the ladies' room, and then home to the security of Ruthie's waiting arms. Ruthie understood. What she understood was that I had to bid adieu to my little-girlhood and advance to the next level.

'She taught me how to put up my hair, got me my first grown-up, sort of grown-up, dress. She showed me dance steps and said it was important always to follow, never to lead the man. Not leading the man was something I found I had to think about consciously the rest of my life. I can tell you at my next dance, everyone thought I was a new girl, there for the first time. They didn't remember me from before, and I was the most popular girl at the dance — by far. I was fourteen, and I knew both sides of the coin, and I knew which side I liked better. It was a lot more fun being popular than not being popular.

'It was the beginning of my learning how important physical appearance is in our society. Too important.'

Betty, however, didn't learn everything from Ruthie that she needed to know. 'I was a total dolt about the birds and the bees. Still am. I don't have the foggiest notion what birds and bees do, though I have had my share of experience with what men and women do.

'I've always preferred the company of men, but Ruthie was my best friend. I could talk with her about anything. Well, almost anything. We always pretended sex didn't exist. Always. I was supposed to assume I was born by immaculate conception, and my sister the same way. Even when I was past twenty, I still hadn't quite grasped how sex was done. When you're very young, you assume that sex comes naturally to everyone else, and you're the only dummy in the world who doesn't know how.

'I had a Puritan upbringing, so I was dedicated like any good Puritan to preserving my chastity long before I knew what chastity was. I was my mother's daughter as she was the daughter of her mother. Ruthie was a 'woman of the world' in so many respects, but when it came to sex, she was a total Puritan. I don't know what my mother thought about my induction into womanhood. I suppose she didn't think about it. The Pilgrims had managed somehow, or we wouldn't *be* here.

'I was extremely curious and extremely romantic about it all, that vague feeling. Moonlight had a tremendous effect on me. Still does. At the age of thirteen, influenced by that moonlight, and a very nice boy, I allowed myself to be kissed. Well, I *did* meet him halfway. It was only a sweet kiss, lips closed, but I enjoyed it tremendously. I realized that kissing held great promise. It was only later, at home, that I began to worry.

45

'A nagging thought crept into my mind. Was I pregnant? Was that how babies happened? Was that what had happened to my mother? If only I had someone to ask, someone more reliable than my classmates, but I couldn't go to Ruthie. Disgracing myself didn't matter to me, but disgracing Ruthie . . .

'A few days later, my tummy seemed to swell, and I was convinced I was pregnant. My horror was indescribable. Then, when I had my first period, I absolutely thought I was dying.

'There was nothing to do except be patient and wait, and I've *never* had any patience, and I've *always* hated waiting. I don't ever want to experience terror like that again. If I had been a Method actress, which I am not, I could have drawn on the memory. It always amazes me how much of what one experiences exists only in one's head, but it makes the experience no less penetrating in its moment, or even in memory.

'There was no alternative. Ruthie had to be told that the world, *my* world anyway, had come to an end. Ruthie always had an answer or found an answer to save us, but this time I knew even Ruthie would be lost. I was preparing to bid a tearful adieu to the world when Ruthie intervened and explained at least *that* fact of life to me.

'She seemed undaunted. That was Ruthie. I thought she must be pretending. She would never let me see how badly she felt. She always protected me as much as she could.

'The first thing Ruthie did was to reassure me that kissing was *not* how babies were made. It

46

was a first step in that direction. Kissing could be dangerous, but not in itself, as long as one had willpower. There had to be 'more,' she said, but she didn't explain what 'more' was. I couldn't even imagine what it was, but at that moment, I was too tortured a soul to ask any questions.

' 'Falling off the roof' was our charming little euphemism for monthlies in those days. Ruthie told me it was the price women paid for having babies. I had to learn the rest of the mysteries of womanhood from my schoolmates, whose information was as unreliable as my own.

'I was happy. I was only 'falling off the roof,' rather than being a fallen woman. I was also proud that I was able to impart my new hard-won knowledge to my younger sister, who would not have to face the Great Unknown as I had.

'When I explained it all from my superior position of age, Bobby didn't seem very happy. I consoled her by telling her it would also go along with her developing a shapely figure, though I must say in Bobby's case, it never happened.'

In 1921, Betty changed her name to Bette. 'I owe my name, spelled as it is, to my father,' she told me, 'as I believe so much of what I am I owe to his negativity and lack of interest, as well as to my own insubordinate nature.

'It was actually a neighbor on West 144th Street, a friend of my mother's, who suggested I end my name with an e instead of a y.

'I was born Ruth Elizabeth Davis and had been briefly called by my middle name to avoid

47

confusion with my mother, who was also a Ruth. So, well before I can remember, I became Betty with a y until this neighbor suggested I spell it with an e because she'd been reading Balzac's *La Cousine Bette*. 'It will set you apart, my dear,' she said. Well, that sounded good to me.

'So I signed a letter to my father that way, and he wrote back, 'You'll get over it.' That did it! From then on, I was irrevocably Bette with an e. It wasn't until some time later that I read the novel and found out Monsieur Balzac's Lisbeth was rather a bitch. Oh, well — too late now.

'What hooked me was when she said, 'It will make you different.' That did it. It appealed to my black-sheepness. I never wanted to be a white sheep following the others to be fleeced or invited *for* dinner. I never really wanted to fit in. I wanted to fit out. Little did I understand that I didn't have to try. My desire to be special and to be different already showed that I was.

'The person I wanted 'to show' was not my dear, doting mother, who appreciated everything about me, but my impossible-to-please father, who simply didn't care. I was never able to gain Daddy's full attention, but I never gave up trying until he died — not even then.

'When I wrote Daddy that letter informing him of the change in the spelling of my name, it produced, I'm sure, only a yawn and a sneer. Condescending. I couldn't bear being patronized. He refused to take my announcement seriously. He said it was just a phase I was going through. As you can see, that was a long time ago, and I made Bette with an e pretty famous, and I don't think I'll be changing it anytime soon. I showed him!

'Young Ruth Elizabeth, me, wanted all kinds of things — a gold wedding band and a silver thimble, a good man and an ivy-covered cottage filled with babies. But very deep inside me, I'd always heard the sound of the music I was going to march to and I wasn't going to let anyone or anything stop me. No guts, no glory. Poor Ruth Elizabeth! She thought she only wanted to be happy. As if that weren't the hardest thing to get. Personal happiness is so much harder to achieve than professional happiness.

'You can't take classes or get a degree. There is no school for it, and you don't just pass or fail. My romantic enthusiasm, naïveté, optimism, to put the best name on it, led me into a trap of doomed hopes. It's difficult, impossible to attain the unattainable. The white cottage with ivy, the domicile of my dream was, alas, an 'enchanted cottage,' dependent on everlasting magic. Personal happiness is so based on your own expectations and dreams.

'In the overall picture, as regards my professional life, I'm the luckiest human being in the world. It brought me everything — and more. In my professional life, you know, I never headed for the glory part of it, I just headed for the fun of the work. I think a lot of the disappointment is those who have as their goal seeing their names in lights, little sports cars, beautiful clothes, a projection room in your home, all the outer glitter.

'That is nothing when you have it. That's when you are among the lucky few who achieve the goals of stardom, but just being a star isn't fulfilling. Those are people who seem on the outside to have everything, but they aren't satisfied, fulfilled. Of course, I had some unhappy moments as I went along. I cared so *much* about *everything*. Intensity of feeling has its rewards and its price. But lucky I was. So much so, I can hardly believe it myself, that I lived that life. Sometimes I have to pinch myself.

'Of course, a career *does* affect your personal happiness, professional and personal happiness being such quite separate things. I think it's very difficult for a famous woman. Just the time. It takes a lot of time getting famous and being famous. To be famous and, at the same time, have a proper personal life, you have to be two people. I *tried* to be two people.

'When I started in this profession, I was working very hard to keep my two people, Ruth Elizabeth Davis and Bette Davis. In the long run, I had to go for one or the other. Obviously, I chose Bette. I didn't have time to be two people.'

Bette later came to believe that the changing of her name had something to do with the drive to change her destiny. She wondered out loud with me as we spoke about her life, would it have changed her sister's life if she had chosen to spell Bobby with an ie at the end?

* ★ ★ ★

In 1924, Bette and Bobby, financially unable to attend college, were sent to the Northfield Seminary for Young Ladies. This was a religious finishing school in Northfield, Massachusetts, which had originally been established for farm girls whose families couldn't afford the tuition and board at other such schools. After a semester, Ruthie took her daughters out of Northfield and enrolled them in the Cushing Academy, a coeducational finishing school in Ashburnham, Massachusetts. Bette found Cushing much more congenial to her temperament than Northfield, especially its coeducational aspect.

'Believe it or not, in my graduating class at Cushing Academy in Massachusetts, I was voted prettiest girl. Oh, yes I was! And I played the lead in the senior play, though I can't for the life of me remember what it was. I had *many* beaus, among them Ham Nelson, who became my first husband. I've carefully saved all of my love letters from this period in a scrapbook. Love letters represent some of our most cherished memories. I don't think people write such wonderful letters now. You can't put a phone call in your scrapbook. Even in those days, love was so very important in my life.

'My first undying love was Ham. Harmon O. Nelson. I never found out what the O stood for until years afterwards.

'When I met Ham, we were in our teens. He was tall, lean, dark, curly-haired — and

51

funny-looking! But with such beautiful brown eyes. Those eyes! I was always attracted by eyes. Of course, he also had other attributes. He had a hard body that was wonderful-looking, especially from the rear view. I was vain about my brain, but at that age, I didn't think about his intelligence when I looked at a man.

'Ham was a musician working his way through school playing at our Saturday dances. Once he asked me to sing with him. I sang 'Gee, I'm Mighty Blue for You,' a popular song of the day. Sometimes I find myself humming that tune to myself. It still takes me back to those early years with Ham.

'I still have my program from the 1926 graduation ball, each dance marked with an X. I danced every one with Ham. The night before, we'd starred together in Booth Tarkington's *Seventeen*. That's it. I've remembered the name of the play. *Seventeen*.

'Then, Ham went away to college, and I met . . . Fritz. Proximity is always an important factor when one is young. 'A beau on hand is worth two in the wish.'

'I'd constructed a white cottage in my mind that I was going to live in with Ham. Then, I started imagining myself in that same white cottage with Fritz *instead* of with Ham. When Fritz had to leave for Yale, Ham returned for the Christmas holidays. Seeing him again made me forget Fritz. I used to furnish that white cottage, the one in my mind, even down to the perfectly white, freshly laundered antimacassars on the backs of the chairs. When Fritz moved in, temporarily replacing Ham, I quickly had to refurnish it, though I kept the white antimacassars. Even in a fantasy, it didn't seem proper for Ham and Fritz to use the same bed.'

2

Becoming an Actress

In January 1926, Ruthie took her daughters to the Repertory Theater of Boston, where Bette had what she regarded as 'a magical experience' that 'transformed' her.

'The first time I *truly* knew I wanted to become an actress was when I was eighteen and saw Blanche Yurka's production of Ibsen's *The Wild Duck*. Ruthie had taken Bobby and me to Boston to see Miss Yurka play Gina. Lovely Peg Entwistle was Hedwig, and I so *totally* identified with her that afterwards I told Ruthie, 'Mother, someday *I* am going to play Hedwig. *I* am going to be an actress just like Peg Entwistle.

'I thought I always knew I'd do something special, even important, but I never thought (I was sixteen then) exactly how or what it was. But Peg Entwistle and I, we were twins, and I identified with her, plus it was the *kind* of a part I would love.'

Young Bette was not just stunned by the performance, but she felt her own body go onstage and enter Hedwig. She felt herself a part of the story taking place on that stage. 'I was on that stage. When Hedwig died, *I* died. When the lights come up in the theater, I knew what I *had* to do. Before that performance, I *wanted* to be an actress. When it ended, I *had* to be an actress.

'With *The Wild Duck*, everything in my life fell into place and I saw myself in focus for the first time. I knew then that nothing was going to stop me from becoming an actress. Nothing. Someday I would play Hedwig and many other roles on the stage, I told Ruthie.'

Bette remembered making a wish as they left the theater: 'I want to be exactly like Peg Entwistle.' Usually Bette didn't wish to be *exactly* like anyone, but this was an exception.

'I was overwhelmed by the performance and the magical world of theater. Ruthie understood this, and *my* mission became hers. My energy and enthusiasm came from my mother's side. She wrote to Daddy, dear ever-optimistic Ruthie, convinced he would understand, too. Instead, he was his customary scornful, scorning self, and he gave me his usual vote of no confidence. 'Let her be a secretary,' he wrote back. 'She'll earn more money, and besides, Betty will never be a successful actress. She doesn't have what it takes.'

'As usual, Daddy inspired me — to prove him wrong. If Ibsen wasn't enough, Daddy was. I might add that he was still writing to me as Betty with a y. Daddy was as stubborn as I am. I must say, however, that if I had followed his advice, I believe I would have been totally successful as a secretary, too.

'Daddy's words stuck in the back of my mind, and while I was studying to become an actress, I was also studying shorthand and typing, my fallback position. As it turned out, however, those skills were very useful. During vacations. I was able to add to Ruthie's income. In high school I had helped pay my tuition by waiting on tables, even though it's always been hard for me to take orders from anyone. There was always something insubordinate about me, so if anyone gave me a direct command like, 'Get me scrambled eggs,' a little voice inside of me said, 'Give them fried.'"

Following Bette's graduation from Cushing in 1927, Ruthie took the family to Ogunquit, Maine, a rustic resort on the Atlantic coast where she rented a fisherman's cottage for the summer. It was at Ogunquit that nineteen-year-old Bette fell in love with Francis Lewis 'Fritz' Hall, a Yale senior, who asked her to marry him. Meanwhile, Ruthie was making plans for her daughter's future that did not include Fritz.

'I was very fortunate to have a mother who allowed me to spread my wings. She saw to it that I went to New York to a dramatic school, which is the proper training, really, which they do much more in England than they do in America. I sort of went on from there.

'Ruthie wasn't a stage mother. She was never around where I worked at all. She was extraordinary. Her belief in me was extraordinary. It's very hard to go forward without someone who believes in you.'

★　★　★

'In the autumn of 1927, Ruthie and I drove down to New York. It was so beautiful. I always loved the changing colors of the leaves. She had arranged for me to try out at Eva Le Gallienne's Civic Repertory Company. If I were accepted, it meant the start of my career as an actress, and, best of all, there were no tuition fees. Students paid their way by acting in the company's productions, exactly what I wanted to do. Ruthie couldn't afford any tuition, nothing. It was a wonderful opportunity, and it seemed it just had to be because it was so wonderful and because we didn't have any other possibility. At that time, I had perfect faith in miracles. Part of having a miracle was having it happen when you needed it.

'Miss Le Gallienne greeted me stiffly, asking a lot of questions like, 'With whom will you be living in New York?' and 'To whom can you turn in the event of an emergency?' The answer to both of these questions was 'My mother.' She made me feel exactly like the little amateur I was. My tryout was an utter abomination. I have never functioned well with someone who doubts my ability to do something. When I protested that I had not been given a fair opportunity, Miss Le Gallienne informed me that my approach to the 'the-a-*ter*' was not serious enough to warrant admission to her school. I still did not understand that in life there are arguments you cannot win, just as there are people you cannot win.

'I returned to Boston defeated, heartbroken, and furious. Especially furious. Every rejection is terrible. Don't let anyone fool you. Ruthie said to me, 'You mustn't ever take it personally.' But there *is* no other way you can take it. It's always personal, and you never forget. If I'd had a good crystal ball, I could have looked ahead and known what kind of career I was going to have. Then, I could have just enjoyed it and not wasted my time worrying and fretting.

'Speaking of crystal balls, when I was eighteen, I went to a Gypsy fortune-teller in York, Maine. I remember she had big gold earrings. I see them in my dreams. She checked out my palm without committing herself. Then, she turned to her tarot cards and scrutinized them. After a long silence and a lot of head-shaking, she told me that someday I would be famous all over the world. I went home and told Mother. We couldn't figure this out at all. We sat up until the wee hours of the morning never thinking of the most likely answer — motion pictures.

'Years later, after the prediction had become an incredible reality, and I was far better known than Miss Le Gallienne, I had my moment, the one I had been waiting for. Who hasn't waited for that moment when you could show someone who didn't think you were worth a row of pins that they were wrong. I walked up to her at a Broadway opening and I announced triumphantly, 'I guess I was serious enough, after all.' She looked blankly at me and said, 'What a pleasure to meet you, Miss Davis! I *so* admire your work.' It was clear she hadn't the vaguest notion what I was talking about! The hurt I'd been carrying around with me for years, she'd completely forgotten. You can't *show* people; it's a waste of your time.

'Ruthie wasn't like me in that respect. She had a wonderful trait. She never bemoaned the past about which nothing could be done. Dear, constructive Ruthie, as positive as my father was negative. She quickly found a job retouching photos in Norwalk, Connecticut, only an hour from New York, and we moved again, this time to a rooming house. Mother worked across the street in a little storefront. I would see her in the window, where she could get more light, all bent over, trying to see through bloodshot eyes, retouching negatives.

'I have to admit I began to lose my confidence and my belief in myself. I couldn't afford to do that, and I should never have wavered in my belief in Ruthie. What you *don't* know is often the most important thing. Fortunately, very fortunately for us, neither of us ever understood anything about the odds against my achieving our goal.

'I was so bored. I wondered if I would lose my sanity. It was then that Ruthie awoke me early one morning. I'd taken to sleeping late, as late as I could, hiding in sleep, trying make the long days seem shorter.

' "Get up, Bette," she said. 'We're going to New York.' I looked out the window. It was raining. 'Hurry,' Ruthie said. 'Rain is always good luck for you.' I tried to think: Was it? I remembered. I was born in the rain. Well, my being born at all was certainly lucky, considering what my father had in mind for me. Ruthie was always right, at least in those days. I heard her saying, 'We're going to get you into acting school.''

Bette's mother refused to tell her what their exact destination was. From Grand Central Terminal, they splurged on a taxi for what Ruthie was convinced would be a defining moment in her daughter's life. Bette realized how momentous the appointment had to be for her mother to take a taxi.

Ruthie had made an appointment at the John Murray Anderson School of Theater and Dance on East 58th Street. Speaking with the brother of John Anderson, Hugh, who ran the school, as far away as possible from where her daughter waited, she made a plea for Bette's acceptance. She wanted to spare Bette any sense of humiliation. She was not concerned for herself, only for Bette.

'The John Murray Anderson School of Theater was one of the most prestigious in New York,' Bette continued. 'Believe it or not, Martha Graham was one of our teachers, and George Arliss was a lecturer. Knowing Ruthie could not possibly afford the tuition, I hardly dared to hope as I waited in the reception hall for my mother.

'I later learned that Ruthie had told Mr. Anderson outright, 'My daughter Bette wants to be an actress. I haven't the money for her tuition now, but I assure you that you will eventually have it. I shall work for it as long as it takes. Will you accept her as a student?' He sat there for a moment. I know he must have been stupefied by Ruthie's guts. Then, weakly, overwhelmed by her

60

passion, he said, 'Yes.' Afterwards, he always told people he never knew what possessed him. But *I* knew. *Ruthie* had possessed him.

'She opened the door to my dream, as she always had. But Ruthie never pushed me through that door. I had enough push for the whole family.'

It was immediately necessary to move to New York City so that Bette wouldn't miss any classes. Ruthie left her job, packing their few belongings and leaving Bobby with family, and drove with Bette to New York.

'I moved to New York, into a brownstone on 58th Street right next to the school. Ruthie got another job, this time as a housemother at a girls school in New Jersey. My mother made it possible for me, not thinking about herself.

'I had a roommate who spent all her time dancing the Charleston. She was so totally different from me. I was totally serious and dedicated, and she was just there, I don't know why, but it seemed her aim was to work the least possible. She wasn't neat, and she talked a lot, and she liked to play her ukulele. Ruthie thought her nonchalance might distract me, but I liked her.

'One day, she said to me, 'You could be the bee's knees if you didn't take life so seriously.' I was very flattered to know that I could be 'the bee's knees,' if I wanted to be, even though I didn't *want* to be. She was strumming on her ukulele as she made this observation.

'Even as a little girl, I'd taken life seriously. I wanted to be Somebody, and I thought I *was*

Somebody, but I didn't want to be the only one who knew it. I was a little nobody, but I was an *independent* little nobody.

'I was always trying to go above myself. Of course, such determination has its negative side, too. What if no one wanted to taste your cookies, even though you baked the best cookies in the world? That happened to poor Peg Entwistle, the wonderful English actress who had inspired me so. With a promising stage career behind her, she went to Hollywood where no one much noticed her until early one morning in 1932. I think after just one film, she climbed to the top of the Hollywood Hills where the big letters spell out the name of the magic town, and she jumped off at the letter H. All that beautiful talent, all those glorious dreams crushed in a second on the rocks below, her undeserved and probably temporary obscurity interrupted momentarily in a blaze of sensational headlines. Then, it was all over. She was my age exactly.

'I was very sad. But I couldn't ever imagine committing suicide. No matter what. It's the most supreme example of quitting, and I can't imagine ever quitting.

'I not only sympathized, I empathized with her. When I was that age, every minute was *the* important minute, and whatever was happening right then seemed like it always had *been* that way, and always *would* be that way. I understood what it was like to feel disappointed in the parts you were offered. An actress's life is one of such utter dependency. Others must write what you do, and others have to make the gamble that pays for it, or you knit. Or worse, you have so much time on your hands, you learn how to crochet.

'At the Anderson school, we performed in a play a week. We even made a two-reel movie. We learned about voice. When we began, my small voice and my New England accent made me a poor candidate for success. All regional accents limit an actor's possibilities.

'For me, there was no one more important than Martha Graham. From her, I learned how to move with grace. 'To act is to dance,' she would tell us. It was she who showed me the importance of the entire body in acting. She was an authentic genius, one of the great people of the twentieth century. I worshipped her. Still do. I learned how to use every part of my body in subtle ways to enhance the words I was saying, or even to belie them. It was the ultimate in body language before that term was used.

'Do you know what I learned from Miss Graham that gave me my career? How to fall, most especially how to fall without looking down.

''Don't look down!' I can still hear her voice in my head from so long ago, admonishing me, 'When you fall, *don't look down!*'

'That's a change in human nature, you know. I learned the lesson so well that decades later when I tripped in the street, not for the cameras, but in real life, I never looked down as I fell. I got up gracefully, unhurt, which astounded the small audience of passersby who had watched my mishap, and I thought, 'Thank you, Miss Graham.'

'People talk about the importance of cigarettes in my films, but are you conscious of the presence of stairs? I've spent a lot of film time on stairs, and ever since my days with Miss Graham, I've been comfortable going up or coming down. It's she who took me step by step, up and down those stairs.

'At drama school, I learned how to talk, how to move, how to sit and stand as well as to fall without hurting myself, how to have total confidence onstage in front of an audience. Anyone can learn the basics of acting, but only a few will become real actors. There are audiences who sit there like stone, daring you to breathe life into them. The real actor, like any real artist, has or finds a direct line to the collective heart.

'Drama school provided me with the rudiments of my chosen profession. From John Murray Anderson and George Arliss, I learned to speak like an actress. I came to the school with a high, tiny voice that couldn't be heard beyond the first row. And my New England accent, you really could not be-*lieve* it! The first day in speech class, I was given a sentence to read: 'Parker parked the car in Harvard Square.' The class would still be laughing if the bell hadn't rung. It looked like my only possibility would be as a comedienne, the kind people laugh at rather than with.

'Rosebud Blondell was one of my fellow students. She later became Joan Blondell, but I always called her Rosebud, her real name, I think. Can you believe it? Nobody does. Whatever were her parents thinking? And she called me Ruth Elizabeth. It was as if Ruth Elizabeth was still alive whenever Rosebud and I were together.'

Bette didn't even *think* about a social life. There was too much to learn, and she needed all her time and energy for her studies. Even so, at least *thoughts* of romance were never totally absent.

'At about this time, I became engaged — for three days. Fritz, my boyfriend from Ogunquit, asked me to marry him, but only on the condition I give up the theater. How could he love me and ask for such a sacrifice? I would have said no right then and there, except he produced the most gorgeous diamond ring I had ever seen and slipped it on my finger. Well — why not think it over for a few days while I wore his ring? After three days he demanded an answer, and I gave the ring back to him.

'Of course, I *had* to return it, but doing so made me realize I would miss the ring more than I would miss Fritz, and that wasn't at all a good way to begin a 'till death do us part' relationship. I could never abide an ultimatum. Besides, I had just received a letter from Ham and decided to renew our romance.

'Romance was always an important element in my life, especially in those days when my virginity was intact. I was hopelessly Puritan, helplessly passionate.

'I moved from crush to crush to crush, always declaring myself eternally bound to whomever I was involved with at the moment. And I believed it, at that moment. I was bursting with youthful energy and a passion that would surely have overcome me if I hadn't been so much in love with acting, too. I was able to divert my passion — physical, emotional, intellectual — into my work, which I felt was the most important thing in my life then. And so it was, and so it remained.

'I was a naïve girl. Maybe I'm still a naïve girl. I believed that romance and love, when I found the right person, would last forever.

'In my case, it lasted fornever. Fornever is the opposite of forever.

'Perhaps it could have lasted, if I had found the right person for me and I had been the right person for him. Dear Willie [Wyler] was the closest I ever came.

'Ruthie taught me an important lesson about men when I was still in high school. Whenever she sensed I was about to go off the deep end with this or that fellow, she would suggest I invite my latest over as a houseguest for a few days. That did it! Overexposure accomplished what a motherly lecture couldn't. After a day or two, I would come running to Ruthie. 'When is he going home? Will he never leave?' It never occurred to me that Ruthie had asked him over for precisely this response.

'Ruthie also tried to teach me that I should hide my intelligence. It was a lesson I failed to learn. Deliberately. I didn't wish to pretend to be dumb. This was an instance in which Ruthie's advice wasn't right for me.

'I owed so much to Ruthie, and I wanted to make her proud of me. Every year, Mr. Anderson gave two five-hundred-dollar scholarships to the most promising girl and boy. I made up my mind to win one to help Ruthie pay my tuition.'

Not only would it be what Bette called 'a plume in her chapeau,' and good for her career, but more important, she was always determined to assume some of the financial burden. At the moment, Ruthie was working hard as a housekeeper.

The final test was the play *The Famous Mrs. Fair*. 'One guess who won the part of Sylvia Fair, and if you don't get it right,' she told me, 'you'll have to leave this apartment.' I didn't have to leave.

'Toward the end of my first term, I won the lead in *The Famous Mrs. Fair*. I hoped to win the scholarship with my performance. Even if I didn't, the invited audience would be made up of important theater people, and they would see me.'

Two days before the performance, Bette felt a terrible cold coming on, the worst of her life. Her greatest fear was that she would lose her voice entirely. She had worked so hard preparing the part that she thought that was what had lowered her resistance and led to the cold.

'I could barely talk, much less project to an audience from a stage. Ruthie took time off from her job at the New Jersey girls school to take care of me. She wore a path down from the brownstone where I was suffering to the corner drugstore. She would get the pharmacist to open up after hours to get my medication. She insisted on sleeping on an improvised bed of three chairs tied together so that I could get my proper rest on the bed.

'Of course, she was wrong. I couldn't sleep a wink knowing she was so uncomfortable, though she was always cheerful and uncomplaining. Anyway, her efforts and sacrifices worked, and on the day of the performance I seemed to be miraculously recovered.'

The full force of the cold held off during the first act, and Bette was able to carry on with the role, much as she had conceived it. The part called for Bette to change, because of World War I, from an innocent girl to a mature, bitter woman. As the character of the heroine disintegrated, so did the health of the actress playing her.

'My voice held up for two acts. Then the cold really came back, full force. As the third act progressed, I heard myself getting hoarser and hoarser. I looked down in the audience and saw Ruthie offering up silent prayers. Her prayers were heard.

'As luck would have it, the character I was playing was a fallen woman, much like Mildred in *Of Human Bondage*. It appeared to the audience I was gasping in a baritone voice on purpose. They were utterly astonished by my vocal range. And so was I.'

As Bette's voice deepened, the audience attributed it to the disintegration of the character, accepting her husky, failing voice as part of the characterization. Again she had won the collective heart of the audience.

'Winning the audience is difficult, but that's what it's all about,' Bette said. 'Once you've won them, they will go a long way with you.'

That night, the winner of the scholarship was announced. Bette told me that winning it meant more to her than winning any other award in her career, even the Oscar.

Because she cared so deeply, she froze and didn't hear the name that was announced. She was watching her mother's face in the audience. When she saw her mother's look of pride, she knew. Ruthie was glowing. The scholarship had been awarded — to Miss Bette Davis!

'Then, as it turned out, I never used it. The director of the play, James Light, was also a director at the Provincetown Playhouse in the Village. He wanted me to be in a new play he was going to produce there. The only catch was I would have to leave school.'

She had won the scholarship, the answer to all of her dreams — only her dream had changed. This could be her first professional opportunity as an actress, but it meant leaving the protective environment of the school.

'I had to choose between accepting my scholarship or accepting my first real acting job. It was a very difficult decision for me, but Hugh Anderson, who had accepted me at the school, only laughed when I told him my dilemma. Of course I should accept the part. 'Use your wings to fly,' he said.'

Ruthie, for once, had no advice. She wanted

Bette to choose. Bette weighed the possibilities. She decided that while there might be something more to learn, there was more to learn by doing than by studying how to do it. There was also the possibility that she might complete her studies and not be offered such an opportunity. The decision was made.

'I attended a few more weeks, then dropped out when Mr. Light told me to get ready for rehearsals. Then, the production was postponed, first a week at a time, then longer. Finally, they decided to postpone it until fall, three months later. I couldn't go back to school. I'd burned my bridges behind me. So I decided to try and get another job in the meantime.'

Through a letter of recommendation from director Frank Conroy, who had been impressed by Bette when she danced at the Mariarden Arts Colony in New Hampshire in 1925, Bette met director George Cukor, who was casting for a production of Philip Dunning and George Abbott's hit play *Broadway* at his Temple Players stock company in Rochester, New York. This was Cukor before Hollywood.

The smallest part in the play was not yet cast, and as a favor to Conroy, Cukor, with some trepidation and low expectations, hired a girl named Bette Davis.

Bette was interviewed by Cukor, but she felt he didn't seem impressed. When I spoke with Cukor many years later, he remembered the meeting and confirmed that Bette's intuition had been correct. She won one week's work, however, and was ecstatic.

70

'The director George Cukor — 'That's 'Cu' as in cucumber,' he always used to say — played a very important part in my life. He was the first person to fire me. You never forget the first person who fired you. He also gave me my first professional engagement. When the production at the Provincetown Playhouse was postponed, Mr. Cukor ended up giving me the smallest part in *Broadway*, a play he was producing in Rochester for his own successful stock company.'

Ruthie, who hadn't thought ahead for herself, always thought ahead for Bette. 'Mother couldn't go. She saw me off at Grand Central Station, and as the train was pulling out of the station, she called out, 'Learn the part of the lead. The actress may have an accident.' I respected Ruthie's clairvoyant powers. Since my part was that of a chorus girl who said only, 'That's swell!,' learning both parts wasn't too much of a challenge.

Ruthie had been reading the play with Bette, and knew that her daughter was well qualified to play the leading role. Though Bette didn't give serious credence to the possibility, she began studying Pearl's part as soon as she boarded the train.

At the Lyceum Theater in Rochester, she was given a skimpy costume and instructed to chew gum vigorously for her part as one of the chorus girls. 'I was a little let down when it seemed the major criterion of my professional acting debut was going to be how well I did, or did not, chew gum. I didn't have to rehearse chewing gum. Although I never chewed gum, I was a quick study and learned with my first package. What would Martha Graham have thought?

'I also had to learn the Charleston. I was a good dancer, but I had never done the Charleston. I had to sort of fake it, which, in truth, was more difficult than really doing it.'

Bette said she had many young men interested in dating her because of the part she was playing, that of a chorus girl wearing 'skimpies.' They hoped she was what was called those days 'fast.' She was happy to disappoint them. 'It was something that followed me all of my life, the idea people have that your stage or onscreen performance is the real *you*. I put myself into the character. The character doesn't put herself into me.'

On the Wednesday matinee, only two days after opening, the leading ingénue, Rose Lerner, had to fall down the stairway as a part of the story. She fell badly and twisted her ankle. She managed to get through the show and do the evening performance, but it was a disaster for the actress and for the show.

'I let it be known I knew Pearl by heart, and Mr. Cukor bellowed to the stage manager, 'Get me that dame with the smallest part right away.' He couldn't even remember my name.'

Cukor later told me that while it was true he didn't remember her name at the moment, he definitely had noticed young Bette Davis. 'She was hard to miss,' he said. A great many people would think that over the years.

The stage manager didn't have to search for her. Bette was right there. She had learned early that being right there was an important part of luck and success.

'I thought he would have me recite a few of the lines, but he just asked me, 'Can you fall down a flight of stairs without breaking your leg?' I said yes. He said, 'Prove it.' Thanks to Martha Graham's training, I fell effortlessly, and I was Pearl for the rest of the week. I was so successful, in fact, that Mr. Cukor engaged me for the next season — as lead ingénue of his stock company!

'In my very first job, there I was working with actors like Wallace Ford, Louis Calhern, Frank McHugh, and Miriam Hopkins! Miriam had the prettiest blond hair I'd ever seen, and she'd drive us all crazy with envy when she'd emerge from a shower and simply toss her golden curls dry. She seemed oblivious, but she knew what she was doing. I was to learn later she *always* knew what she was doing. It sort of kept all of us who didn't have golden curls in our places. A decade later, in *The Old Maid*, she drove me crazy again, shaking those curls whenever we had a scene together.'

At the time, Bette told me, she believed they were naturally golden, their wonderful color unlike Bette's own pale, blond hair, which photographed darker than it was. She said she never knew whether Hopkins's hair was natural or the result of 'a bottle and some divine permanent.'

Bette remembered that Miriam was extremely attractive to men, 'not only her looks, but her southern way, her easy confidence. She was older

73

than I, which at that moment seemed to me an advantage she had. Later, she was welcome to her extra years.'

In the play, Hopkins was the young, decorative wife of tightrope walker Wallace Ford. 'She stood by in tights throughout his act,' Bette said.

Except for a faux pas of one night, Bette was successful in her part. She was supposed to shoot her lover twice, and he would then stagger offstage to die. She shot him so many times that he couldn't justify being alive long enough to stagger offstage. He had to lie onstage for the entire act, trying not to breathe visibly.

The first play of the next season was *Excess Baggage*, a comedy by John McGowen. 'You won't be familiar with most of the plays of that time,' Bette explained to me. 'While there are a few classics which have survived the test of time, there were literally *thousands* of plays which did not. Some of them very successful, too. It was a heyday for the theater. You cannot *imagine* what halcyon days those were!

'I had very good notices. In a play called *Yellow*, the well-known actor Louis Calhern, who was twice my height and twice my age, was not pleased by my being cast as his mistress. It was the part that went with being the ingénue for all of the plays, but he complained that I was *too* ingénue and that I looked more like I was his daughter.' Calhern was actually thirteen years older. 'I don't know if that was the reason I was fired, but it may have been.'

Since critical and public reaction to her performance was favorable, Bette had assumed that she would be performing with the Temple Players for the whole summer season, and she informed James Light that she wouldn't be able to begin early rehearsals of *The Earth Between*. Her assumption proved incorrect. Life in the theater could be unpredictable.

'Mr. Cukor often criticized my work, and I, being a know-it-all, always defended it, never admitting I was wrong, even when I was. Perhaps that's why Mr. Cu-kor, as in cucumber, fired me the first chance he got. I'll never really know why, because I was never told. Some people said it may have been my determined virginity. I was *perfectly* virginal, though it would have been difficult to be 'imperfectly' virginal, wouldn't it? Stock company ingénues were supposed to be available for love scenes offstage as well as on, though not, of course, with Mr. Cukor.'

I told Bette that when I mentioned her to George Cukor, he said of her, 'She's no Planny Annie. That means she's not a bitch. She's gallant, but foolish.'

Bette was pleased by those words.

I was with Bette at a party in Beverly Hills when I saw George Cukor, whom I knew, standing nearby. I invited him to join us. It was the first time they had spoken since he had fired her, more than fifty years before.

He said, 'Hello, Bette. It's been a while.'

'Yes, it has, George. Well, what do you think about my career since you fired me? I didn't do so badly, did I?'

'Due to me, my girl,' Cukor said.

Afterward, Bette sniffed, 'Not exactly Philip

Barry dialogue, but very Cukor.'

They never met again.

Cukor told me that even in Rochester as young as she was, Bette had star quality. 'Do you know what the secret of star quality is?' he asked me.

'It's being irritating. The great women stars have an irritating quality, each in her own way, individually irritating. It's a part of what makes them distinctive. My great friend, Miss [Katharine] Hepburn, Garbo, Olivia [de Havilland], with all that sweetness of Melanie, each had that oh-so-irritating quality.'

As he spoke, Cukor touched the ring he always wore, one that had been bequeathed to him by his good friend W. Somerset Maugham. 'That girl [Bette],' he said, 'did justice to Maugham in *Of Human Bondage* and *The Letter*.'

★   ★   ★

'I was out of a job and heartbroken,' Bette said, 'but Ruthie never had any doubts I would be successful. Ruthie told me it was perfect timing, though I didn't see it that way. I wasn't so sure. I'd gone from being the happiest person in the world to the unhappiest. Nothing-to-lament was Ruthie's feeling. It turned out Ruthie was right again.'

Bette left Rochester and Cukor's Temple Players in search of a job for the summer. She fervently hoped it would be with a summer stock company. She wanted acting experience, but her greatest need was to earn money. She knew that if her hopes failed, she would have to call on her experience as a waitress.

She went to agencies, to casting offices, all in vain. She began to feel shattered by the weight of so much rejection. Bette not only needed to earn money, but she knew that only by working could she master her craft.

Finally, she was told that she would be taken on for the summer at the Cape Playhouse. With Ruthie and Bobby, she drove up to Cape Cod, and Ruthie rented a small house for the summer. They paid the rent in advance for a month. Then Bette went to the theater only to find herself 'unexpected.' Apparently the person who had told her to come to the theater had no proper authority to hire her, and all the parts had been cast. People felt sorry for her, but what could anyone do?

Someone *could* do something, and did. The owner of the theater, a Mr. Morris, asked, Would it help if he offered her a job for the summer as an usher?

Bette was overjoyed. They were financially rescued, and she had the job next best to being onstage. She was in the theater, watching, if not performing. She memorized all the parts she might perform, but there were no mishaps. She contented herself with being the best possible usher.

Then, at the end of the season, Laura Hope Crews, who was starring in, as well as directing, A. A. Milne's *Mr. Pim Passes By*, didn't feel the company's ingénue was right to play the young British girl. Bette was an actress playing an usher, but she was anxious to return to being on the stage.

Able to find the song the girl had to sing 'by scrambling with Ruthie's help,' Bette won the part of Dinah. The audience loved her because she was perfect in the part, and also because she was *their* usher who had made good! Then, the summer season ended, and the Davis troupe returned to New York.

'The Provincetown Playhouse was now ready for me. *The Earth Between* was ready to start rehearsals. My salary was thirty-five dollars a week, and I was *thrilled*.' Bette knew that Eugene O'Neill had been introduced there and that Katharine Cornell had performed there. It was time to begin feeling a little nervous. 'If not Broadway, this was New York,' she recalled thinking.

The play went on and got roundly panned, but the critics liked Bette's performance. 'Mr. [Brooks] Atkinson of the *Times* wrote, 'Miss Bette Davis, who is making her first appearance, is an entrancing creature who plays in a soft unassertive style,'' Bette remembered perfectly. 'Even Daddy sent flowers, a lovely little basket of spring flowers, with a card engraved 'HARLOW MORRELL DAVIS.' He was always in character. My father was not a truly loving person unless you count the way he felt about his dog.

'I had no more doubts about my direction. And I had a new beau named Charlie. I'd met him in Rochester, and we'd become engaged. Unlike Fritz, he adored my career and came to every performance. Now that I was having some success, I thought of my future as Charlie's wife. In my daydreams, I saw myself bowing to the applause of adoring audiences, then stepping offstage into the kitchen of a little white, ivy-covered cottage where I'd bustle around making a pot of chowder and steamed clams for my husband. Then I would step back on the flower-strewn stage for the next performance. Charlie was tall, lean, and strong, and I did adore him. I adored a lot of boys in those days.

'I call the Provincetown Playhouse my Opportunity Theater. I had to reward my mother's sacrifice, but even more important, I had to confirm her perfect faith in me. The one thing she never gave me was advice on my acting. She knew that I knew better. An intuition. There was something more than studying and learning. Definitely something more.

'What Provincetown gave me was not only the opportunity to succeed, but the opportunity to fail. What is important is having the opportunity. Not everyone is that fortunate. Even the opportunity to fail is worth something, especially if you get another opportunity to succeed, if the flop doesn't mean you stop.

'You must realize that success is built on disappointment, and disappointment is inherent in all success. I learned this lesson early.'

Toward the end of the run of *The Earth Between*, Bette received a note from The Repertory Company, which starred Miss Blanche Yurka. An actress had to be replaced in *The Wild Duck*, and Miss Yurka wanted to know if she would be interested.

'*Interested?*' Bette said. 'Ever since I'd seen Peg Entwistle in *The Wild Duck*, I'd dreamed of someday playing Hedwig, but I had no idea it would be *that* soon!

'The next morning I raced breathlessly uptown to the Bijou Theater, where the great star greeted me. I read a few lines. 'That's fine, my dear,' she said in a resonant voice that was remarkably gentle. 'We'll have one week of rehearsal after you close in *The Earth Between*.'

'I rode back on the open top of a Fifth Avenue double-decker bus as Hedwig. The conductor thought I was crazy, and the other passengers gave me a lot of room, but I was Hedwig, and I was truly in heaven as the bus moved through the city I was conquering.

'Just before the curtain that night, I broke out in a cold sweat and a pink rash. Somehow I got through the performance, though near the end of the third act, the spots were showing through my makeup. How I ever got through that evening is a mystery to me. Truly, I was feeling *so* sick. As I collapsed backstage in a chair, Daddy came walking into my dressing room, as stiff and formal as ever. He'd hardly changed at all — just a little gray at the temples and even more impersonal, if possible. He had reached the pinnacle of what the United Shoe Company offered and was now a leading patent consultant for the government.

'Daddy gave a brilliant discourse on everything in the play — except my performance, which he didn't mention at all. I was already feeling awful, but this really hurt. Then he came to the point. 'Uh — would you care to, uh, go out with me and have a little — supper?' I didn't realize until that moment how inarticulate he could be when he was really nervous. The thought of food appalled me, but I knew if I said no, he would be crushed forever.

'"I'm sorry, Daddy. I feel so wretched,' I heard myself saying. 'I have a chill and I'm soaking wet . . . '

'I call myself an actress, but that was my least convincing performance. 'I see,' he said stiffly. He refused to believe I was really ill. My heart started to ache, and I suppose his did, too, but I was just too weak to care. He had come to New York for a reconciliation, and I had seemingly rebuffed him.

'The doctor diagnosed my illness as measles, the worst case he'd ever seen. I was immediately put into quarantine. Not only would I not be able to finish out the last week of *The Earth Between*, but my dream of playing Hedwig was over. I surely wouldn't be able to attend rehearsals for *The Wild Duck*, and Miss Yurka would have to find another actress. I felt like dying, but Ruthie had other plans for me. She bought out a drugstore, then called Miss Yurka's manager to explain that with or without rehearsal, I would be ready. If the actress whom I was replacing would agree to stay until she *had* to leave the company, Ruthie promised that I would be ready in time to step in. All that remained was for me to get well and learn the part in a fortnight.

'The next two weeks were a nightmare of work. I had always loathed being read to, but the measles had weakened my eyes, so Ruthie sat beside my bed and read the part over and over again until I thought I'd go mad. I was so irritable that, in spite of my weakness, I threw Mr. Ibsen's *Duck* across the room. But Ruthie remained the steadfast, patient New Englander.

'Bobby was away at college, but when she heard about my illness, she sent me a little duck with a message around its neck. It said, 'If you must have childish diseases, here's a toy to play with.' If only I'd been able to cheer Bobby up later, when she needed it, the way she cheered me up then! It was the only smile that passed my lips the whole time.

'The day of reckoning arrived. Well or not, I was to be at the Bijou Theater, nine A.M. sharp the next morning. Ruthie was supposed to set the clock for seven A.M. At nine, I was dreaming I'd been cured at Lourdes. Ruthie had forgotten to pull out the thingamajig on the alarm! My guardian angel had failed me. I sank back into my pillow and — I assumed — my deathbed, anyway, my professional deathbed.

'But Ruthie wasn't ready for me to die just yet. She ripped off my bedclothes and dragged me out of my sepulcher. The next thing I remember is we were in a taxi speeding up Sixth Avenue. Ruthie conveyed to the driver that his tip was contingent on how fast he went.

'We arrived at the Bijou an hour late, and Ruthie tried to explain how it was all her fault. I saw this wasn't going to take, so I turned to her

82

and said, 'Get out, Mother! And stay out!' It worked. The director was pacified, and Ruthie understood. She backed out to the stage door, and I walked onstage.

'When the rehearsal went without a hitch, all was forgiven. I was handed my costume and told to be ready for a matinee that afternoon. It was filthy and ragged. Unbelievable. I crawled off to lunch, hoping to keep it down until after the performance. When I came back, the costume was laid out for me, exquisitely pressed, the collars and sleeves crisp. The whole room was immaculate. Obviously *not* the management. *Ruthie's* work.

'There was a lot more to do, and I still didn't feel right. I knew the lines letter-perfect, but I'd never handled the props, and I wasn't sure I had the stamina to last through four acts of raising flags on flagpoles and running up and down ramps in my constraining peasant costume. The matinee curtain went up. I raised the flag successfully, and all went smoothly for four acts. But to find myself onstage after two weeks in bed was a bit much.'

By the time Bette went on tour, she was definitely recovered.

'Philadelphia, Washington, and finally Boston — I knew from the applause I had made it. I was *good* as Hedwig. Good taste, not false modesty, prevents me from quoting some of my notices. Suffice it to say, I could have written them myself!

'Boston had a special significance for me. It was not only my hometown, but it was where I had first seen Peg Entwistle play Hedwig. Everyone turned out to see me — even Daddy. When I arrived at the theater, there was a letter on my dressing table from Charlie. It seemed nothing could go wrong. Then, I read his letter.

'My heart sank. Charlie had broken our engagement, just like that! He said we were too young, and, besides, his father disapproved of actresses. He hoped I would understand and forgive. He was so sorry, but he was helpless against his family.

'However he put it, I was *dumped!* I was angry as hell, but I wasn't going to let it spoil my triumphant return to Boston. I tore up Charlie's letter, but I couldn't tear it out of my mind.

'I've always been inspired by anger. I think I gave a great performance that night, but my mind kept drifting back to Charlie's letter. His father disapproved of me because I'm an actress! Why didn't Charlie have the backbone to stand up for me? Why didn't he even bother to talk it over with me? He never loved me. I never wanted to see him again! Then there was tremendous applause.

'The play was over, and we were taking our curtain calls. The curtain came down and, as was her custom, Miss Yurka stepped through the curtain to take her solo bow. The cast had started toward the wings when the stage manager motioned us back onstage. This was no ordinary ovation, and when the curtain opened again, the whole cast once more joined the star.

'I had never seen such a responsive audience. Their ardor was persistent, their passion insatiable. The curtain went down again, and Miss Yurka took me by the hand and led me out with her. This was a tremendous honor and extremely generous of her. Then, she let go of my hand, smiled that grand smile of hers, and stepped off the stage — leaving me all alone before that loving audience.

'I couldn't believe what was happening. The theater shook with applause. People stood on their chairs, cheering and waving. And it was all for *me!* Waves of love flooded the stage and washed over me. I started to cry. The sweetness of such a moment is impossible to describe. One is both lover and beloved. I forgot all about Charlie and his silly letter. I'd found the one true, enduring romance of my life.

'I looked down at Ruthie, glowing with pride for me. She had quite literally given the best years of her life to me and Bobby.

'My mother always complimented me. She told me that I was pretty, that I had talent, that I was special, and that I could achieve whatever I wanted, if I wanted it enough. All I had to do was to determine what it was I wanted to do, and then to work hard.

'It was very reassuring, and it gave me great confidence to know that my mother believed in me that way. I can never understand parents who undermine their children.

'Mae West told me that her mother never said a cross or sharp word to her. Never in all her life. Neither did Ruthie, though she may have said a few firm ones, but only to encourage me and pull me through. Anyway, I never needed any firmness, because I was firm with myself. I wanted only to do my best.

'My mother always said positive and encouraging things to my sister Bobby, too. But Bobby didn't believe them when she heard them. I wondered why. Perhaps it was because my mother didn't really believe them when she said them.

'Ruthie's belief in me meant everything. Her belief in me was so all-pervasive, I couldn't help but catch it. And, of course, I had my own confidence genes. If there is such a thing as confidence genes, I got them.'

The Wild Duck tour ended at the Shubert Theatre on Broadway, but it was 96th and Broadway. 'It was as close as you could come to being on Broadway and not being on Broadway at the same time,' Bette said.

Returning to the Cape, Bette was recognized this time as a promising young actress. She was given her first opportunity to play a woman, rather than a girl, in The Constant Wife. She was so frightened by the opening night that she fainted onstage. 'It was only a small faint, and I recovered quickly,' she remembered. The actress with whom she was performing was able to act as if the faint was in the script. 'The audience was unaware that anything untoward had transpired when I had practically expired.'

As the lead in The Patsy, a comedy, Bette experienced her first major audience laugh, 'an unintentional laugh,' she pointed out. It was the first line she spoke, and thus she was able to fully enjoy the rest of the performance. She found it wonderful eliciting a response of laughter from an audience. 'Later,' she said, 'it would be tears and two handkerchiefs.'

It was during the rehearsals for George Bernard Shaw's *You Never Can Tell* that Bette experienced what she referred to as 'the divine rapture' of falling in love with her co-star, a not uncommon occurrence in the theater and in film. In this case, Bette's 'crush,' not true love, came to a rather abrupt end when, too distracted to have her lines firmly in mind, she almost failed to open. She came to her senses and with her good memory and Ruthie's work with her on the lines, at the last moment, they saved Bette's opening. 'Now I can't remember anything about him, even his name.'

★   ★   ★

The next fall, Bette and Ruthie faced, if not starvation, hunger pangs. Harlow's checks never covered what they felt were even basic needs, such as eating, and it didn't stretch through the month.

With the help of an agent who sold the uncertain producers on Bette, she opened in the part of the ingénue in *Broken Dishes*, which was officially her Broadway debut. 'I think often that we actors cannot judge ourselves and our performance,' Bette told me. 'Of course we do, but it doesn't mean anyone else agrees with us.

'When I was very young on the stage in New York in *Broken Dishes*, one night I knew I'd been wonderful. I was *so* happy. I'd really put out. I'd given my all. My only regret was that my mother hadn't been there to see me excel in my shining moment.

'I said, 'Mother, tonight, I was simply marvelous.'

'Not a word. Silence.

''I was there, dear. Bette, it was the worst performance you have ever given.'

'After she said it, I understood. I'd lost control because I was having a ball and enjoying myself too much.

'I tried never to let that happen again. I had learned that if I had too much fun, maybe the audience wouldn't have *any*.'

The play opened during the Wall Street crash of 1929.

The star of the show, Donald Meek, arrived and said he had lost all of the money he had in the world. 'He was in his sixties, and I was only twenty-one. I didn't have any money to lose, but I suffered with him that night. Poor, dear Mr. Meek. Well, at least the play was successful, and the next year we went on tour with it.

'The stock market had never interested me because I never really had any surplus money, so I didn't have to worry, except New York was an expensive city, and I wasn't a gold digger. In fact, I was just the opposite. On rare occasions when I was invited to go tea dancing at the Biltmore, I made an effort not to be the economic ruin of my beau. I became known as a cheap date because I do adore potatoes. I could be happy anytime with potatoes. 'Spuds' became my nickname.

'Yes, I dearly loved potatoes. Still do. I love them in any way, shape, or form. I even love potato skins. Yummmm. If all other food disappeared and there was a famine and they left me only potatoes, I could live forever. French fries are the ones I like the least because you really can't taste the potatoes as well. Mashed, hash-brown, potato pancakes. Oh, boy! Can you imagine, there are people who don't eat their potato skins! I could never get along with that kind of person. I get so angry when I make a beautiful crusty potato, and they just leave the skin.

'At this point in my career, I hadn't thought much about the movies. A lot of people in the theater were snobs about the movies. But because of sound, more Broadway actors were being scouted for Hollywood, where they could enjoy the relative financial security of the studio system. One night, Arthur Hornblow from Samuel Goldwyn was in the audience to look at me for a part in *Raffles* opposite Ronald Colman. Needless to say, I didn't win *that* raffle! When Mr. Goldwyn saw my test, he is reported to have said, 'Whom has done this to me?' Years later, I was briefly considered for the part of Cathy in his 'Withering Heights,' as Mr. Goldwyn always called the Brontë story.

'In my test, I noticed a crooked tooth I had never been aware of. After that, I felt everyone was looking at my tooth. I got braces in case I was ever offered a Hollywood test again. But they interfered with my speech in the theater, so I couldn't go on with them. Anyway, the time they were on seemed to take care of the problem.

'In a way, it's strange I ever became a motion picture actress. I hated being photographed. Being my mother's model for her photographic classes had not made me feel any easier in front of a camera lens. I came to detest it, but I couldn't tell my mother.

'Well, I wasn't unwilling. You might say I was hesitant. I was one of her subjects, her primary subject. She used me as a model, to get work. She was always so full of enthusiasm. Sometimes I got sick of posing. But I couldn't let Ruthie down. So her enthusiasm carried over to me.'

When we met in California in 1981, Bette showed me some of the photographs her mother had taken of her when she was very young. 'As you can see,' she said, 'I wasn't a bad subject.'

I commented that in one of the photographs her mother had caught the defiant spirit of Bette, even as a young girl. She laughed.

'You see that look on that girl's face. My daughter B.D., of course, is my twin. Every now and then, she looks at me just like that, with that kind of cold look, as much as to say, 'Don't you fool with me!' I obviously didn't want to be photographed, and I couldn't hide it.' This was said a few years before B.D.'s book.

★ ★ ★

During the Broadway run of *Broken Dishes*, Bette was 'absolutely heartbroken' when she heard the news of Fritz's marriage. Her despair, however, was soon ended by a resumption of her romance with Ham. She met him again while she was doing *Broken Dishes* in summer stock at the Cape Playhouse. He was playing in a band to help him pay his tuition through the Massachusetts Agricultural College in Amherst.

'I was always very good at wearing blinders. My own brand of rose-colored glasses. I saw only what I wanted to see where my personal life and romance were concerned.

'I'm good at giving love. I'm not bad at getting love. But I was never very good at keeping it.

'I think I was in love with being in love and looking for a man I could cast in the part opposite me. Being in love isn't something anyone can do properly alone, with the exception, of course, of a few men I've known who were in love with themselves, the Errol Flynn type, Howard Hughes . . .

'Compatibility. That is the most important word in any relationship. Passion passes, you know. Passion is easier to find than compatibility.

'I wish that someone could have explained the facts of life, the ones that matter, not the ones in biology books. My mother didn't know much about either, and would have been too embarrassed to talk about that kind of thing with anyone, especially her own daughter.'

While Bette was doing her next play on Broadway, *Solid South*, a Universal talent scout arranged for another screen test to see if she would be suitable for a part in the upcoming film of Preston Sturges's play *Strictly Dishonorable*. This time she was offered a Hollywood contract for three months at $300 a week. She and her mother would be given a round-trip train ticket to Hollywood. The scout mentioned to Bette that he didn't understand how someone who looked like her could hope to succeed in Hollywood because she wasn't at all typical of the way starlets looked. It didn't disturb Bette. 'I wasn't planning to be a starlet,' she told me. 'I was planning to be a star.'

After Bette left Broadway for Hollywood, she never missed live theater, as do many stage actors. 'The theater is a selfish life. All you think about is yourself and staying healthy.

'Once you become very well known, a star, if you catch a cold, you let down so many, the cast, the audiences, the people who risked their money. And once I became so famous, I couldn't really have an understudy. Audiences had not come to see my understudy. That's the truth of it.

'Then, it's a strange thing when a show closes. It's all gone. A desolate sight. Is there anything more forsaken than a theater with the closing notice posted?

'The movies are forever, though I must admit, we had no idea how long forever was when we were just making them.'

3

Early Hollywood

'Would you like to know about the first dick I ever saw?' Bette Davis asked writer Harry Haun.

Haun told me that this hadn't been one of his prepared questions.

'I was twenty-three,' Bette went on, 'and just starting out at Universal in Hollywood. Everyone in the crew was kidding me because I was so virginal and innocent, even sort of retarded in that way, about sex. They told me that the baby I was going to give a bath to was a boy baby.

'Well, it was a black and white picture, but even in black and white, you could see my face was gray.'

*   *   *

On Monday, December 8, 1930, Ruthie, Bette, and a wire-haired fox terrier named Boojums left Grand Central Terminal on the *20th Century Limited*, with one change in Chicago, for California. In 1930, it took almost five days to cross the country. Bette and Ruthie arrived at Los Angeles's Union Station on Friday, December 12.

'The train arrived on time,' Bette recalled, 'just a little after noon, and I was very excited. I hadn't expected a star's reception, but we did expect there would be *someone* from the studio to meet us. We waited an hour and I've never had much patience. When I called them to ask what happened, they said there *was* a studio representative on the platform, but he didn't see anyone who looked like an actress. 'How could he not?' I told them. 'I was carrying a dog!'

'When I arrived in Hollywood, according to their standards, I wasn't 'glamorous' enough. Now, this was *really* in the very beginning of talking pictures, and all of us who came out from the theater were not actressy kind of people. We had our own color hair and maybe a couple of teeth crooked. We looked *totally* different from the Hollywood starlets, and we were very, very puzzled about this standard they were looking for. And offscreen, we didn't go around all dressed up, like a Harlow or somebody like that would, you know. They just did not understand us, at all.

'I was referred to as 'the little brown wren.' Nobody helped me about makeup or about the camera. It's a wholly new profession, really. Finally, they find out the best way for you to wear your hair. They put a makeup on you that does the best for you, but it's just a slow process of getting to look on the screen like what you really thought you looked like in life!

'I was often told, 'Be natural!' Natural in front of a camera, in front of all those people. It's the hardest thing in the world to be natural, to seem natural, in an unnatural situation.

'Then, some genius at Universal got the bright idea to change my name to 'Bettina Dawes.' And to be a little vulgar, I told them I certainly would not allow myself to become known commonly, and I do mean 'commonly,' as 'Between the Drawers' all my life! A little humor sometimes takes care of things! That did it. Otherwise, I would have refused and refused and refused. I was lucky they had such an absurd suggestion because even *they* saw the absurdity. I was never asked to change my name again.

'After my first picture, *Bad Sister*, I remember sitting in the outer office when Mr. [Carl] Laemmle, Jr., was talking to somebody, and he was talking about me, not knowing I was there. He said, 'She's got as much sex appeal as Slim Summerville.' This was no compliment to any young lady. In case you've never seen Slim Summerville, he looked and talked like Bull-winkle.

'Then he said, 'Who wants to get *her* at the end of the picture?' Oh, I was defeated! Heartbreak. It was absolute heartbreak. This really does *catastrophic* things to your ego, and I didn't have a lot of ego. Never have had lots. This is a big misnomer about actors. We have very little ego, basically, you know. I think it has something to do with why we want to play other people.

'It's very important to be able to keep what confidence you have no matter how dire the circumstances. You have to learn how to shelter and protect it from the onslaught. I had my pride in doing my work the best I could.

'There was another young Broadway actor in the cast of *Bad Sister* they didn't like. His name was Humphrey Bogart. They didn't think he looked right for films either.

'Universal was going to drop me, but the great cameraman Karl Freund told Mr. Laemmle, 'Davis has lovely eyes.' My contract was renewed with the admonition I be limited to certain roles.'

Bette had originally been brought out to Hollywood with the thought of starring her opposite Paul Lukas in *Strictly Dishonorable*. After she arrived, she was not considered right for the part. While waiting for an assignment, she was told to report to wardrobe. There she was outfitted to be tested for another film, *A House Divided*, starring Walter Huston and directed by a newcomer, William Wyler.

'My first meeting with Mr. Wyler was really rather grim. I was under contract to Universal, and it was his first truly important picture. I was sent down to make a test for it, as a new little kid from New York.

'They outfitted me in a little cotton dress that was far too revealing in front. It was what I called 'a chest dress.' Nowadays, of course, no one would consider a little décolletage risqué. It would just look ridiculous, probably showed *this* much, about one inch. Nowadays, one's bloody well *expected* to go absolutely starkers for the whole *world* to see. It was an unbelievably different time.

'I was very, very embarrassed. I was a little

Puritan from New England, so you can imagine how embarrassed I was. It made me look common, but I wasn't listened to when I complained.

'I was rushed onto the set where a dark, brooding little man stared me up and down. He was an ex-prop man, a relative of Mr. Carl Laemmle.

'He stood behind the camera and said, 'What do you think about these dames that come onstage and show their chests, and think they can get jobs?' He dismissed me with a sneer.

'I didn't get the part. *That* was my introduction to Willie Wyler.

'Well, I'm not a very vengeful person, but this I *never* forgot. Because it was just terrible for me. And I said, 'One day, God willing, I shall tell this man.'

'So came the day when Mr. Warner said, 'You are going to have a *great, great,* privilege, Mr. William Wyler is directing *Jezebel.*' I said, '*Really?*'

'I had my first meeting with him. I said, 'Mr. Wyler, I hear I'm to be very privileged to work with you. When did you ever see me before?'

'He had no memory of it, of course. That's all. This was maybe seven years later. I just sat down and explained why I hated him. He kind of got red in the face, and he said, 'I was *horrible* in those days. I'm much nicer now.' So, that's where my revenge went. He had a fine sense of humor, and he always knew how to turn things his way. Willie was to play such an important part in my life, in every way.'

One of the experiences Bette never forgot was being called on to lie on a couch 'to act as a test girl for thirty or forty men, more or less, give or take a few, and these tryout actors would plop themselves on my bosom, flattening it and me. The minutes flew like hours. Some of them ought to have thought of going on diets. Only one, Gilbert Roland, he was a gorgeous guy, had a few words to reassure me I wasn't just a rug. He said, 'We actors here at the studio all have to experience humiliations.'

'It was feudal serfdom. If we didn't behave ourselves, we got lashed, tongue-lashed, that is, but lashed nonetheless, and if we slaves revolted, we could have our contracts canceled. The only thing worse than *having* a studio contract was *not* having one.'

Since Bette was being paid $300 a week, she was assigned a supporting role in a remake of Booth Tarkington's *The Flirt*, retitled *The Bad Sister*.

'Would you believe it, I wasn't the bad sister? I was the good sister. Humphrey Bogart was in the picture, too, but I didn't really get to know him until we were both at Warner Brothers. He'd been on the Broadway stage, too. I've heard that he got noticed in a play where he played a character who only had one line. He kept repeating, 'Tennis, anyone?''

The Bad Sister (1931)
Small town temptress Marianne Madison (Sidney Fox) elopes with confidence man Valentine

Corliss (Humphrey Bogart), after he has swindled the whole town with the unwitting help of her respectable father (Charles Winninger). After Corliss jilts her, Marianne returns, pretending to be repentant, but her long-rejected suitor, Dr. Dick Lindley (Conrad Nagel), finally sees her for what she is, and appreciates the more enduring values in her shy sister, Laura (Bette Davis), who has always secretly loved him.

'It was believed at the time,' Bette said, 'that Sidney Fox was going to be a big star.' Bette was still being called 'the little brown wren' by some at Universal. Her next assignment was the smallest part of her screen career.

Seed (1931)

Bart Carter (John Boles), a successful novelist, goes back to the family he abandoned ten years earlier. Finding his five children grown, he invites them to come and live in Paris with him and Mildred (Genevieve Tobin), the glamorous publisher who lured him away and made him famous. Their future as a family, however, remains uncertain.

'I played the part of one of John Boles's daughters. If you blinked at the wrong moment you would have missed me. I should have joined the extras union.'

In spite of this, Universal picked up Bette's option. Besides Freund's comment on her eyes, the editor of Seed, Ted Kent, thought she 'had something,' according to Bette. Her next picture was *Waterloo Bridge*, directed by James Whale, who directed *Frankenstein*.

Waterloo Bridge (1931)

In World War I London, chorus girl Myra (Mae Clark) and Canadian flier Roy Cronin (Kent Douglas/Douglass Montgomery) meet and fall in love during an air raid. When Roy leaves for the front, Myra realizes she cannot escape her past and admits to Roy's mother that she is really a prostitute. Sadly, Myra wanders back to where she and Roy met, Waterloo Bridge, and she is killed during an air raid.

Bette was loaned out to RKO for her next picture, *Way Back Home*, which was based on a popular radio serial, *Seth Parker*, starring Mr. and Mrs. Phillips H. Lord. Lord would later create the long-running radio series *Gangbusters*.

Way Back Home (1932)

Goodhearted Maine preacher Seth Parker (Phillips H. Lord) and his wife (Mrs. Lord) take in runaway Robbie Turner (Frankie Darro). When his cruel drunken father, Rube (Stanley Fields), tries to get his son back, Seth adopts him. Rube kidnaps Robbie after attacking Mary Lucy (Bette Davis), a neighbor who is trying to protect the boy, but David Clark (Frank Albertson) saves her. Then Seth rescues Robbie when Rube is killed by a train.

Frank Albertson will be remembered as Cassidy, the bragging Texas oilman in Alfred

Hitchcock's *Psycho*. The film's composer, Max Steiner, a pupil of Gusav Mahler, employed a style of Hollywood film music that traced its origins back to Viennese opera of the early twentieth century. His contribution to many Bette Davis films was exceedingly important. Bette later said, 'Sometimes I felt Max Steiner was one of the men I was married to.'

While film reviews were considerably less important than they later became, Bette was conscious of the power the reviewers had on her early Hollywood career. 'When I started out,' she told me, 'it was amazing. The first film I did, I got a great review in *Variety*. I thought, 'Ah, a piece of cake.' Then I read some more reviews. No cake. I was crushed. I understood right away that somehow I had to get a thicker skin.

'Those who say they don't read what the critics say about their work and aren't influenced by it, ha! I don't believe this for a minute and a half. Less.

'I *can* accept a critic giving his honest appraisal. Anyway, I like to *think* I can. What I don't approve of is a reviewer writing something just to show himself as brilliant for his own aggrandizement, at the expense of a performance. This is naughty.'

Bette was next loaned out to Columbia for an adaptation of Edgar Wallace's *The Feathered Serpent* called *The Menace*. The film was directed by Roy William Neill, who would later become associated with the popular Sherlock Holmes series.

The Menace (1932)

Escaped convict Ronald Quayle (Walter Byron) returns to his ancestral estate in England, hoping to clear himself of murder. Unrecognizable after plastic surgery, Quayle is able to prove that his stepmother (Natalie Moorhead) conspired with an accomplice to murder his father.

Bette plays the part of Quayle's former fiancée, Peggy. In the cast was Murray Kinnell, a character actor and good friend of George Arliss. Arliss would soon be casting for *The Man Who Played God*.

★ ★ ★

Bette's last picture for Universal would also be a loan-out, this time to B. F. Zeidman Productions, Ltd. The film, *Hell's House*, starred Pat O'Brien and Junior Durkin, a popular teenage actor of the early 1930s. Durkin's career would end at twenty when he was killed in an automobile accident in 1935.

Hell's House (1932)

When the headquarters of bootlegger Matt Kelly (Pat O'Brien) is raided by the police, they arrest a teenager, Jimmy Mason (Junior Durkin), who is only working there as an errand boy. After Jimmy is sentenced to three years in reform school, his girlfriend, Peggy (Bette Davis), becomes Kelly's girlfriend. Jimmy escapes and confronts Peggy, who explains that she was only trying to help get him out of reform

102

school. The police arrive, and Kelly clears Jimmy.

The title refers to the reformatory where Jimmy is sent. Originally, the film was called *Juvenile Court*. It was shot in fourteen days.

In September 1931, after six pictures, Bette's Universal contract ran out, and Junior Laemmle, now in charge of Universal, did not exercise the option.

'They dumped me,' she told me. 'My career was almost over before it had really begun, like Peg Entwistle's.

'I'd come to love making films. I hadn't known I would love it the way I loved the theater. I loved it more, with its infinite possibilities, but now Mother and I were packing up to go back. I felt a failure. I'm not a good loser. Worse yet, we were going to be broke again.

'Just as we finished packing and were about to leave for Union Station, the phone rang. It was someone who claimed to be George Arliss.

'I couldn't imagine that the great George Arliss would be calling me, so idiot that I was, I assumed it was some friends ribbing me. What a cruel sense of humor some people have, I thought.

'I took the phone from Ruthie and a very cultured British voice on the other end said, 'Hello, this is George Arliss. I'd like to speak to Miss Davis.'

''This is Miss Davis,' I said in my very best stage diction. 'How are you, Georgie, old boy?'

'Very positively, very calmly, he said, 'Miss

Davis, this is George Arliss.'

''Oooo, Mr. Arliss, how lovely of you to call me.'

'Well, after three or four exchanges like this, it hit me.

'It really *was* the great actor. Himself.

'I was mortified, then overwhelmed. He wanted to interview me for the female lead in his next picture. He'd been desperately looking for the right girl and thought I might be the one. He asked me if I could come over to Warners immediately.

'When I realized it really was he, I could have flown there without a plane. He asked me how I got there so fast, and then he talked with me about a part in *The Man Who Played God.*

'I was very nervous because it was everything I dreamed of. It wasn't only that I wanted desperately to stay in Hollywood and act in films, but the idea that I could learn from this great man of whom I was in awe . . .

'He had such a beautiful voice, it made my heart beat faster. I'm certain he understood how nervous I was, but he pretended to ignore it while I gradually calmed down. He didn't say a word that would embarrass me about how I acted on the phone when I had been fooling around and failed to recognize him.

'He wanted to know how long I had acted in the theater, and I told him it was about three years, and he said to me, 'Just enough to rub the rough edges off.' Isn't that beautiful? I thought that was the most beautiful remark I'd ever heard.

'I was cast as leading lady in *The Man Who Played God*. As I tell you about it, I can remember exactly how I felt at the moment. Better than remember, I can *feel* it.

'I was jumping up and down for joy. I tried to control my excitement because I didn't want people to think I wasn't professional, or worse, childish, or worse yet, a lunatic. I actually told perfect strangers there. 'I've got a part with Mr. Arliss.' Enthusiasm. I had it. Enthusiasm is one of life's great blessings. And I think it's somewhat contagious. Some of these perfect strangers seemed happy for me.

'Mr. Arliss not only kept me in Hollywood and saved my screen career, but he gave me an opportunity to get a Warner Brothers contract. And you know what *that* led to! I became known as 'The Fourth Warner Brother,' though not to Jack Warner, thank you very much.

'Mr. Arliss was the man who played God for me, and may I add, he was absolutely the most beautiful man, beautiful on the outside, and even more beautiful inside.

'Eighteen years. That's what Mr. Arliss gave me because that's how long I stayed at Warner Brothers.

'Wherever I am, I always have Mr. Arliss with me in a silver frame, and in my heart.

'Thank you, Mr. Arliss.'

Bette was paid $300 a week for her appearance in *The Man Who Played God*, which was well enough received for Warner Brothers to offer her a twenty-six-week contract at $400 a week, with a five-year renewable option. It was the beginning of her eighteen years at Warner Brothers.

The Man Who Played God (1932)

Concert pianist Montgomery Royale (George Arliss), deafened in an explosion, learns to read lips so proficiently that with binoculars he can eavesdrop on conversations in Central Park from his Fifth Avenue apartment. Some of the people he observes are needy, and Royale, being wealthy, helps them anonymously, changing their lives.

He takes great pleasure in playing God until he observes his youthful fiancée, Grace (Bette Davis), telling Harold (Donald Cook), the young man she loves, that she cannot leave Royale because of his handicap. He won't allow her to make that sacrifice, so he breaks their engagement, finding happiness instead with Mildred (Violet Heming), a friend who has always loved him.

Bette was the one who suggested that her character say, 'I won't be a quitter,' and George Arliss contributed his own comment on her 'beautiful eyes.'

Bette's style of acting was quite different from most of the cast. While they spoke slowly and deliberately, she spoke quickly enough for critics to complain that she spoke too rapidly for the microphone. It wasn't Bette or the microphone that was at fault, but the playback amplification equipment in the theaters, some of it dating back to the first sound films and well behind

Hollywood's then-current state-of-the-art recording facilities.

This film anticipates Alfred Hitchcock's *Rear Window* (1954), in which a man with a broken leg observes his neighbors through binoculars.

'At the end of the film,' Bette told me, 'Mr. Arliss, as he was billed above the title, said to my character, 'I'll always be your friend.' And he always was.

'After *The Man Who Played God*, I was firmly entrenched in Hollywood. I was successful, and success means doors open for you magically as if you were a queen. And behind each door is a promise. There are special people behind those doors, the great of the world. I thought they would be different from mere mortals, and they were. F.D.R., Carl Sandburg, Tennessee Williams, all larger-than-life people. When I was with them, I could *feel* the difference, and it made me nervous. When I felt that nervousness, I knew I was with someone special, someone who affected me, someone who affected the world.

'With success, you go everywhere first-class, and you aren't dependent on others. You don't have to wait around anymore. People wait for *you*. But one thing success does *not* guarantee is happiness, although as Joe Mankiewicz said, 'Happiness doesn't buy money.''

4

The Warner Years
(1932–1937)

'In the beginning, the first two or three years, we did eight and ten films a year,' Bette told me. 'The contract system meant that month after month, we were able to make films. If a film we made flopped, we'd made another before anyone knew about it. We knew we were doing some ghastly stuff, but that's how we were learning our trade, and this is the way it *had* to be. Many scripts I knew weren't great. Nothing ever turned out to be great that I thought wasn't good. No surprises. So we just learned our craft and didn't worry about the crap we were doing.

'You don't learn through the parts that are easy for you. You don't learn through just doing parts you love. You don't.

'As you learned your craft, the audience became familiar with you, and if they liked you at all, this familiarity endeared you to them. They could go to the box office and spend their money and have a pretty good idea what to expect. I was so anxious never to disappoint them. Only the public can make a star. The studio could only give you the chance to try out for audiences. It is the public that must embrace you. They take you 'unto themselves' or they don't. We were permitted, allowed, to make films. It was a privilege. Today the time between films leaves too much space in a career.

'The thing that is hard and wrong now is that there is no place to struggle. There is no place to hone your craft. At current budgets, you can't afford a failure.

'One thing I'm proud of, I can tell you, is that I always gave my best. That is what a professional does. That is what is called passing the crap test.

'Only when you've done your best in a bad film have you passed the crap test. I think the test of a real professional is doing your very best even when you feel what you've got to work with is crap.

'I'm very proud to say, *I* never failed the crap test.'

There was, however, more to being a Hollywood actress than learning lines and hitting marks. 'You were being fashioned into a salable piece of merchandise, often at great personal sacrifice. Oh, the sacrifices we actresses make! Oh, the sacrifices we *women* make!

'You see, I thought I was fairly attractive until I got to Hollywood, but I didn't go on thinking that for very long. But then they would want to go too far in their efforts to 'glamourize,' according to their conceptions. Hepburn, Margaret Sullavan, and I were the three who really fought it.

'I'd have given anything to look like Katie

Hepburn. Oh, I adore her face! It's so interesting! Mine is just kind of round. I always *hated* my face.

'I never was a cutie. But I had shapely legs and nice 'bulbs,' as Jack Warner referred to them.

'When I went to Warners, they made me bleach my hair. Really, I was lucky it didn't all fall out. Some of it did. And it never grew back. And they actually thinned my hair. I knew the dye job was going to limit my parts, so I snuck down one day and had Perc Westmore put it back — the color, not the hair — the ash brown I'd always had. And one year later, Mr. Wallis sent for me. He said, 'You've had your *hair* redyed!' One year later!' Hal Wallis was the executive producer of Warner Brothers under Jack Warner.

'He'd never even noticed! But if I'd gone for permission, he wouldn't have allowed it, you see. And I didn't *want* to go through life with this very bleached head of hair. When I looked in the mirror, it was as if someone else was looking back at me, someone with a slight family resemblance.

'Excessive torturous bleaching of my hair caused it to become so thin I have to sometimes resort to wigs. Terrible to have to wear a wig. The extreme bleaching was especially hard on fine hair. Dyed hair just fell out. I could have cried.

'As for my eyebrows . . . Ruined forever. Over-plucked or shaven to give them a fashionable arch, they never grew back, but for a few hairs which remain and which may or may not be fashionably arched.

'Probably they didn't know that most of the time, eyebrows don't grow back as thick as they were, or ever grow back at all. My own eyebrows certainly were never the same. Before I went to Hollywood, I didn't know what an eyebrow pencil was. In Hollywood, I all too quickly found out.

'They thought anything artificial was superior to anything real. If *they*, the producers, studio executives, Mr. Warner, had known the possible cost to us, still they wouldn't have cared. You were their property. Of course, they didn't want to damage their property as long as they thought they had use for it. They didn't really care about you, but they didn't want to damage your value, as long as you belonged to them. We actors were their chattel, or perhaps more correctly, to paraphrase Mr. Hitchcock, their cattle.

'Of course, we didn't know much about those things in those days, about eyebrows, I mean. If we understood, maybe some would have made the choice to take the risk anyway. Most of us would have chosen our careers over our eyebrows. You could live with the hope your eyebrows would grow back, but you *knew* your career never would. So, I sacrificed two eyebrows for one career.'

'Glamour is so mysterious and fragile. It's a fascination with the unknown. But how is glamour possible now when we know everything there is to know about our celebrities? Now we know what they look like without their clothes, who they're sleeping with . . . *everything!* In my day, I wouldn't flaunt my 'bulbs'! They weren't the biggest, but they weren't bad!'

Bette's second and third Warner Brothers pictures, *The Rich Are Always With Us* and *So Big*, were shot simultaneously, the first by day, the second by night. The first released, *So Big*, was based on an Edna Ferber novel and starred Barbara Stanwyck. William Wellman directed. This was a remake of a 1925 film with Colleen Moore and Phyllis Haver that was remade again in 1953 with Jane Wyman and Nancy Olson. *So Big* was one of Bette's favorite early films.

So Big (1932)

As a child, Selina Peake (Dawn O'Day/Anne Shirley) loses her father (Robert Warwick) and his fortune, but not his idealism. The grown-up Selina (Barbara Stanwyck) pursues her own mission in life as a schoolteacher in the rural Northwest.

There she meets an immigrant Dutch farmer, Pervus deJong (Earl Foxe), who shares her ideals, and they marry. After they have a child, Dirk (Dickie Moore), Pervus dies. She hopes her son will become an architect, but the grown Dirk (Hardie Albright) disappoints her by becoming a bond salesman.

Selina finds consolation in Roelfe Poole (George Brent), a young man whom she has inspired to become a sculptor. Meanwhile, Dirk has fallen in love with a girl, Dallas O'Mara (Bette Davis), who shares his mother's ideals, and Selina hopes she will change the course of her son's life.

Alfred E. Green directed *The Rich Are Always With Us*. This was the first of many Bette Davis films with cinematographer Ernest Haller, Bette's favorite.

'I had the same three cameramen through the years: Ernie Haller, Tony Gaudio, and Sol Polito. They were the three greatest, plus the nicest people, but Haller was the genius. He was such a doll. Tony Gaudio was *beautiful*.'

A version of the famous two-cigarettes-on-a-match, so well remembered from *Now, Voyager*, was first used between George Brent and Ruth Chatterton in this film. In real life, the couple was married for several years. Bette particularly noticed Brent.

The Rich Are Always With Us (1932)
The seemingly happy marriage of Caroline (Ruth Chatterton) and wealthy stockbroker Greg Grannard (John Miljan) ends in a divorce when he falls in love with Allison Adair (Adrienne Dore). The scandal, however, affects Greg's business.

A famous newspaper columnist, Julian Tierney (George Brent), admits that he loves Caroline, but doubts her feelings toward him when she expresses such concern over her ex-husband and his failing business fortunes. A younger woman, Malbro (Bette Davis), comes into Julian's life, and Caroline fears she has lost him.

In an accident, Allison is killed and Greg seriously injured. Caroline nurses Greg through his convalescence. Julian is touched by Caroline's compassion and realizes he loves her. He asks her to marry him, and she consents, but only after Greg has fully recovered.

In all of Bette's Warner Brothers films up to this point, she had played supporting roles. With her next film, *The Dark Horse*, she received star billing with Warren William. She described him as 'a bargain-basement John Barrymore who imagined himself the ultimate ladies' man.

'The giggle around the studio was that he had an erection ninety percent of the time and had to wear special underwear in order to conceal it. I think *he* started the rumor. Anyway, I never bothered to find out if it was true or not.'

The Dark Horse (1932)

Election worker Kay Russell (Bette Davis) persuades her party to hire her boyfriend, Hal Blake (Warren William), a brilliant campaign manager, to help elect an incompetent candidate, Zachary Hicks (Guy Kibbee), as governor. First, however, they must pay Blake's fine and back alimony payments to his ex-wife, Maybelle (Vivienne Osborne), in order to get him out of jail.

Blake's ingenious strategies succeed brilliantly until the opposition party forces him to remarry Maybelle to avoid a scandal. Hicks wins the election, and Blake's marriage is ruled invalid, leaving him free to marry Kay.

At tea in her New York apartment, Bette reminisced with composer-conductor Marvin Hamlisch and me about *The Dark Horse*. It was a film Bette remembered as 'not exactly a brilliant plot, but I was happy to be moving forward in my career.' Picture by picture, she was doing the groundwork for her future. This led Bette and Marvin to some personal recollections of the perquisites of fame.

Marvin asked her, 'Do you know Carvel ice cream? It's that kind of . . . '

'Yes! Yes! I do!'

He went on. 'My friend and I were on Long Island, and we were getting a Carvel, and the person behind the counter getting us the ice cream said, 'Hey! You're Marvin Hamlisch! Wow! Would you please sign this.' And he gave me a paper napkin. I signed it. He said, 'Please let me give you this.' And he gave me a free Carvel. Then, he gave my friend a Carvel, too.

'We walked out and my friend said, 'Now when you don't *need* it, they give it to you free. If you're dying, do they give you a free Carvel?''

'Yes, yes,' Bette responded. 'They most certainly do.

'When we were first here in New York, looking for a job, living in a little room, you know, no money, no nothing, we went into this little restaurant one night, my mother, my friend, and I. We ate these delicious things, and it was a big splurge, all we could afford, but not as much as we wanted.

'Well, this very nice man who seemed to own the place came over and said, 'Did you ladies enjoy the food?'

''Oh, we did!' we said in unison. 'It was

115

delicious.' Well, you could see that. You just had to look at how we'd cleaned our plates so you couldn't tell there'd been any food on them.

'He said, 'Wouldn't you ladies like seconds?'

'We didn't speak. He'd read our minds.

'We couldn't order any more because we'd spent all our money. Well, we had *something* left, but if we spent that, we'd have to have starved the next day.

'He looked at me, and he said, 'I believe you're trying to be an actress.'

'I said, 'Yes. Oh, yes!'

'He said he loved the theater, and he would like to help. He wouldn't take any money. He gave us our dinner free. And moreover, he invited us to come back whenever we wanted and have our meals free.

'Then we left, and I said, 'I wish we *could* come back, but we *can't* accept his offer.'

'And my mother said, 'Of course we can. You're going to be a great star. As soon as you're successful you'll come back and pay him, and he'll be happy to have played his part in the life of an important star. Bette, your guardian angel is watching over us, and you can't hurt your guardian angel's feelings.'

'It was easy to persuade me in those days. I was always hungry.

'Well, we went back many times, and that dear man often was all that stood between us and starvation or, anyway, hunger pangs.

'I've never liked owing a debt, so I couldn't wait to be successful enough to pay him. I kept very careful account of what we owed. He gave us dinners free during a six-month period. Imagine.

'The first time I came back from California was on a promotional tour for *The Dark Horse*, my biggest part yet. I'd brought the money for our dinners and a heart full of thanks. I wasn't exactly a star, and I didn't know if he'd recognize the name of Bette Davis, but I wanted to tell him what his gift had meant to me.

'But I couldn't find him. The little place had gone. I wondered if that dear man and his delicious little restaurant had existed only for me. I tried to find him.

'Over the years, I would have given almost anything to have found him, to have paid my debt, and to have asked him if he realized, you know, that the young girl he helped was now Bette Davis.'

Marvin said, 'Wow! That was even better than Carvel's.'

★   ★   ★

The Cabin in the Cotton was another turning point in Bette's career, and it was the first time she worked with director Michael Curtiz, about whom she had mixed feelings.

'Mr. Curtiz, I must say, monster as he was, was a great European moviemaker. He was not a performer's director. I made quite a few pictures with him. You had to be very strong with him. And he wasn't fun. He could humiliate people, but never me. He was a real *BASTARD!* Cruelest man I have ever known. But he knew how to shoot a film well.'

In this film, Bette had the opportunity to show what she could do with the part of an independent woman. Her character was summed up in the memorable line she drawls: 'Ah'd love to kiss you, but Ah just washed mah hair.'

The Cabin in the Cotton (1932)

Wealthy planter Lane Norwood (Berton Churchill) takes an interest in Marvin Blake (Richard Barthelmess), the ambitious son of a sharecropper. He employs him as bookkeeper in his general store, where Marvin falls in love with Norwood's flirtatious daughter, Madge (Bette Davis).

Norwood hopes to learn from Marvin about a sharecroppers' rebellion. Meanwhile, Marvin finds irregularities in Norwood's books that prove he is cheating them.

The sharecroppers rebel, burning down the store and apparently destroying the incriminating books; but Marvin has kept a duplicate set, and Norwood is forced to accede to their demands.

Marvin goes back to his former girlfriend, Betty (Dorothy Jordan), but Madge believes she will win him.

'Because of my performance in *Cabin in the Cotton*,' Bette told me, 'Warners picked up my option.

'When I did *Cabin in the Cotton*, I was still a virgin. Yes, that's absolutely true. No question about it. But my part called for me to exude raging sexuality. Well, if they had known I was

118

still a virgin, they wouldn't have believed I could carry it off. They wouldn't have trusted me if they'd known, but no one asked. It was assumed that a young actress had lived a bit of a loose life.

'In case you're interested, I can name every man I'd ever slept with up to that time. Don't worry. I'm not going to embarrass you. It won't take long:

'Not one! Not even *one!*

'I not only wasn't getting any, but I didn't even know yet what I wasn't getting. I thought I understood what sex was all about in a kind of general way from books Bobby and I had devoured, but I was obsessively preoccupied with how it felt. That was what I couldn't imagine.

'I could hardly wait. But I had been brought up to believe that I had to bring my virginity to the marital bed.

'Eventually, I did just that, but I don't know if my husband, Ham, appreciated my sacrifice. He didn't mention it. I think there were two virgins in that bed.

'My husband was rather embarrassed by sexuality — mine, not his. He hadn't been brought up to believe that a woman could care as much about it as a man, enjoy it, need it.

'We just did it. We didn't talk about it.

'It's believed that men need sex more than women. Well, that's not believed by me. I think women need sex more than men.

'For me, it was a pressure-cooker effect. I'd been waiting so long, I didn't need much to make me happy — and I didn't get much. It was more precious.

119

'But I didn't know then, so it was enjoyable. I didn't learn until later why people made such a fuss about sex.

'It was in the spring of 1932 that Ham wrote telling me he was coming to California that summer after he graduated from college. I was looking forward to seeing him, but I was a little apprehensive. After all, we hadn't seen each other in almost three years, and a lot had happened in my life. I had become a movie star. A real movie star. I was pictured in all the fan magazines next to Jean Harlow, Constance Bennett, and Madge Evans, if you remember who *they* were. You've probably heard of Jean Harlow.

'They were right on top, and *I* was there with them. I could hardly believe it myself. But I was self-conscious about my increasing fame. I was afraid it would make Ham feel insecure. I wondered about it. Well, I'd soon find out.

'I needn't have worried. The male ego is more often than not elephantine to begin with. Ham wasn't a bit deterred by my movie star status. He arrived, and we just picked up where we'd left off.

'Ham stood taller and more genuine than ever. I was homesick for the world I was brought up in, and Ham meant home. Ham was my first love — and my youth.'

Bette always thought a lot about marriage and babies. 'Every girl did then,' she told me.

'Ruthie was actually getting worried about me, and so was I. 'You can't go on like this. Marry him!' If only Mother had been wise enough to suggest we have an affair first — but that was too much to expect. She came from another time.

'I wasn't that smart myself, and Ham had too much respect for me to suggest it. So, on the eighteenth of August, 1932, in a hundred and ten degrees of heat, I found myself standing before a preacher at an Indian mission in Yuma, Arizona, being married to Ham, with Ruthie and Bobby as our witnesses.

'It was Ruth Elizabeth's moment. It was, in fact, her greatest day. It was the day she had been waiting for — the union under God of a pure bride and the approved bliss of the wedding night, all that kind of thing. This was what Ruth Elizabeth had been saving herself for. We, Ruth Elizabeth and Bette, could offer ourselves to Ham in pristine condition. 'Pristine,' that was the key word. Ruth Elizabeth and I could enjoy formalized passion, ritualized love, proper and sanctified. It was just the way my mother and society said it was supposed to be. We were Mrs. Harmon O. Nelson. We were thrilled, as though we were the absolute first, and it had never happened to anyone before.

'I had the man I loved and I had my work, and I was finally released from my maddening curiosity about physical sex. It was natural, and it was fun. All my dreams seemed to be coming true.

'We even had a white ivy-covered cottage, and it wasn't all that easy to *find* one in Hollywood. Mansions were more common, but I only longed for a cottage. Mother and Bobby had a guesthouse in back. I wanted all of us to be together, and I failed to ask Ham how he felt about it. In a way, Ham found himself married to the bunch of us. Very cozy.

'I was now a proper wife, but Ruthie continued to treat me like a child. Well, she *had* been in charge for twenty-five years, so it had become a habit, and I guess she found it hard to give up the reins. She could not accept that my husband now held that right, especially since it didn't seem to be a right he expected or wanted.

'The first casualty of our situation was Bobby. Her security seemed to be totally shattered by my marriage. Her anxieties took on the proportions of a nervous breakdown. She was a true Scorpio, so she had her own tremendous need for love and passion and success, and here I was getting everything, while she was getting nothing. It had become a real problem. There were people who thought she needed profes- sional help, but we certainly weren't going to commit her to a sanatorium, so Ruthie took her back east. My contract with Warner Brothers, four pictures and a cross-country tour, had left Ham and me no time for a real honeymoon. This idea of a traditional honeymoon seemed important to me, as did all aspects of a traditional marriage. As if all of this weren't enough, Ham had to travel constantly with the dance band he had organized and led. I accepted that fully. That was his career, and I assumed it meant to him what mine meant to me.'

★ ★ ★

122

Bette continued her screen career as a member of the Warner stock company, making at least five or six films a year. *Three on a Match* reunited her with her friend from the Anderson School, Joan Blondell. Bette said, 'I always called her 'Rosebud.' She was forced to change her name because the powers-that-be, or rather, the power-that-be, Mr. Warner, thought no one would *believe* that was her real name. Well, of course, they wouldn't. Sometimes, there's nothing harder to believe than the truth.'

Three on a Match was directed by Mervyn LeRoy, who wasn't impressed by Bette. 'He told people I had no future,' she said. 'I guess Miss Lana Turner was more *his* cup of tea.'

Three on a Match (1932)

Three school friends, Mary Keaton (Joan Blondell), Vivian Revere (Ann Dvorak), and Ruth Westcott (Bette Davis), reunite, vowing never to lose touch again. Vivian, unhappily married to a successful lawyer, Robert Kirkwood (Warren William), plans an ocean cruise with her young son (Buster Phelps). At a bon voyage party, Mary introduces her to Mike Loftus (Lyle Talbot), a gambler to whom Vivian is immediately attracted. When she runs off with Loftus instead of taking the cruise, Kirkwood is granted a divorce and custody of their child. He hires Ruth to take care of the child, then falls in love with her, and they marry. Vivian becomes an alcoholic and drug addict.

Loftus loses all his money and tries to blackmail Kirkwood. Failing, he sends three thugs

(Humphrey Bogart, Jack La Rue, and Allen Jenkins) to kidnap Kirkwood's son. Vivian, taken prisoner when she tries to save her son, writes a message to the police on her dressing gown, and then jumps out of an upper-story window, killing herself, but saving him.

When I mentioned Bette Davis to Joan Blondell, she remembered Bette as someone who never changed in their friendship, 'even when she became just about the biggest star in the world and even when we didn't see each other for years. Once you were friends with Bette, you were always friends. She was a straight-shooter, never jealous, never catty or a gossip. She was a true friend, and those don't grow on any trees I've known, especially Hollywood trees.

'Bette broke her back in 1957 looking at a house and not paying attention. She was in terrible pain for a long time, but she was terribly brave. I don't know how she got through it, but she was never a whiner.

'She had kind of a hard time when she was growing up because her mother didn't have much money and there were the three of them, the mother, Bette, and Bette's sister. They had to struggle, and that changes you. It takes its toll.

'She avoided athletics when we were young because she said she couldn't afford an injury. Most of us didn't think like that.

'Bette had great energy. I had plenty of energy myself, but I was lazy. I spent my energy mostly on having fun.

'Bette and I weren't exactly the same, but we

really got along. I always had a lot of respect for her. She was a very serious person, dedicated, and she knew what she wanted, which was to be an actress, the best actress she could possibly be.

'Bette always called me Rosebud, but my real name was Rose. Sometimes when she said it, I almost wondered who that was she was talking to. Most people only knew Joan Blondell. That's what the movies do.

'She had to take a lot of cracks about her looks. She wasn't regular-looking, but that worked to her advantage.

'I never met a woman who loved men more than Bette did, but she didn't trust them. She kind of dared them to let her down, and sooner or later, they did just that.

'I was a blonde with a very nice figure, and men thought I was cute. They liked cute, nonthreatening, you know. Everything came easier to me, and I didn't have her unquenchable ambition.

'When you have that kind of ambition, it's a lot of pressure. You're always afraid of losing what you have. Bette hung on hard for a long time. She had the greatest talent, but you can have that and still not make it, or not be able to keep it, so being an actress isn't a very secure profession.'

★ ★ ★

Bette told me, 'There were a lot of leading men I would like to have worked with, Gary Cooper or Clark Gable for example, but it wasn't often you got to work with people who had contracts at other studios, and Mr. Warner felt that if you could carry a picture, which he knew after a certain point that I could, he didn't need to diminish his profit by adding a male star to the budget.'

Among her early films, Bette especially cherished *20,000 Years in Sing Sing* because it was the only time she ever worked with Spencer Tracy. 'I wish I could have worked with Spencer again, when we were both big stars. We worked well together, and we shared the same birthday, April 5th. I considered having the same birthday a very important sign. I'd always admired the way [Katharine] Hepburn looked, and then she got Tracy for all those pictures, not to mention quite a bit more. Of all the male actors I worked with, Spencer Tracy appealed the most to me. I saw everything in him that Hepburn saw in him.'

Originally, James Cagney had been cast for Tracy's part in *20,000 Years in Sing Sing*, but he was engaged in a contract dispute with Warner Brothers. Michael Curtiz was assigned the film. Though there are seeming improbabilities in the film, such as a warden temporarily releasing an inmate from Sing Sing on the prisoner's word of honor, the script was based on a book written by a former warden of Sing Sing, Lewis E. Lawes.

20,000 Years in Sing Sing (1932)
With organized crime having forgotten him and escape too dangerous, Tom Connors (Spencer Tracy) loses hope of ever getting out of prison. Only his girlfriend, Fay (Bette Davis), continues

to believe in his innocence. When she is injured in an automobile accident, a sympathetic warden (Arthur Byron) allows him to visit her unguarded.

At her apartment, he finds Joe Finn (Louis Calhern), the man responsible for sending him to prison. Finn is there to intimidate Fay, who has continued to fight in Tom's defense. When a fight ensues, Fay grabs a gun and shoots Finn.

Tom is tried for his murder and, despite Fay's confession, sentenced to death in the electric chair.

This ending would not have been possible two years later, with the Motion Picture Code, which would have required that Fay be punished.

Parachute Jumper, Bette's fourteenth film, co-starred Douglas Fairbanks, Jr., and a lot of leftover aerial footage from World War I. Two decades later, Fairbanks would be her producer for *Another Man's Poison*. When he met her, he thought she was 'individual' and a much better actress than was required for her part in *Parachute Jumper*. He said, 'I could easily have imagined that she would have a good career, but not one that would be as great as it was.

'In 1933, she was already Bette Davis,' Fairbanks told me. 'Very much so. The only change in her over all those years was that she became even *more* Bette Davis. I was kind of her confessor, confidant.

'She was already very strong, sharp, *definite*, not tactful.

'She was very flirtatious. She conveyed she was rather keen on the sport of sex.

127

'But she was not lovable. She had a rather hard quality, not affectionate. For me, a woman couldn't be really sexy without being attractive to me in other ways as well.'

Parachute Jumper (1933)

During Prohibition, unemployed ex-marine pilot Bill Keller (Douglas Fairbanks, Jr.) finds work flying liquor from Canada, and then discovers he's really smuggling illegal drugs. Bette Davis plays his girlfriend, Alabama, who helps him. With co-pilot Toodles (Frank McHugh), they outwit racketeer Weber (Leo Carrillo) and send him to jail.

At sixty-five minutes and on a low budget, this kind of action-comedy-romance filled the Saturday programming needs of the growing chain of Stanley-Warner theaters, and included a serial, cartoon, short subject, newsreel, and trailers. In 1962, clips from *Parachute Jumper* were used in *What Ever Happened to Baby Jane?*

★　★　★

Bette didn't believe in displaying photographs in her home that belonged only to her public life. She kept a silver-framed picture of George Arliss among her personal possessions. The photographs in her home represented her personal feelings rather than just her professional life. The memory of George Arliss meant a great deal to her.

'It was always such a great pleasure, as well as an honor, working with Mr. George Arliss, because whatever was happening on his set, at four P.M. sharp everything stopped for a half hour while we had tea. I think he had it in his contract. Mr. Arliss helped pour, and everyone, to the lowliest grip, participated. I especially enjoyed knowing instinctively that Mr. Jack L. Warner was sitting in his office having a fit during this expensive daily homage to a civilized way of life he would never understand because it wasn't in the least bit cost-efficient.

'Besides working with Mr. Arliss again, *The Working Man* involved a subject close to my father's heart, shoes. He, too, had worked with a shoe company.'

The Working Man (1933)

Benny Burnett (Hardie Albright) takes charge of the Reeves Shoe Company when his uncle, John Reeves (George Arliss), retires. On a fishing trip in Maine, Benny meets the idle rich heirs to his rival company, Hartland Shoes, brother and sister Tommy and Jenny Hartland (Theodore Newton and Bette Davis). Not knowing who he is, they generously offer him a job in their factory.

Benny's competitive spirit is so great that he rapidly advances in their company, finally taking over the factory and offering serious competition to his own company. In so doing, he inspires Tommy to become a useful person and Jenny to fall in love with him. A merger may be in the future.

Robert Florey, who directed the Marx Brothers in *The Cocoanuts*, was assigned Bette's next picture, *Ex-Lady*, of which she had a low opinion, as did the critics. The film, made before the Production Code, features an unmarried couple living together and a seduction scene under a restaurant table. In the spirit of Lubitsch, the audience sees only the table wobbling violently, but can guess what is happening underneath. The film treats the idea that women can think and act like men. 'In certain respects, the picture was ahead of its time,' Bette said.

Ex-Lady (1933)

Commercial artist Helen Bauer (Bette Davis) convinces advertising copywriter Don Peterson (Gene Raymond) that they will be much happier if they just move in together rather than getting married. The arrangement works well until Don decides to start his own ad agency and convinces Helen that they must get married or face the disapproval of potential clients.

The agency thrives until the couple leaves for a postponed honeymoon. When they return, they find the agency in deep financial difficulties. Don pursues a wealthy advertiser (Kay Strozzi), who finds him attractive, and Helen becomes jealous. Without really meaning it, she suggests they return to their premarital sexual freedom, and Don, too enthusiastically accepts. Angrily, Helen encourages the attention of Don's chief competitor, Nick Malvyn (Monroe Owsley).

After an argument, the couple is reunited in a more conventional marriage.

Ex-Lady was the first film in which Bette received principal billing. A clip from this film was used in *What Ever Happened to Baby Jane?*

Although Bette receives star billing in *Bureau of Missing Persons*, she appears in only one of the stories. She said of her segment, 'It was a plot that wasn't. I can't remember it, and I can't forget it.'

Bureau of Missing Persons (1933)

In Bette's segment, she goes to the bureau to locate her missing husband. Detective Butch Saunders (Pat O'Brien) finds that she is really Norma Roberts, a missing person herself, wanted by the Chicago police for the murder of her first husband. Norma disappears. Saunders lures her back by claiming he has found her husband's corpse. Her supposedly dead previous husband (Alan Dinehart) also appears, but he turns out to be a criminally insane twin brother. He had murdered Norma's husband, hoping she would be blamed.

As Bette's career with Warner Brothers progressed, her marriage to Ham deteriorated.

'When you have a project that energizes you and doesn't enervate you, that's wonderful, whether it's a film or cooking a pot of chowder.

'When I was making a film, and I was proud of the film, doing work I knew was good, I would have a constant rush of adrenaline. I was never tired while I was working. It only hit me when I stopped, when I went home at night and closed the door behind me. It wasn't exactly what a husband wanted.

'I can't deny I was pretty hard to get along with. After a hard day's work as a southern belle or a gangster's moll, I was ready to explode, which I frequently did. I came home like a tired businessman, expecting to be soothed by a tender, loving spouse, and I would find Ham relaxing with his pipe and slippers expecting the same kind of treatment. I suppose what I really needed was a good wife. Unfortunately, so did Ham.

'I worried about my career twenty-four hours, no, twenty-*five* hours a day, and I always brought my worries home with me. I did adore Ham, but he seemed strangely distant from my crises. He couldn't seem to understand how I felt about my work. I came to believe he didn't feel as intensely about his as I had once thought. But luckily, our battles usually ended up with us under the sheets.'

★ ★ ★

'When director John Cromwell chose me to play Mildred in *Of Human Bondage*, that was wildly lucky for me. She was the first really *evil* heroine that had ever been on the screen, so none of the beautiful, glamorous leading ladies of that day would play her. Many actresses are afraid that being typecast as a villainess can injure one's reputation. It's so much more fun to play someone mean. But one doesn't have to be a bitch to *play* a bitch, you know. They said playing Mildred would ruin an actress's career, but it *made* mine. It was my ambition to play people exactly like her. So when I was offered that part by Mr. Cromwell in 1934, I told him, 'The right arm? Or the left?'

'At the time, however, Warner Brothers had other plans for me. They thought they needed me desperately for such immortal classics as *Fashions of 1934*, *The Big Shakedown*, and *Jimmy the Gent*.'

Bette was to be turned into a blond bombshell. Her hair was dyed platinum, her eyebrows plucked, according to the movie star fashion of the day, and then eyebrows were penciled in.

'In *Fashions of 1934*, they tried to recast me as Jean Harlow, and I did the best I could to play Miss Harlow. I did such a good job, there was nothing left of Bette Davis. But I decided then and there that there was only one Jean Harlow and only one Bette Davis, and they could never be the same actress. Never so against type for me again.'

Fashions of 1934 (1934)

Sherwood Nash (William Powell), a notorious fashion thief, is caught photographing the new Paris collection of famed designer Baroque (Reginald Owen) and threatened with arrest. Because Nash was aided by an old friend now posing as a phony duchess (Verree Teasdale) who is engaged to Baroque, the charges are dropped. Instead, Nash and Baroque put on a successful joint fashion show with songs and dances. Nash enjoys being legitimate so much, he considers marrying his assistant, model Lynn Mason (Bette Davis).

Bette was next supposed to play Josephine in a biography of Napoleon directed by Robert Florey. When Edward G. Robinson rejected the part of Napoleon, the project was abandoned. Bette was then cast as the good girl in *The Big Shakedown*, a picture with a theme that is still relevant, adulterated drugs.

The Big Shakedown (1934)
Gangster Nick Barnes (Ricardo Cortez) persuades pharmacist Jimmy Morrell (Charles Farrell) to make counterfeit drugs, thus replacing his lost bootlegging operation. With his increased profits, Jimmy is able to marry Norma Nelson (Bette Davis), a clerk in his pharmacy, who disapproves of Barnes.

When Jimmy tries to quit, he is beaten, and then ordered to dilute the drugs. One of the victims of these diluted drugs is Norma, who almost dies in childbirth. Their child does die, and Jimmy vows to kill Barnes, but the president (Henry O'Neill) of the legitimate drug company ruined by sales of the cheap diluted drugs has already killed him. Jimmy is exonerated.

Norma was the kind of saccharine good-girl role Bette was about to rebel against. Her next part was not much better, except that it was opposite James Cagney, whom she considered a great talent as well as a friend. *Jimmy the Gent* was the first of two films she would make with him.

Jimmy the Gent (1934)

Joan Martin (Bette Davis) tires of working for uncouth, unethical missing-heir finder Jimmy Corrigan (James Cagney) and joins his chief competitor, the gentlemanly Charles Wallingham (Alan Dinehart). Furious, Corrigan tries to win her back by dressing like Wallingham and emulating his refined way, but he only makes a fool of himself until he is able to expose Wallingham as the phony he really is in a missing-heir hunt that uncovers a murder. Joan rejects Wallingham's marriage proposal and goes back to work for Corrigan. The implication is that they have a future together.

'I always wanted to work with Cagney,' Bette told me, 'but whenever we *did* get together, the result was catastrophic, though no fault of his.' Bette admired the way Cagney stood up against the studio after the big success of *The Public Enemy*, threatening to retire if they didn't renegotiate his contract.

* * *

'I recall so vividly that day in 1934 I found out I was going to have a baby. I'll never forget it. Problems at the studio suddenly seemed insignificant. I was absolutely the happiest person in the world, as happy as a clam at high tide. I was bursting with the news, but I simply had to tell someone right away. Ruthie and Bobby were back east, and Ham was up in the Bay Area with his orchestra. Even if Ruthie and Bobby had been there, I thought Ham certainly ought to be the first to hear the news. It was his right, and it was the right thing to do, and it was what I wanted to do. If I told Ruthie first, and if she'd been there, I might have blurted it out, and then if Ham ever found out I did that, he might have been hurt and resented it.

'Since something so wonderful couldn't be entrusted to a mere telephone, I drove straight up to San Francisco to deliver the marvelous news to Ham in person. I made up the scenario in my mind as I often did. I just knew he'd be overwhelmed to find out he was going to be a father.

'Well, he was. But it was so very different from what I'd expected. 'You'd be a fool to jeopardize your career by having a baby,' he said coldly. Suddenly he reminded me of my father. Had I followed in my mother's footsteps? Daddy himself couldn't have been colder. 'And you can't possibly think I'd let you pay the hospital bills,' he added. It was an incredible blow. Until that moment, I hadn't noticed how shabby his motel room looked. Ham looked different, too. I'd thought him handsome, but he wasn't handsome anymore. Indeed, I wondered *why* I had ever thought him handsome, and I wondered if he'd ever look so handsome to me again. I must tell you, he never did.

'I felt seven years old, and Papa had left. Only this time, I wasn't glad. We weren't going on a picnic, and we weren't going to have a baby. I was dumbfounded. I thought it was *our* money, *our* career — our baby. I saw clearly now what, until that moment, I'd only sensed in the back of my mind; that while Ham was perfectly content to live on the fruits of my career, he resented it. Worse than that, he resented *me* — and our baby. Our baby was in the way of the life he wanted, just as I had been in Daddy's way.

'I turned where I had always turned before — to Ruthie. I wrote to her about the baby and about what happened when I told Ham. I knew that she of all people would understand, because she had had the same experience that I was having. She had felt what I was feeling. I knew Ruthie perfectly, but I found out that maybe no one ever knows anyone else perfectly, it being so difficult even to understand oneself. The encouragement of which I was so certain was not forthcoming.

'She wrote back that a child now might be harmful to my career. How *could* she, after the way Father had treated her?

'I was emotionally shattered. But I got the abortion.

'Now I ask myself, why? Why did I so meekly do what I was told to do? Ham suggested it. Ruthie agreed. But I was old enough to make up my own mind. I was established professionally. I was properly married. I could easily have afforded a baby. And I *wanted* a baby! I wanted a family so desperately.

'I wonder what that child would have been like? I've wondered through all the years. There would probably be grandchildren. Ruth Elizabeth would have been so happy! But what about Bette?

'Bette would have missed the biggest role in her life thus far, the turning point in her career: Mildred in *Of Human Bondage.* Would she then have missed being Jezebel, Judith, Elizabeth, Charlotte, and Margo Channing?

'But I didn't miss any of these roles, and I didn't miss having a family. Still, I wonder what my life would have been like if I hadn't had that first abortion . . . '

★ ★ ★

Although she received top billing, Bette played what amounted to a supporting role in *Fog Over Frisco.* It marked the end of her early Warner Brothers period, before she established herself firmly as a star in *Of Human Bondage.*

Fog Over Frisco (1934)

Thrill-seeking socialite Arlene Bradford (Bette Davis) finances her extravagant lifestyle by using her fiancé's access to accounts in her stepfather's brokerage firm to sell securities stolen by crime boss Jake Bello (Irving Pichel). When the fiancé, Spencer Carleton (Lyle Talbot), is exposed, Arlene plans to leave San Francisco with Mayard (Douglass Dumbrille), her father's Honolulu director. Mayard, instead, rejects her, demanding the return of his love letters, and Bello won't let her leave his gang, making clear his own interest in her.

Arlene disappears, and her stepsister, Val (Margaret Lindsay), is kidnapped by Bello when he attempts to recover some incriminating papers from her. She escapes after he is murdered.

Arlene's body is found, strangled by Mayard, who was actually her ex-husband. Carleton commits suicide, clutching her returned engagement ring.

Fog Over Frisco was produced by Henry Blanke and directed by William Dieterle, 'both of whom I deeply respected,' Bette said. 'Blanke was an intelligent man of consummate taste who was always there to help you, and Dieterle was an actor's director. I understand that he'd been a famous film actor himself in Germany before he came to Hollywood. A brilliant man, but he gave in to his stars later on. That's wrong.

'*Fog Over Frisco*, I thought, was an interesting script, and I loved my part. But I still hadn't forgotten *Bondage*.

'I spent six months on Mr. Jack Warner's doorstep, arriving in the morning with the shoeshine boy and manicurist. I begged, cajoled, implored, even threatened. Faced with a nervous breakdown because of my persistence, he said, 'Yes! Yes! *Anything* to get rid of you. I'm so sick of listening to you, go ruin yourself.' By then, he believed I really *was* the terrible Mildred.

'Mr. Cromwell had liked me so much in *Cabin in the Cotton* and *The Rich Are Always With Us* that he had perfect faith in my ability. I

139

always do my best work when someone truly believes in me. Mr. Leslie Howard, my co-star, was less impressed. He and his English colleagues on the picture were appalled at the idea of an American girl being cast as a cockney. I hired an English maid at home who spoke with what I thought was just the right accent for Mildred. She taught me cockney English. I didn't tell her why she was really there, because I didn't want her to become self-conscious about how she spoke.'

Of Human Bondage (1934)

Clubfooted medical student Philip Cary (Leslie Howard) falls obsessively in love with Mildred Rogers (Bette Davis), a cockney waitress. When he becomes jealous, she tells him scornfully she could never love a cripple, and she leaves him.

Philip meets Norah (Kay Johnson), an attractive writer. She offers him her love but cannot erase his memory of Mildred.

When Mildred returns, pregnant and penniless, Philip supports her, planning marriage when her child is born. Mildred leaves Philip again, this time with a fellow medical student (Reginald Denny).

As an intern in a charity hospital, Philip meets a patient, Athelny (Reginald Owen), who introduces him to his daughter, Sally (Frances Dee), with whom Philip feels instant rapport.

Mildred returns with her baby, and Philip cannot refuse her shelter. She offers sex in payment, but he rejects her. In her anger, she destroys the securities he needed for tuition.

Philip is forced to drop out of medical school and take a job he hates. When he has a breakdown, Athelny and his daughter nurse him back to health. While he is recuperating, he receives an inheritance that enables him to return to school and have corrective surgery on his foot.

He learns Mildred has died in a charity hospital, freeing him of his obsession and allowing him to marry Sally.

'I insisted on doing my own makeup. *My* Mildred wasn't going to die of a dread disease looking like a debutante who'd missed her afternoon nap. I've simply never understood why Hollywood actresses allow themselves to be made up to look like Hollywood actresses no matter what the part calls for.

'Because of Mildred, there were some who considered me the female Marlon Brando of my generation. Even Mr. Howard changed his attitude toward me. In my *Bondage* close-ups, he would casually throw me lines while reading a book. In our next picture together, he was more attentive, I assure you!

'Speaking of Marlon Brando, I must say something about acting technique. Though I admire him tremendously, I don't for one moment subscribe to the Method school of acting. I never became so totally absorbed in a part that I 'lost' myself in it. Never. I prepared for a role by simply learning my lines and hoping for the best! When I was playing Mildred, I was always totally aware that I was Bette Davis playing a loathsome creature who thought she was a 'lai-dy.' Mr. Brando is a great actor not because of any Method but because of talent. Yet, I must admit that at the time I was playing Mildred, there was an anger in me, which I drew upon like a proper Method actor — an anger toward my father, and toward Ham and Ruthie, who wanted the abortion.

'I believe Ham could've been a big success if he'd had my drive to reach the top. I had more than enough for both of us, but it's difficult for a man to live with a woman who has so much drive.

'I was a worker bee with a queen bee complex. That's why our marriage didn't last. But you cannot ever really get a divorce from the person with whom you share your early memories.

'Ham taught me how to play one song on the piano, 'I Can't Tell You Why I Love You, But I Do.' The graduation song was 'Moonlight and Roses.' The most popular tune of the day was Irving Berlin's 'Always.' These were what we called 'our' songs, and they still are mine. My mother requested that 'Always' be played at her funeral. How I cried! Not just for Ruthie, but for all of us, each dead in a different way.'

Bette lit another cigarette. 'Ham chose to show his manhood in the only way he knew. He couldn't earn more money. He wasn't a good lover, although I didn't know it then. But he did have the power over me to make me unhappy. He couldn't give me happiness, but he *could* give me *un*happiness.

'One of Ham's merits was his fidelity. He was absolutely faithful — I think. At the time, however, I was very innocent and trusting, so how would I have known the difference? After I'd been married for a few years, Ruthie told me I'd never have to worry about Ham being unfaithful. Nobody else would want him! A fine time to tell me, after she was the one who encouraged me to marry him.

'She believed he'd never give me any trouble. What she didn't realize was that he wouldn't give me anything else, either. Ham was the first man I'd ever known, in the biblical sense, so he seemed an adequate lover. But I had no standards whatsoever to define or measure 'adequate.''

'Is the much-told story true that you named the Oscar after him?' I asked.

'Well, *I* say so. I certainly do. But the Academy quarrels with me very heavily about this, so I've finally given up. Yes, I have. I do that sometimes, you know. But I *did* name Oscar. The backside of Ham looked just like Oscar's. His name was Harmon O. Nelson, and I never knew what the O stood for. He wouldn't tell me. I guess because he hated it so. Then, I found out Ham's middle name was Oscar. So I said to him, 'The backside of the Oscar looks just like you.' Oscar and Ham both had flat rear ends. I told them at the Academy, and I swear that's how it happened. But I'm tired of arguing the case.

'I was the first woman president of the Motion Picture Academy, you know. I took it very seriously and had numerous excellent ideas, but I was too young when it happened and I didn't have any patience. I came to believe they only wanted my name and public image, and not my ideas. So I resigned the position in order to *show* them, but then nobody cared. It's usually a mistake doing something just to *show* someone, and such a waste. Resigning as president of the Academy is something I truly regret. Many of my ideas were later incorporated. Darryl F. Zanuck [producer and head of Twentieth Century Fox] never totally forgave me because he had supported me for the post.'

On December 27, 1934, Bette signed a seven-year contract with Warner Brothers that doubled her salary. She was also assured better roles and more control over what she did and with whom she did it. The picture that followed *Of Human Bondage* was *Housewife* with George Brent. 'I would rather have followed *Bondage* with *It Happened One Night*,' Bette said.

'Did you know that [Frank] Capra considered me for Claudette Colbert's part? But Mr. Warner wouldn't lend me out for another picture after *Bondage*. And he never even thought *that* was a performance! Not his cup of tea.

Housewife (1934)

Encouraged by his wife, Nan (Ann Dvorak), advertising copywriter Bill Reynolds (George Brent) opens his own agency. It is unsuccessful until Bill's former girlfriend, Patricia Berkeley (Bette Davis), writes a popular jingle that makes his agency profitable. Bill thinks he is still in love with Patricia, and Nan agrees to a divorce, but an accident to their young son makes him realize how important his wife is to him.

Not only was Bette's performance in *Of Human Bondage* ignored by the Motion Picture Academy, but the film was as well. It received no Oscar nominations. 'Can you imagine that?' Bette asked. '*It Happened One Night* won everything that year. Best picture, best actor and actress, best director, best everything. There wasn't *any* Oscar performance in it, just charming, charming performances. I couldn't even *vote* for our picture because it wasn't nominated.

'There was a big write-in vote for *Bondage*. The next year, they hired Price Waterhouse to count the votes and keep them secret.

'There was a rumor that the studios used to split up the Oscars. They'd say, 'This year, we'll have it, next year, you.' I don't think there was any truth in that. I can't imagine those people getting together that way. I think the advertising for Oscars is so revolting! I disapprove. The money they spend! And I'm afraid the advertising absolutely is affecting people. I don't feel Oscars should be given to an actor. It's the part that wins the Oscar. Every time an Oscar is given out, an agent gets his wings.'

★ ★ ★

In 1935, Bette Davis made *Bordertown*, with Paul Muni, *The Girl from 10th Avenue*, with Ian Hunter, *Front Page Woman* and *Special Agent*, both with George Brent, and *Dangerous*, with Franchot Tone.

'I met Paul Muni on *Bordertown*,' Bette told me. 'One of the most intelligent persons with scripts I have ever in my life known. At the end of *Bordertown*, Mr. Muni said to me, 'Don't ever bother with a director again. You don't need it.'

'Now, I'm a kid, but I said, 'Mr. Muni, the day will never come that I won't need a director and not want one.' And to this *day*, I can get through anything because I've had enough experience. I can be a *hundred* times better than some directors. But believe you me, I do not want to do it *alone!*

'My director on *Bordertown* was Archie Mayo. Archie was never a great director, but he was a very proficient motion picture maker. Fat, jolly, cute man. For Muni with an Archie Mayo, it was self-preservation. All those Warner directors, Lloyd Bacon, Archie Mayo, Alfred Green, Michael Curtiz — all smashing moviemakers, but if you were an artist like Muni, you had to protect your own performance.'

Bordertown (1935)

Mentally unstable Marie Roark (Bette Davis) kills her husband (Eugene Pallette) because she wants to marry Johnny Ramirez (Paul Muni), his partner in a bordertown cabaret. When Johnny shows too much interest in Dale Elwell (Margaret Lindsay), an attractive and wealthy customer, Marie confesses to the murder and implicates him. Her trial testimony is so confused, however, that Johnny is found innocent. He proposes to Dale, who rebuffs him and then is killed in a car crash. He sells his part of the cabaret, donating the proceeds to charity.

'I'll never forget, when I did the insane scene in *Bordertown*, it was the first time, I believe, that anyone in motion pictures didn't tear their hair out and *look* insane. So Mr. Wallis sent for me, and he said, 'You have to retake this scene. No one will know you're insane.'

'I said, 'Mr. Wallis, if you preview this, and nobody knows I'm insane, I'll redo it.' I never heard of it again.

'I knew instinctively it would work because I knew that every talented actor has to play two things at one time. You don't just play one thing, standing there head-on into a camera. There's something going on in the back of your head that makes you say this. And in your head, you've got to project this other thing that's going on.

'The camera catches thought. And if there's ever a moment with any actor when there's no thought, the audience does not know why, but they are just not interested.'

Bordertown was Bette's twenty-fourth film. Her name and face were familiar to the public, and in spite of the wide range of characters she had played, she had progressed from being a talented, versatile actress to a well-defined personality whose roles were somewhat limited by audience expectations. Bette didn't like being typecast, but she understood the reasons for it.

'In our business,' she said, 'some critics say about me, 'She's always the same.' This is certainly not true. But if there isn't some label on the personality for the public to recognize *you*, you'll never be a big star. They have *got* to find *you* each time as someone they already know. Now, for example, John Barrymore played many great parts. Bernhardt played many great parts, but there was always a Sarah Bernhardt underneath, a John Barrymore underneath, and the public grew to know that person.

'You cannot disguise yourself so much that you cannot be recognized. It just doesn't work. I believe that. And I've thought about it, as it pertains to me. Even though I've worn millions of makeups and millions of wigs, underneath is always the same person. The public recognizes Bette Davis, and they know they are going to get a Bette Davis picture. I hope that means they will get their money's worth.

'Now, Paul Muni,' she said, 'I never knew him well enough to know why he started hiding himself. Why did he hide? I believe he wrecked his career with it. I know he was influenced by Stanislavski. *I* like Stanislavski, but Stanislavski was for reality in your character, not hiding. Muni was carrying to an extreme what all of us actors love to do, hide our own personalities behind a character.

'I have a theory about this, and it's taken me many years to say this, and I say it about anybody who goes into acting. I don't think any of us who went into acting seriously loved playing characters like ourselves. We hid behind other characters. It's a paradox, but true. I heard this from Hank Fonda, too. And it's taken me years to figure this out. I used to say, 'Why do I love playing other people?' You hide in public!'

A guiding force in Bette's career was producer Hal Wallis, whose close association with her began when he was the associate executive producer on *Bordertown*.

'Wallis was one of that rare breed in Hollywood,' Bette said, 'an intelligent producer. To him, I owe a great deal. I can't say enough about him. In my heart, I never stop thanking him.

'I've had fantastic luck. I *hand* my career to the ex-*traordinary* properties that Mr. Wallis bought for me. For two years, I never stopped. Every one was one of the great movies, five in a row, I ended up eighty pounds plus a little. Went to New Hampshire and never came back for six months. I was gone. But *that* was the year [1939] that made *it* PERMANENT! That's what you have to do to have a career. But Wallis gave me these things, and I had enough physical health to get through it. But Wallis I will always hand it to.

'I think under Hal Wallis, Warner Brothers, for ten years, was a studio that will never be equaled again. He was smashing. I repeat myself: It was he who bought all those great properties for me. What a debt I owe him! After I'd worked for him for ten years, I was in his office one day, and he said to me, 'I have to tell you something. I *loathe* the parts you play. But as long as you can sell 'em, I'll buy 'em.' Because he really loved a kind of trashy comedy, but what a smart man! He made Warners. And then, of course, he lost his job at Warners.

'You know, he came to the studio one day, and

the cop said, 'You can't get in today, Mr. Wallis. You can come back at three o'clock this afternoon and pack up your office.' And that afternoon they came and took all of the sound equipment out. That was it. But I'll say something for Hal Wallis. At that *unbelievable* tribute they gave to Jack Warner when he sold Warners, Mr. Wallis sat right down there in front in honor of Jack Warner. And I went up to him, astounded, and said, 'How are you making it through this?' He said, 'It's not easy, but I should.' And he'd been *FIRED!*

'Those ten years under Wallis — Muni, Cagney, Bogey, me — that was when all of us made our great movies. Absolutely. All of us who were actors, under Wallis, had our great years. You know, I used to make five, six of those huge pictures at a time. He bought *Old Acquaintance*. He bought *The Old Maid*. He bought *Jezebel*. He bought *Dark Victory*. He bought *all* these films for me. *The Corn Is Green* was a loan-out. But that was the only other loan-out besides *Bondage* in the eighteen years.' Bette wasn't thinking of *The Little Foxes*.

'The studio system made stars. Nobody can be made a star again in the same way without that studio system. Ninety men in the publicity department. By the time Warner films came out, the whole world knew it.

'Today they don't know what a star is. A star is not just a big name that supposedly can act. A star runs a set. They make the whole cast feel comfortable. They are *in charge* of a set, a star is. As a kid, *Bordertown* was a great experience for

150

me, because I feel Paul Muni was the first real honest-to-God star I ever worked with. And *Bordertown* was the first good part I ever had at Warners. No question about that. Well, it took me a while until they realized that this was my medium.

'Muni appreciated, for instance, when my character woke up in the middle of the night with grease on her face and curlers in her hair. I had a two-day fight with Warners. Wallis came on the set and said, 'You can't look like that on the screen.'

' 'Well,' I said, 'you don't want me to look like this, I'm going home. That's how this bitch would look in the middle of the night.' You see, nobody did that in those days. I think that's why Muni thought I really had something, and he stood up for me. I think of him many, many times during my life.'

After *Bordertown*, Bette was disappointed to be assigned to three films that scarcely reflected her powerful *Of Human Bondage* performance. For *The Girl from 10th Avenue*, Bette at least received top billing, the first time since *Ex-Lady*.

The Girl from 10th Avenue (1935)

On the rebound from being jilted by his debutante fiancée, Valentine Marland (Katherine Alexander), Geoffrey Sherwood (Ian Hunter), a socially prominent lawyer, awakens one morning after drinking too much the night before to find he is married to Miriam Brady (Bette Davis), quite literally 'the girl from 10th Avenue.' This wasn't what he had in mind. She offers to let him out of the marriage, but he sees something sincere and lovable in Miriam that he does not see in Valentine, even when he is given a second chance to make 'the appropriate marriage.' In spite of Miriam not being acceptable in his social circle, he remains happily married to her.

'The original title of *Front Page Woman* was 'Women Are Bum Newspapermen,'' Bette said. 'Can you imagine?'

Front Page Woman (1935)

Reporters on rival newspapers, Curt Devlin (George Brent) and Ellen Garfield (Bette Davis) plan to get married, even though Devlin cannot accept women as journalists. When Ellen scoops him on a story, he retaliates by feeding her the wrong information on a trial verdict that gives him the scoop while disgracing her. On her own, she finds out that she was right, after all, winning back her job and a grudging admission from Devlin that women can be as good reporters as men.

'I don't know if it was a coincidence or not,' Bette said, 'but after I played in *Front Page Woman*, William Randolph Hearst started inviting me up to San Simeon. Somebody told me he thought I'd make a good newspaper-woman. What a great review! I was complimented wildly.

'Ham gave me a great review, too, sort of. He said the way I looked at George Brent in that film and in *Special Agent* meant I just *had* to be

152

in love with him. He didn't believe me when I said that's how an actress is *supposed* to look at her leading man. But he wasn't far wrong.'

Special Agent (1935)

As an undercover agent for the IRS, newspaper reporter Bill Bradford (George Brent) goes after racketeer Nick Carston (Ricardo Cortez) through his bookkeeper, Julie Gardner (Bette Davis), whom Bill has charmed. Carston finds out and has Julie kidnapped so she cannot testify, but Bill saves her, and the racketeer is sent to prison.

In early 1936, while she was in the second year of her current contract, Bette was nominated by the Motion Picture Academy as best actress for her performance in *Dangerous*, and she won. 'That was a consolation prize,' Bette said, 'for *Bondage*. But that year, I could have won for 'Mother Goose.' She was to win one more Oscar, for *Jezebel*, out of ten nominations.

Dangerous (1935)

Joyce Heath (Bette Davis), a forgotten stage star, has her career revived by wealthy architect Don Bellows (Franchot Tone), who produces a new Broadway play for her. In love with Joyce and not realizing she is already married, Don asks his fiancée, Gail Armitage (Margaret Lindsay), to release him from their commitment so he can marry Joyce. When Joyce's husband, Gordon Heath (John Eldredge), refuses to give her a divorce, she tries to kill him in an apparent accident, but he survives, crippled. Hearing of the accident, Don agrees to go on with the play, but returns to Gail. Joyce becomes a star again and, accepting her guilt, tries to salvage her marriage to Gordon.

'It's important to get your Oscar-losing face right for when they *don't* give it to you, especially nowadays when the whole world is watching you in close-up. Everyone practices for winning, but when you win, whatever you say, you'll carry through. What's more difficult is carrying on when you lose, if you aren't naturally a good loser.'

The Oscar for *Dangerous*, combined with her triumph in *Of Human Bondage*, gave Bette reason to feel that her value to Warners had increased and that she deserved a new, more generous contract. The studio was opposed to such a renegotiation, although they had set the precedent earlier with James Cagney and with Edward G. Robinson. At the time, it had seemed a turbulent period in her life, but in talking about it with me a half century later, she was nostalgic.

'Do I ever miss the big studios and my endless fights with them? 'Ever'? *Always!* The studio was my family. Warners was my bad home. Oh, how I longed to get away from it! Then, after it was all over, how I missed it! Those glorious years!

'We were treated like serfs, but we got to do picture after picture. With the concentrated publicity, not only did the public come to know you, but you had the possibility, the opportunity to hone your craft.

'In those days, the studio owners were basically great gamblers, and they gave us our opportunities. *That* we have lost, that kind of gambling spirit.'

★　★　★

Bette seldom played parts for which she had any prior life experience. *The Petrified Forest* was one of those rare instances. 'I knew how to play a waitress who wanted to be an artist,' she said, 'because I *was* one, back in my school days. Though as I've said, I'm not at all enamored of Method acting, I had plenty of memories of customers who'd stiffed me to draw on for my character.

'And did you notice? My hair changed back to its natural color for that picture. I'd been a blond bombshell long enough.'

The Petrified Forest reunited Bette with Humphrey Bogart. Both had had supporting roles in *Bad Sister*, and in *Three on a Match*, he was third man through the door after Warren William, and Bette was the third girl in the billing after Ann Dvorak and Joan Blondell. Warners had not wanted Bogart, but Leslie Howard, who had starred in the Robert E. Sherwood play on Broadway, insisted that Bogart, the stage Duke Mantee, play the role on the screen, too. Howard was also able to persuade Warners not to film the play with a happy ending.

The Petrified Forest (1936)

Among the group being held captive in an Arizona service station café by desperado Duke Mantee (Humphrey Bogart) and his gang are world-weary poet Alan Squier (Leslie Howard) and aspiring artist, currently working as a waitress, Gabby Maple (Bette Davis). Believing he is going to be killed by Mantee, Alan signs his insurance policy over to Gabby. After a gun battle, Alan dies in Gabby's arms, consoled by the knowledge that she will now be able to afford art school in Paris.

After appearing in three pictures of which she was 'wildly' proud — *Of Human Bondage, Bordertown,* and *The Petrified Forest* — and another for which she won an Oscar, Bette was disappointed with her next assignment. She described it as 'a dilly.'

The Golden Arrow (1936)

Reporter Johnny Jones (George Brent) is so eager to get a story on eccentric heiress Daisy Appleby (Bette Davis) that, at her suggestion, he marries her. When he tires of being 'Mr.' Appleby, she fears he will find out that she isn't really an heiress, but has been hired to play one as a publicity stunt by the Appleby Cosmetic Co. Johnny does find out, but he also finds out he loves her. Besides, her apparent fortune will allow him enough income to write his novel.

'I was a pioneer in trying to break the studio system's hold on actors. In 1936, I rebelled. I wanted more say in the choice of my scripts. I was getting things like *Housewife*, *Special Agent*, and *The Golden Arrow*. Oh, it was terrible! I wanted a chance at the great directors and the best available actors. And I wanted to be able to accept outside work when it was offered, and more money. Mr. Warner made some minor concessions and said, 'Just be a good girl, Bette, and everything will work out.' Well, he was only partly correct. I *wasn't* a good girl, and it worked out anyway. I won't bore you with how they suspended me for three months, and I ended up in an English court being sued by the Brothers Warner. They won, of course; but I paved the way for Olivia de Havilland's eventual victory over the studio system.'

The film that precipitated Bette's decision to break her Warner Brothers contract was *Satan Met a Lady*, a remake of the first *Maltese Falcon*, which had been made in 1931. There were many changes, including new names for the original Dashiell Hammett characters.

Satan Met a Lady (1936)

Private eye Ted Shayne (Warren William) is hired by Valerie Purvis (Bette Davis) to find a woman named Madame Barabbas (Alison Skipworth). When he locates the woman, she offers to pay him to reveal Valerie's whereabouts. Barabbas wants her to return a bejeweled ram's horn, which Valerie, as her agent, stole from her after years of tracking it down.

Shayne has his partner, Ames (Porter Hall), shadow Valerie, and he is killed. Valerie then asks

Shayne to pick up the ram's horn, which has just arrived by ship. As he does, the package is taken away at gunpoint by Madame Barabbas, and then from her by Valerie. Valerie is apprehended by the police, and confesses that she killed Ames because she thought he was Barabbas's agent.

Just before this film, Bette had rejected a part in *God's Country and the Woman*, in which she would have been a queen of the lumberjacks. She was also arguing 'wildly' with Jack L. Warner about the parts she was being offered and her salary. Warner tried to placate her with the promise of the part of a lifetime.

'Did you know I almost was Scarlett O'Hara? 'Almost,' one of those terrible words. As a matter of fact, I was the *first* one offered the part. When I threatened to leave for England, Mr. Warner said, '*Please* don't leave. I've just optioned a wonderful book for you.' 'Ha!' I said. 'I'll bet it's a pip!' Famous last words. It was *Gone With the Wind*, and Errol Flynn had been selected as Rhett Butler.'

The part of Scarlett O'Hara was dreamed of and sought after by many actresses, anyone who might have any of the requisite qualifications and quite a few who didn't.

In a nationwide poll to determine to whom the part of Scarlett should go, the first choice by a landslide was Bette Davis. One of the reasons was Bette had won their hearts with *Jezebel*, and then she had won an Oscar for that performance.

Exactly what had made her number one on the list for audiences took her off the list of

David O. Selznick, who had acquired the property. Once Bette had become so identified as Jezebel, she could no longer be Scarlett.

Selznick had always hoped that someone truly could *become* Scarlett, and that meant not having an actress who already had too strong a public identity.

Bette blamed George Cukor, who was scheduled to direct *Gone With the Wind* and was Selznick's friend. She believed that Cukor 'interfered and blackballed' her, and that it was he who didn't want her for the part of Scarlett because he hadn't liked her in Rochester all those years before.

Cukor denied saying he didn't want Bette. He didn't remember being asked, but if her name had been seriously considered, he would have used any veto power he had during the time he was still on the film. 'Bette wasn't at all right for that part,' Cukor said. 'She was too identified with other parts, and she wasn't beautiful enough. Vivien [Leigh] was perfection.'

After Selznick and Cukor parted ways, and Cukor was replaced as director of *Gone With the Wind*, he coached Vivien Leigh and Olivia de Havilland, whom he liked and thought perfect for their parts, at his home on Sundays

Bette told me, 'I should have bitten my tongue when Mr. Warner offered me the role of Miss O'Hara. Well, I didn't then, but I made up for it in all the years to come. Whenever I think of it, I have a very sore tongue, such as right now.

'With my special sense of dramatic timing, I left for England on the next boat. If there had been the Concorde then, I would have left on *it*. The same thing happened with *The African Queen*. It was bought for me, and I left the studio. Such a marvelous role! I would have done it with John Mills, who was absolutely perfect for the part.'

An offer from a producer in England convinced Bette she had had enough of Warner Brothers, so she and Ham left for London. Ludovic Toeplitz, who had produced *The Private Life of Henry VIII*, wanted her to appear in two films to be shot in England and Europe.

'They've called me 'difficult.' Well, 'they' were correct. But what it meant was I absolutely cared about getting it right, not wrong. There are a lot of people who don't want to take any risk. Some of them are just bloody lazy. Lazy is more rampant than you can believe. Then there are the ones who don't *know* any better. I got into trouble because I was a perfectionist. It doesn't mean I did things perfectly. It just means I *wanted* to.

'Being a perfectionist means you can't watch rushes without feeling sick, sick, sick. You can't see your own movies without wanting to go back and redo them. Then, if you ask and expect others to reach for your standards, they hate you. On those rare occasions in life when finally you *do* please yourself, no one notices. But until you are called 'difficult,' you *aren't* anyone.'

Jack Warner, who was in Europe at the time, rushed to London, where the studio had served an injunction to stop Bette from breaking her contract and appearing in *I'll Take the Low*

Road, the first of the two films Toeplitz intended to shoot with her. Warner was not able to talk her into settling out of court, and the case went to trial. Bette was left to face the court case alone when Ham accepted a job offer in New York.

'Nobody believed I was fighting for my artistic integrity,' Bette told me. 'The whole trial centered around how much money I was getting, and how grateful I ought to be. That the studio had the power to order me to appear in a burlesque show or face suspension wasn't taken into consideration. They actually did have an ad in which I was pictured almost nude. Well, the only thing I objected to about that was the artist didn't make me look as good as I really *looked* in the nude at that time.

'When you got right down to it, I was challenging the whole studio system, and I lost. Well, no wonder. I wasn't even thirty.'

Warner Brothers won an injunction for the duration of her contract, and Bette owed her lawyer, and court costs for herself and the studio, too. She considered appealing, but was advised against it by George Arliss.

'Dear Mr. Arliss once again to the rescue. Quite unannounced, he appeared at my hotel and we had tea. He told me to go back and face them proudly. I'd lost a battle, but not the war. He predicted a wonderful future for me, and I'm overjoyed that he lived to see it happen.' George Arliss died in 1946 at seventy-seven.

'I heard a rumor that Warners was negotiating with England's biggest star, Jessie Matthews, to come to Hollywood and replace me. If I'd won, that might have happened, but I doubt it. They'd have had to bring her husband, Sonnie Hale, over, too. He directed and starred with her, and they were inseparable.'

She returned to Hollywood, where Warners assigned her to her next picture. 'Coincidentally,' Bette said, 'it was about women who are held in virtual slavery, and it ends in a trial.'

Marked Woman barely passed the Production Code because the unspoken assumption is that the heroine is a prostitute, as are all of the women of the Club Intimate. This sympathetic portrayal of 'women who are forced by economic pressures to be at least part-time hookers' appealed strongly to Bette, who saw parallels between Mary Dwight's day in court and her own in the English court fighting Warner Brothers.

Marked Woman (1937)

Mary Dwight (Bette Davis), hostess in the Club Intimate, a clip-joint nightclub, threatens to change her testimony that led to the acquittal of the boss, Johnny Vanning (Eduardo Ciannelli), on a murder charge after his involvement in the death of her beloved younger sister, Betty (Jane Bryan). Sheltering Betty and providing a good life for her had been Mary's reason for working as a hostess. Vanning's thugs beat Mary, deliberately scarring her face and sending her to the hospital. In spite of this, she appears in court, disfigured, inspiring the other hostesses to testify against Vanning for the prosecuting attorney David

162

Graham (Humphrey Bogart), thus sending the racketeer to prison.

'In those days,' Bette said, 'all movie head injuries were treated with an attractively bandaged hood. I wanted something more stark, so I left the set and drove to my doctor. I said, 'I've just been beaten up severely around the face. Treat me.' He did a good job. I looked just *awful*.

'When I passed through the studio gate on my way back, the guard phoned ahead that Miss Davis had been in a terrible accident. Mr. [Lloyd] Bacon took one look at me and said, 'You can't go on like that!''

Bette laughed at the memory of her director's consternation. 'And I loved it. I knew I'd been successful.

'I said, 'I go on with this makeup, or you go on with somebody else.' He went on with me.

'*Marked Woman* was a damned good picture.'

* * *

Since most of Bette's pictures were intended primarily for women, she was delighted to be assigned a prizefight story as her next film. She had only one reservation, 'kissing Edward G. Robinson.'

'He was a fine actor and lovely man, but do you remember his lips? He had liver lips. When we did *Kid Galahad* together, I pretended I was being kissed by Clark Gable. It took a lot of imagination, but I made it work. I dare any of you to say I looked like I wasn't enjoying my love scenes. I wanted to be in the movie because it was a man's movie, and I wanted that different audience.'

Kid Galahad (1937)

When Ward Guisenberry (Wayne Morris) knocks out champion Chuck McGraw (William Haade) at a cocktail party, Fluff Phillips (Bette Davis) suggests to her boyfriend, fight promoter Nick Donati (Edward G. Robinson), that he should back the young man, whom she dubs 'Kid Galahad.' Fluff is sent along to supervise the training of the young boxer.

Nick asks her to marry him, but she tells him she can't because she's fallen in love with 'the Kid,' as he has become known. Furious, Nick arranges for the Kid to meet the champion and throw the fight after taking a terrible beating.

The young boxer obediently follows Nick's instructions, but Fluff and Ward's girlfriend, Marie (Jane Bryan), prevail upon him to allow the Kid to win, and he knocks out McGraw.

A big-time gambler, feeling double-crossed, shoots Nick, who dies in Fluff's arms. The Kid, having promised Marie he will give up boxing, leaves with her, and it is Fluff who goes out into the night alone.

This film is one of those in which Bette Davis's character goes home alone.

* * *

After almost three years of constant work, and the court case, Bette began to show signs of severe fatigue. Ruthie rented a house on the beach in Santa Barbara for her to rest on weekends and between films. There, Ruthie tried without success to nurse her daughter back to health with the spiritual healing principles of Christian Science, which had become Ruthie's new religion. Bobby was on a honeymoon cruise.

Bette's next film was based on an original screenplay by director Edmund Goulding, a remake of his 1929 Gloria Swanson film, *The Trespasser*.

That Certain Woman (1937)

Mary Donnell (Bette Davis), trying to escape a sensational past in which she was married to a gangster, goes to work as a secretary for attorney Lloyd Rogers (Ian Hunter). She falls in love with Jack Merrick (Henry Fonda), the son of Rogers's wealthiest client, and they elope. Merrick Sr. (Donald Crisp), however, has the marriage annulled without knowing that Mary is pregnant. Mary tells only her boss, who loves her, but is married.

Jack marries someone of whom his father approves, but she (Anita Louise) is crippled in a car accident with Jack driving.

Rogers dies, including Mary and her son in his will, and causing his widow to believe the child was her husband's. Newspapers sensationalize the story, and Jack returns to help Mary. When Merrick Sr. hears of his grandchild's existence, he tries to take him away from Mary. Mary agrees to let Jack and his wife adopt him.

Mary leaves for England alone, realizing she still loves Jack, and terribly missing her son.

Jack's wife dies, and he finds Mary. Free now to remarry, they are reunited, together with their child.

This was the first time Bette had worked professionally with Henry Fonda, but not the first time their paths had crossed. Bette recounted her memory:

'You'll never guess who gave me my first *serious* kiss. Henry Fonda! Not on the screen, in life. In my teens, one of my first dates was with Hank. It was a blind date. We were both in school. Neither one of us even knew we were going to be actors. He was very shy, but even so we somehow ended up very late at night in the Princeton Stadium. It was the most beautiful moonlit night. He was so handsome.

'He kissed me.

'I knew I was in love.

'I wished I could be beautiful for him, because he had the pick of all the girls. I was just a plain little thing as far as Hank was concerned. He never called back. I sent him a love letter, but he never answered it. When we did *The Certain Woman* together, he didn't even remember our first date.'

When I spoke with Henry Fonda, he told me *his* account of the episode.

'The mother of a friend of mine in my hometown, Omaha, asked me if I'd drive east with her son to Princeton to keep him company.

166

In return, she would give me a week in New York.

'I jumped at the chance. I'd never traveled, and New York was the place I most wanted to go, to see the plays. I went there from Princeton and saw nine glorious plays in six days.

'My friend picked me up to drive back to Princeton. In the car with him, he had a Mrs. Davis and her two teenage daughters, named Bobby and Bette. We drove through a pea-soup fog all the way, but we got to Princeton. The girls and their mother stayed at a hotel, and my friend and I spent the night in his dormitory.

'Being a very juvenile type, my friend suggested that we play a kind of game to see which one of us could kiss the most girls, and there'd be a prize of some sort. I was painfully shy at that time, still am, but I've learned how to cover it over so it doesn't show too much. I've tried to play the part in life of someone who isn't so shy. Anyway, I agreed, because I figured I was hired to go along with him.

'On Sunday after dinner, we left Mrs. Davis at the hotel and drove with the girls to the Princeton Stadium. She trusted us, I guess, or she trusted her daughters. My friend got out of the car with Bobby and left me in the rear seat with Bette. I'd just learned that my friend was 'pinned' to Bobby, an expression they used in those days for people who were going steady. It meant more than that, because the girl got a fraternity pin, which was preliminary to getting a ring. A fellow's pin meant a lot to him. So I knew damned well he was kissing her in that empty stadium out there in that moonlight, and he was making points.

'In college I dated a girl steady, going out with only her for two years, and I never kissed her. It's hard to believe now, but it gives you some idea of my predicament sitting in that back seat with Bette. I don't think I even put my arm around her. Finally, I gave her a little peck, or a kind of a kiss, just to keep the score even with my friend. I can't say I didn't enjoy it, because I did, and I thought Bette did, too. Next day, we put the girls and Mrs. Davis on the train for Boston. Before I left Princeton, I got a letter from Bette that she must have written on the train and mailed at Grand Central Station. She said that she'd told her mother everything, and they would be announcing the engagement when they got home.

'It was about three years later, when I was the third assistant stage manager, which was so low on the scale it hardly existed, and Bette was an apprentice at the Cape Playhouse on Cape Cod. I often walked her home at night. We'd sit on the screened porch and drink lemonade. You know something? All those times over lemonade, she never mentioned that kiss. Neither did I.'

Because Bette's two previous pictures with Leslie Howard had been critical as well as box office successes, she looked forward to *It's Love I'm After*, especially because the cast included her friend Olivia de Havilland.

It's Love I'm After (1937)

Stage idols Basil Underwood (Leslie Howard) and Joyce Arden (Bette Davis) appear to be the ideal couple, but their offstage life is far from romantic. Their upcoming marriage has been postponed eleven times, clearly not a promising sign.

When asked by friend Henry Grant (Patric Knowles) to disillusion Henry's fiancée, Marcia West (Olivia de Havilland), who has a serious crush on Basil, Basil is delighted to exercise his natural proclivities for bad behavior. Basil demonstrates for Marcia how totally obnoxious he can be, but she becomes even more infatuated with him, and she breaks her engagement to Henry.

When Marcia announces she is going to marry Basil, Joyce shows Marcia fake pictures of Basil's 'children.' Then, Joyce has him all to herself again.

When Bette, pleading sunstroke, failed to report for her next scheduled film, *Hollywood Hotel*, the studio suspended her. Rather than do *Hollywood Hotel*, she entered the hospital for a month-long stay.

5
The Warner Years
(1938–1944)

Miriam Hopkins not only had performed the lead in *Jezebel* on Broadway, but she owned rights to the play along with playwright Owen Davis, Sr., and the producers. Thus, when she sold her rights to Warners for instant cash, she hoped she would be the first actress considered for the screen role, and she was — the first considered and the first rejected. It hadn't occurred to her that the role of a southern beauty, *her* role, would go to Bette Davis, who was neither southern nor a beauty.

'The part was something I could feel,' Bette told me. 'Wearing a red dress to a white dress ball? Of course! It seemed to me that *Jezebel* was something of an extension of my character in *Cabin in the Cotton*.' When *Jezebel* opened in March of 1938, Bette became a superstar overnight. She won the Oscar for best actress. (Fay Bainter won for best supporting actress in *Jezebel*.)

William Wyler, who had recently achieved distinguished successes with *Dodsworth* and

Dead End, was the director. Though Bette had been directed by him briefly for a test in 1931, this was her first experience having him direct her for a feature film.

'I think Mr. Wyler is, without doubt, through all the years, our greatest American director,' she told me. 'Anyway, to me he is. *Jezebel* was the first time I worked with him. And he was very tough. But that's gone out of our business, the toughness. In those days they *were* tough. He was tough with everybody.

'*Jezebel* was one of those defining moments in my career. I owe so much to Willie. He was the director who helped me achieve my full potential. Because of him, my name was above the title for the first time, and it's stayed there ever since.

'He was the most exciting man I'd ever known. Oh, we fought hard professionally, but it only made us closer. When I did a lot of takes, I'd feel I was doing them all the same, but Willie would catch the one that was different, special. He had a great eye. He also had great eyes.

'The work was our bond. Other people couldn't really understand what our work meant to us. Over and over again, Willie and I fought and made each other miserable, then made up and made each other happy. He was *everything* I ever dreamed of in a man, so love and passion soon followed.' Wyler had recently been divorced from actress Margaret Sullavan.

'An affair between the stars, or between the director and star, produces an electricity in a film that the audience feels. You can still feel it in

Jezebel when you see the picture.

'The time in my life of my most perfect happiness was with Willie directing me in *Jezebel*. I had the film of a lifetime and proximity to Willie. My work and Willie. Willie and my work. I knew true happiness. I cherished the moment. The only flaw was that nagging doubt in the back of my mind, 'Could it last?'

'I've found that happiness is a way station, a place to refuel and go on again.

'After the *Jezebel* premiere, Hedda Hopper came up to me and whispered, 'I could tell you *were* in love with Henry Fonda. In the close-ups I could see it in your eyes.' What she didn't see was Henry Fonda. At the time they were shooting the close-ups, he was in New York with his wife, who was having Jane. His wife had him put it into his contract that he could go back to New York for the birth of their baby.

'What I was looking at was Willie Wyler, who was standing behind the camera. The cameramen and still photographers immediately noticed the new radiance in my face. 'You're beautiful, Bette,' they said. 'You must be in love. The camera never lies.' And it didn't. I was indeed in love.

'Whatever pain was involved, I'm glad I experienced that feeling. Romance, passion, respect, and consideration. Sex is flat without that.'

At the end of *Jezebel*, in mid-January of 1938, Bette discovered she was pregnant. She said she never told Wyler. She had her second abortion. 'I killed a part of myself, but I couldn't win Willie

172

by making him feel forced to marry me.' After *Jezebel* wrapped, Wyler returned to Goldwyn and Bette went on to *The Sisters*.

Jezebel (1937)

For the 1850 New Orleans Olympus Ball, willful Julie Marsden (Bette Davis) defies her inadequately attentive fiancé, Pres Dillard (Henry Fonda), by wearing a red gown instead of the required white. Pres punishes Julie by forcing her to dance while everyone shuns them from the sidelines.

Pres breaks their engagement, announcing he is leaving New Orleans to work in his family's New York bank. Angrily, Julie turns to aspiring beau Buck Cantrell (George Brent).

Certain that Pres still loves her, Julie is shocked when Pres returns a year later with his bride, Amy (Margaret Lindsay). At the Halcyon Plantation, Julie flirts with Buck to arouse Pres' jealousy.

After Pres has been called away to New Orleans, his younger brother, Ted (Richard Cromwell), feels his family's honor has been compromised, and challenges Buck to a duel. Buck is killed, but before dying, he tells Ted that he knows Julie has been using him to win back Pres.

In New Orleans, cannon shots announce yellow fever. When Pres collapses, everyone moves away from him, exactly as they had from Julie at the ball.

Julie runs the quarantine blockade to reach Pres. Amy arrives to find Julie nursing her desperately ill husband.

Determined to accompany Pres to the quarantine island, Julie persuades Amy that she is far better qualified to fight for Pres' life. Amy agrees when Julie assures her that Pres loves her, his wife. Julie leaves with Pres on the wagon to the island of the dying.

'I like black and white pictures,' Bette said, 'but this is one that would have been more effective in color, I think, for showing the red dress. Julie was the best part I'd had since Mildred in *Bondage*.

'Many people who saw the film and spoke with me about it over the years remembered seeing it in color, the illusion of color was so great.

'The dress couldn't *really* be red, because in black and white, red would have photographed black. Actually, it was a sort of rust color.'

Julie Marsden is in many respects what is considered an archetypal Bette Davis part, yet by no means was it the only kind of character she played.

'I've played quite as many calm, heroine-type women as I have a Jezebel-type person. But the Jezebels are always remembered more, because people are fascinated by a woman like that more than by just a heroine. I was always challenged by women like this, because it was really something to work with, and it did become known as a Bette Davis part.

'I have no regrets about that because I believe unless you get a category, you just have no hope.

You must have an identification of some kind. It doesn't mean that you always have to play this, and I work very hard to play other kinds of parts. This is *my* identification. Personally, I've *never* been able to figure out really what I am like or what I'm *not* really like. I could always understand my character on the screen better than I could understand myself. And when I had to play myself in *Hollywood Canteen* and *Thank Your Lucky Stars* I was utterly lost, utterly. You cannot imagine.'

Bette had one lingering regret about *Jezebel*. 'I wanted my father to see the film. I wanted to hear him say I was a great actress and that he had been wrong not to believe in me. I really wanted to hear him say, 'I am proud of you. I am very proud of you. I love you.''

That never happened. During the shooting of the film, Harlow Davis died of a heart attack at the age of fifty-two.

'I couldn't go to the funeral back in Boston without shutting down production, so I finished the film. I knew Daddy would *not* understand.

'I had let him down again. When I was free, I cried for days.

'I could sometimes postpone a cold when I was working. I was so determined. Then, when I had time, after the film wrapped, I would have a humdinger of a cold. I had tried in the same way to postpone my grief.

'I was heartbroken, but I don't know exactly why. At the time, it seemed normal to care when your father dies, even though I hardly knew him. He was, after all, my father. But looking back, I wondered if it was because it meant that my long struggle to gain his attention, to win his admiration, was over. He had played a part in my life, and a greater part in my thoughts. I had failed to win his love, period.'

★ ★ ★

After being awarded an Oscar for her performance in *Jezebel*, Bette expected better roles than the ones she was offered. She complained vigorously and was put on suspension, during which time she received no salary. 'I really needed the money, but I couldn't afford to risk my career on what I was being offered.' With *The Sisters*, she found the part and another director to respect, Anatole Litvak.

The Sisters (1938)

Louise (Bette Davis), the eldest of the three Elliott sisters of Silver Bow, Montana, elopes with Frank Medlin (Errol Flynn), a peripatetic newspaperman. They go to San Francisco where Frank abandons her just before the earthquake of 1906. She survives the subsequent fire, but suffers a miscarriage.

Afterward, she goes to work in a department store where the owner (Ian Hunter) falls in love with her. Frank returns, however, and Louise forgives him when he says he still loves her.

In a memorable visual ending, the three sisters come together from different places on the dance floor, almost floating toward each other. They are

176

oblivious to and apart from the jubilant crowd, which darkens and fades into the background.

Together, they turn. In a striking elevated reverse-angle shot, they are seen, arms locked, apprehensive, looking upward.

We don't see the person at whom they are looking, but we believe he is Frank, the charming rogue played by Errol Flynn, whom Louise has just taken back.

In the four years since they were last together, the sisters have become the women they will be for the rest of their lives. It seems as if they are looking into their own futures, not just the future of Louise.

This is a different ending from that of the novel, the one originally shot by Litvak. In a preview, the audience didn't like Bette Davis leaving Errol Flynn for the dependable Ian Hunter, so a 'happy' ending was shot, with Bette taking back Flynn, who had promised to reform. The actors considered it unrealistic, but the studio hoped it would satisfy audience expectations.

'This is not at all a happy ending,' Bette said, 'because it would be out of character for Frank to become a steadfast husband. That would be as foolish as thinking *Errol Flynn* would make a longtime husband. Who would be so foolish? Well, Louise, my character, would, of course. Louise is a romantic and believes, or at least hopes, it will be permanent.

'It was a very Bette Davis thing to do. Romantic foolishness is almost certainly doomed. The Flynn character would never change, He couldn't even if he wanted to, and he certainly didn't want to.

'My character was a romantic fool like me.'

Her marriage to Ham had been deteriorating, 'disappearing for years,' as Bette described it. 'Admitting defeat was always difficult for me. Ham and I weren't really right for each other. We had just *seemed* right for each other. It was the end of many of my girlish dreams.

'Without mentioning any names,' Bette said, 'I'll tell you about a man I met after our marriage had failed, but before Ham asked for the divorce.'

'I met this man at Tailwaggers, the animal welfare organization. I've always loved dogs — my own, all dogs — and it broke my heart to think of them homeless, unwanted, held as prisoners, under inhumane conditions when some of them are more human than we are.

'Since they are dependent, it's up to us to do what we can for them. I think all of us who have so much in life have to put something back. If you can give a home to a dog or cat, they desperately need you, especially the ones in the shelters. And if you can't adopt, you can always give money.

'Well, anyway, in 1938, I was a Tailwagger. In fact, I was *the* Tailwagger — president of the organization. We had the most glamorous black-tie party in Beverly Hills, and I remember what I was wearing — a pink lace gown, *very* low cut. Very.

'A tall, slim man approached me. He seemed reserved, even shy. He spoke softly, and I had to lean close to hear him. When he introduced himself, he looked into my eyes, not down my dress. That really impressed me, though if I didn't want men looking, why didn't I wear a higher-necked dress? Always the ambivalence. Ruth Elizabeth and Bette.

'He bought me a ton of raffle tickets. Impressive, though none of them won. And he asked me for a date. I was flattered. I was married. I was bored. I accepted.

'By that time, I was married to Ham only in name. We were usually separated because of his work or my work, or both. When we were together, there was nothing left between us. Any happy days we had had were in our memories almost entirely before we married. The terrible distance when we were together was harder to bear than when we were apart. We no longer communicated with each other at all. And our sex life had disappeared. A woman who's been with just one man for a long time is practically a virgin again.

'With this man, I had to be the aggressive one, because he really was reserved. He was a few years older than I, but he seemed younger. He brought out a side of me, sexually, that no one else had, at least up to that time.

'We had to be very careful. Even though he wasn't an actor or a director, he was just as famous as I, certainly more important. We couldn't be seen at restaurants together, so we ate at home, and he liked that. He was surprised I was so domestic, and he said it was exciting to have me cook for him. It was also convenient.

'At the time, I thought he wanted to avoid gossip. Now, I wonder if he only liked my cooking because it saved him money. He never carried much cash. The rich seldom do. This was in the days before credit cards, and sometimes I'd have to let him have some money. *I* always bought the groceries. At the time, I thought it was funny.

'This man *had* to have his way. He never really listened to you, though he *seemed* to be listening. Perhaps it was because he was having hearing problems even then, and he'd taken to just nodding his head when he saw you speaking. I think he heard what he *wanted* to hear. His hearing was better when you were saying what *he* wanted to hear.

'In his later years, he became the world's foremost hermit. I never knew if he retreated from the world as he became increasingly deaf, or if he became deaf because he was retreating from the world.

'The most revealing portrait ever made of me was taken by George Hurrell on the set of *Dark Victory*. It's an extreme close-up that shows *such* pain, especially in my eyes. I was in absolute agony that day, convinced my career was over.

'Having discovered my affair, Ham was in a rage. I was surprised he minded. If positions had been reversed, I wouldn't have cared what he did, because at this point we were only married legally. Well, I don't *think* I would have minded. Ham took it very big, or at least he acted that way. I think he was looking for an excuse. Maybe he had found somebody else. Anyway, he got greedy when he heard who it was.

'Ham wanted a divorce, and he needed money, so I borrowed it from the studio to give to him. My marriage to Ham had *endured* for six years. Anyway, that was the end of Ham — and, in a way, the end of my youth. I had just turned thirty.' They were divorced on December 6, 1938.

'That man I was having the affair with didn't offer any money to help with my problems with Ham, and I assure you, he was not, by any stretch of the imagination, needy. It was a warm rather than a hot affair, and I suppose it would have run its course without Ham's intervention, but it ended abruptly when Ham found out, and it took what was left of my first marriage with it.

'I always had to believe I was special for any man I was with. This man and I weren't in love in that magical way, but I couldn't have done it at all if I hadn't felt there was love between us. Perhaps I missed out on passion by always looking for romance. But we are what we are. I couldn't imagine sharing my white cottage with a stranger — even that cottage in my mind.

'Speaking of cottages, ten years later, when I was married to Gary Merrill, he rented a house in Malibu, and it was the funniest thing . . . Well, maybe it *wasn't* so funny, after all. He'd chosen the exact house where I used to meet Hughes . . .

'There! I've said it. But I'm sure you'd already guessed it was Howard Hughes. Anyway, I thought it was better not to mention the house and what had transpired there to Gary.

'I suppose the affair with Hughes happened because my marriage had really already ended. I just didn't want to admit it. The marriage had been a mistake. I couldn't forgive Ham for not wanting our baby, for acting coldly, as my father had.

'I wanted to be free of a husband I didn't love or respect anymore.

'Hughes sent me a rose every year after that for a long time. Very romantic. He probably had one of his secretaries do it. Maybe once you were on, it was hard to get off the rose list. Can you imagine I was so naïve I thought that rose was romantic?

'He was a very stingy man. He never gave me even a small gift. I wasn't the kind of girl men gave gifts to. The gift they gave me was themselves.

'You know, I was the only one who ever brought Howard Hughes to a sexual climax, or so he said at that time. No, of course you don't know. It's true. That is to say, it's true that he said it. Or, let's say, I believed it when he told me that. I was wildly naïve at the time. It may have been his regular seduction gambit. Anyway, it worked with me, and it was cheaper than buying gifts. But Howard Huge, he was not.

'I liked sex in a way that was considered unbecoming for a woman in my time. The way I felt was only considered appropriate for a man. It was both a physical and emotional need. Of course, it had advantages in the pleasure it brought me. No question about that. But it also made me a victim. Dependent.

'My professional timing was always better than my personal timing; but then, I was always finding professional happiness is a lot easier than finding personal happiness, especially for a woman. Women are supposed to wait for the right man to come and ask us. Well, the men who asked me were usually the wrong ones. *That* they were. Personal happiness is magic and can't be planned.

★ ★ ★

'I loved *Dark Victory*,' Bette told me, 'and it got me another Oscar nomination. The life I have led is unbelievable. I am the first to admit it. I'll tell you another unbelievable life. Did you see *Dark Victory?*'

I nodded that I had.

'Well, did you ever think Ronnie Reagan would become the most famous actor of all time? Of course, it wasn't for being an actor.

'I used to think of him as 'little Ronnie Reagan,' not because he was short. He wasn't. He was tall and well built. The 'little' was for his acting talent. He wasn't totally lacking, but it appeared to be a small range, although I would be the first to admit that it's difficult to hone your craft if you don't get the chance. His part had been written to move along the story and avoid characters having to talk with themselves. He was very good in that picture where he loses his legs [*Kings Row*].

'Not too long ago, I had the chance to see *Dark Victory*, and I revised my opinion of the

Ronald Reagan performance. I don't see how he could have been better. Geraldine Fitzgerald — magnificent! George [Brent], dear. As for Judith Traherne, my character, well, I cannot have false modesty. I am proud of her and of me.'

Dark Victory was originally produced on Broadway. It was written by George Emerson Brewer, Jr., and Bertram Bloch, and starred Tallulah Bankhead. David O. Selznick owned the screen rights, but nothing was done about making the play into a film until Bette read it and decided that the story of Judith Traherne would be right for her. She persuaded Hal Wallis to buy it for Warners despite Jack Warner's resistance.

'The day I started *Dark Victory*,' Bette told me, 'Mr. Warner sent for me. He said, 'We bought this for you. We'll let you make it. But not one fellow will come into the theater. Who wants to go to the movies to see some dame dying?' Well, apparently *he* didn't go, but fortunately, a great many others *did*. Our picture was successful and memorable.'

Dark Victory (1939)

The privileged, fun-loving existence of Judith Traherne (Bette Davis) is threatened when her recurring headaches signal the possibility of a brain tumor. Following an operation, she is not told that she has at most eight months to live. She is told she will feel well until near the end, when she will lose her sight.

She falls in love with her surgeon, Dr. Frederick

184

Steele (George Brent), and he with her. When Judith learns that the operation was not a success, she rejects his proposal of marriage as an act of pity. She retreats to her stables, where her only company is her thoroughbred horse, Champion. An Irish stable hand (Humphrey Bogart), himself long in love with Judith, inspires her to seize the moments left to her.

She marries Dr. Steele and lives out a happy lifetime in one summer on his Vermont farm, where he devotes himself to finding a cure for diseases like hers. When her failing eyesight indicates the end is near, she doesn't tell him, and encourages him to leave without her for a medical conference in New York. Judith knows she is going to die, but she feels that she has won her own brief dark victory over death.

When Bette went up the stairs for the last scene, she stopped in the middle of the take and asked director Edmund Goulding, 'Who's scoring this film? Max Steiner?'

Goulding answered that he thought so.

'Well,' Bette declared, 'either *I* am going up those stairs or Max Steiner is going up those stairs, but not the two of us together.'

Bette was referring to composer Max Steiner's music, often as important a dramatic element as the actors themselves. In the finished film, his music *does*, indeed, go up the stairs with Bette. Forty-five years later, she told me, 'Dear old Max Steiner. I'm glad we went up those stairs together.'

Judith's secretary, Ann King (played by

Geraldine Fitzgerald), was not in the original stage play. 'It was Eddie Goulding who put my character into the screenplay,' Geraldine Fitzgerald told me. 'It was a great invention. I was written in so that Bette's character wouldn't have to complain.'

'It's important not to have a character indulge in so much self-pity that she loses the sympathy of the audience,' George Cukor once told me. When I went with him to a Columbia University acting class where he was a guest speaker, he told the young actresses, who were proud of their ability to produce tears, 'If you cry for yourself, the audience won't cry for *you*.' In *Dark Victory*, Judith shows her mettle, and doesn't cry for herself.

Dark Victory had a great emotional impact on Bette. 'For weeks after we finished filming, I slept badly, and when I woke up, I was too afraid to open my eyes.' She was afraid, she said, that when she opened her eyes, there would be only blackness.

'*Dark Victory* really affected me. I was personally so upset about *being* so upset, that after the first week, I went to Hal Wallis and asked if I could give up the part. Hal said to me, '*Stay* upset.'

'The question I'm most often asked is 'What was your favorite part?' so I'll answer it before you ask. It was Judith Traherne in *Dark Victory*.

'I haven't the foggiest which is my favorite film after *Dark Victory*. Oh, I suppose I'd have to choose *Eve*. Mankiewicz was truly a genius. I always think it's better not to have your favorite film at the very beginning of your career, when you don't need it. When you're very young, you don't need so much. Poor Orson Welles. Imagine having to top or equal *Citizen Kane*!

'I hope there won't be a remake of *Dark Victory*. I've always felt it belonged to me.'

* * *

In December 1938, between *Dark Victory* and *Juarez*, Ham divorced Bette on grounds of 'cruel and inhuman treatment.' He cited in particular the importance she gave her career over their marriage. 'You might say he named my career as co-respondent,' Bette said.

After Ham divorced Bette, and her relationship with Hughes ended, it didn't matter to her, because the man she was thinking about was still William Wyler.

'Willie was the perfect man for me in every respect except one. He had everything I admire: his brilliance, his talent, his personal charm, his wit, his sensual appeal, everything I prized. There was only one quality he didn't have. He didn't want to marry me. Certainly not enough, because he married someone else.

'When we met, I told him I didn't want to get married again. Well, I *didn't* want to at that time, and I didn't want to marry just anyone; however, very quickly, I knew he was the man I wanted to marry. But I couldn't let him know that. Men don't like to feel you're looking to catch them. If they feel that, they are likely to swim away, and Willie, especially, was a man any woman would want. I felt I had to play a little hard-to-get. Well, I was too good an actress. I overplayed my part.

'I fantasized endlessly about Willie asking me to marry him. In my mind I said yes in so many different ways. I wondered why he was taking so long. Was he ever going to ask me? Then he did ask, and fool that I was, I said, 'I have to think about it.' I didn't want him to feel I was too anxious. He was everything I wanted, but I wasn't certain I was everything *he* wanted. I loved the way he directed me on the screen, but that didn't mean I wanted him directing me in real life. He was a perfectionist, no lily guts, and I had a feeling he'd want to change me.

'I sensed he was proposing to Bette on the set and expecting to get Ruth Elizabeth around the house. Even so, my answer could only be yes. But I'd been waiting a long time for him to ask me, and he'd taken his good old time about it, so I wasn't going to rush into my yes. Besides, I didn't want him to think I was overanxious, that no one else wanted me. I wanted Willie to appreciate what he was getting, to realize just how special I was. He'd never find anyone else like me again. It didn't occur to me that he'd never look.

'I let him wait. I had to fight with all my strength to keep from picking up the telephone. Instead, I stayed by the phone every minute waiting for him to call. Terrible. Terrible. There's nothing worse than waiting for a phone to ring with that call from someone you can't live without — and it doesn't. You wonder if it's out of order. Then you decide *you* are. The temptation to call him was absolutely over-whelming, but somehow I resisted. I felt I had to test him.

'Then, a letter arrived. It was from Willie. I was about to tear it open when I decided, 'No, I can wait.' I set the letter aside, though it tortured me. I was dying to know what was in it. Of course, if I opened it, no one would know. But I would know. Finally, I couldn't stand it any longer. I opened the letter. It said if I didn't call him and give him an answer, it was all over.

'Love makes such fools of us. Really. I who never play games, never pretend! I began to call Willie. I called desperately, but I couldn't find him.

'Then, I heard on the radio he'd married somebody else. So, the only person I taught a lesson to was myself. The trouble with playing hard-to-get is that the other person may choose not to play. Just this once, I acted this way because I cared so much. I was never able to profit from the lesson. There never was another Willie. So all these years I've had my precious pride, and now — I have *it* to keep me company.

'Willie was the love of my life. No question. I've always wished I'd married him. I would have had some wonderful times, and perhaps I would have had Willie's child. Oh, how I would have loved that! I suppose the films we made together are our children. We made three: *Jezebel, The Letter*, and *The Little Foxes*.

'Willie was the only man I ever met whom I respected in every way. Lust with trust. I cherished the moment, but Willie's strength and brilliance overwhelmed me, and I felt threatened. Here was a man who would run my life from sunrise to the next sunrise. How thrilling! Ruth Elizabeth was enthralled. I, Bette, resisted this loss of sovereignty. Then the man of my dreams married someone else. At the time, I thought I missed him, but what I really missed was Us.

'I saw Willie many years later, in 1959. I'd looked forward to it for a long, long time. I could feel my heart beating harder and faster. I wondered what he was thinking. I wondered how it would be, that first moment when our eyes met, when we were once again together. Would that old magic be there? Would he notice I was older? I lived the moment over and over again in my head.

'I walked on the set where he was directing *Ben-Hur* in Italy. I didn't want to interrupt, so I waited until there was a break, then I stepped dramatically into his line of vision. 'Hello, Bette,' he said. 'Glad you could come by. Just take a seat.'

''Glad you could come by, just take a seat.' It was as if there had never been anything between us, as if he hadn't given me a thought during the years which had passed. Well, I knew it then. He hadn't. There had never been a day I hadn't thought of him. But once I realized that Willie had gotten on with his life, I made up my mind it was high time for me to get Willie out of my mind. The strange thing is the more desperate you are to get rid of a thought, the more it persists.

'When they wanted me to appear for Willie at

the American Film Institute, I thought about doing it. He'd been *so* important in my life. I didn't know whether to do it or not. Then, at the last moment I knew I couldn't do it. I pleaded illness. There were those who said derisively, 'A Bette Davis cold.' When it was over, I was sorry, but you can't get yesterday back for any price.'

Bette said that she had another reason that had made her feel nervous about attending the AFI tribute. She knew that at Willie's side would be the woman with whom he had shared his life, Talli [Margaret Tallichet], his wife and the mother of his children. 'Oh, I do envy Talli that,' Bette said. 'I don't know how I would feel sitting at *their* table.'

The next year, when Bette was honored with the same award by the AFI, Wyler was there with Talli. Bette saw them and somewhat to her surprise, she felt happy. 'I was happy for him, happy that he had found a good life. So, you see, I really *did* love him.

'And I was pleased to find that I'm not at all a bad person.'

Bette was the first woman to be so honored by the AFI. 'I was proud indeed, and excited about it. I even went to one of those diet places to get in shape — six hundred calories a day and decaf. Ugh! They asked Willie to speak for me, and he did. I hadn't braved it for him, but he stood up for me. As always, he was the better man.

'He said I was difficult in the same way *he* was difficult, that we only wanted the best. He said that I would probably be willing to leave the ceremony right then and there to go back to

191

Warners to reshoot a scene from *The Letter*. I nodded my head forcefully in the affirmative.

'I've told myself it wouldn't have worked out if I'd married Willie. Can the magic of being together last? I don't know. I'm afraid it always has to wear off. Too much to hope for. Well, at least, if I couldn't find magic in life, I found it on film. If I couldn't be Jezebel in life, I could be Jezebel on the screen for a while. I thought to myself I could exist without Jezebel, but she couldn't exist without me. No — that's not true. She *will* exist without me. She'll always be there, and she'll never get wrinkles. Of course, Baby Jane will never have anything *but* wrinkles.'

Wyler remembered the affair somewhat differently. He told me that Bette had claimed she didn't *want* to get married again, and he had believed her, probably because he *wanted* to believe her. He described her as 'a unique and wonderful actress and person.'

'She was very passionate and emotional,' Wyler said, 'with more energy than anyone I'd ever known. Too much for me.'

Wyler added that he had infinite respect for Bette Davis the actress and an enduring affection for the woman. 'But she was the *most* emotional person I had ever met.'

At first, it was flattering to him, the depth of her feeling for him, until he realized she could, in just a moment, become what seemed to him 'equally emotional over the slightest, the most inconsequential thing.'

'After a while, it became rather draining,' he remembered. 'Arguing seemed to stimulate her and especially her enjoyment in making up.' But it didn't stimulate him, it exhausted him. Her endless wellspring of energy sapped his, he said, and he felt it eventually would have ruined his career. He couldn't imagine going home every night to all that turmoil and being at the service of her career, as well as his own. 'Two big careers, equal, and constantly shifting up and down, probably it's one career too many. If she got what she wanted, I felt it wouldn't be what she wanted anymore. It seemed it was always about having to pass a test, until you failed.'

He said that he had enjoyed being with her and didn't understand that she was looking forward to a future he hadn't envisioned and for which he had not made plans. Once again Bette's white cottage in her mind had remained only for single occupancy.

★　★　★

Geraldine Fitzgerald reminisced with me about Bette during a lunch at Le Cirque in New York.

'Bette was the most generous actress I've ever worked with. She helped me a great deal when I first came to Hollywood, and we remained lifelong friends.'

She told me about crossing the country with Bette during World War II. They found themselves on the same train in adjoining bedroom compartments. Bette insisted that the wall between them be removed. It was possible, but a cumbersome task, especially with the train in motion. Bette made a tremendous fuss, however, and after a huge commotion, a conductor who was a Bette Davis fan had some porters do the job.

During a twenty-minute stopover in Kansas City, Bette decided it would be pleasant to take a stroll with Geraldine on the platform. Everyone else on the train followed a short distance behind, straining to catch every word that was spoken. 'There was no one who could enunciate and project like Bette, and, at the time, I was terribly self-conscious,' Geraldine recalled.

'Bette had one favored subject over all others. Sex.

''Now, Fitzy,' she asked me, 'What do you think of George Brent?'

'I said, 'I think he's a very talented actor.'

''No, I don't mean on the screen,' Bette said. 'I mean in bed.'

'The crowd following us looked at the ground, pretending they hadn't heard, which meant they had.

''But I've never been to bed with him,' I said.

'Bette looked at me, amazed, and said for the benefit of everyone else, 'Then you must be the only one on the Warner lot who hasn't!''

During *Dark Victory*, Bette did have an affair with George Brent, 'one of the few men who gave me something besides himself,' she told me.

'People think actors and actresses have affairs with *all* their co-stars. I wasn't so lucky — or, perhaps, so unlucky. But George Brent and I *did* have something going. He helped me through *Dark Victory*, and we fell in love.

'We were both single at the time, and that was

194

rather a pleasure. We could be seen together in public places. Hal Wallis was pleased by our affair. I suppose he thought it would help the picture at the box office.

'George was notorious as one of the tightest men in Hollywood. He liked me, but he *loved* his money. Oh, I always knew how to pick 'em! Once, he gave me a bracelet with B-E-T-T-E spelled out in diamonds — you know, the tiny chip diamonds. He said he was glad I had such a short name. I laughed and I said, 'Well, my name is *really* Ruth Elizabeth.' He didn't think that was funny at all.

'Thirty years after our affair, I was playing onstage, and I received a bouquet of white orchids from George. On a card, he wrote he would be coming backstage after the show to see me. We hadn't seen each other in years and years. I was in a dither. Would I still look good to him? I was more nervous about seeing George than about doing the show.

'There was a timid knock at the door, and this incredibly ancient old man came hobbling in. He was portly, bald, and long in tooth, though not long in teeth. I didn't know it was George until he giggled. I couldn't ever have forgotten that funny, out-of-character giggle.

'We hugged and chatted a bit, but I was so shaken, I hardly knew what to say. It seems heartless, I know, but I couldn't help thanking God I hadn't married him. When he was thirty-five and I was thirty-one, that four years difference hadn't meant anything, but time plays strange tricks.

'I was very involved with George Brent. I found him an exciting man on and off the screen. Onscreen he was a leading man, but he didn't have that extra something that makes a star, what Bogey had.

'I was always trying to cast the man of my dreams. There were some who said I just couldn't be pleased, that I had an unrealistic idea, in my life and in my bed.

'My favorite actor with whom I never played, professionally or personally, was Laurence Olivier. I admired everything about him. He was a great actor, and he was my dream man. Literally and figuratively. Larry was my fantasy lover, the perfect man, or at least I thought he would be. He was not only beautiful, but intelligent.'

★　★　★

Warner Brothers lavished unusual care on the production of *Juarez*, which is essentially two stories about two men who never meet each other. Because the more important and complex story excluded the star of the film, Paul Muni, he insisted that his character, Juarez, be made more important than Brian Aherne's character, Maximilian. Reviewers and audiences, however, found the tragedy of Bette Davis's character, Carlota, the most important and the most sympathetic.

'The real problem,' Bette said, 'was we were shooting two movies at the same time, and we'd already shot one of them, that with Brian and me, before Paul even walked on the set. When he saw what we had done, he and Bella [his wife] had different ideas, and our part got cut. That's what star power will get you.'

Juarez (1939)

Maximilian von Hapsburg (Brian Aherne), the Archduke of Austria, is appointed the Emperor of Mexico by Napoleon III (Claude Rains). In Mexico, he is fiercely opposed by the forces of President Benito Juarez (Paul Muni). Maximilian's rule, though just and equitable, is appreciated by neither the Mexicans nor the French, and he is forced by the French to adopt harsher methods. To complicate matters, the United States supports the forces of Juarez, and requests that Maximilian leave. The Empress Carlota (Bette Davis) returns to France to plead with Napoleon III for military aid to save her husband. It is refused, and she goes mad. Maximilian stays in Mexico to the end, and is killed by Juarez's army. At the end, Juarez, understanding Maximilian's noble motives, pays private homage to his enemy.

As was his custom, director William Dieterle insisted that important members of the cast and crew gather at the studio at the moment deemed most propitious by his astrologer, even if it was before the start of production. For *Juarez*, that time was eight A.M., Saturday, October 15, 1938. Actual shooting began two weeks later.

★ ★ ★

Bette Davis would co-star with Miriam Hopkins for her next film, *The Old Maid*. Bette denied that there was any antagonism between the two actresses. 'Miriam and I got along fine — socially. Even with her overdone southern accent, she was a charming woman. Professionally, you just had to accept that she was going to try to steal the scene from you in any way possible. But I was used to this from our days together with George Cukor in Rochester. Her favorite trick was never looking at you when you were speaking. She would be looking all over the set, 'catching flies' as they used to call it on the stage. Then, she would change the business in our close-ups together so that mine didn't match hers. I didn't mind this because I can get across an emotion with my back, if necessary, and with Miriam it often *was* necessary. She would keep moving upstage so that I would have to turn away from the camera, even at the expense of her getting out of the light. But nothing she could do could erase the fact that, for a change, I was the sympathetic character, and she was the bitch.

The Old Maid (1939)

Charlotte Lovell (Bette Davis) falls in love with dashing Clem Spender (George Brent), the rejected suitor of her cousin Delia (Miriam Hopkins). When Clem is killed at Vicksburg, Charlotte leaves Philadelphia to have his child secretly.

Several years later, Charlotte starts a school for war orphans. Delia learns that one of the children, Tina, is her cousin's daughter, and becomes jealous of Charlotte for having been loved by Clem. Spitefully, she ruins Charlotte's chances of marrying her brother-in-law, Joe Ralston (Jerome Cowan).

When Delia's husband, Jim Ralston (James Stephenson), is killed in an accident, little Tina and 'Aunt' Charlotte come to live with Delia. As Tina grows up (depicted in a memorable transition montage of changing shoes), she comes to hate her strict, puritanical, 'sour old maid' Aunt Charlotte, and love her unofficial foster mother, Delia. To help the adult Tina (Jane Bryan) marry well, Delia adopts her.

On the eve of Tina's wedding to wealthy Lanning Halsey (William Lundigan), Charlotte intends telling her daughter the truth, but cannot bring herself to do it. Tina leaves on her honeymoon after making her 'old maid aunt' happy by kissing her good-bye.

Bette remembered women in the audience crying when the lights went up after *The Old Maid*. 'That was thrilling for me. When I was acting in the theater, and I got my first laugh, I thought that was wonderful. But when I first saw people crying at one of my films, those tears were even more special. They had been drawn into the world of our film and shared my experience so fully, but without having to pay the price.

'Why is everybody so afraid of sentiment nowadays? Sentiment is going. I think it's a terrible thing that's happening to people that they're so afraid to be sentimental. Any

199

sentiment at all is called being 'overly sentimental.' This worries me. If this trend continues, it will be a cold and unfeeling future, or if one does have those feelings, one will have to pretend not to.'

★ ★ ★

'I really had my crust to attempt *Elizabeth and Essex*, I must say,' Bette told me. 'But I was so tempted to play this woman who is the woman in history I adore the most and have read the most about. I have very mixed emotions when I see it. The court scene, the Queen part of it, that is magnificently written. But I don't believe Elizabeth was quite like this on the human side, and that made it very difficult to play. I suppose I was too young, because I hadn't experienced enough in my own life, so I didn't have *that* to draw on. A lovely thing happened, though, something which meant a lot to me at the time and which I have remembered ever since.

'Charles Laughton came on the set one day when I was doing Elizabeth, and I said, 'Hi, Daddy!' because he'd done that wonderful Henry the Eighth.

'It was the first time I'd ever met him. He was an actor I absolutely worshipped, and one of my great regrets is he and I together couldn't have played two of the meanest people that ever lived, Henry the Eighth and Elizabeth the First.

'So, I went over and chatted with him. I said, 'Mr. Laughton, I really have my nerve at this age to be playing Elizabeth at sixty or so.' And he said a marvelous thing to me which I never forgot.

'He said, 'Never not dare to hang yourself. That's the only way you grow in your profession. You must continually attempt things that you think are beyond you, or you get into a complete rut.' He was right, and this is true, I think, for all actors' careers.'

The Private Lives of
Elizabeth and Essex (1939)

Queen Elizabeth (Bette Davis) is angry at her beloved Earl of Essex (Errol Flynn) because in a great victory over the Spanish, she believes he has placed personal glory above serving his Queen. She appoints his rival, Sir Walter Raleigh (Vincent Price), to a higher post, and Essex leaves London angrily, returning only when she apologizes.

Though concerned for his safety, she is forced to send him to Ireland to put down a rebellion. While he is away, his enemies conspire to alienate the Queen's affection for Essex by having a lady-in-waiting (Olivia de Havilland) withhold his correspondence to her.

Essex is defeated in Ireland, but returns as a popular hero, and some expect him to take over the throne from Elizabeth. She appears to capitulate, but after he is disarmed, she has him imprisoned. She offers to spare his life if he will give up his ambition to be King, but he refuses. Heartbroken, she has him sent to the Tower and beheaded.

'I acted with Errol Flynn as Essex, and he could be a *perfectly* delightful person, and he himself said he really was not an actor. I would be the first to agree with him. He really wasn't. And if he was sitting here with us, he'd die laughing, on the spot. But you know, those long approaches of Essex toward the throne, I used to just sit there as he came toward me, and daydream, and say, 'Oh, Sir Larry, why isn't it you?'

'I only met Olivier once, but that was enough. Stunning. He was an Adonis. I was so attracted to him, I never got over it. I imagined working with him — and more. I dreamed about him for years, not only when I was asleep, but in my waking dreams, as well. I used to close my eyes and pretend he was there in bed with me. The ecstasy of having sex with him was utterly unimaginable.

'Men think women aren't the same as *they* are, wanting a gorgeous man in the way they want a gorgeous woman. Ha! I saw in Laurence Olivier exactly what men saw in Marilyn Monroe. Men thought about her when they were making love to their wives. Maybe in real life if they'd had the chance, they wouldn't have *really* wanted to go to bed with her. Too threatening. But if Laurence Olivier had asked *me*, I would have said *yes!* As it was, I had sex with him dozens and dozens of times — in my head, alone in bed or sometimes when another man was making love to me.

'If I'd been able to do the casting for my pictures, I would have enjoyed the kissing scenes more. A beautiful leading man made all the difference. When I did *Elizabeth and Essex*, I wanted Olivier to be Essex.

'Errol Flynn liked to put his tongue in your mouth after he'd been drinking all night. Ugh! I always kept my lips tightly closed. He must have been a terrible lover. I wouldn't know firsthand. He invited me to find out, but I didn't think I'd like being compared to all those cute little contestants in the private beauty contest he was holding.

'How could any woman in her right mind be attracted to a man who was such an egomaniac, who could only make love to himself, a heartless womanizer? Well, *I'll* tell you how. Easily! Because a woman doesn't choose with her mind. I wouldn't admit it at the time — I wouldn't have given Flynn that satisfaction — but, yes, I suppose I *was* attracted to him, in spite of his faults. No, probably *because* of them. But, of course, nothing happened. I had my pride, and it was greater than my passion, with Flynn anyway. Why are we women attracted to the wrong man? We know we're supposed to look for security, and instead we're fascinated by *in*security. But no question about it — Flynn was a beautiful thing.

'In a very difficult performance, like Queen Elizabeth, Mr. Warner often let me do the first two days over at the end. It's pretty hard to walk on a set and just be Queen Elizabeth the first morning, *especially* in the morning. But at the end of the film, you've played her so many times, you're used to playing her.'

This was her first color film. It was to have been *The Miracle*, a Max Reinhardt project that was never realized.

★ ★ ★

After *The Private Lives of Elizabeth and Essex*, Bette went to New England for a holiday. 'Four major movies in one year was an exhausting schedule,' she said. 'No question about it.' Ruthie recommended Peckett's Inn in Franconia, New Hampshire, for her overworked and lonely daughter.

There, Bette met Arthur Austin Farnsworth, the desk clerk and assistant manager of Peckett's Inn. Bette told me that she was 'in a searching mood.'

Farnsworth was a few years older than she, and she found him most attractive. He came from an old Vermont family, which meant, as Bette said, 'He was geographically correct.'

'I called my second husband 'Farney.' Everyone did. We were married for only a couple of years. He was my husband between Ham and Sherry.

'I was working a lot in those days. I hardly ever saw Farney. I married him knowing little about him. Farney never talked much, but in my simpler days, I took this as a manly trait, and that way I could imagine him the way I wanted.

'He traveled sometimes, but after he died, I felt guilty because it seemed I should have known him better. He was a pilot, and he told me he'd survived a bad crash. *That* I knew, but not much else.

'When we were together, we weren't genuinely compatible, and quarreled. He drank more than I knew. Maybe if he'd lived longer, we would have worked things out and settled into a comfortable marriage, and I would have missed two divorces. Maybe not.'

★　★　★

All This, and Heaven Too started out expensively, even before a single scene was shot. The Rachel Field novel was bought by Warners for $100,000 in 1938 before publication. Then, the studio had to invest in an uncommon number of period costumes and sets, as well as a large cast. The result was a very long film, 140-plus minutes, directed at a leisurely pace by Anatole Litvak. 'Rachel Field told me she liked Casey Robinson's screenplay, with all its flashbacks and whatnots,' Bette told me. 'She was a lovely lady, who often visited the set. I got to know her very well. She died a few years later, very young. Sad!'

All This, and Heaven Too (1940)
Mlle. Henriette Deluzy-Desportes (Bette Davis) accepts a job as governess to the children of the Duc and Duchesse de Praslin. The Duchesse (Barbara O'Neil) becomes jealous of her children's affection for Henriette and suspects that her husband (Charles Boyer) is having an affair with her.

Henriette is discharged by the Duchesse with the promise of a letter of recommendation that never arrives. When the Duc hears of this, he argues violently with his wife, and the next morning she is found murdered. The Duc is arrested, but he takes poison and dies. Henriette, suspected of being an accomplice, is tried and found innocent.

The French public, however, continues to believe her guilty. She is forced to flee to New York, where, with the help of a mysterious benefactor, she finds a teaching position in an exclusive girls school.

When her pupils learn of the scandal, they taunt her until she tells them the true story. They believe her and are totally sympathetic. Her benefactor turns out to be an American minister (Jeffrey Lynn) whom she met on her way to the de Praslin home. It is implied that there may be a happy future for them together.

'Anatole Litvak was a marvelous director,' Bette said, 'but I think he made one serious, *serious* mistake in *All This, and Heaven Too*. Barbara O'Neil had wanted to play the Duchesse as insanely jealous and unattractive, which would have given Charles Boyer some reason for acting the way he did toward her. But that, Mr. Litvak said, was not the proper way to portray a French aristocratic lady from Corsica. It's a weakness of the film, because the Duc doesn't have sufficient motivation for murdering his wife, I do believe. I respect Tola [Anatole Litvak] *deeply*, but he was a very, *very* stubborn man.'

The Letter reunited Bette with two of the people she respected most, author Somerset Maugham and director William Wyler. Bette's future friend Gladys Cooper had created the part of Leslie Crosbie in London's West End in 1927, and Jeanne Eagels had played Leslie on the screen shortly before her death. In the 1929 Paramount film, Herbert Marshall played the role of Hammond. Bette had seen Katharine Cornell as Leslie on Broadway in 1927.

The Letter (1940)

Leslie Crosbie (Bette Davis), wife of Malayan rubber plantation manager Robert Crosbie (Herbert Marshall), is accused of murdering Geoffrey Hammond (David Newell). Robert believes she was defending herself from an attempted rape, but after a letter written by her to Hammond is offered to Robert for $10,000, Leslie admits to her sympathetic defense attorney, Howard Joyce (James Stephenson), that she was having an affair with Hammond and that she killed him, carried away by her passion. The incriminating letter, sent by her to Hammond, invited him to visit her on the night of the murder.

Through Joyce, Robert gives his life savings to Hammond's Eurasian widow (Gale Sondergaard), to buy the letter, not knowing its contents, only that it will save his wife. After Leslie is acquitted, she reveals to him what the letter says. Then, she tells him that she still loves Hammond. Despite all of these admissions, Robert is able to forgive her.

Later that evening in the garden, Leslie is stabbed to death by Hammond's widow.

The ending of the film differs from the stage play, in which the woman's punishment is not death, but life with the husband she has betrayed. The studio was forced to bow to Production Code demands for 'justice.'

'The only satisfaction I got out of *The Great Lie*,' Bette told me of her next film, 'was seeing Mary Astor get an Oscar. How she deserved it! Do you know she actually *played* those concertos? Absolutely.'

Bette was only partly correct. Astor, who was a trained classical pianist, could provide the correct fingering for the virtuosic concerti by Anton Rubinstein and Tchaikovsky played in this film, and thus be filmed with her hands on the keyboard while another pianist provided the actual music on a playback recording. For this 'finger-syncing' and a fine performance as the beautiful, spoiled, selfish Sandra, Astor won the best supporting actress Oscar for 1941.

The Great Lie (1941)

After the elopement of concert pianist Sandra Kovack (Mary Astor) and wealthy aviator Pete Van Allen (George Brent) turns out not to be a valid marriage, Pete marries Maggie Patterson (Bette Davis), his former fiancée; but Pete is called away on government business, and Maggie learns that Sandra is going to have his baby.

Pete is reported killed in a plane crash. Maggie, heartbroken, offers to adopt Sandra's baby. Pete survives and assumes the child is his and Maggie's. Sandra returns from a foreign concert tour and insists Maggie tell Pete the truth, thus hoping to win back her former husband. Pete really loves Maggie, so Sandra lets them keep the child, and she returns to *her* real love, her career.

Bette married Farney on the last day of 1940 at Jane Bryan Dart's Arizona ranch. Bryan, Bette's actress friend, had given up a promising Hollywood career to devote herself to marriage, which Bette found perplexing. Bette believed a woman could 'have it all' long before that concept became popular. Farney had been married once before, to a Boston socialite who was a pilot, as was he.

He had been in a serious accident, presumably while flying, in which he suffered head injuries that had led to recurring headaches. Bette described Farney as 'muscular and well built.' 'His mother was from an old, respected New England family,' and he told Bette that one day he would come into a substantial inheritance, though he didn't elaborate, and she didn't care.

Bette bought an old house in New Hampshire, which worried Jack Warner. He was uneasy about his star spending too much time away from the studio. Farney later found a position with Minneapolis-Honeywell.

* * *

'I think the main attraction for the press who came to Death Valley to cover me and Jimmy

Cagney shooting *The Bride Came C.O.D.* was Farney,' Bette told me. 'He was a total surprise to everyone, and they wanted to know about him. They should have called it 'The Bridegroom Came C.O.D.''

Bette came to do *The Bride Came C.O.D.* quite by accident. Director Vincent Sherman was partly responsible.

'Hal Wallis sent me a script he wanted Bette Davis to do,' he told me. 'It was called 'Caesar's Wife,' something like that. I thought it was a very bad script, and I didn't want to do it, and I didn't know what to say. I didn't want to say to Bette Davis, 'I don't like this, and I don't want to do it with you.'

'So, I got a call from Wallis, and I went up to his office. He was the top man there, and here I was, just having made one or two pictures as a B director. He said, 'You mean to tell me you're turning down a Bette Davis picture?'

'I said, 'I'm turning it down because I don't want to be the one who causes her to make a bad picture.' So he said, 'What I want you to do is write her a letter and tell her that you're tickled to death to have a chance to direct her, but that you don't think that you have enough experience to do this picture.'

'I wrote a letter trying to make it not sound stupid, but I don't know whether Bette Davis ever got that letter or not. She never mentioned it to me, and I didn't go over it with her later.

'But what happened was that I knew the Epsteins [brothers Julius and Philip], and I told them about it, and they laughed. They thought it was funny as hell. They were doing a script for Jim Cagney, called *The Bride Came C.O.D.* So when they heard I didn't want to do the picture that Wallis had for Bette, they called and asked if they could have Bette for the Cagney picture. Well, Bette was glad to play in *that.* And I was relieved, too.'

The Bride Came C.O.D. (1941)

On a dare, heiress Joan Winfield (Bette Davis) agrees to elope with bandleader Allen Brice (Jack Carson). They charter a plane from Steve Collins (James Cagney), whose company is near bankruptcy.

Joan's father, Lucius K. Winfield (Eugene Pallette), hires Steve to deliver her unmarried to his Texas ranch instead. Joan assumes she is being kidnapped and offers to pay Steve to take her back to Los Angeles, but he refuses because she can't match her father's offer.

Steve makes a forced landing in the desert near a ghost town inhabited only by Pop Tolliver (Harry Davenport). Believing Joan, Pop jails Steve and provides her with a room in an abandoned hotel.

Allen arrives with a Nevada justice of the peace, and he and Joan are married. Her father arrives, and they discover that the marriage is not valid because they are still in California. Hardboiled Steve proposes to Joan, but not wanting to appear sentimental, he tells her that even though he loves her, he is really marrying her for her father's money.

If *The Bride Came C.O.D.* ranks as one of Bette's most forgettable films, her next picture, *The Little Foxes*, is one of her more memorable.

When William Wyler first saw Tallulah Bankhead playing Regina on Broadway in 1939, he thought immediately of Bette, and approached playwright Lillian Hellman with this in mind for a screenplay. The resulting script was shown to Bette, who was less impressed by it than she was by the prospect of making another film with Wyler, whom she regarded as the best director in Hollywood. Wyler intended to make the film for Samuel Goldwyn.

Warners, however, was not enthusiastic about lending out their top female star to another studio. Finally, a deal was struck allowing Bette to make *The Little Foxes* for Goldwyn in return for Goldwyn lending Gary Cooper to Warners to make *Sergeant York*. The real reason, it was rumored, was that Samuel Goldwyn cancelled a huge gambling debt Jack Warner owed him in return for the actress.

The look of *The Little Foxes* is brilliantly enhanced by the deep-focus photography of Gregg Toland. Toland is best remembered for having photographed Orson Welles's *Citizen Kane*.

The Little Foxes (1941)

Regina Giddens (Bette Davis) needs $75,000 to invest in a business venture being started by her brothers, Ben (Charles Dingle) and Oscar (Carl Benton Reid), but her sickly husband, Horace (Herbert Marshall), refuses to give her the money. Meanwhile, Leo (Dan Duryea), a nephew who is a bank employee, steals enough negotiable bonds from Horace's safe deposit box to finance their business without Regina's participation. She finds out, and threatens to blackmail her brothers into giving her a full share. When they ignore her threat, she tells Horace, but he refuses to expose Leo.

Horace suffers a heart attack, and Regina withholds his medication. On his deathbed, Horace implores his daughter, Alexandra (Teresa Wright), to marry her young suitor, David Hewitt (Richard Carlson), with whom she is in love and whom Regina has deemed unsuitable, and to leave with him.

After her father dies, Alexandra overhears her mother and uncles arguing over their business interests. From what they say, she understands that her mother, in effect, has murdered her father.

As Alexandra leaves the house, her mother is seen watching from an upstairs window, alone.

A line in the film, said by Regina to her grown young daughter, her only child, 'I don't want us to be bad friends,' predicted something of Bette's future relationship with her own child, B.D.

One of Bette's misgivings about Lillian Hellman's screenplay for *The Little Foxes* was that she was too often offscreen. In her next picture, *The Man Who Came to Dinner*, she is offscreen a great deal of the time, yet she *requested* the part, and was even responsible for the Broadway play by George S. Kaufman and

Moss Hart coming to Hollywood.

She saw it on Broadway and envisioned playing in the film version opposite John Barrymore. When the ill Barrymore was unable to accept the role, Bette agreed to play Maggie Cutler to Monty Woolley's Sheridan Whiteside. Even though Woolley had created the part on the stage, Bette remained convinced that Barrymore would have been better. Barrymore died the next year, 1942, while Woolley, who had gone unnoticed in films since 1931, became an overnight star whose screen and television career would last until his death in 1963.

Edited out of the final version of the film was Laura Hope Crews, who had given Bette one of her first acting opportunities when Bette was an usher at the Cape Playhouse.

The Man Who Came to Dinner (1941)

While on a lecture tour, author-raconteur Sheridan Whiteside (Monty Woolley), world-famous for his sardonic wit, grudgingly accepts a dinner invitation from the matriarch (Billie Burke) of a prominent Ohio family. Entering their home, he injures himself when he slips on the icy steps and becomes an unwanted house-guest. Certainly, he doesn't wish to stay, and very soon, the family is even less happy about his extended visit.

While his leg is healing, he cunningly interferes in the lives of his hosts and even of his secretary, Maggie Cutler (Bette Davis), until she realizes what he is doing and threatens to resign. Nonetheless, he continues, even bribing the local doctor (George Barbier) with the promise of having his memoirs published if he does not reveal that Whiteside is really not so critically injured.

Whiteside's ruse is discovered, and he is ordered out of the house by the long-suffering husband (Grant Mitchell). As he is about to leave, Whiteside recognizes an aunt (Ruth Vivian) as an accused, but acquitted, ax murderer, and he blackmails his way into an extended stay. Triumphantly, as he finally leaves the house, he slips on the icy steps, this time *really* breaking his leg.

As they were about to begin filming *The Man Who Came to Dinner*, Bette, seeing an adorable dog, a Scottie, bent down to pet him. She liked all dogs, but she found the Scottie 'an adorable breed.'

To her shock, the Scottie bit her on the nose. Bette said she was especially disappointed that this would happen to the president of the Tailwaggers Association, raising money 'to aid dogs in need.' It was 'most unfair.'

'This particular dog wasn't particular when he singled me out. I had always loved dogs, my own, and *all* dogs.

'Well, after this experience, I still loved dogs, except the one who bit me. I'm not really a turn-the-other-cheek person, and besides, I didn't have another nose to turn.'

Bette had to leave to recover. The studio would have preferred that she stay in Hollywood, but Bette preferred to be in New England. Bette left. Finally, her nose healed.

'I loved it best in New England during the late fall, the winter, and the early spring when the 'fudgies' weren't there. You know who the 'fudgies' are? Those tourists who come to New England from all over the country, only in season. Then, the local people make fudge in their kitchens to sell.'

She didn't look for her friends in the world of show business. She felt that it was full of false values and she fervently believed people with her New England roots were different and would be 'real' friends.

'Actors as a group are not my passion. Socially, that is. No, socially, I always love writers and directors. They're much more interesting. A group of actors together can be rather tiresome. Whose rushes were what, and all this, you know? I never sort of lived my profession when I wasn't actually working in it. You know, I just always went off to New England whenever I could.

'There is a very old French saying: 'An actor is always less than a man, an actress more than a woman.' I have to be very honest. I don't think you can make generalizations, and I think there are very, very many exceptions to the rule. Certainly that beautiful man, Claude Rains. Mr. Spencer Tracy, Mr. Gary Cooper, and Mr. Clark Gable were certainly not less than men. But, it's a strange profession for a man, truthfully.

'Steve McQueen, for instance, always did motorcycling to keep sure he's a man. Steve McQueen told me that one night. I said, 'Why do you take a chance? You're one of the few

216

smashing young men that have come along, and we *need* you *desperately*.' He said, 'Because it's a strange profession for a man, and I just want to stay in something else to keep being a man.' Interesting.'

★ ★ ★

Just as Bette was about to start *In This Our Life*, she learned that Farney had been hospitalized in Minneapolis with pneumonia. She wanted to fly to his bedside right away, but the bad October weather of 1941 had grounded what few scheduled flights were operating at that time. Above the vehement protests of Warners, who didn't want the picture postponed or their leading actress injured, she chartered a plane to Kansas City and then Minneapolis with the help of Howard Hughes. As soon as she determined Farney was going to be all right, she returned to Los Angeles by train, where a Warner Brothers car was waiting to take her straight to Burbank and *In This Our Life*.

The film's director, John Huston, had recently done *The Maltese Falcon*, and as a joke, he assembled most of that picture's cast as background in his current picture. The scene is a tavern where Walter Huston is the bartender and the patrons are Humphrey Bogart, Mary Astor, Peter Lorre, Sidney Greenstreet, Elisha Cook, Jr., Ward Bond, and Barton MacLane, all uncredited.

217

In This Our Life (1942)

Terribly spoiled, self-centered Stanley Timberlake (Bette Davis) kills a child while driving at high speed, but places the blame on a family servant's son (Ernest Anderson). One of Stanley's jilted suitors, attorney Craig Fleming (George Brent), believes the story of the mother (Hattie McDaniel), who swears her son was at home when the accident took place. Agreeing to defend her son, Craig finds evidence of Stanley's guilt, and demands that she confess.

Stanley turns to her wealthy uncle (Charles Coburn) for help. He has always adored her, but now, even though she begs, she cannot reach him. He has learned that he has a few weeks to live and can only think of his niece coming to care for him. She drives off at high speed, and is killed when her car crashes during a police chase.

The scene most often excerpted, that of Charles Coburn telling an unfeeling Bette that he only has a short time to live, was not directed by John Huston. He had been called to Washington for war duty after Pearl Harbor, and Raoul Walsh had taken over for him near the end of the film.

Bette prepared to take a twelve-week vacation, for which she would receive no salary. Before leaving the lot, she visited the publicity department to pose for promotional photographs. She was made up for the pictures, but someone arrived who told her she couldn't work since she was technically off the payroll. This made Bette so angry, she rushed into Jack

218

Warner's office, where she demanded more money for fewer pictures, and then left for Mexico, threatening never to return. 'I always wore my dark glasses when I spoke with Mr. Warner,' Bette told me. 'He never said anything about it, but I think it bothered him not to see my eyes. This time, I wasn't wearing them. I was wearing my makeup for the photos, and I think it scared him. When I got back from Mexico, he raised my salary to twenty-five hundred a week and limited the number of pictures I made a year to two.'

* * *

'The more successful an actor, the less he or she gets to act,' Bette told me. 'People come to expect a personality, and that's the kind of parts you get offered, ones to suit audience expectations of your star's persona. That's why I'm so proud of my Charlotte Vale in *Now, Voyager*. With her, I get to act and be Bette Davis at the same time.'

Now, Voyager was directed by Irving Rapper, who had previously worked as an assistant director on *Kid Galahad*, *All This, and Heaven Too*, and *The Sisters*. He also had been a stage director in England before coming to Warner Brothers. I talked with him in New York City near the end of his life.

'I went to work at Warner Brothers in the mid-1930s as an assistant director to the great Michael Curtiz. He did films like *Casablanca* and *Yankee Doodle Dandy*. He should be much more famous. I owe most of my knowledge of the cinema to him.

'*Kid Galahad* was my first Bette Davis picture. She had just come back from England where she had lost a lawsuit against Warner Brothers. We became great friends and remained so. I worked on *All This, and Heaven Too* and *The Sisters* with her, too.

'Her pictures were made for Hal Wallis and Henry Blanke. Blanke was one of the most sympathetic and intelligent producers in Hollywood. These people encouraged us to make our films slowly and with care, giving special attention to the photographing of the great stars. It would take hours to set up the shots. And the stars would often take an interest in the direction and technical details in a creative sense.

'I remember in particular that Bette Davis had a marvelously probing intelligence in this respect, which some directors didn't like, but I did. She wanted to know and understand. It gave me a great strength to work with her.

'As a joke, she once did a bit part, walking on as a nurse in a small Geraldine Fitzgerald film I directed called *Shining Victory*. She would do that kind of thing.

'I used to preplan my pictures very carefully, though not quite in the sense that Hitchcock did. He did it with drawings, every shot. I wanted to leave a little room for flexibility, but I knew I could act best spontaneously if I was very well prepared. I'd plot out the opening and closing of a scene, with its highest dramatic point. Then, I'd come on the set with fully detailed plans, and

Bette or someone would yell, 'What the hell is all that?' And I'd forget them.

'I improvised a good deal, but I always tried to follow the scripts I was given as much to the letter as I could. At Warners you got a finished script, and if you refused to do it, you were suspended. I had ten suspensions in seven years, but I was lucky. Influential people like Henry Blanke and Bette were in my corner.

'Just before *Voyager*, I faced suspension if I didn't do *The Gay Sisters*, with Barbara Stanwyck. So, I came into *Voyager* with less than two weeks of preparation. One week of that was taken up with test scenes of Paul Henreid, a refugee who had just come over from Europe. You could hardly understand him, so I figured audiences were going to be lost and not like the film. I wondered how Bette would react to his heavy accent.

'She reacted very well because she immediately liked him. They got along famously, and he was a good actor. He was a quick study and got his lines right so everyone could understand them, though off the set, he sounded sometimes like he was speaking German when he was speaking English.

'Michael Curtiz was supposed to have directed this film, but he didn't like the subject or Bette, so it went to me. I insisted on casting *Voyager* myself because I had some unconventional ideas, and I felt casting was the key. I think I was right, too, because what made the picture great was the brilliant acting.

'Hal Wallis asked me why I cast Ilka Chase

and Bonita Granville, and I told him, 'Because they will needle Bette Davis.' I couldn't have people who were in awe of her. When Bette heard about this, she said, 'Irving, you son of a bitch!' That was Bette.

'With *Now, Voyager* I began my rain trademark, which is at the beginning. I've had an important rain scene in every film I've made since then, sort of like Hitchcock's cameo appearances. Rain creates such a mood of tension. When I was a kid, it always seemed to be raining at important moments. Bette told me that rain was lucky for her and that when she was born, it was raining.

'There is a scene that was cut from *Voyager*. The girl, played by Davis, is on a cruise with her mother when she's young, and she imagines herself dressed like a princess. A handsome young ship's officer invites her to a dance, and she becomes aware for the first time that she's desirable. It was shot silent and was probably too long, so it was cut, which was too bad because I thought it was a nice scene.

'Bette was a big, big star, so she had a lot of power. My getting to work with her again meant she liked me and what I did. That meant a lot to me, personally and professionally. She was very serious about her work, and if she had only liked me, but not respected my work, she would have asked for another director.

'As a person, she had a good sense of humor, but where her work was concerned, she didn't fool around. We had such good rapport because we both cared so much about what we were doing and always wanted to do our best. She made a great difference in my career, and I like to think I was good for her, too, on the films we did together.'

The producer, Hal Wallis, who had produced seventeen of Bette's films for Warner Brothers before *Now, Voyager*, had greater independence under a new agreement with Warner Brothers. Bette believed he had bought *Now, Voyager* with her in mind as Charlotte Vale, the ugly duckling heroine. Ginger Rogers told me that she was Wallis's first choice.

The image most people recall from *Now, Voyager* is the lighting of the cigarettes. 'It was Paul's idea, you know, to light the cigarettes from one match,' Bette told me. 'Paul Henreid's. The script for *Now, Voyager* had it another way. I think they should have given our cigarettes an award!

'Recently, somebody told me George Brent had already lit two cigarettes that way in an earlier Warner Brothers epic. I'll still maintain till my dying day that we did it first. Absolutely.' The film was *The Rich Are Always With Us*, and Bette, who had only a supporting role, didn't remember much about her ninth film when I spoke with her, half a century later.

'Cigarettes were so important to my characters, and to me, too. People are always asking me why I don't give up smoking. I have. Many times. But my friends wouldn't let me stay with it. They couldn't stand me. I actually overheard someone say, 'She's a monster when she doesn't smoke.' And the other person responded, 'How can you tell the difference?' Well, if I hadn't had the cigarettes, I'd've eaten a package of Oreo sandwich cookies instead.

'The cigarette was my character prop. Miss Crawford might have said it *was* my character. I used it for showing anger, to make a point or to emphasize a reaction, to show nervousness. There was *no one* who could put out a cigarette like I could. One thing I understood. If I played a character who smoked, she wasn't going to be a namby-pamby smoker and take a puff or two. She was going to chain-smoke her way through the film as any serious smoker worth her tobacco would. Once Dean Martin said, 'Nobody swings her butt the way Bette Davis does.' I *think* he was talking about my cigarette . . .

' ''Oh, Jerry — we have the stars, let's not ask for the moon.' Dear Charlotte! That was her great line. A great line. It was the way she felt, but not the way I feel. She was always willing to compromise. But I wasn't willing to enjoy just the stars. I had to have the moon, too. Then, I wouldn't settle unless I also had the sun.'

I asked Bette to speculate on what she thought happened to Charlotte afterward. As it turned out, she had given some thought to Charlotte's future.

'It seemed to me Charlotte's romantic dreams with Jerry were fine — for a while. After all, she *had* been a bit retarded in *that* side of her life, and everyone should have the experience of romance. Whatever the price — and love does exact a price — it's worth it. The price is losing it.

224

'My theory is that the thing with Jerry wore off, the way *that* does, and she went on to find lasting happiness with Dr. Jaquith. She helped him with his work, making her life *really* count. Charlotte doesn't go on waiting around for Jerry, who just uses her when he likes. She takes courses in psychology, and when Dr. Jaquith asks her to marry him, she does, and she has a brilliant career, too. Do you like that?

'I *did* love the character, but Charlotte was more noble in her love for Jerry than *I* could ever have been. I think if the truth were known, she was undersexed. Otherwise, *honestly* — the whole thing just couldn't have worked out.

'The director, Irving Rapper, and Paul Henreid didn't get along. As Paul began feeling his oats and taking over his character, the actor-director relationship deteriorated terribly, but Irving tried to contain himself. He really tried. Then, when he absolutely felt he couldn't stand it any longer, he'd shout 'Lunch' and we'd take a break even if it was ten in the morning or four in the afternoon. These days, no one could get away with that. Today, there isn't any room for eccentricity. Eccentricity isn't cost-efficient. The accountants will get you.

'I received more fan mail for *Now, Voyager* than for any other film. The mail was really for Charlotte, from women who were plain, or fat, or just unhappy — unable to find fulfillment, unable to find the man they dreamed of.'

Now, Voyager (1942)
Repressed spinster Charlotte Vale (Bette Davis)

escapes the tyranny of her domineering mother (Gladys Cooper) after being treated for a nervous breakdown at a sanatorium by Dr. Jaquith (Claude Rains), a psychiatrist. On a cruise, the new Charlotte falls in love with Jerry Durrance (Paul Henreid), a man who is dutifully committed to an unhappy relationship with his invalid wife.

Charlotte returns to Boston, heartbroken, but meeting Jerry again, she realizes she still loves him. She breaks an engagement to a man (John Loder) approved by her mother. During an argument with Charlotte, the mother dies. Feeling responsible, Charlotte returns to Dr. Jaquith's sanatorium, where she encounters Jerry's troubled twelve-year-old daughter, Tina (Janis Wilson). Helping Tina with her emotional problems reunites Charlotte and Jerry. He feels guilty about always accepting from her without giving anything, but Charlotte is satisfied with their relationship as it is.

The critical reception for Now, Voyager was positive, but not enthusiastic. Though Bette's performance was praised, the film itself was perceived as just another Bette Davis woman's picture. It did a fair business at the box office but was a disappointment to the studio and Warners' owned-and-operated distributor-exhibitor, the Stanley Corporation. More was expected of a Bette Davis film, especially during the wartime boom in movie attendance. No one predicted that Now, Voyager would become one of Bette's best known and most beloved films.

During the shooting of Now, Voyager, Bette had been approached by John Garfield, who had been rejected for military service and wanted to do something for the war effort. He wanted Bette to help him set up a Hollywood Canteen for servicemen like the Stage Door Canteen that actress Jane Cowl had set up in New York. Bette became the prime mover in the creation and operation of the Hollywood Canteen.

She embraced the project enthusiastically, enlisting the aid of Music Corporation of America head Jules Stein to manage the financing. As chairwoman, Bette persuaded studio craftsmen to donate their labor to renovate an old stable, while familiar Hollywood actors were invited to do all the work needed to operate the canteen. Bette remembered Marlene Dietrich in particular.

'I met Dietrich at the Canteen. When she came out on the dance floor, there was never anyone so glamorous. Then, the next night, she'd be working in the kitchen without her eyelashes and wearing a hairnet, peeling vegetables, even scrubbing the floor.'

After Now, Voyager, Bette went on a government-sponsored tour through Missouri and Oklahoma, where she sold $2 million worth of War Bonds in two days.

★ ★ ★

For *Watch on the Rhine*, Bette accepted a secondary role, although she got top billing. 'I complained wildly about this to the studio, but they wouldn't budge. Paul Lukas, they argued, 'wouldn't put the asses in the seats.' Well, Mr. Lukas proved them wrong and me right by winning an Oscar.'

Most of the Broadway cast was brought west to make the film, as was the play's director, Herman Shumlin. The screenplay was written by Dashiell Hammett and Lillian Hellman, who wrote the original play.

Watch on the Rhine (1943)

Ailing ex-architect Kurt Muller (Paul Lukas), leader of an anti-Nazi underground movement, leaves Germany with his family to recuperate with his American wife's mother (Lucile Watson) in Washington, D.C. A fellow émigré, Count de Brancovis (George Coulouris), suspecting Muller's true identity, threatens to expose him to a German intelligence agent (Kurt Katch) unless he pays blackmail. Enraged, Muller kills Brancovis, and then leaving his family, he returns to wartime Germany. Tearfully, his wife, Sara (Bette Davis), must accept that their eldest son, Joshua (Donald Buka), will soon follow him.

Bette's appearance in the wartime revue *Thank Your Lucky Stars* has become a classic, while the film itself is barely remembered. She sings the song 'They're Either Too Young or Too Old,' and does a jitterbug dance with Conrad Weidel, a champion jitterbugger. For this, she was paid $50,000, which she gave to the Hollywood Canteen.

Thank Your Lucky Stars (1943)

Two unknown performing songwriters (Joan Leslie and Dennis Morgan) display their talents in a World War II charity show, which includes many famous Hollywood stars. Bette Davis sings and dances.

Bette told Weidel that she didn't want to rehearse because she was afraid she would only be able to get through the dance once. 'I'd never jitterbugged, so I said to the young man, 'Look, I'm not a movie star. I'm just some dame you picked up in a dance hall.'' Though slightly injured during the dance, Bette went on until her performance was completed. 'I hurt my leg, but I wasn't going to spoil that take and have to do it again. I *couldn't* have! I just limped my way to the porch and finished the song.'

★ ★ ★

Although *Old Acquaintance* was released a month after *Thank Your Lucky Stars* in November 1943, it was actually made first. Edmund Goulding was scheduled to direct *Old Acquaintance*, but he suffered a heart attack and was replaced by thirty-six-year-old Vincent Sherman after Julien Duvivier turned down the job

Sherman had come to Hollywood as an actor in 1933 to play one scene opposite John

229

Barrymore in Elmer Rice's *Counsellor at Law*. He had been chosen by Rice himself from the Chicago company of the stage play. William Wyler was the director of the film and had selected Sherman over the New York company actor playing the part.

Old Acquaintance (1943)

The critical success of Author Katherine 'Kit' Marlowe (Bette Davis) inspires her best friend since childhood, Mildred 'Millie' Drake (Miriam Hopkins), to write a novel aimed at popular tastes. When it becomes a best-seller, Millie follows it up with a series of similar novels while Kit continues to write a few critically-acclaimed, but less successful, books and plays.

Success alienates Millie from her dependent husband, Preston 'Pres' Drake (John Loder), who falls in love with Kit. Unable to tolerate Millie anymore, he leaves her and their small daughter, Deirdre (Francine Rufo). Kit rejects his proposal of marriage.

Kit meets Pres again, during World War II in New York. He is now a major in the army, and she is involved with a younger man, Rudd Kendall (Gig Young), a naval officer. Learning that Pres is in New York, Millie tries to win him back. When Pres admits that he once loved Kit, Millie accuses her best friend of breaking up her marriage. They have a heated argument which ends with Kit violently shaking Millie.

Meanwhile, Rudd and Millie's daughter, Deirdre (Dolores Moran), have fallen in love. Kit sadly realizes she has lost him.

Kit and Millie reconcile, toasting their turbulent friendship over the years with flat champagne. Millie plans to write *Old Acquaintance*, a book about their long relationship, and Kit approves.

Director Vincent Sherman remembered his first meeting with Bette Davis several years after he had turned down Hal Wallis's offer to direct her. She approached him in the Warner commissary. 'She was very small, but she took long strides just like a long-legged model. She said, 'I'm Bette Davis.' As if anyone didn't know.

'She told me that George Brent had enjoyed working with me. I'd just directed him in a film neither one of us had really wanted to do, *The Man Who Talked Too Much*, but we got along fine.

'She asked me if I'd read a script, and if I liked it, perhaps I'd direct her in it. I was thrilled and I thanked George. I was only a B film director until that moment, and it wasn't likely that I would have been thought of for a Bette Davis picture.

'I received a script from Warners, but when I read it, I felt the script needed to be rewritten and said so. The picture did not get made. After that, whenever Bette passed me, she didn't say hello.

'Then, I received a script for *Old Acquaintance*. While it was not my cup of tea particularly, I thought it would make a nice picture.

'Two years had passed since I'd first met

Bette. In the time that had passed, she had made *Dark Victory*, *The Little Foxes*, and *Now, Voyager*.

'The *Old Acquaintance* director, Edmund Goulding, had a heart attack, and I was asked to do the film with Bette Davis and Miriam Hopkins. I wasn't certain how Bette was going to feel about my directing, but obviously she'd accepted me, or I wouldn't have the job. Bette was a big star, and if she had vetoed me, I wouldn't have been considered. I knew that until we got started and had a lot of film in the can, she could easily have me replaced even after that.

'While Bette finished resting in Palm Springs, I began filming with Miriam. Miriam was fun to work with, a very good actress, very talented, very *bitchy*, by the way. She and Bette despised each other. Miriam had the lead in *Jezebel* on Broadway, and it flopped. Bette did it on the screen and won an Academy Award.

'Bette finally arrived. She visited the set accompanied by her agent, Lew Wasserman. She was an awesome force.

'I walked over to greet them. Bette said to me, 'How is it going?'

'I asked her if she would like to see what we'd been shooting. If she didn't like what I'd shot, she had the power to get another director, and I'd be out. I said, 'Why don't you take a look at what we've shot so far? We've been shooting for about five or six days.' And she says, 'Oh, *may* I?' It was a gamble, I was well aware.

'Well, I knew damn good and well that's the reason she came to the set with her agent. She

232

was going to look at the rushes. If she liked what she saw, it was okay. If she didn't like it, she'd say to Warner, 'I don't want to make it with this director. I don't like what he's doing.' Well, that was all.

'Bette watched the rushes. Wasserman didn't stay. Bette had established her position and she knew what she was looking for. When she finished watching the rushes, she gave me a cool look. I couldn't read it.

'Then, she said, 'What time do you want me for work? It's just wonderful!'

'She asked me about her character. I told her that I felt that Miriam's character, Millie, was well intentioned and a friend, but jealous and not very easy to get along with. And I thought that Bette, as a writer, was a very mature, sophisticated, intelligent woman, who didn't have any of the female tactics that Millie had.

'I said, 'I think my feeling is that the character of Kit is very much like you are.' She looked at me as though to say, 'How the hell do you know what I'm like?' But she didn't say anything. She said, 'I see. Well, let's see,' and that's the way we started off.

'She suggested that her character might use a cigarette holder. Otherwise, she didn't have anything intrusive to suggest. Then, she warned me about Miriam's tricks. She said that she thought that the way I had filmed Miriam was fine, but as we got more into the film, Miriam would be using her feminine wiles on me to get me to favor her in close-ups, that she would use every scene-stealing device, that in general, she would try to get me to favor her in my directing.

'I didn't want to show preference to one of them. I just wanted to do it for what I thought was right for the scene. I wasn't going to favor Bette over Miriam, or Miriam over Bette. Sometime during the picture, Miriam said to me, 'Well, I'm sorry if I caused you any trouble, but this is Bette's home lot, and I was just a visitor, so I was trying to protect myself.'

'For the wrap party, Bette had a picture made of a boxing ring. She was in one corner, and Miriam was in the other, and I was the referee. That was Bette's sense of humor.

'On the last night of the picture, I drove her home. She was spending the night with her mother in Laurel Canyon. It was late at night, and we stopped at a restaurant on Ventura Boulevard.

'She said, 'Well, Mr. Sherman, it's been a lot of fun working with you. And I love you.'

'I said, 'I love you, too.' I thought meaning I approve of you. I didn't know that she meant anything personal.

'And she said, 'You don't understand,' and she put her hand on mine and said, 'I mean I really love you.'

'Well, I was absolutely dumbfounded. I didn't know what the hell to say. She was married to a very handsome guy, and I was married and had a daughter who was only two or three years old, and I was happy. And while I found her attractive and it was flattering to hear it, the idea of me putting my arms around Bette Davis and kissing her was a million miles away. I mean, I

234

never even dreamt of that.

'I said something very banal, like, 'Well, I'm flattered beyond words,' and I was. Anyway, this was around three o'clock in the morning, and we're sitting in my little Plymouth outside the mother's house on Laurel Canyon, on one of the hills, and the front door opened. Mrs. Davis came out in her bathrobe, and she said, 'Is that you, Bette Davis?' And Bette said, 'Yes, Mother.' She said, 'Well, you know what time it is? Now, you get into this house right now.' Well, I laughed, and Bette said, 'What's so funny?' I said, 'Well, I haven't heard anything like that since high school.' She said, 'Oh, don't mind Ruthie. But it's getting late. I'll go in.' I gave her a kiss on the cheek, and she got out of the car and walked up to the house.

'I drove home that night, and I thought what the hell am I going to do? I said, 'What am I gonna do?''

Sherman's dilemma was solved by Warner Brothers. Bette took a vacation in Mexico, hoping he would join her, but Warners asked him to edit *Old Acquaintance*. Forthright and frank, Bette had told her husband what she was planning. Their marriage was deeply troubled. Farney asked Sherman not to meet his wife in Mexico. Sherman was relieved to assure Farney that he had no such plans.

Shortly afterward, on August 23, Arthur Farnsworth was walking to his car on Hollywood Boulevard when he suddenly cried out and collapsed. Unconscious, he was rushed to a hospital, and Bette was called. She gave instructions to have her husband immediately transferred to Cedars of Lebanon Hospital.

Bette sat at his bedside until he died two days later, on August 25, 1943, without ever gaining consciousness.

Bette believed he might have been doing secret war work. He had implied as much to her and used it to explain why he couldn't talk much about himself. Evidence was discovered of a previous injury to the head. Otherwise, there seemed no explanation of exactly what had happened.

A statement was issued saying that Bette recalled his falling down the stairs in their home months earlier. He had struck his head, but didn't complain, and they accepted that it was only a minor injury.

Bette was offered the opportunity to delay the start of *Mr. Skeffington*. After the funeral, however, she asked for only one week. She said she preferred to go back to work.

It was considered brave of her, 'but work was exactly what I needed,' she told me. 'I was not only sad, but I felt a tremendous sense of guilt about his death because we had quarreled shortly before.'

Mr. Skeffington (1944)
Beautiful Fanny Trellis (Bette Davis) marries Jewish financier Job Skeffington (Claude Rains) to prevent her brother Trippy (Richard Waring) from being prosecuted for stealing money from Job's bank, where he had been employed. An angry Trippy is killed in France during World War I, and Fanny blames Job.

When her daughter, young Fanny (Marjorie Riordan), is born, Fanny is not happy but Job loves his daughter. Fanny and Job are divorced, and he departs for Europe. Not really wanting to be encumbered with a child, Fanny allows their daughter to live abroad with her father. In New York, Fanny continues to reign as a sought-after wealthy beauty. At the start of World War II, her daughter returns.

After a bout with diphtheria, Fanny loses her latest romantic fling, Johnny Mitchell (Johnny Mitchell), to young Fanny. She also loses her youthful appearance. The men who were part of her life are no longer young themselves, but when they see Fanny after her illness, they no longer find her attractive.

Job returns from Europe, a concentration camp survivor. Old and penniless, he hopes to meet with Fanny. Being no longer beautiful, she hesitates, but then relents. Finding out that he is blind, she is ready to take care of him. She will not be alone, and he believes her to be as beautiful as ever.

When Bette returned to do *Mr. Skeffington*, Sherman noticed a change in her. 'Everything was 'Why should I do that?' 'Why are you putting the camera there?' Almost an argument. And there was something distant.

'One thing we agreed on was Claude Rains for the part of Skeffington. Warner wanted John Loder, but I thought that Claude would have the ironic quality that was necessary to play this character.

'Bette was being so difficult, I asked Warner to take me off the picture. He said, 'Don't pay any attention to her. She's gone through a lot, losing her husband. You know Bette. She's emotional. Just go ahead and do your job, and don't worry about her.'

'We were working late one night. I took her to dinner, and she confessed that she was taking out her guilty feelings on me. She felt so guilty about Farney, because their marriage had so deteriorated before his death. 'I didn't get married to get a divorce,' she said.

' 'I go home knowing I've been terrible to you, but I couldn't help myself. So, I suppose I'm blaming you. But I know it's not your fault.' It was like an open confession.

'And that night I took her home, and we went to bed.

'The next day when she walked into the set, it was like a different human being. Ernie Haller said to me, 'My God, she's like a new woman this morning!' Nobody knew what I knew. Anyway, they were so happy that everything was going nicely. And she'd be all right, by the way, for four or five days, and then begin to tighten up again. The only time she'd relax is after we'd been to bed again. About every four, five, or six days. I had about four weeks to finish the picture, and it went on until the end.

'We finished the picture, and I saw her on the lot one morning. She said, 'I just saw J.L., and he's very happy with *Mr. Skeffington*. He wants us to do the next picture together.' It was *A Stolen Life*.

'I said, 'Well, Bette, I'll be very happy to make it with you, but with an understanding.' She says, 'About what?' 'Well, Bette, darling, we can't *both* direct the picture. One of us has to be in charge.'

'We had an argument right then, and she says, 'You mean to tell me you don't want to do it?' I said, 'Not unless we have an understanding.' She says, 'Well, if *that's* the way you feel about it!' Boom!

'Angry, she turned, walked away, got in her car, slammed the door, drove off the lot, and that's the last I saw of her. That was the end. I never talked to her again. Except once.

'After I did a picture with Debbie Reynolds, I get a call inviting me to come to a party at Debbie's house one night. My wife was still alive, and we went. Of course, Debbie didn't know anything about what had happened in the past. All she knew was that I had directed Bette in a couple of pictures. So she put me at the table with Bette Davis.

'Well, of course, Bette said nothing the whole evening. She was polite. She was sitting on my right, and my wife was sitting on my left, so it was a very awkward evening. My wife knew all about it. But she was very sophisticated and a most intelligent woman. Anyway, that was the last I saw of Bette.'

★   ★   ★

Hollywood Canteen was written and directed by Delmer Daves. He also wrote the earlier *Stage Door Canteen*, directed by Frank Borzage. Like the first film, the story centers around servicemen who visit the canteen, but in Hollywood instead of Manhattan. The entire Warner Brothers 'stock company' appear as themselves in cameos. Bette appeared in it at the same time she was making *Mr. Skeffington*.

Hollywood Canteen (1944)
Two soldiers (Robert Hutton and Dane Clark), finishing sick leave and about to be shipped out to active duty in the Pacific during World War II, find themselves honored guests of the Hollywood Canteen when one of them becomes the millionth GI visitor. Bette Davis and John Garfield appear as themselves, as do various Hollywood stars in cameos or as performers.

'I always firmly maintained that the blacks got the same bullets as the whites,' Bette told me. 'This was at a time when the racial situation was quite different from now. I absolutely refused to do as some people thought, to have some soldiers segregated in a corner of the canteen. There were those who didn't like it, but I knew what I believed. Every one of the military young men was there because he had joined to protect our country.

'They made me so proud, and the only thing I couldn't bear was that I would look out and see all those happy young faces with their heroism and dedication shining forth, and I would know that some of them weren't coming back home, and knowing that they knew it, too.'

One consequence of her work at the

Hollywood Canteen was a romance with a young soldier, Lewis A. Riley, son of a wealthy New York family and a corporal in the Second Army Signal Corps. She visited him at Fort Benning, Georgia, just before he was shipped overseas.

'We talked about marriage, and then we wrote about it. After a while, I felt like a male-order bride. That's spelled M-A-L-E. We had most of our short affair by mail, and censored V-mail, at that.' During World War II, letters from troops abroad were photographed on 35mm film and shipped as V-mail, short for 'Victory' mail. 'Not very intimate.'

While in Georgia, Bette accepted an invitation from Franklin D. Roosevelt to have dinner with him in Warm Springs. The President had extended his invitation when Bette first met him, at the White House during a War Bond tour. 'FDR was one of my idols. Still is.

'I only barely remember Lew. He just faded away in my reality and in my mind. Just an interlude, you might say. But FDR, he was unforgettable.'

6

The Warner Years
(1945–1949)

Bette began *The Corn Is Green* while she was still busy with the Hollywood Canteen. She was thirty-six, and the part had been performed to great acclaim onstage by Ethel Barrymore, who was sixty-five. 'I should have been older, no doubt about it,' Bette said. 'Even Miss Barrymore said so.' The playwright, Emlyn Williams, however, disagreed when I spoke with him at the Savoy Hotel in London.

'The age of the actress who plays Miss Moffat is unimportant. What's important is the dedication and compassion that has to show through in the character she is playing, and Bette Davis is herself that kind of woman. Let me give you an example of her dedication and compassion.

'There was a young actress in the cast who was quite nervous. I think it was her first film. Anyway, Bette had been very helpful to her early on, and they were doing a scene together. The director decided to do the close-ups the next day, which was a Saturday, so Bette wouldn't be there for the young actress to speak to

242

Even as an infant, those Bette Davis eyes were extraordinary. In those days, however, they were Ruth Elizabeth Davis eyes. *(Museum of Modern Art)*

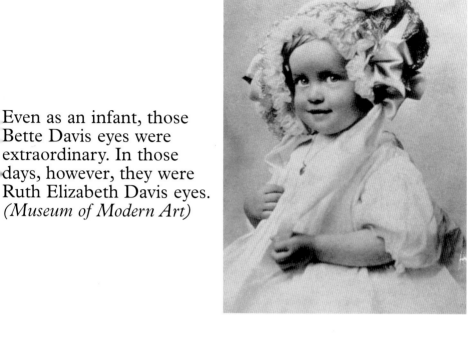

Teenage Bette with a friend. Her mother said that it was impossible to take a bad picture of Ruth Elizabeth. *(Museum of Modern Art)*

Young Ruth Elizabeth
Davis in a portrait by
her photographer
mother.
(Collection of Bette Davis)

Bette with sister Bobby
in a picture taken by
their mother, Ruthie,
who supported the
family for many years
as a professional
photographer.
(Museum of Modern Art)

Bette was never fond of cheesecake photos. Even though she was proud of her figure, she wished to show off her talent, not what Jack Warner called her 'bulbs.' *(Museum of Modern Art)*

A glamorous Hollywood publicity portrait in 1931. Universal was not impressed, and soon dropped the actress they chose to call 'the little brown wren.' *(Museum of Modern Art)*

Bandleader Harmon O. Nelson was Bette's favorite beau in high school, and he became her first husband in 1932. They were divorced in 1938. *(Museum of Modern Art)*

Bette and George Arliss in *The Man Who Played God* (1932). Arliss, she believed, was the person who saved her career in Hollywood. All her life, she kept a silver-framed picture of him in her home. *(British Film Institute)*

For *Fashions of 1934,* Jack Orry-Kelly was brought out from New York to design the wardrobe. His look contributed to the Bette Davis persona throughout her long Warner Brothers career. She is with Etienne Girardot and William Powell. *(Museum of Modern Art)*

Bette and Humphrey Bogart in *Marked Woman* (1937), one of her favorite pre-*Jezebel* Warner films. *(Museum of Modern Art)*

Henry Fonda and Bette in *That Certain Woman* (1937).
They had met years earlier on a blind date.
(British Film Institute)

Director William Wyler
was for Bette Davis 'the
lost love of my life.'
(American Film Institute)

Bette in *Jezebel*
(1938), for which she
won an Oscar.
*(Museum of
Modern Art)*

Humphrey Bogart,
Bette, and Geraldine
Fitzgerald in *Dark
Victory* (1939). She
often said that this
was her favorite film.
*(Museum of
Modern Art)*

Bette Davis's Queen Elizabeth smokes a cigarette off-camera during the filming of *The Private Lives of Elizabeth and Essex* (1939).
(Museum of Modern Art)

The most mysterious of Bette's four husbands was Arthur Farnsworth. She married 'Farney' in 1940. This photo was taken by Bette's mother at the wedding. *(Museum of Modern Art)*

With Paul Henreid in *Now, Voyager* (1942). Charlotte was one of Bette's favorite roles. *(Museum of Modern Art)*

Miriam Hopkins and Bette drinking flat champagne. *Old Acquaintance* (1943). *(Museum of Modern Art)*

Bette, cigarette in hand, sings for World War II servicemen at the Hollywood Canteen. *(Museum of Modern Art)*

Bob Hope, Frank Sinatra, and Jimmy Durante rehearsing a War Bond promotion radio show in 1943. *(Museum of Modern Art)*

Bette appeared with Glenn Ford in two films, here in *A Stolen Life* (1946) and later in *Pocketful of Miracles* (1961). *(Museum of Modern Art)*

Ruthie took this photo at her daughter's third wedding, in 1945, in Riverside, California. Bridegroom William Grant Sherry is at far right. Their daughter, Barbara Davis (B.D.) Sherry, was born in 1947. In 1949, Bette filed for divorce. *(Museum of Modern Art)*

Bette performing on CBS radio in the late 1940s.
(Museum of Modern Art)

Bette with her mother in 1950. *(Museum of Modern Art)*

Bette as Margo Channing with Anne Baxter, Marilyn
Monroe, and George Sanders in *All About Eve* (1950).
(Collection of Joseph L. Mankiewicz)

Husband Gary Merrill
and Bette, early in their
marriage, during happy
days in Maine.
(Museum of Modern Art)

When Frank Capra remade his 1933 *Lady for a Day* as *Pocketful of Miracles* in 1961, he cast Bette Davis as Apple Annie. Bette always enjoyed playing characters older than she was at the time.
(Museum of Modern Art)

Bette and Joan Crawford as they appeared in *What Ever Happened to Baby Jane?* (1962). Bette particularly loved the character of Jane and felt she would 'wipe the linoleum with Crawford.' *(British Film Institute)*

Cinematographer Ernest Haller's last Bette Davis film, *Dead Ringer* (1964), involved some difficult split-frame photography because she played twin sisters. *(Museum of Modern Art)*

Hush…Hush, Sweet Charlotte (1964) was an attempt to duplicate the success of *What Ever Happened to Baby Jane? (Museum of Modern Art)*

Bette with her daughter shortly before B.D.'s marriage at sixteen.
(Museum of Modern Art)

Bette, meticulously attired, coiffed, and made up, though gravely ill, shortly before her death in 1989. The long ash on her cigarette indicates her hand was still steady. 'I never wanted to be the object of envy,' she said, but even less did she want to be the object of pity.
(Collection of Robert Lantz)

off-camera. Bette had Saturdays off.

'The actress appeared on Saturday morning, more nervous than ever, because it's very difficult to speak lines to nobody. But she wasn't alone. Bette was already seated beside the camera, in full makeup, ready to listen to her and reply. Now, *that's* dedication and compassion!' The young actress was Joan Lorring, who was nominated for an Oscar for her portrayal of Bessie in the film.

The part of Morgan was supposed to go to Richard Waring, who had played Trippy in *Mr. Skeffington*, but he was drafted into the army. His replacement was John Dall, who won an Oscar nomination for his performance and later starred in Alfred Hitchcock's *Rope*.

The Corn Is Green (1945)

Miss Lilly Moffat (Bette Davis), an English schoolmistress, meets with strong resistance when she tries to reform education in a backward Welsh mining town. Only one student, Morgan Evans (John Dall), shows promise, and she tries to prepare him for an Oxford scholarship.

Threatening his chances is Bessie (Joan Lorring), a young woman of low morals who tells Miss Moffat he is the father of her child-to-be. Miss Moffat pays her to leave town.

After Morgan has passed his scholarship examinations and is about to leave for Oxford, Bessie returns with his child. He feels that he must marry Bessie to give his son a name, but Miss Moffat stops him from ruining his chances for a better life by adopting the child herself.

Bette lit another cigarette from the one she was smoking, then rose and spoke with animation as she moved around.

'It was at a party I regretted going to in October of 1945 that I met an artist named William Grant Sherry. If only it had stopped there!

'Have you ever regretted going to a party? First, let me tell you what makes a good party: It isn't the menu, it's the men you sit next to. If you want to have a good party, always invite beautiful women and intelligent men. If you want to have a lousy party, invite intelligent women and beautiful men. I married Sherry exactly a month after that lousy party at Laguna Beach. A year and a half later, my daughter, Barbara Davis Sherry, was born.

'We lived happily never after.'

★ ★ ★

'When we were making *A Stolen Life*,' film editor Rudi Fehr told me, 'I always looked at the rushes of the film every day after lunch with Jack Warner. And he liked what he saw. He really liked the rushes. So I told Bette that Jack Warner really liked the picture. And she said, 'Then it probably stinks.''

'I never could *bear* myself on the screen,' Bette told me. 'I did not want to see myself in the rushes. The rushes could make me ill for three days, picturing this awful creature I saw yesterday on the screen. I couldn't *stand* myself.

'I did go to see the finished pictures. I've seen nearly all of mine.

'The finished picture depends upon the script, the director, how well the cast did it, and how well it's put together. Because when we finish a film, Leslie Howard said this: 'It's sixty percent ours at that point. Forty percent is what they do with it, over which you get no control.' And many heartbreaks come in that area by bad editing or whatever. Many heartbreaks. The thrill of the work you do is when, on the screen, it's the script you dreamed about. And if it came out the way you dreamed when you did it, well, it doesn't happen often.

'It's very dependent on how great the director is. The great director is a great editor. And in the final analysis of the project, I cannot say enough about how important the editing is. The heads of studios, like Warner and Mayer, and all those men, they were not good editors. They all had their taste in the films. Jack Warner, for instance, couldn't stand to have one minute of silence on the screen. You might be, say, giving a look that would spare you ten pages of dialogue, but he would say, 'Come on. Slow, slow, slow, slow.'

'Jack Warner wasn't a man of subtlety. And that was not the business they were in, subtlety.'

A Stolen Life (1946)

Kate Bosworth (Bette Davis), an aspiring artist, falls in love with Bill Emerson (Glenn Ford), a handsome marine engineer, but he prefers her more outgoing twin sister, Patricia (Bette Davis). Bill and Patricia prepare to go to Chile, where he has been offered an engineering post.

Kate goes to study with Karnock (Dane Clark), an artist she respects, but she soon realizes she will never achieve her ambition to become a first-rate artist, and she returns to Martha's Vineyard. There she encounters her sister, who has not gone to Chile with Bill, after all.

In a sailboat accident during a storm, Patricia is lost and Kate saved. Mistaken for her sister, Kate takes on Pat's identity. Bill returns from Chile, and Kate thinks she can keep him as Patricia, but he recognizes who she really is and accepts her for herself. She did not realize that Bill had come to hate the unfaithful Patricia, and he realizes that it is Kate he has always loved.

A Stolen Life was the only film Bette produced. It seemed a natural step for her, since she had always endeavored to be involved in every aspect of her films, beginning with their selection. She always had script ideas, especially for her character. She wanted to be able to choose her director, or at least to have veto power. She had many ideas and opinions, and she wanted the director and the producers to listen to them, but as she explained, 'I didn't want them just to do what I said. I wanted them to *consider* it. I wanted them to defend their positions, not just to give in. Then, I wanted the director to *direct* and for me to be an *actress*.

'I discovered that being the producer, too, didn't free me. It encumbered me.'

★　★　★

'Paul Henreid couldn't play the cello,' Irving Rapper told me, 'so we had to tie his hands behind his back for close set-ups, where you could see his fingering and bowing. Then, a real cellist would sit behind him and do the real playing. I can't watch *Deception* now without squirming when I see Paul playing Haydn with somebody else's hands. When you do shots like this, it's best to distract audiences with something else happening at the same time or with camera movement.

'The way John Collier originally wrote *Deception*, it had a Lubitschstyle ending, nonchalant, you know, with Bette, Paul, and Claude walking away as friends. But this didn't suit Bette at all. She insisted on a dramatic conclusion, and she got it.

'She also insisted on Ernest Haller as cameraman instead of my usual one, Sol Polito. Haller was very concerned with making female stars look beautiful, especially aging ones, and that's what Bette was very concerned with, too. She was approaching forty at this time, so I gave in to her wishes. I actually preferred Polito, who was a wonderful no-nonsense technician, but I let Bette have Haller on *Deception*. I didn't want her worrying about how she looked. It might affect her performance.

'Now, this story has been told very, very often, always about Garbo or Dietrich, but it really happened with Bette. After about a week of shooting, she came up to me and asked if I'd seen the rushes. I tried to reassure her about her performance, but that wasn't what she wanted to

247

know. She was worried about how she looked. I couldn't reassure her enough, so she went to Haller and said, 'Ernie, why can't you make me look the way I looked in *Jezebel?*'

'And he said, 'Bette, I was seven years younger then.'

'But Ernie did a very good job, because he got all those wonderful deep-focus shots that were essential to tell the story. Bette and Paul are on the screen in so many scenes, and the extreme depth of the focus allowed me to move them about more freely.'

Deception was drawn from a two-person play by French playwright Louis Verneuil. It was first produced in Paris in 1927 as *Monsieur Lamberthier*, the name of an important character who never appears onstage. He is the rich old man who had been keeping the woman in the cast who marries an artist and doesn't want him to know of her previous affair. The play appeared as *Jealousy* on Broadway and in a film starring Jeanne Eagels, who had just done the first Hollywood version of *The Letter*. The stage play, starring Basil Rathbone and Eugenie Leontovich, was revived in 1946 as *Obsession* and played for a short run on Broadway after a national tour. When Warner Brothers bought the play, it was extensively rewritten, adding the rich old man, Hollenius, the composer, as an active character. For his portrayal of this newly important character, Claude Rains appeared above the title for the first time in his Warner Brothers career.

Deception (1946)

After World War II, Christine Radcliffe (Bette Davis) is reunited with the man she loves, European cellist Karel Novak (Paul Henreid), whom she had given up for dead. Although he still loves her, he becomes jealous when he finds her living too luxuriously for a music teacher. To convince him of her love, she marries him.

A man from Christine's past appears, Alexander Hollenius (Claude Rains), a famous composer and conductor. With seeming generosity, Hollenius offers Karel the opportunity to perform the solo part in the premiere of his new cello concerto.

Christine suspects that Hollenius's generosity is false, and she confronts the composer with her suspicions. He maliciously suggests that he could ruin Karel's career by telling him before the concert about their own affair. Enraged, she shoots him.

Karel's debut is a success. Afterward, Christine confesses to him what she has done, admitting her relationship with Hollenius. In spite of everything that has happened, Karel still loves Christine, and he will stand by her.

The 'Hollenius' cello concerto, written by Erich Wolfgang Korngold for this film, was later expanded by the composer and published as his own opus 37. There have been several commercial recordings.

★ ★ ★

After the completion of *Deception*, Bette took maternity leave from Warner Brothers. Barbara Davis Sherry was born by cesarean, and thus Bette was able to choose the date. She chose May 1, 1947. Bette, who was thirty-nine, was told she shouldn't have any more children. To avoid confusion with her Aunt Barbara (Bobby), the seven-pound baby girl was called B.D.

'What I wanted most for my daughter was her happiness. I wanted so much for her to be happy in life.

'I remember when I bought her first doll. Then, her first adorable kitten. She loved the perfect pony I bought for her. For her honeymoon, though I hadn't wanted her to marry so young — only sixteen and I had to give my permission — I bought her the most beautiful silk nightgown and peignoir in the world.'

★   ★   ★

Bette reported for work at Warners at the end of July 1947. She was supposed to select and produce her next film, but she decided to leave this to the studio, and *Winter Meeting* was chosen for her. It would be directed by Bretaigne Windust, a highly regarded Broadway stage director who had no cinema experience. He is famous for one picture, *The Enforcer*, which was directed partly by Raoul Walsh, who would not accept directorial credit.

Winter Meeting (1948)

Susan Grieve (Bette Davis), finds solace and satisfaction in writing poetry and doing charitable work until Slick Novak (James Davis), a young naval hero, comes into her life. They meet at a party in his honor, where he leaves the beautiful woman he has come with, Peggy (Janis Paige), to go with Susan to her apartment.

The next morning, she takes him to her parents' Connecticut farm, where she explains why she finds it so difficult to love. There, her father committed suicide after her mother ran off with another man. Novak also has a problem. He wanted to be a priest, but feels himself unworthy of serving God.

Susan encounters Novak again, this time at a restaurant where he is back with Peggy. The next day he comes to her apartment to explain that he was only using Peggy to stop himself from falling in love with her. She forgives him, telling him not to abandon his dream for the priesthood. She also forgives her mother, who is in a hospital dying.

Richard Widmark, who had just attracted attention for his outstanding portrayal of a sadistic killer in *Kiss of Death*, was considered for the part of Novak. Bette was the only star in the picture. It was the first of hers to lose money for Warner Brothers. She desperately had wanted to do Edith Wharton's *Ethan Frome* or a film based on the life of Mary Todd Lincoln, Abraham Lincoln's wife.

'The story of Mary Todd Lincoln was,' Irving

Rapper lamented, 'the film that got away,' the one he most wanted to direct, with Bette Davis starring.

'Mrs. Lincoln was a strong influence on her husband, and a strong personality. Some people thought she was sort of mad. She was, anyway, high-strung. She had a black friend, her seamstress, something unheard of at that time.

'She was always worried about Mr. Lincoln going out without proper protection. She felt he was in danger, and she was the one who heard there was a conspiracy to kill him.

'After the death of both her son and her husband, she had a breakdown and was committed to a mental institution by her family.

'There was a script, and Bette and I met. She loved the idea. It would have brought her a sure Oscar. No matter how great the performance, an actor or actress needs the award-winning part. This was it. It might have happened, except that Jack Warner never liked to do biographies. Mary Todd Lincoln didn't have a chance with him.'

June Bride, based on a successful Broadway comedy, was Bette's next picture. Windust was again the director. Bette described her costar, Robert Montgomery, as 'a male Miriam Hopkins.'

'He was an excellent actor, but addicted to scene-stealing,' Bette said. 'He would add business in his close-ups which didn't match mine, so that there would only be one way to cut the film — his way. Mr. Montgomery understood films. Windust, who was not a film man at all, never noticed, and I couldn't have cared less.

Montgomery was welcome to all the close-ups he wanted. I act with my whole body.'

June Bride (1948)

Carey Jackson (Robert Montgomery), a war correspondent between assignments, is hired by publisher Carleton Towne (Jerome Cowan) to assist Linda Gilman (Bette Davis), editor of his glossy women's magazine. The trouble is, Carey was once in love with Linda, but they didn't marry because she would not give up her career for him and his way of life.

Knowing his distaste for convention, Linda takes Carey along as her assistant to cover a typical middle-American wedding at the Brinker home in Indiana for the magazine's June issue. She hopes Carey will be so bored, he will quit. Instead, he finds out that the bride (Barbara Bates) and groom (Raymond Roe) are mismatched and each should be marrying someone else. He sorts out the mismatched couples to everybody's satisfaction except Linda's, whose feature article is now ruined. She fires Carey, then realizes that the *real* story of the Brinker family is an even better subject for her magazine than the one they had expected to find.

Linda also realizes she is still in love with Carey, and resigns her job to follow him on his next overseas assignment.

One of the teenage girls in the cast is Debbie Reynolds. This was her first picture. Later, she would appear with Bette in *The Catered Affair*. *Beyond the Forest* was Bette's last film for

Warner Brothers. It wasn't supposed to be that way. She still had ten years left on her contract, a contract that allowed her to make a certain number of pictures a year on her own as well as those for Warners. This film, however, made up her mind. If *Beyond the Forest* was the kind of movie the studio had in mind for her during the next decade, then she had no future with Warner Brothers and she asked to be let out of her contract. She did more than ask, she demanded, threatening not to finish *Beyond the Forest* if they didn't acquiesce. 'I was too old for the part and what woman would ever want to leave Joe Cotten?' Joseph Cotten was her co-star.

'I made over fifty films in eighteen years at Warners. When I announced I was leaving, it was like getting a divorce. What I didn't consider was that I was giving my ultimatum late, like a wife giving an ultimatum to a husband when he already wants to leave her for a younger woman. I was forty and had a small child when I gave the ultimatum.

'It's strange how much you can miss a bad home.'

Beyond the Forest was based on a best-selling novel by Stuart Engstrand, written for the screen by Lenore Coffee, and produced by Henry Blanke. It was directed by the legendary King Vidor.

Beyond the Forest (1949)

High-spirited Rosa Moline (Bette Davis), bored with her dull existence in a Wisconsin milling town, has an affair with Neil Latimer (David

Brian), a vacationing Chicago millionaire. Determined to follow Latimer to Chicago, she tells her husband, Dr. Louis Moline (Joseph Cotten), that she must have a vacation from him. To finance the trip, she pressures his patients into paying their past-due bills.

In Chicago, Rosa learns that Latimer is engaged to marry a socialite. After Rosa has returned home to Louis, Latimer appears in town, no longer engaged. He asks Rosa to divorce her husband and marry him.

Rosa becomes pregnant. By accident, the caretaker (Minor Watson) at Latimer's lakeside lodge learns of this and threatens to tell Latimer. Rosa, fearing he won't want her if he knows she's pregnant, shoots and kills the caretaker in what appears to be a hunting accident.

Rosa hopes her husband will perform an abortion, but when he refuses, she tries to induce a miscarriage. She is successful at this, but contracts peritonitis. Delirious, Rosa leaves her sickbed and tries to catch the night train to Chicago. As she reaches out to board it, she dies.

On location at Lake Tahoe, Bette almost lost an eye when her rifle recoiled. She also contracted tick fever. 'Location shooting can be very taxing, not to mention dangerous. It's hard when you have to die all day without any coffee.'

Beyond the Forest has one of Bette's most famous lines, 'What a dump!'

When Bette left Warners, she said 'No one waved good-bye. There was no party. There was no gold watch.

'One of my last lines, the one I had to loop afterwards, was, 'If I don't get out of here I'll just die!' How prophetic!'

★   ★   ★

Enjoying his favorite lunch, a hamburger and French fries at Hamburger Hamlet in Beverly Hills, King Vidor poured on a heavy ration of ketchup as he talked about *Beyond the Forest*.

'You have to fall in love with the project. You don't *have to*, but it's better. None of us was in love with this project.

'I had often been 'in love' with my leading lady in a film I was directing, before or during. There is no doubt this caused complications, during and especially after.

'All of this falling in love seemed very hard to avoid, but I must say, this didn't happen on *Beyond the Forest*. There was no attraction at all between Bette and me.

'Of course, I speak for myself, but in this instance, I feel I can speak for Bette, too.

'Before we began, she told me that she was very happy to be working with me, and I believed her. She wasn't the kind of person who would just *say* something like that. Neither was I. We both meant it, but we didn't mean it as much by the time the film wrapped. She was badly cast, and she knew it. She was extremely angry about it.'

Of *Beyond the Forest*, Bette said, 'It's not a film I talk about. I can't say I'm ashamed of it, but I can't say I'm proud of it.'

7

After Warner Brothers

Payment on Demand was originally called 'The Story of a Divorce,' a title that Bette described as 'the state of my domestic existence at that time.'

Sherry wasn't adjusting to the role of 'Mr. Davis.' He was especially sensitive about it when a fan of Bette's called him that. Bette said that he frequently became violent toward her at home, and that she was afraid of him.

'He was a bully, so he became worse after I told him that I was becoming afraid of him. He seemed to enjoy that.'

This film's most distinctive moments are in the staging of flashback sequences. Walls disappear as characters are transported into the past. These effects were the conception of writer-director Curtis Bernhardt, which he said were based on effects he had seen early in his career in Germany.

Payment on Demand (1950–51)
After twenty years of an apparently happy marriage, Joyce Ramsey (Bette Davis) is told by her successful husband, David (Barry Sullivan), that he wants a divorce. In reviewing their

marriage, Joyce realizes that her driving social ambition has alienated David, and he has found someone less demanding (Frances Dee). Joyce threatens to expose his adultery, and he grants her everything she demands, including large trust funds for their two daughters, Martha (Betty Lynn) and Diana (Peggie Castle).

Joyce tries to forget David on a Caribbean cruise, but on shipboard she is confronted with the problems of being a divorced middle-aged woman. A cablegram from Martha arrives, announcing her intention to marry, and Joyce rushes home. She wants to advise her daughter not to make the same mistakes in marriage that she has made.

Joyce and David meet again. Realizing they still love each other, they decide to think about a reconciliation.

RKO owner Howard Hughes insisted on this relatively upbeat ending. In the original ending, it's evident that whatever Joyce says during their reconciliation, she won't change.

Though *Payment on Demand* was made before *All About Eve*, it was released afterward, on February 15, 1951, thus helping its box office. *All About Eve* was released October 13, 1950.

★ ★ ★

Joseph L. Mankiewicz, who had just won two Oscars for *A Letter to Three Wives*, was looking for his next project at Twentieth Century Fox in

April 1949, when he was offered a property about Broadway. It was a short story about ambitious actresses that had appeared in *Cosmopolitan*. 'I missed the Broadway theater, and women are more interesting and complex than men,' he told me, 'so this project caught my interest.'

While still on the set of *Payment on Demand*, Bette received a life-changing phone call from Darryl Zanuck.

'It would have been very exciting, historic even,' Bette told me, 'if I had *believed* it was Zanuck. He hadn't spoken to me for years, so I might not have recognized his voice, though it was distinctive, as was his speech. Zanuck hadn't approved of me as a person ever since I'd resigned after only a short time as president of the Motion Picture Academy. Because he had strongly recommended me, I'd embarrassed him.

'Well, with my career in the doldrums, going nowhere, this call from Mr. Zanuck came at a critical moment, and my reaction was the same as it had been with Mr. Arliss. I did a George Arliss encore. Apparently, I hadn't learned much in the interim. I decided it must be some idiot playing a very unfunny joke on me. I went along with what I thought was the game, being my most sarcastic self, inherited from my sarcastic father. I was lucky. I came to my nonsenses before Mr. Zanuck hung up. My guardian angel was around when most needed.

'Mr. Zanuck would never have kept talking to me when I was acting the fool if he hadn't been very, very anxious. When I understood it really *was* he and what he had in mind, I was even more anxious. He told me he had a script by Joe Mankiewicz that was in need of me due to Claudette Colbert's accident. I hadn't heard about her back injury.

'Joe had just won two Oscars. I was in need of his script, and *I* was in need of *him!*

'I had to be ready in a few days. Fortunately, my part in the film I was doing was almost complete.'

She read the script and loved it. The only problem was that her work on *Payment on Demand* would leave her little time to prepare. The new film was to begin shooting in mid-April 1950, in San Francisco at the Curran Theater, in only two weeks. She was able to study the script, and have makeup tests and wardrobe fittings for *All About Eve* while completing *Payment on Demand*, then still called 'The Story of a Divorce.'

There were several changes in Zanuck's thinking and planning during the creation of *Eve*, but from the beginning he saw only one possibility for the role of Karen Richards, the show business 'civilian' wife, Celeste Holm.

Nancy Davis, who was later to become Mrs. Ronald Reagan, was on a short list if Holm had been unavailable. A few years before he married Nancy Davis, Ronald Reagan himself was on a longer list of actors considered for the part of director Bill Sampson.

Thelma Ritter, who had been in Mankiewicz's *A Letter to Three Wives*, was Zanuck's, as well as Mankiewicz's, first choice for Birdie, Margo Channing's acerbic dresser. She and Bette became good friends.

Claudette Colbert had been the first person chosen to sign a contract to play Margo, and she had done so 'with grand élan,' as she told me. When she was injured and couldn't do the film, Bette was the next person seriously considered.

'I wasn't supposed to play Margo Channing at all, you know. I was a replacement, a desperate last-minute replacement for Claudette Colbert, who had injured her back. A few years later, I met Miss Colbert for the first time, and I said, 'I thank you all my life!' So, her bad luck was my good luck. No question about that.'

When I spoke with Claudette Colbert about *All About Eve*, she winced, as if in pain. 'Oh, it still makes my back hurt, just to remember it.

'It was one of the greatest parts in the history of films, and I was offered it before Bette Davis. It wasn't as if I didn't know it was a great part. I did, and I grabbed it. I said yes before I asked what I was going to be paid. I didn't care. But then, foolish girl that I was, I injured my back very badly, very badly, and I couldn't do the film. I was in terrible physical pain, and on top of it, the mental pain of losing the part.'

At the time of our meeting, she was accompanied by her close friend, the Russian-born French Art Deco artist, Erté. Though famous as an American actress, Colbert was born in France, and she and Erté, when alone, sometimes spoke in French. She said she didn't want to forget her first language. They had just returned from her home in Barbados.

Erté knew the film and the Bette Davis performance. 'She was very good,' Erté said to Colbert, 'but for me, you would be best.'

'No,' Colbert said. 'I wouldn't have been. Bette was best, but I wish I'd had the part, if they had let me play it in a wheelchair.'

'Willie Wyler encouraged me, very strongly, to cast Bette Davis as Margo Channing,' Mankiewicz told me. 'He said, 'She's the perfect actress for the part, and whatever you expect from her, she'll give you more. She's the hardest worker you'll ever find, and you couldn't find a finer actress.''

Other directors, when they heard that Mankiewicz was considering Bette, rushed in with their opinions. Mankiewicz said the words varied, but the reaction basically could be summed up in 'Oh, no!' What Mankiewicz quickly realized was that the chorus of warnings came mainly from directors who had not worked with Bette Davis. They were the ones who said she would be 'too difficult to work with,' based on hearsay.

'I was told Bette would appear with a yellow legal pad and pencil, and a marked-up script, and she would have changed every line I wrote, and there wouldn't be a line of mine as I wrote it when the film actually made it to the screen. To the contrary. It was exactly the opposite.

'Bette was not only perfectly behaved, but she was appreciative, encouraging. I don't really remember her changing a word. And when she had a question or a thought, she only mentioned it privately to me, with courtesy and respect, and she was able to inspire my thinking or add a good bit of business for herself.

'Willie remained her staunchest supporter and defender. He said, 'Joe, she'll be fine and not cause you any trouble.''

Mankiewicz said that Wyler was absolutely right. 'If there was anything he wasn't right about, it was that she would be 'fine.' Well, she was a lot more than fine. She was great.

'I thought that Anne [Baxter] was going to steal the film. I was personally very impressed by Anne as an actress, as a person, and in the performance of Eve, our title character. I was worried that when the film was shown, critics and audiences would be stunned by Anne, and Bette would be hurt by having the lesser part. Well, I couldn't have been more wrong.'

Mankiewicz said he had chosen Anne Baxter, 'not only because she was a lovely actress, but because she resembled Claudette Colbert, and that gave another dimension to the story. We lost that shading, but the film seems perfect as it turned out. Bette was perfect.

'As soon as I had the picture put together, I knew that not only was it Bette's film, but that she would long be remembered as Margo Channing. Anne was perfect as Eve, but she would only be noted as part of the wonderful company of actors. It was then, forever, Bette's picture.'

'I can give you a perfect example of the kind of collaboration between an actor and a director which is ideal,' Bette told me. 'The basis for it is trust. One must have trust in the director, and one must have respect. You have to believe he can surprise you.

'I went to Joe in the morning before we started shooting, and I said, 'There is a scene which is necessary for exposition to advance the plot. I understand that. But it is talky, so I don't know how to do it. What do I do so it doesn't seem talky, which it does now? This is the only scene I find talky.'

'There are directors I couldn't have spoken to that way. But they weren't the directors I wanted. I was never good at couching my words diplomatically.

'Joe understood me as an actress and as a person. He didn't miss a beat:

''As you get angry, you want a piece of candy. The angrier you get, the more desperately you want the candy. You look toward the candy jar on the piano.'

'I interrupted. 'But there *is* no candy jar on the piano.'

''There *will* be. And then, finally, passionately, you *eat* the candy.'

'Genius. I always was especially good at creating business for my characters, but I never would have thought of that.'

In 1944, an eighteen-year-old Barbara Bates was discovered in her hometown, Denver, when a visiting Hollywood press agent was struck by her beauty. He helped her get a contract with Universal, where she became a starlet and appeared on the cover of *Life* magazine. She married the press agent.

Among her earlier parts, none in especially memorable films, Bates played the title role in *June Bride*. Then, in 1950, at twenty-five, she was cast by Mankiewicz as Phoebe in *All About Eve*. Her relatively small part became the entire last scene, and the final shot of her standing in front of her mirrored reflections, one of the great iconic images of cinema.

She made fifteen more Hollywood features, usually playing supporting roles, mostly in forgettable films, as well as some television commercials. In 1967, after her husband's death, she returned to Denver, where few recognized her as a former movie star. She married her childhood sweetheart. In 1969, she committed suicide, a few months short of her forty-fourth birthday.

*   *   *

It was Mankiewicz who chose Marilyn Monroe to play Miss Caswell.

'I was pleased by Marilyn's performance,' he told me. 'At the time I selected her, I had no allies. Everyone wanted someone else, from long lists of blondes, natural and bottle. There was no one else who was at all right, but I was warned not to select Marilyn Monroe because she was 'too neurotic' and had already shown herself to be undependable. I was warned about her as I had been warned about how difficult Bette Davis could be.

'Bette and Marilyn were exact opposites. Bette had perfect confidence, and Marilyn had perfect insecurity.

'I had had my own experiences with neurotic actresses, and I found that it was really insecurity and that, if they felt I believed in them, it made all the difference. They responded to encouragement and praise, especially when they knew their performances merited it.

'From the first moment I met Marilyn Monroe, I felt that she had a potentially great future on film. She was beautiful in life, but on film, she was magical, and she radiated a vulnerability which made a man want to protect her. Marilyn Monroe was like a mermaid in shark-infested waters.'

Mankiewicz said he selected her because of masculine intuition. She had, he said, a quality of 'innocence and, of course, that vulnerability.' He felt she had a genuine talent and he didn't understand why others didn't see it, except 'they were too dazzled by her looks.'

'The rumor was that Marilyn Monroe dyed her pubic hair,' Bette told me. 'That was very shocking gossip for then. I don't know anyone who'd seen the evidence, but they were happy enough spreading the hearsay.

'Someone who knew Marilyn once told me she really didn't like men and sex all that much, because she was tired of men always trying to get her into bed — theirs or hers. Lucky girl. Secretly, I wished I could be a *femme fatale*, but my audience was chiefly women — the handkerchief crowd. Now instead of tearjerkers, they have *fear*-jerkers. Anyway, what I really wanted to be was an actress, and I'm happy to have been Bette Davis. To *be* Bette Davis!

'I felt a certain envy for what I assumed was Marilyn's more-than-obvious popularity. *Here* was a girl who didn't know what it was like to be lonely. Then, I noticed how shy she was, and I think now that she was as lonely as I was. Lonelier. It was something I felt, a deep well of loneliness she was trying to fill.'

★ ★ ★

Edith Head, who designed Bette's clothes for the film, saw Bette as perfectly confident. In her experience working with stars, Head said, 'The actresses, every one of them, even the most beautiful, even Grace Kelly, always took that last look in the mirror to make certain everything was right, to remove any doubt.

'Bette Davis was the one who never did that. She never took that last look. She didn't have to, because she had true confidence.'

Bette had a different explanation. 'I was thought to be someone of perfect confidence just because I was outspoken. Being outspoken has come to be equated with intelligence. It's often really just foolishness.

'Edith was my mirror. I could see the

267

expression on her face, and knew that she had made me look as good as I could for the part, and that was what I wanted. She would walk all around me, looking at every angle. It was more than I was able to see, and she never made the clothes too tight to inhibit my movements.'

All About Eve was based on a Cosmopolitan story by Mary Orr, then titled 'The Wisdom of Eve.' Orr was a young actress about to marry a successful director, Reginald Denham, when they visited actress Elisabeth Bergner and her director-husband, Paul Czinner, for a country weekend.

The Two Mrs. Carrolls was a successful play on Broadway in 1943 and 1944. Elisabeth Bergner was the star. She had been a star in theater and film in Germany, and then in England, after the rise of the Nazis forced her to leave Germany.

While Denham and Czinner talked about a new leading man for the tour of The Two Mrs. Carrolls, the two actresses, one almost a legend, the other just beginning her career, chatted.

Bergner told Orr about a young, aspiring actress who had turned up at the stage door every night after The Two Mrs. Carrolls, and matinees, too. The girl was 'apparently shy,' Bergner recalled, but not too shy to approach the actress and tell her that she saw every performance. Bergner, at that time, never questioned the girl's story. Only later did she think about what it would have cost to see so many performances, even in the worst seat.

Bergner invited the girl to visit her in her

dressing room. The girl was flattering, and she told a story about having come from England because of the threat of war, and being alone in New York.

Bergner felt sympathy for the girl and created a job for her as a kind of coffee girl assistant to her husband, who was producing *The Two Mrs. Carrolls*.

When the actress Irene Worth decided to leave the cast, the fan was given a chance to read for the part and, if she read well, to fulfill all her dreams. She read well. She won the part, even though she was really too young for it, and even though it turned out she had lied and wasn't English, but American.

Bergner decided that what the girl really wanted was *her* starring part — and her husband.

Orr wrote the story, told in the first person by the character later played in the film by Celeste Holm. Orr's husband thought it was a great story, but she didn't find it easy to sell. Finally, someone who knew her husband bought it for *Cosmopolitan*.

The story was sent to Joseph Mankiewicz, and that led to the acquisition by Fox of 'The Wisdom of Eve.'

Mary Orr told me that she wasn't pleased by the film Mankiewicz had made based on her story. She was prejudiced against it, she said, because she wasn't included in the film's credits. She blamed Mankiewicz, though it was a studio decision, based on her not having asked for film credit in her contract when she sold the film rights. 'Written for the Screen and Directed by Joseph L. Mankiewicz' is the only on-screen writing credit.

Orr did retain theatrical credit and a participation in theatrical rights. Because she and her husband worked so much in the theater, she thought in those terms. Many years later, when *All About Eve* was adapted for the theater as *Applause*, Mary Orr received the credit for her story, and it was Joseph L. Mankiewicz's name for the film script that was missing from the credits.

Adolph Green, who with Betty Comden wrote the book for *Applause*, remembered Bette going backstage in 1970 at Broadway's Palace Theatre to congratulate Lauren Bacall, who played Margo Channing. 'She told Betty [Bacall], and you know how Bette Davis emphasized her words, 'You're the *only* one who could have played the part.' And Betty believed it, because Bette Davis always told it like it was. The truth.'

★ ★ ★

Bette had an extremely sore throat when she reported for work and an extremely husky voice, so she was in a state of panic. She was terrified for the picture.

Mankiewicz showed at least a calm exterior. He reassured his star, telling Bette that her husky voice could be incorporated into Margo's character, if she felt she could keep that lower voice until filming was completed.

Indeed, Bette's voice did get better, and she

had to be conscious of keeping it lower than usual.

Mankiewicz, a student of Shakespeare, said that there were elements in *All About Eve* of *The Taming of the Shrew*, 'in fact, of the taming of the *shrews*.'

A number of people suggested that he had put himself into Addison DeWitt's character, and into the critic's acerbic dialogue, and said that they could tell 'I had put my heart into writing for him.' Mankiewicz admitted that he did enjoy writing for DeWitt, but really no more than for the other characters. The DeWitt character was partly modeled on George Jean Nathan, a famous Broadway critic noted for his caustic wit.

Margo Channing was Mankiewicz's favorite character for writing dialogue, and he believed he had put more of himself into her character than into any other. He really didn't see himself as DeWitt, or as Lloyd Richards, the playwright, but 'there was some of me in Bill Sampson.'

Bette said, 'I gave a lot of thought to the character of Margo. I knew she was a fabulous character, and I wanted to give her my very best. Of course, I pride myself on always giving my best, but Margo was a treat, and I wanted really to understand her. I decided that she was suffering from an inability to love or be loved, a very serious condition.'

All About Eve (1950)
As actress Eve Harrington (Anne Baxter) receives the annual Sarah Siddons Award for distinguished achievement in the theater, her rise to

fame is seen in flashbacks.

A year earlier, legendary Broadway actress Margo Channing (Bette Davis) is so touched by Eve's sincere devotion as an innocent young fan that she employs her as an assistant. It soon becomes apparent that Eve's innocence is a pretense, as she insidiously takes charge of Margo's life. When the actress notices Eve's interest in Bill Sampson (Gary Merrill), Margo's director and lover, she arranges to have the young woman given a job in the producer's office.

Margo is late for a reading with an aspiring young actress (Marilyn Monroe), and Eve reads in her place. Bill and playwright Lloyd Richards (Hugh Marlowe) are impressed by Eve, and they choose her as Margo's understudy. Margo finds out and turns her wrath on Bill and Lloyd. Lloyd's wife, Karen (Celeste Holm), who first befriended Eve, decides to teach Margo a lesson.

Karen delays Margo so that she misses a performance, and Eve goes on in her place. Influencial critic Addison DeWitt (George Sanders) writes a rave review, with allusions to Eve's 'refreshing and appropriate youthfulness.'

Eve tries to seduce Bill, but he rejects her. She turns to Lloyd, persuading him that she would be a more suitable lead for his next play than the middle-aged Margo. Addison, well aware of Eve's scheming, is intrigued by her.

Eve gets the lead in Lloyd's new play when Margo declines the role because she and Bill are to be married, and Margo no longer wishes to play ingénues.

Eve confides to Addison that she plans to marry Lloyd after he divorces Karen. Addison tells her that she belongs to him. He then informs her that if she doesn't obey him, he will expose her sordid past and her lies. Eve must accept Addison's demands, or have her career destroyed.

The flashback ends with Eve receiving the Sarah Siddons Award and thanking her 'friends,' Karen, Margo, Bill, and Lloyd, while Addison looks on, amused.

In Eve's apartment, a young, worshipful fan waits, as Eve once waited. Phoebe (Barbara Bates) appeals to Eve, who allows her to stay a while and perhaps for the night.

As she puts things away for Eve, Phoebe models Eve's elegant cape in front of a three-way mirror, with its multiple reflections, imagining that *she* is the one accepting the Sarah Siddons Award . . .

'I played three roles on the screen that Tallulah Bankhead had created on the stage,' Bette told me, 'and then in *All About Eve*, my character was said to have been inspired by her. I'd never met her.

'One evening at a party, I saw her stalking menacingly across the room, right toward me. She was definitely not sober and she was obviously looking for a quarrel. She said, '*Dah*-ling — you've managed to play my best parts, but not as well as *I* did.'

'I wasn't in the mood to oblige her with an offstage confrontation. so I simply responded, 'Miss Bankhead — I agree with you *absolutely*.'

That took the wind out of her sails, and she didn't have anywhere to go with it, so she just retired from the scene.'

The Stork Club was a fashionable nightclub in New York City when *All About Eve* was made. Mankiewicz knew what the restaurant looked like, but since an important scene is played in the ladies' room, he wanted that to be authentic, too. His friend Robby Lantz remembered how Mankiewicz scouted the ladies' room.

'Joe, my wife, and I went to the Stork Club one night because Joe wanted Sherlee, my wife, to go to the ladies' room and give him a full report of what she saw in there. That was her mission. So, Sherlee was a spy to get all the information that Joe needed to re-create that ladies' room in *All About Eve*.'

★ ★ ★

'I know some of the people who worked with me said I was 'difficult.' Well, they were right, I suppose, from *their* point of view. If it was true of me sometimes, it was only because I always wanted the *world* for our film,' Bette would tell me.

'I have frequently been described as rude. Well, I don't think I'm rude. I certainly have never *wished* to be cruel. But I have never had time for affecting foolish manners. It always seemed more honest not to.'

Celeste Holm was to discover this side of Bette at their first meeting. I spoke with Celeste at Gracie Mansion, the New York City mayor's residence, at a film party being given by then-mayor Rudolph Giuliani.

'We were on location in San Francisco for *All About Eve*,' Holm told me, 'and I was thrilled to be working with Bette Davis. I'd never met her, so first chance I had, I went up to her and said, 'I'm so thrilled to be working with you, Miss Davis. I've always admired your work so much.'

'Without smiling, she turned to me, took a long, long drag on her cigarette, exhaled, and then said as only Bette Davis could say it, 'Oh, shit. Manners.'

'Then she turned away. I was so crushed, I just backed away without saying anything. I didn't realize then that I'd just become a victim of the Oh, Shit Club.'

In the Hollywood of the late 1940s, it was a fad to listen to someone talk seriously about something, and then say 'Oh, shit' in a normal conversational tone without changing your expression. Celeste said she didn't learn about the Oh, Shit Club until much later.

'I guess there was something in life she wanted she didn't get. The word I would use for her is 'irascible.'

'I remember we were all sitting around. Most of making movies is sitting around. It can be very trying. Sometimes you say stupid things, just filling up the time.

'I said something about a man who made Pyrex teapots. He found out people were mixing martinis in the glass pots, and he was a teetotaler.

'Bette said, in the exaggerated way of diction

275

she had, 'I don't know *how* I existed without knowing *that*.'

'Well, that's the way she was. I felt pretty foolish in front of everyone.

'She seemed to feel she had a license to be rude. Well, maybe she did. I thought it was bad manners on her part.

'I never understand all the Bette Davis nuts. I think she was over-acclaimed, over-praised, over-indulged.

'Why does everyone always ask me about *All About Eve*? I preferred *Gentleman's Agreement*, and I got an Oscar for that.' She won the Oscar for best supporting actress in 1947, was nominated in 1949 for *Come to the Stable*, and nominated again in 1950, for *All About Eve*.

'I'm very proud of the parts I've played. I was Ado Annie in the original stage production of *Oklahoma!*, and I was nominated for an Oscar three times. Karen was just one of the parts I played.'

★   ★   ★

Joseph Mankiewicz ended his contract at Twentieth Century Fox, and decided to return to New York City. His older brother, Herman J. Mankiewicz, had brought him out to Hollywood in 1929, when Joe was twenty years old. Herman was a highly successful writer-producer, most remembered as the co-writer with Orson Welles of *Citizen Kane*.

Despite his own two decades of accomplishments as a director, writer, and producer, and the great respect accorded him in Hollywood, he had never felt at home in Hollywood. In truth, he told me, he had never felt comfortable living anywhere but New York City. He hadn't ever fully adjusted to the different lifestyle of southern California. 'I think the smog has a bad effect on creative thinking,' he said. In Hollywood, he had written or directed, among other films, *The Ghost and Mrs. Muir, A Letter to Three Wives, The Barefoot Contessa, Sleuth*, and *All About Eve*. Although he became a real presence in the film world there, all the while he maintained a negative approach to Los Angeles, which he himself characterized as 'a sour view, a kind of snobbishness.'

He had hoped it was going to be a great new beginning for him, the start of a wonderful time, his new life in New York City. He was certain that living in New York would fill him with adrenaline, and he believed the Broadway theater would be the scene of his most significant accomplishments.

He packed all his possessions, sending them on their journey from one coast to the other in two moving vans. One of the vans carried the Mankiewicz household furnishings — furniture, rugs, dishes, pots and pans, the usual household goods — all replaceable rather than treasured possessions.

The other van contained what Mankiewicz called 'my life.' It was all the personal and professional memorabilia and paraphernalia of his lifetime up to that time. There were the family pictures, the letters he had exchanged with Herman and other members of his family, and his address books filled with the guarded private telephone numbers of the Hollywood elite. There were also scripts of the films he had written, his diaries, and his rare book collection.

There were, even more important, all of the contemplated writing projects for the future, more ideas than he could ever develop, the jottings of bits of dialogue that he had heard in conversation, or in his mind.

During the cross-country journey, one of the vans was involved in an accident and caught fire. All of its contents were destroyed. When Mankiewicz received the horrifying phone call, he prayed that it was the van with its contents of no great consequence to him. Far from it. The van with the priceless possessions, irreplaceable documents and souvenirs, was the one that had burned. Not a single photograph or scrap of paper survived. It was a tragic loss, all the more tragic, because emotionally Mankiewicz was never able to escape his sense of loss.

'Until then, I had considered myself a lucky person, and I had approached life in an optimistic, even gambling way, without weighing things. Afterwards, I was tormented by the 'What if's?' and 'Why me's?' My life became measured for me in 'before the fire' and 'after the fire.'

'The question that stuck in my mind was, 'Why wasn't it the other truck?' Why wasn't it the truck with the things that didn't matter, instead of the one with everything I cared about?

'Why hadn't we sent the things one day later? Or one day earlier?

'I've never been a total believer in destiny. I've always been more likely to blame myself. I punished myself for being punished.

'Throwing precious time after precious possessions . . .'

The real pain came over the years whenever Mankiewicz looked for something familiar that he needed or wanted. It began as a reflex, and finished, almost always, in despair, a renewal of the pain, which did not fade with the years. 'In fact,' he told me, 'it seemed that the pain, the sense of loss, the sinking feeling, did not grow less, but more. I suppose it became a kind of obsession.'

Mankiewicz had dreamed about working in the theater in New York, but he never directed for the Broadway stage, nor did he write a play that was produced on Broadway.

* * *

In *All About Eve*, professional happiness and personal happiness once again coincided for Bette, with Mankiewicz in her professional life and Gary Merrill in her professional and personal life. It was reminiscent of the time when William Wyler was the man in her life as well as, she felt, the director of her best work.

'Movies make for strange bedfellows. I'm referring to my relations on- and offscreen with Gary Merrill.

'I'd made up my mind that I would not marry again. It was an easy statement to make. I had reached a point where there was no line around the block to my front door.

'Joe Mankiewicz played such an important part in my professional life, and personal life, too. I told Joe, 'You resurrected me from the dead.'

'Gary was Joe's choice for the part of Bill Sampson. Joe insisted, and Joe was right. Gary was perfect — in the part, forever, and in my life, at least for a while. As I said once to Joe, 'You never told me about the sequel!'

'Gary and I lived out the sequel, which didn't have Joe to direct it, and it was more of a bittersweet soap opera with a poor ending.

'I was very sexually satisfied during the shooting of *All About Eve*. Gary was a wonderful lover. By then, I'd had enough experience to know the difference. He was tender, considerate — and athletic.

'We had the honeymoon before the marriage. I thought that our marriage would be the frosting on the cake. It would only make what we had better. Well, I was wrong. Instead, it was the crumbs.

'I had the horrible feeling of desperation that accompanies the thrill of finding someone you want, and then wondering how to make it all permanent. I didn't know how to do that. I didn't know that it's impossible. That you can't own anyone. Legally, yes; their feelings, no.'

'The first time I met Gary was when we were both doing makeup tests. It was important that Margo look older than Bill. I did, naturally. That wasn't any problem. I was older. I *looked* older. But it was important not to have it look like too *much* age difference.

'There is nothing more terrifying for an actress than having to play opposite your romantic leading man who is younger than you are.'

He was particularly impressed when he first met her. She had come during the weekend for makeup tests. 'I had been asked to do that,' Merrill noted, 'but she didn't have to.'

When I spoke with Gary Merrill, he described Bette as 'perfectly cast, a true star, just right for playing Margo Channing.'

In July 1950, Gary Merrill and Bette Davis were married, or as Bette said, 'Bill Sampson married Margo Channing. The marriage *endured* ten years.

'Gary's was the marriage that *should* have worked. Like Ham and Farney, Gary was a New Englander. I always had a weakness for those.

'Gary Merrill and I fell in love during *All About Eve*. We married for love. Margo was in love with Bill. Bill was in love with Margo. And you know *they* will always be in love.

'The names on the marriage license should have been Margo Channing and Bill Sampson. It might have worked out if we'd both stayed in character. The only problem was we fell in love with each other's characters in the picture, and then — the picture ended. But we didn't understand that, so we had to go on playing the leads in an overlong real-life soap opera. Wrong script, bad casting.

'During our first *All About Eve* rehearsal, I took a cigarette out, and naturally, I waited for him to light it. I kept waiting. Finally I asked him if he planned to light my cigarette. Looking me squarely in the eye, he said, 'No. I don't think Bill Sampson would light Margo Channing's cigarette.'

'I looked at him for a moment, then said, 'Of course he wouldn't, Mr. Merrill. You're quite right.'

'At the time, I wondered if it was Gary Merrill talking to Bette Davis, establishing his territory, like a lion with a lioness. I think he wanted me to know that in *All About Eve* he wasn't going to be Paul Henreid. Much later, in real life, he wasn't going to be Mr. Davis. A lot of the wonderful attraction I felt for Gary began there.

'I was pleased because apparently Bette Davis had been crushing to male egos. I appreciated the independence and strength of Mr. Merrill.

'So often, an actor and an actress acting out a love affair in a movie carry their roles into real life. I know. I've seen it, and it happened to me. *More* than once, although for me, it was just as likely, *more* likely, that it was with my director I would be smitten. Our passion would endure as long as the making of the film. Then, it was a 'wrap,' both for the film and the passion.

'In spite of the fact I'd vowed I'd never marry an actor, I eloped with Gary to Mexico, less than a month after I'd divorced Sherry. People said I acted impetuously. I agree absolutely! That's the most wonderful thing in life — to be carried away. To turn off thinking, not to weigh and be practical, just to feel. It wasn't very often in my life that feeling ruled my head. Those were precious times for me. Usually, I paid a high price for those moments — such a high price that looking back in the short term, I regretted the times I acted on impulse. I understand now that those are the moments I would most like to relive. And those were the moments the Ruth Elizabeth side of me was most hopeful. She was the side of me that was most impulsive and most vulnerable.

'A question I'm often asked is, 'Do you still pay Gary Merrill alimony?' The answer is *no!* And I never *did!* That was one husband back — Sherry, although it wasn't called alimony. The only thing Gary and Sherry had in common, besides me, were names that rhymed.

'Gary was an imperfect husband, and Sherry was absolutely perfect — a perfect shit! He cost me a pretty penny, but it was worth every cent — for a few minutes', or rather a few seconds', performance. It was he who gave me my daughter.

'I think sex is spoiled when the man is dependent on the woman as the family breadwinner. It just isn't the right relationship, going back to our days in the caves. What if the woman had been the one to go out and hunt the animals for food and skins? Maybe what I've really wanted is a caveman, dragging me by my hair to his lair. But my hair was always too short and too thin for that. Sherry came the closest to my image of that caveman, but he dragged me into *my* lair.'

Not long after the divorce of Sherry and Bette, the young nursemaid for B.D., Marion Richards, became the second Mrs. William Grant Sherry. She was twenty-two.

★ ★ ★

'Our movie characters fell in love,' Gary Merrill told me. 'Bette became the character in the film, but the character didn't necessarily become her.

'At home, she liked to play the part of a homebody. It was one of her many parts. And whatever she did, she threw herself into it, head-first. If it was a bucket of soap suds for the kitchen floor, her attention to getting that floor clean was obsessive and compulsive. Getting everything clean seemed to mean something special to her, more than just getting it clean in the normal way.

'We married late, and we brought too much baggage with us. We didn't have the perfect marriage. She wasn't the perfect wife. I surely wasn't the perfect husband. But no doubt about it, we had some good times together.'

John Springer remembered a weekend he spent at Bette's home in Maine. She cooked dinner for him. They listened to music, read. There was no sign of Gary Merrill.

'Then, at about two A.M.,' Springer said, 'I was awakened by shouting and screaming, and what sounded like glass and bottles breaking. I heard Bette's and Gary's voices. The quarrel grew louder and sounded increasingly violent. It went on for a few hours. Then, it stopped.'

Springer went back to sleep. 'The next morning,' he continued, 'there was no sign of

Merrill. Bette cooked a lovely breakfast, and we went out shopping for lobsters. On our return, she cooked the lobsters. She seemed in good spirits, nothing at all wrong.

'And she never mentioned the arrival and departure of Gary Merrill.'

★ ★ ★

'When I was making *All About Eve*,' Bette told me, 'I wished I could have looked better, younger. I saw the film recently, and I thought how lovely I looked, and not old at all. Time.

'There comes a time in a famous and successful woman's life when there's no point in having false modesty about fame and success, and when she no longer can trust a man's protestations of desire purely for her. Too old.

'Even if you look young for your age, and I didn't — every one of my years showed — one of the disadvantages is everyone knows your age. Everyone. Television shows wish you a 'Happy Birthday!' Well, I can tell you it would be a far happier birthday if they didn't feel they had to *wish* me one and, incidentally, if they didn't have to mention specifically exactly *how many* birthdays I had already had. I had enjoyed playing an old woman, but when I was a young woman.

'There is always talk about remaking *All About Eve*. I think it would be discourteous to remake *Eve* while I am alive. I believe I own that part while I am living, not legally, but morally. Margo was not *me*. But *I* was Margo. But after I'm gone, I'd like to look down, or up, and see

285

Meryl Streep playing Margo.'

Meryl Streep is an actress Bette held in great esteem. Bette frequently mentioned her as someone who could have played some of the Bette Davis roles.

At an American Film Institute event in New York City, Meryl Streep told me that she treasured a note Bette Davis had sent to her saying, 'I am very proud of you.'

'It was amazing,' Streep said. 'She wrote as though we were closely related. I always hoped we would work in a film together, but it never happened that way. But what I feel is that we have been working together. She was that great an influence on me.'

★ ★ ★

'I am the greatest admirer of Mr. Mankiewicz as a writer,' Bette told me. 'Utterly brilliant. No doubt.

'In conversation, the same was *not* true. He was disappointing, to say the least, ponderous I thought. The problem was, I suppose, he was talking as a person rather than as a writer. He wasn't writing dialogue for himself.

'As a director, I was not as impressed by his style as I expected to be. But then I saw the film.

'I could not have been *more* impressed. He was a genius and he saved me. He gave me a new life.'

He also gave Bette what is generally considered to be her most famous line: 'Fasten your seatbelts, it's going to be a bumpy night.'

8

Mid-Career Crisis

Douglas Fairbanks, Jr., who had been Bette's co-star in *Parachute Jumper* two decades earlier, was her producer for *Another Man's Poison*. I asked him how she had changed between the two films.

He said I would have to ask the young Douglas Fairbanks, Jr., about *Parachute Jumper*, and the middle-aged man he was then about *Another Man's Poison*, because he had probably changed more than she had. For him, her outstanding characteristic both times was her confidence. She was only attractive to him as a movie star, 'definitely not as a woman.'

'When she was in London to make *Another Man's Poison*,' he said, 'she insisted as part of her agreement on having top-quality steak provided every day. This was not easy because England was still suffering some of the leftover wartime deprivation, and no one was enjoying the quality or quantity of fine meat Bette demanded.

'Because fine beef wasn't plentiful, we had to have it flown over. We really didn't mind the expense, but it wasn't very good for morale on the set, especially when she and Gary Merrill ate their steaks in front of the others. It was bad enough just to smell them cooking. Some of the technicians had been through so much during World War II — the battlefield, the Blitz . . .

'Some years later, I asked her about it. She was astounded. She said she hadn't known. The war was over. It had been over for a long time, and in America it was different.

'Bette was actually very patriotic. She'd helped establish the Hollywood Canteen and then been active there entertaining the servicemen. She said she admired the British so much for the way they had endured, survived, and fought on to victory in World War II, and that she was fully aware of what they had gone through. She said she would never have eaten meat if she had known about the shortages. She asked me why I hadn't told her.

'I'd just assumed she knew.'

Another Man's Poison (1952)

Mystery writer Janet Frobisher (Bette Davis) lives on an isolated estate on the Yorkshire moors. She has fallen in love with Larry (Anthony Steel), a young man engaged to her secretary (Barbara Murray). He is infatuated with her, but the unexpected arrival of her husband (Reginald Beckwith), an escaped convict, threatens their romance. Her husband and an accomplice have robbed a bank and are fleeing the police.

When her husband demands that Janet hide him, threatening to tell Larry the truth if she doesn't, she kills him. Then, his accomplice,

George Bates (Gary Merrill), appears. Janet admits that she has killed her husband, and Bates helps her dispose of the body in a nearby lake in return for her allowing him to hide from the police in her home.

Bates's unexplained presence inhibits her romance with Larry and arouses the suspicion of Dr. Henderson (Emlyn Williams), a visiting veterinarian who is treating her beloved horse, Fury. When Bates kills Fury, Janet tries to kill him in an apparent car accident by the lake where they dumped her husband's body.

Bates survives a crash into the lake, but the police drag the waters for his vehicle, and Janet, fearing her husband's body will be found, poisons Bates's brandy. Janet intends telling Dr. Henderson that she killed her husband when he threatened her life. Before she can explain all of this to Dr. Henderson, he tells her that he has informed the police that he suspected Bates was holding her prisoner.

Shocked, she faints, and the doctor attempts to revive her with the brandy he doesn't know is poisoned. Awakening, she understands what has happened, and she dies laughing.

Irving Rapper, who directed *Another Man's Poison*, continued to be impressed by Bette's concentration and flexibility.

'One of the interesting things about her was that she could be involved in the most emotional, high-intensity, hysterically passionate scene, and when I said 'Cut,' she turned off her character immediately. She could do the same when she began a scene. She didn't have to get into the mood and find her character. She was always prepared. She never had to go into the dressing room for twenty minutes, or to sit in the trailer, to find her character. She found her character at home and brought her with her.'

★   ★   ★

When Bette and Merrill returned to the United States, she was asked to accept a rather small part in *Phone Call from a Stranger*. It was to be produced by Nunnally Johnson for Twentieth Century Fox, and Jean Negulesco would be directing. 'The frosting on the cake was Gary,' Bette told me.

'The film would star Gary, but my part was very nice, and it meant we would be working together. *Another Man's Poison* had been a disappointing experience in terms of the finished film, but personally it was wonderful because it offered us the chance to be together.

'I, of all people, could understand that Gary cared about his career and that sometimes our careers would keep us apart, take us in different directions, but I preferred not to think about it for the moment, rather just to be able to luxuriate in our togetherness. Those were the moments I would most like to relive. And those were the moments when the Ruth Elizabeth side of me was exceedingly hopeful.'

Phone Call from a Stranger (1952)
During a cross-country flight, David Trask (Gary

Merrill) meets three people who are making life-changing journeys to Los Angeles.

Binky Gay (Shelley Winters) is abandoning her ambition for a Broadway career and returning to her husband, Mike (Craig Stevens), in spite of a meddlesome mother-in-law (Evelyn Varden).

Dr. Fortness (Michael Rennie) is going back to accept responsibility for a car accident in which three people were killed. He hopes by doing so he will regain the respect of his son, Jerry (Ted Donaldson).

Eddie Hoke (Keenan Wynn), an overbearing traveling salesman, is returning to a wife whom he describes as a bathing beauty.

Trask himself has left his unfaithful wife and plans to start a new life in California.

Hoke suggests that the four get together for a drink in Los Angeles, but the plane crashes, and only Trask survives.

In Los Angeles, Trask contacts the people who were waiting for his three acquaintances, and he tries to complete the intentions of each.

When he visits Hoke's wife, he finds not a bathing beauty, but a bedridden invalid (Bette Davis). Marie Hoke tells him how her husband forgave her when she ran off with another man (Warren Stevens), who left her after she was paralyzed in a swimming accident. Mrs. Hoke pleads with Trask to forgive *his* wife, too.

Trask calls his wife to tell her he is returning to her and their children, making Mrs. Hoke very happy, and Trask and his wife are happy to be reuniting.

'I just described Gary as a lion,' Bette continued, 'but he was really more of a tomcat. Male cats like to go away for weeks at a time, you know, and then they return tired, hungry, and bedraggled, with no explanation whatsoever for their absence. I admit that at the time I thought it might be other women, but I think now it may have been other bottles.

'He'd come back all bedraggled from a binge, having disappeared for a couple of weeks and scaring the life out of me. I would think each time, if only he comes back, I'll be so glad to see him, I won't say a cross word. I made my plan. I'd just overlook it, like with a big male cat, if you've ever had one of those. I'd show him his food and water, and his bed, and leave him alone to sleep it off. Then, I'd be all brightness and cheer, and not rebuke him, and he'd love me. Then Gary arrived, the rat! How dare he to do that to me?

'I'd scream at him. And he'd scream louder at me. I'd out-scream him. I realized later, too late, that the only way to love Gary was exactly the way he was. If I'd understood that, we wouldn't have had to endure our ongoing battle. Other men had tried to change me, but Gary accepted me as I was. I was the one who wanted to do the changing. I succeeded all too well, but the problem was I couldn't change what I considered his faults. All that changed was what I'd loved about him.

'We quarreled about the unexplained separations which led to separations readily explained. I thought these separations were a cause of our divorce. Probably, to the contrary, they stretched *out* our marriage. Though we had so much in common, we were not suited to being constant companions. It's a good thing *All About Eve* ended where it did. Gary and I went on to bore everyone, especially ourselves, with our incompatibility. Left on our own, Bill and Margo reverted to Gary and Bette. Pity.

'Gary was one of twins, but his sister died at birth. Someone once told me it might have been some feeling of guilt that he survived, and she didn't, that later led to his drinking problem. I myself have never liked the easy answers of amateur psychiatrists.

'In his defense, however, I must say that he was usually away in the pursuit of his own career, which improved noticeably after he married me. I don't begrudge him that, and I don't believe he ever begrudged me my being Bette Davis. I wanted to be known as Mrs. Merrill. Remember that marvelous line from *Eve*, about Margo wanting to be 'a downright, upright, four-squared married lady'? Well, that described *me*, too.

'Gary's absences became longer, and so did our arguments. We both loved to take on responsibilities. And once taken on, we never shirked a responsibility. The little girl we adopted, Margot, was one such responsibility.

'When Gary asked me to marry him, I told him doctors had advised me not to have any more children. The abortions and a cesarean birth had taken its toll. I was forty-two, he was thirty-five. He said it didn't matter at all, and we could adopt a family. Since I already had a daughter, we agreed that our next child would be a boy. But while Gary was on location in the Caribbean, I was offered the most beautiful baby girl, who had just been born. I couldn't resist, although Gary very much wanted a son.

'When Gary got back, he was as taken with her as I was. Well, perhaps he wasn't really. He had wanted a boy, a son. We had definitely agreed on that. Then, I had gone ahead on my own, as if we weren't two, but only me. Perhaps Gary, who was a very good actor, was an even better actor than I knew.

'He suggested we call her Margo, after Margo Channing. Of course. How perfect. But we spelled it with a final t so people wouldn't notice we'd named her after my role in Eve. It seemed the right thing to do. After all, she *was* the child of Margo Channing and Bill Sampson — the product of their love affair in *All About Eve*. The t in her name was silent.

'Margot was a lovely baby, but our joy was short-lived. First, we noticed she cried a lot. B.D. had been such a good-natured, happy baby, no trouble at all. Margot wouldn't just cry — she'd scream! She sounded terribly wounded, desperately hurt. It was a terrified and terrifying sound. We couldn't discover the cause of her pain. We were certain if we just gave her more love, she'd get over it. The nights were very hard. We couldn't seem to comfort her. Many of our arguments, Gary's and mine, grew out of the strain over Margot. In my heart, I knew the problem was my fault for having acted so precipitously on my own, without consulting with Gary; but I never spoke the words to Gary, that I knew I had been unfair to him, and was sorry about that. I must say that never once did he ever say one word to me about the problems with Margot being my fault, or of my doing.

'I had adopted a severely retarded child. I tried to hide from it. I refused to believe what they said. I was certain that love could make the difference, *would* make the difference. I was wrong. Margot showed us that all our love could not overcome her handicap, and we did not know that she was going to be a danger to B.D. and the boy we adopted, Michael.

'I must say for Gary that he felt just the way I did and fully assumed the responsibility for something I had gone out and done on my own. Of course, he had to sign the papers, but I was the one who wanted this beautiful little girl, only a few days old, a little sister for B.D., when I had promised Gary we would adopt a boy.'

*   *   *

The Star is the story of a fallen star who sees herself as a falling star.

Rumor had it that the story was based on Joan Crawford. 'There certainly were elements of Miss Crawford,' Bette admitted, 'but I played a character who was not *just* Joan Crawford. If for one minute I'd have thought the character *was* Miss Crawford, I would *never* have accepted the role, because I couldn't have done *in*justice to her character. Any role I played drew upon everyone I had ever known who fit, and on something of me, but there was something else which even I could not define. That was the difference between me and the Method people. I guess that 'something else' you could call 'inspiration.' I thought *The Star* was a better picture than it was given credit for being.' It was a *flop d'estime*.

The Star (1952)

Margaret Elliot (Bette Davis), a fading Hollywood star, runs into Harry Stone (Warner Anderson), her agent, as she passes an auction house. Inside, her possessions are being auctioned off to pay creditors. Stone is carrying the purchase he has just made at the auction, explaining that someone would have bought it, and his wife always liked it. She tries to persuade him to find her another role, one that will revive her sinking career.

Facing eviction from her modest apartment, she tries unsuccessfully to borrow money from those she has helped in the past. Only her young daughter, Gretchen (Natalie Wood), now living with her father and his new family, continues to believe her mother is a star.

Despondent, Margaret takes out her Oscar and decides to get drunk. She succeeds.

After a wild, drunken ride with her Oscar, she is arrested and put into jail. The next day, she is bailed out by one of her former leading men, Jim Johannson (Sterling Hayden), who left acting and owns a marina. Of all the people she has helped, only he remembers her in her time of need. He encourages her to find another career outside Hollywood, but she doesn't last long as a lingerie saleslady in a department store when she is recognized by two unpleasant female customers.

Margaret is offered a role in a film, but she fails the screen test because she cannot accept that she is no longer the star of the picture, and no longer 'young and dewy.'

At a party, she is offered the part of an older actress who, in her climb to stardom, forgets she is also a woman. She recognizes the parallel to her own life and goes back to Jim, taking Gretchen with her.

'My heart broke for her,' Bette said, talking about the character of Margaret. 'Of course, many of her mistakes were of her own doing. But we all make mistakes. Some of us have to pay more for them and some of us hardly at all. That's the luck factor. She got caught up in wrong priorities and self-obsession.'

Bette was particularly fond of the fourteen-year-old Natalie Wood and thought the young actress showed brilliant talent, 'something shining through.' She predicted a great future for Natalie.

'I loved having Natalie Wood as my daughter in the film. What a wonderful girl! And she was already a fine actress, very professional, talented, a special person. She was a lovely, lovely child. How I would love to have had her *really* as my daughter.

'I was very happy to have been able to help her. I don't mean with her acting. She didn't really need that kind of help.'

Natalie Wood related the incident at the 1977 American Film Institute lifetime achievement tribute to Bette Davis:

'I'd been acting for some time, and pretty much going from one picture to the other, playing somebody's child, and pretty much doing what I was told. But when I was told that in the next picture, the leading lady was going to be Bette Davis, I was absolutely thrilled to get the chance to work with her. The picture was called *The Star*, and somehow, I never got introduced to the star, although I was playing her daughter.

'So, the first day, we were filming on Sterling Hayden's sailboat, and all of a sudden it turned out that I had to jump off the boat and swim to a faraway raft. So, there I was, faced with the threat of being flung into the ocean or losing the part, and I went into hysterics. It must have been heard all the way to Catalina. In any case, Miss Davis certainly heard them.

'She came out of her dressing room to find out what all the commotion was. This was the only time I ever saw the famous Bette Davis temperament, and it was not on her own behalf. But she did tell the director that she wouldn't stand around while he threw some terrified kid into the ocean, and if he'd wanted a swimmer, he should have gotten Johnny Weissmuller.

'I never saw her again for quite a few years. And then, at a party, I spotted her across the room, and I wanted to go over to her and remind her of the incident, and thank her. Then I thought, 'Oh, well. It was a long time ago, and I had a small part, and she probably won't remember.' So, I didn't.

'A little while later, somebody tapped me on the shoulder, and I turned around, and it was Bette, and she said, 'I'm sure you don't remember me, but we worked together once.''

The script was changed so that Gretchen just has to lean precariously over the side of the boat. Jim then says of her, 'She's a good sailor.'

This scene became especially poignant when the grown-up Natalie Wood, many years later, lost her life by drowning. Natalie's future husband, Robert Wagner, was to become one of Bette's best friends after she appeared in his television series, *It Takes a Thief*, and in *Madame Sin*, a 1972 TV film produced by him.

★　★　★

After *The Star*, Bette returned to Broadway for the first time in twenty-two years in a musical revue called *Two's Company*, with words by Peter DeVries and Ogden Nash, music by Vernon Duke, and directed by Jules Dassin, with the musical numbers directed by Jerome Robbins.

Robbins was a legendary director of Broadway musicals, a great choreographer. Among his Broadway shows were *On the Town, Call Me Madam*, and later, *West Side Story*. Bette was overjoyed when John Murray Anderson, her school mentor, was brought in to restage the revue during out-of-town tryouts. 'He did it just for me, and then we hardly ever saw each other. I was ill from Detroit to Broadway, and I was mortified when, in tryouts, I collapsed onstage after several days of strenuous rehearsals and no sleep. But I got right up, apologized to the audience, and went on.'

Robbins told me, 'Miss Davis — she asked me to call her Bette, but I always thought of her as Miss Davis — did not have the talent or training, but she had the personality, charisma, and the loving support of her fans, and that carried the show.

'She asked me to give her strong direction, but I was careful. I didn't want to direct her to do what her bones and larynx couldn't do. She needed my reassurance, but she was too savvy to be impressed by my simply telling her in some trite ways that she was doing well. She wouldn't put up with 'That was good' or 'You did that very well.' She looked to the expression on my face and my body language.

'The show had to be built around what she was able to do, not what *we* wished she could do, because the audiences were coming to see *her*. That was the reason they were buying all of those tickets. Devoted fans they were.

'I, personally, was surprised that she had agreed to do the show. I heard that her husband had encouraged her to do it, but I don't know about that.

'It was clear that the confidence she personified was like mine, not deep-felt. I identified with her. I understood perfectly how she felt, because I felt the same way, even though

I didn't come to know her well; but I felt instinctively that she knew you have to appear to believe in yourself totally, so the others don't have doubts.'

When I spoke with Robbins about Bette Davis at the Venice Carnival in the mid-1980s, he was wearing a golden lion's head with an extremely large mane, and he had a tail. It was a bit distracting for me, but not for him. My own costume was a simple long dress and a mask on a stick.

Two's Company played until March 1953, ninety performances, and appeared to be headed for a long run when Bette complained of a toothache and weakness. An examination revealed that she had osteomyelitis of the jaw. After an emergency operation, she faced a long period of recuperation. She did not work again until 1955, when she returned to Elizabethan times.

★   ★   ★

Richard Todd told me that when he was approached to play the part of Sir Walter Raleigh, the title of the film was going to be *Sir Walter Raleigh*. 'When Bette agreed to be Queen Elizabeth, the film took on a whole new aspect. She was a great star. The title changed. Her role was built up at the expense of mine, but, as I remember the way I felt then, I don't think I was upset. You know, we're in the twenty-first century now, so one's emotions at a particular moment aren't that easy to summon up.

'This wasn't my dream part, I must admit. If it happened to a film of mine I remember with pride, such as *The Hasty Heart* or to *Stage Fright*, which came at an important moment in my career and which allowed me to know Hitchcock, I might have been more upset. As it was, I thought it an honor to work with Bette, and I was a bit nervous in her presence. She had a rather imperious quality, wonderfully appropriate to her queenliness. When we weren't filming, she seemed to have that same imperious quality, but it was, I think, only her way of being guarded. She had a position to maintain, and I think her defense was that bit of guardedness.

'Once, when I 'went up' on my lines and forgot something, which I almost never did and which I personally took as terrible, to let everyone down, she came up to me while we were waiting to retake the scene, and whispered into my ear, 'I'm on your side.' It's a cherished memory of mine. She also said to me once, 'It's easy for me to imagine my character being in love with yours.' Imagine that?'

At the time of filming, Joan Collins wondered why Bette seemed not to like her. At first, she thought she could be mistaken, but others on the set assured her it was apparent to all. 'Why?' she asked.

'It's obvious,' was the response. 'It's the way you look. You're more beautiful than she is.'

Bette had to wear a bald wig, which made her appear almost hairless except for a few wisps of gray hair. She had white makeup, and wrinkles had been added.

Collins was young and beautiful, perfectly made up to enhance her natural beauty, 'to be the *most* beautiful I could be,' she said. 'So it was foolish to say *I* looked better than *she* did.' Collins played Lady Bess, one of the six handmaidens who attended Queen Elizabeth, and the one who was in love with Sir Walter Raleigh.

Collins said she had been warned a great deal about what to do and what not to do in Miss Davis's presence. One admonition was repeated by anyone who knew anything about Bette Davis: Do not chew gum.

Her part as a lady-in-waiting called for her to put shoes on Queen Elizabeth, but, as she remembered it, Bette made it hard for her and criticized the young actress. Finally, Collins got the shoes on.

Thirty years later, it happened that for the *Night of 100 Stars* Joan Collins shared a dressing room with, among others, Bette Davis.

Sometime later, I was with Bette Davis and John Springer at lunch. As we spoke about the *Night of 100 Stars*, Springer mentioned Joan Collins's feeling that Bette had not liked her when they were making *The Virgin Queen*.

'How absurd,' Bette said. 'The poor girl was confused. Of course I didn't like her character. She wanted to take Sir Walter away from me, and as Elizabeth the Queen, I resented that. It was essential that an air of hostility exist between us.

'She was in her costume and her makeup, and I was in mine. If we'd been chummy on the set,

303

some of that softness might have seeped through.'

The Virgin Queen (1955)

Walter Raleigh (Richard Todd) attracts the favorable attention of Queen Elizabeth (Bette Davis) when he gallantly doffs his expensive cape and throws it across a puddle in her path. In spite of the great difference in their ages, she falls in love with the younger man and appoints him captain of the guard against the advice of Chadwick (Jay Robinson), one of her most trusted counselors, who is an enemy of Raleigh.

Raleigh hopes that Elizabeth will commission three ships for him to sail to the Americas in search of treasures for England, but she will consider only one ship.

Finally, she consents to his voyage and knights him on the eve of his departure for the New World. Then, she learns Raleigh has secretly married one of her attendants (Joan Collins). He is imprisoned in the Tower of London and sentenced to death.

Weighing her wounded affections against the wealth Raleigh may bring back to her, she relents. Raleigh is allowed to set sail for America with his new wife.

Perc Westmore repeated Bette's makeup from *The Private Life of Elizabeth and Essex*, moving her hairline back by shaving off two inches of hair and what was left of her eyebrows. 'This time, woefully, my hair didn't all grow back,' she said. 'They did it because

Queen Elizabeth was losing her hair, and they made sure I did, too.'

★ ★ ★

'As my daughter Margot grew older,' Bette told me, 'she couldn't seem to deal with any frustration, and she craved constant praise. She was a strong child, very hostile, and she could be violent. Her alternating temper tantrums and curious lethargy demanded constant attention.

'Shortly after we adopted her, we had the opportunity to adopt a wonderful baby boy. Gary would have the son he wanted. We were both thrilled, and we named our baby Michael. B.D. loved the new baby, but Margot seemed to resent, even hate him. We were afraid to leave her alone with him.

'It was the day Margot attacked Michael with a piece of broken glass, and we saw him standing there, so little and helpless, bleeding, that we knew. We had to face that there was something terribly wrong, something we couldn't under-stand, something we couldn't fix.

'The doctors told us Margot had been brain-damaged at birth. Everything the rest of us take for granted was always going to be a tremendous effort for her — learning to brush her teeth, buttoning her dress, everything.

'There were people who told us we could return her. Can you imagine! Like damaged merchandise. Like a carton of eggs you got at the grocery, and some are cracked. Unthinkable. Both Gary and I felt she was ours. She was the child we chose. Anyway, she was the child *I* chose.

'They told us Margot, no matter how tall she grew, would always be seven or eight years old mentally. The really terrible thing was, that made her bright enough to fully comprehend what she was missing.

'She would want to have a job. She would want to get married, to have babies. She would want what all little girls of seven or eight want — to grow up one day and live the life of a woman. But Margot would never enjoy a fulfilled life. She would have only her dolly, but unluckily, unhappily for her, she would be fully able to understand that a doll is only a doll. Margot's dreams would remain only that — dreams.

'We desperately wanted to keep Margot, but the doctors warned us we would never be able to take proper care of her. We had to find a different answer. We also had the safety and welfare of our other children to consider. We knew we had to protect B.D. and Michael. So, with heavy hearts, we found a comfortable, loving home for her that we could afford and that would provide what she needed. It was sad, but the home for special children seemed to make Margot happier than we did.'

The school they found for her was the Lochland School for Retarded Children in Geneva, New York. Margot was four.

'On the day she left, she looked like a little doll, dressed in her sailor suit and hat. She has been happy at the home, and that, after all, is what life is all about. Over the years, she's spent holidays with us, and has made a better adjustment to life than some 'normal' people I've known.

'Margot placed a great strain on our marriage, but her condition was also a bond between Gary and me, though we didn't realize it at the time. When Margot was gone, the bond was gone. One thing Gary and I could always do, even through the tears, we could always laugh together. We knew our marriage was over when we stopped laughing together.

'Sometimes, I have to admit that my love for practical jokes did get out of hand. Knowing Gary hated nothing more than a birthday party, especially his own, I arranged a surprise one for him on his fortieth birthday. I hired a couple of extras dressed as pastry chefs to carry in an enormous birthday cake. I'd had the prop department make me a cardboard cake with 'Fuck you' written across the top. Gary's reaction was to get very drunk, but not as drunk as the time he ended up taking a shower in the ladies' dressing room of our country club. Fortunately, there weren't any 'ladies' around or I might not have gotten him back.'

* * *

Storm Center was shot before *The Catered Affair* though it was released afterward. The original screenplay, called 'This Time Tomorrow' and then 'The Library,' had been written several years earlier by Elick Moll and Daniel Taradash, and was inspired by an Eisenhower speech that warned against book-burning. Because of the film's controversial theme, and censorship during the Cold War, Columbia was hesitant about joining with Taradash's independent unit, Phoenix. When the picture was finally released, audience and critical reaction was indifferent. Bette thought the film missed its point because of wrong casting.

'The relationship between the boy who burns down the library and my part, the librarian, didn't work because there wasn't any emotional rapport between us, which was absolutely essential. The child who played the part [Kevin Coughlin] was too cool and detached to give this impression.'

Exteriors were shot in Santa Rosa, California, where Alfred Hitchcock had filmed *Shadow of a Doubt* in 1942. 'Would you believe that there were people there who thought we were communist sympathizers?' Bette said.

Storm Center (1956)

Alicia Hull (Bette Davis), a widowed librarian, defies a Kenport City Council order by returning a pro-communist book to circulation after having agreed to ban it. She contends that the availability of such a book reaffirms the ideals of American freedom, but is dismissed. Efforts to reinstate her uncover her membership in suspect organizations. Her claim that she agreed with the principles of these groups only in certain respects is not accepted.

Freddie Slater (Kevin Coughlin), a sensitive child who is devoted to Mrs. Hull and the library, becomes so traumatized that he sets fire to the building. The burning of the library restores equilibrium to the community. Alicia is reinstated. She sets out to rebuild the library, upholding American liberty, specifically freedom of speech.

Mary Pickford and Irene Dunne were originally tested for the Alicia Hull role by Stanley Kramer in 1952. He had bought first option on the script and briefly considered making the film.

★   ★   ★

'You would not *believe* the trouble I had convincing the studio that Ma Hurley shouldn't dress like a movie star!' Bette told me. 'I give full credit to Sam Zimbalist and Richard Brooks for standing up for me when I refused to ruin Paddy Chayefsky's wonderful play with a glamorous wardrobe. I *insisted* on buying my clothes where Agnes Hurley would have bought them — off the rack at Macy's!'

The Catered Affair (1956)

Jane Hurley (Debbie Reynolds) casually informs her parents that she and her fiancé, Ralph Halloran (Rod Taylor), will be married sooner than they had planned. They want to combine their honeymoon with an opportunity to drive a car from New York to Los Angeles, and then go to Mexico for their honeymoon. They did not want a big wedding. Her parents accept the news impassively. Their own marriage has been dull and disappointing.

Then, her mother, Agnes (Bette Davis), suddenly in competition with her more affluent future in-laws, decides Jane deserves a better wedding than the one she herself had, and she plans a catered reception at a hotel, which will cost $2,000. This is all the money her cab driver husband, Tom (Ernest Borgnine), has saved over a lifetime toward buying his own taxicab.

Agnes is uncharacteristically extravagant in planning her daughter's wedding, and the cost of the catered reception soars. Then, the hotel becomes temporarily unavailable, and the wedding has to be postponed for two months. Becoming impatient, Ralph asks Jane to elope, but she refuses, and they argue, almost calling off the wedding.

The catered reception has to be canceled, causing Agnes and Tom to argue, too, but their arguments are as unemotional as their marriage. She accuses him of being a poor provider for his family, then feels badly when he doesn't respond. Agnes has never felt that Tom loved her, but now she realizes that in his way he does.

The young couple make up, and on the day of a small wedding, Agnes surprises Tom by spending the $2,000 on the taxicab he wanted. They are driven to the church in his own new taxicab. It seems that their future together may be the happiest part of their lives.

'When they made *The Catered Affair* at M-G-M Studios,' Debbie Reynolds told me, 'they cast me in the part of the daughter. Bette was a great help to me, because Richard Brooks was not really happy with my being cast in that part. He wanted somebody from New York, someone that was more from the theater rather than a Hollywood personality. He didn't really like the idea of having little Miss Cute, me, Debbie Reynolds.

'I know that, because he said it all to me. He said that he was stuck with me, and that he'd do the best he could with me. He hoped that I could come through all right for him, because everybody else was so great, but he wasn't certain I could keep up with the others. He actually said that he was stuck with me. And he said so in front of everybody, too.

'He *was* cruel. So Miss Davis took me into her dressing room, and she said, in her voice, you know how she spoke, 'Don't pay any attention to him, the son of a bitch, remember this: The only important thing is to work with the greats.' She said, 'I will help you all the way. Pay him no attention. Don't worry about him, only work with the greats.' Those words meant everything to me. She said, 'We'll all be great together.'

'She worked with me on every scene. So did Ernie Borgnine, and they couldn't have been sweeter. Barry Fitzgerald [who played her grandfather] treated me like his little granddaughter. I was only twenty-one and had not had a lot of experience, but everybody was so nice to me. Bette, especially.

'We became friends after that, and continued on after the movie. When I married Eddie

Fisher, she came over and visited the place we had rented. It was called All Hollows Farm. It was a farm out in Pacific Palisades, and she used to bring the children over, and we'd walk around and just talk. At the time, she was married to Gary Merrill, and they were having some problems. In a way, he really was like a third child to her. She was trying make it work, and she always tried very hard at everything she did.

'You know, she made unfortunate choices in men, and I know what *that* means.

'At that time, I had just been married to Eddie, and she came over for dinner a couple of times. Then, I went east, and I drove out to her house in Connecticut. When I walked in the door, she said, 'How's my *daugh*-ter?'

'I've always done her in my nightclub act, I always do her in my show. I loved doing her. She's wonderful to impersonate. Such fun. She was distinctive. Unique. She came to see my act. She thought it was very funny.

'But she said, 'You've got to do me bigger. I'm not big enough. Throw your arms a bit more.' She took what I did as a compliment, which it was.

'If she didn't want to talk to you on the phone, she'd pretend to be somebody else. Imagine! with that voice. 'Miss Davis is not here. Who's calling? Just a minute.' And she'd go away, and she'd come back and say, 'Hello, Debbie dear. I wasn't sure I was here.'

'We weren't able to stay close, because I traveled so much, and I had my two children and my three stepchildren. I was very angry when the daughter wrote the book. I wrote her a letter. I was very upset about it. I didn't hear back from her, but I had to do it because I just wanted her to know . . .

'Bette really took good care of her children. She certainly wasn't mean to them. She didn't deserve to have that happen.

'I thought it really led to her becoming even more ill. That was so cruel.

'I saw her just toward the end of her life. We did a benefit on the same evening for hairdressers awards, and we were able to chat for about three hours.

'She'd had had a stroke, but she was still puffing her cigarettes and ordering me around, you know. I had to do three introductions, and I had a choice of four dresses. 'Ah, the pink one. I like the pink,' she said. I had thought I'd wear the blue. She said, 'Oh, no. Don't wear the blue. I like the pink.'

'So, of course, I wore the pink. I always minded my mother, and Bette had played my mother. She was a good actress and a very kind woman, and just as bright and sharp as could be. Too sharp, I guess, for a lot of the producers. Age was not kind to her at the very end. After her stroke, I think she felt very badly about how she looked, and because of that, she stayed home a lot more than she would have. And it limited her ability to act, which she so wanted to do. The way she looked limited her parts.

'She deserved anything and everything. She was one of the truly great actresses of all time. She and Hepburn, I think they were the greatest.

She was a funny lady, too, you know. She was *very* opinionated. She had her opinions, and if you didn't go along with them, you got a really big argument, but the argument was so much fun, you didn't really mind. I think she received a very hard ending, with what her daughter did.

'Of course, the sickness was one thing, but she took what her daughter did even bigger and harder and worse, I think, than the sickness. She had cared so much. It was unfair and — really cruel. She was very sensitive to people. Her feelings were easily hurt. Everybody thought she was so tough, but she wasn't really. Especially when it came to those she loved.

'She was very dear to me.'

* * *

In October of 1957, Bette and Gary officially separated. She claimed that he had been physically abusive when he was drinking, and he didn't deny it. His contention was that Bette was enough to drive anyone to drink. 'She was the total actress,' he told me. 'Every day was a new performance.' Bette always denied that she could not separate her professional life from her private life.

Bette said, 'We separated by mutual disagreement.'

* * *

Bette was supposed to return to the stage in 1957, playing in Ketti Frings's adaptation of the

314

Thomas Wolfe novel *Look Homeward, Angel*, when she broke her back in a fall. She was looking at a rental house in Los Angeles and opened a door that she thought was a closet. Instead, it was a stairway to the basement, and she fell down fourteen steps. She said she remembered every one of them. When the play opened on Broadway without Bette, it won a Pulitzer Prize.

After a long recuperation, she took what work she could get on TV and radio, including an *Alfred Hitchcock Presents* directed by Paul Henreid and photographed by Ernest Haller called 'Out There — Darkness.' She starred in a striking episode of *Suspicion* based on a Daphne du Maurier short story, 'Fraction of a Second.' A woman is involved in an accident. Apparently uninjured, she goes about her daily routine but finds everything is different. No one recognizes her, and her daughter is no longer a child. Only at the end does it become clear that she is dead and that in her last moment of life she has seen what will happen without her in the years following her death.

'I'm grateful to television,' Bette said. 'I didn't get residuals, but it kept my career alive.

'Besides, as one grows older, there are certain advantages to be being seen in close-up on the small screen. The smaller the better.'

★   ★   ★

For producer Samuel Bronston's *John Paul Jones*, Bette traveled to Europe by ship with

B.D. and Bette's sister, Bobby, taking them for a holiday that she said they both loved. B.D. was eleven, and it was long before her book-writing days. Bette enjoyed ocean voyages, and she was pleased to be playing Catherine the Great of Russia, even if only for a cameo appearance. It was a part she had always wanted to play, and she told me she thought it would have been a part she would like to have played in real life. 'All those *men!* But,' she added, 'I wouldn't have cared for the plumbing in those days.

'I didn't really get along with the director, John Farrow, but years later, I adored his beautiful, talented daughter.' In *Death on the Nile*, Bette appeared with Mia Farrow, the daughter of Farrow and Maureen O'Sullivan.

John Paul Jones (1959)
John Paul Jones (Robert Stack) is denied his plea for a large American navy, so he accepts an invitation from the Empress Catherine (Bette Davis) to command the Russian navy in the Black Sea. He changes his mind, however, when it becomes evident that Catherine's interest in him is not just professional.

Bette's scenes, some of which were shot in the Royal Palace in Versailles, took only four days of shooting.

★ ★ ★

'They say that separations are hard on a marriage, the conflict of two careers that have to be pursued in different places, so you are often apart. Well, that was the best part of my marriages. Peace. It's what made the marriages last as long as they did. I think my standards were too high. My dream of a marriage always was two equals, two people who respect each other. The man would respect my opinion as much as I respected his. Well, many years ago that was even less possible. It's more difficult for a woman to be accepted for her intelligence than to be forgiven for it.

'My arguments with Gary could get physical. Once, he pushed me into a snowbank in Maine. In all fairness, it was after I'd slapped him. It was rather fun in the snowbank. And he did help me out of it.

'When we finally separated for good, there wasn't much china left for us to fight over.'

★ ★ ★

Bette's next film, *The Scapegoat*, was with Alec Guinness, an international star who had won an Oscar for *The Bridge on the River Kwai*.

Guinness told me, 'I was thrilled to be working with Bette Davis. When I heard that we were to be co-stars, I thought to myself, though I didn't say it to the people who were paying me, I would work with her without being paid.

'Well, apparently, she wasn't as happy to be working with me. I don't think she liked me at all.

'I always think it's better if a genuinely friendly friendship is established. For me, it would have

317

been an honor. I invited her to dinner more than once. She ignored that I had spoken. She didn't answer. The first time I didn't know what her failure to respond meant. I wondered if she heard me. I thought she might be shy as a private person. I certainly was.

'The second time, I assumed she had no interest in having any personal relationship with me. I didn't know any other way to explain it to myself.

'The film didn't turn out to be as successful as I hoped it would be, and I can't say that after making it I knew Bette Davis the person. But I did have the experience of working with the actress. So, I *did* know the professional person, But I *can* say that she knew what she was doing.'

Bette said, 'Even when you have only a small part, if you care, you're working so hard, you just don't have time to be friends and socialize, even if you'd like to. But my part was much better than what ended up on the screen after the producers finished with it.'

The *Scapegoat* (1959)

John Barratt (Alec Guinness), a British tourist who is a professor of French, traveling in Le Mans, France, inexplicably meets his exact double, Jacques de Gue (Alec Guinness), who is a French nobleman. Barrett gets drunk and is drugged. He awakens alone next morning in de Gue's hotel room. Despite his protests, he is assumed to be de Gue. Barratt is persuaded to go to the de Gue estate, where he meets a dysfunctional family.

De Gue's eccentric mother, the Countess (Bette Davis), is a bedridden morphine addict. His unhappy wife, Françoise (Irene Worth), is the wealthy member of the family, which has been left with all the accoutrements of wealth but without the money. De Gue's sister, Blanche (Pamela Brown), dislikes him. His teenage daughter, Marie-Noël (Annabel Bartlett), will do anything to attract his attention. His mistress, Bella (Nicole Maurey), is uncertain how he feels about her.

Barratt decides to undo de Gue's thoughtlessness and selfishness. He blocks the sale of his family's money-losing glassworks in order to protect the workers' jobs, and then agrees to give them more money. He promises his wife he will remove a clause in their marriage agreement that puts her in the position of being more valuable to him dead than alive. It makes him a rich man if she dies, and she is frightened. Barratt spends time with the daughter and treats the mistress more lovingly, confirming her intuition that, despite the way he looks, he is not de Gue.

Françoise is killed in a fall from a window of the estate. Blanche believes that de Gue pushed Françoise, but he has a perfect alibi. Barratt now understands that the real de Gue has returned to commit the perfect murder and replace him, one way or another.

Barratt and de Gue meet at the glassworks. Both men have pistols. De Gue is a great shot and Barratt, who has never fired a gun, is also handicapped by his injured right hand. Barratt

319

knocks over the lamp, and shots are fired in the darkness.

Only one of the two men emerges from the factory. He goes to meet Bella. The bandaged right hand of the survivor reveals that he is Barratt, as does his manner and his reception by Bella, who loves Barratt.

Although Bette co-starred with Alec Guinness in *The Scapegoat*, she spends much less time on screen. The film, based on a Daphne du Maurier story, was produced by Michael Balcon, adapted by Gore Vidal and Robert Hamer, and directed by Hamer.

★ ★ ★

'Around 1960, I sat out a whole solid year without one job offer. Not one. Gary was busy working and gone so much, and we weren't getting along all that well anyway, so I finally shut up our house in Maine and moved to Los Angeles with the children. Still no offers. That was one of the low points in my career. I truly thought it was all over.'

Bette returned to the theater in *The World of Carl Sandburg*, a two-person show co-starring Gary and assembled from the writings of Sandburg by Norman Corwin, who was also the director. She saw the seventy-two-city tour as an opportunity to be together with her husband in the world they shared, acting.

Merrill particularly loved the theater and the live audience, a feeling Bette could understand, because, as a girl, she had felt the same way. She told me that she thought 'there was nothing in the world more divine than theater, until I discovered films.'

Sandburg was pleased with the project, and his words meant a great deal to Bette, because she 'totally' admired him. The tour opened at Bowdoin College in Maine, followed by a series of successful one-night stands throughout the country during 1959 and 1960.

Bette quarreled with Merrill shortly before they were to open in a four-week run at the Henry Miller Theatre on Broadway. Merrill was dismissed. Leif Erickson had to substitute for him. It was more than the show, or the marriage, could survive.

'I was totally wrong,' Bette admitted to me. 'I have regretted ever since that Gary didn't open with me in New York. He deserved to open on Broadway. I've regretted that I didn't try harder to do everything I could to make our marriage work. Our marriage and Gary truly deserved that. This is an enormous truth. It was the biggest mistake I ever made because Gary was a fine person and I had no right to expect perfection from him when I didn't give him perfection in return. My last chance.

'In the play, he was wonderful. Offstage, he wasn't perfect, but he was my best husband, by far.

'The show was a reading, and while I didn't like that aspect of it at the beginning, I came to like it very much as we performed it, except that not having to learn lines gave us more time to argue. The New York audience didn't care for it — in advance. They didn't turn up in any great numbers to dislike it. Perhaps Gary could have saved it.'

Bette sued for divorce in July 1960. There was a custody battle over Michael, who wanted to be with his father. Eventually, he did go to live with him.

During this period, Bette worked on a book with writer Sandford Dody. The book, called *The Lonely Life*, would be published in 1962.

Bette said, 'I began my career as a dispensable ingénue, then became an indispensable ingénue, went on to be an indispensable heroine, and I lasted to be a dispensed-with bag lady.'

Pocketful of Miracles, in which Bette appeared in 1961, was based on a great success of 1933, *Lady for a Day*, directed by Frank Capra and starring May Robson as Apple Annie, who sells apples on the streets of New York during the years of Prohibition. Annie is not a beggar, not a bag lady. She is employed, if not gainfully. Based on the Damon Runyon story 'Madame la Gimp,' the 1933 screenplay was written by Robert Riskin, who was married to Fay Wray, star of Erich von Stroheim's *The Wedding March* and Merian Cooper's *King Kong*.

In 1961, Capra agreed to remake the film because, he said, he thought he could do it better.

The script of the remake was written by Hal Kanter and Harry Tugend. Glenn Ford became a co-producer with Capra. It was Ann-Margret's film debut, and Hope Lange, said to be Ford's romantic lead in life, was his romantic lead in the film.

Bette assumed that the best actress dressing room would be hers. It was, briefly. It happened to be next door to Ford. Then, Bette was told there had been a mistake and that she had been given the wrong dressing room. She was moved to a slightly smaller one because, she believed, 'Mr. Ford preferred to be close to Miss Lange.'

Bette later heard that Glenn Ford had given an interview in which he said that he had wanted Bette for the part because he felt sorry for her. He was quoted as saying he was glad to have been able to help her out.

'How dare he?' Bette said. 'I never spoke to him again.'

She didn't say whether they ever met again, or if he even knew she wasn't speaking to him.

Bette believed that she had many times been misquoted in her celebrity life, but it never occurred to her that others might have been, too. When she saw anything in print, she tended to believe it.

Pocketful of Miracles (1961)

New York crime syndicate boss Dave the Dude (Glenn Ford) is about to merge with his Chicago counterpart (Sheldon Leonard), but can't complete the deal until he finds Apple Annie (Bette Davis). She is a street peddler who sells him his lucky apple each day. He locates her on skid row, drunk and contemplating suicide.

Her daughter, Louise (Ann-Margret), is returning to New York from a Spanish convent, where she has been reared with no knowledge of her mother's real life. Louise is coming with her fiancé (Peter Mann) and his father (Arthur O'Connell), a Spanish nobleman, to introduce them to her mother, whom she believes is a wealthy social figure. Annie has been supporting her daughter all these years from the sale of her apples, and she doesn't want her daughter shamed by her.

Dave, impressed by Annie's courage, decides to set her up as a grand lady for her daughter's visit. A Park Avenue apartment is rented and Annie is transformed by beauticians and given an elegant new wardrobe. An alcoholic but dignified ex-judge, George Manville (Thomas Mitchell), is brought in to pose as her second husband, and her guests are recruited from the underworld.

The ruse works until the Chicago mob shows up at the reception. Annie is about to admit everything to her daughter when the mayor (Jerome Cowan) and governor (David Brian) appear with their wives, and a debacle is turned into a triumph.

Louise, her fiancé, and his father return to Spain convinced Annie is a socialite. Dave is so impressed that he and his girlfriend, Queenie Martin (Hope Lange), consider getting married and going straight. Annie plans to return to selling apples on the street, where she intends to organize the beggars, and Blake Manville, swearing off alcohol, proposes to her.

'Bette Davis had a lot to give, and she gave it,' Peter Falk told me. 'I was a beginner, and she was an artist and a professional, but she accepted me and made me feel comfortable and relaxed, so I could do my best. I was overconfident and underconfident, a very poor combination for someone with as small a part as mine. She not only helped to start my career, but she helped me not to end it.'

★ ★ ★

On July 1, 1961, while Bette was finishing *Pocketful of Miracles*, Ruthie died at the age of seventy-five after a three-month illness. 'When my mother died, images of grief, joy, gratitude, recrimination, and guilt all flashed through my mind at the same time,' Bette told me, 'and they have continued to haunt me in the years since. The strongest is that of Ruthie's tired, proud smile when I graduated from Cushing Academy.

'So I could complete my senior year, Ruthie took all the photographs of the graduating class for the yearbook. That meant doing all the work herself — taking the pictures, developing the negatives, and making the prints, working through the night to the point of collapse.

'I vividly recall Mother crouching over negative after negative, hour after hour, day after day, doing her retouching work. She would come home every night exhausted, her eyes strained, her back aching, but always cheerful, always hopeful. It's an image of her gallantry that will stay with me forever.

'In those days, photography was not only hard work, it was dangerous work. The chemicals used in developing were toxic. As long as I live, I'll never forget the sight of my mother sitting in the auditorium as I stepped up to receive my diploma. I couldn't help noticing how thin she was. She only weighed about ninety pounds — and the developer poisoning was very apparent on her face. She was wearing an old hat and last year's dress, and a tired but proud smile on her face. It was plain she was totally exhausted, but there wasn't a prouder mother in that auditorium. I felt like crying, then and now.

'This was my greatest incentive to become a success. As I looked down at her, I thought I must repay her for all those years of blood, sweat, and no tears. I am eternally grateful that I was able to do this, but I could not give her back her youth. She'd given that to me and my sister, years before. For her, the word 'sacrifice' was routine, and the word 'can't' not in her vocabulary. When I looked down and saw my poor tired mother there with the results of the developer poison on her face in her pitiful best dress, looking so proud and happy, I swore to myself, one day, she will never work again.

'Many years later, when Ruthie died, I felt a rush of guilt. Even after Bobby and I were grown women, she had continued to be our mother, and we her little girls. Eventually, I cut the umbilical cord, but not until I was thirty-six. Bobby never did. Bobby suffered nervous breakdown after nervous breakdown, not only because she could never be Bette Davis, but because of Mother's overbearing influence.

'But we didn't have to confide in her. We

didn't have to listen to her, then follow her advice as if we were still children. If she made mistakes in counseling us, they were mistakes of love that we asked for.

'And Ruthie's extravagance! When my success in Hollywood was assured, she went on a spending spree that lasted for the rest of her life. Even longer. Among the papers I found in her desk were instructions for her funeral, ending with the words, 'I intend to die as I have lived. I want my casket to be one of those silver things.'

'Suddenly it seemed Ruthie had to make up for everything she'd missed. The extent of her deprivation had been even greater than anything we understood. It turned out she loved luxury. When people have been very poor, and then get a lot of money, either they can't enjoy spending at all because it's unnatural or they're afraid of being poor again, or they want to spend and spend unreasonably to prove to themselves they really are rich. At first I didn't understand. How could I ever have felt an ambivalence about her spending? Hadn't she more than earned it? How could any amount of money compensate for the sacrifice of her youth or repay her?

'Ruthie always had a plan in life, and dying was one of her most carefully laid out and deliberate. 'I'm tired, darling, so tired of the fight,' she had told me just before her bursting heart gave out. There was nothing wishy-washy about Ruthie. Even her defects were monumental. She could be brutally honest, yet self-deceptive about the most trivial thing. She was the wisest person I ever knew, while at the same time, the most childlike. She was both self-indulgent and endlessly sacrificing, arbitrary yet reasonable, sophisticated yet naïve. There never was anyone like Ruthie.

'How dared I ever expect perfection in such a magnificent creature as you, Ruthie! Why did I fail to tell her that I understood what she had done for me, how much I loved her? When she went to sleep that night for an eternity, Bobby and I wanted to hide in the bathroom as we had done as little girls when grief overcame us. We were orphans. Her joy and vitality were gone forever. No longer could she protect us, no longer could we depend on her . . .

'Ruthie! Oh, my God, how I miss her! I owe her everything.'

Bette, realizing how emotional she had become, stopped, asking me to excuse her for a few minutes.

9

Most Wanted to 'Help Wanted'

Shortly after Ruthie's death, Tennessee Williams asked Bette to play the part of Maxine Faulk in *The Night of the Iguana*. 'It wasn't the lead,' Bette said, 'but it was the best part.' Margaret Leighton and Patrick O'Neal were her co-stars.

Bette felt they didn't like her. This usually meant she didn't like *them*, but which came first could not be ascertained.

'Mutual liking of each other by my actors is not essential to a play,' Williams told me. 'If mutual respect and mutual love were the answer, we could have a lot of doves cooing. Sometimes discord is the best answer.'

Williams said he never regretted his original wish to have Davis cast, but he never celebrated it either. He appreciated her individuality, and while initially he had hoped they would come to know each other better, he later decided 'it was something I could live without. It becomes difficult to distinguish between artistic temperament, simple temperament, and simply temper,' he said. 'In order to get along with me, you have to be like my Frankie, and take a lot. I would guess that Bette's friends had to be prepared to take a lot.' Frank Merlo was Williams's longtime companion, who died about the time of *The Night of the Iguana*.

'My cowardice about the theater is astronomical,' Bette told me. One of her greatest professional disappointments was not getting to do *The Night of the Iguana* on the screen after she had created the part on Broadway. When the film was cast, the leads went to Richard Burton, Deborah Kerr, and Ava Gardner, who won the Davis stage role.

'Ava Gardner got the part, and I was never asked,' Bette said. 'At the time, I said publicly that Miss Ava Gardner was too young for the part, but I knew the truth. I was too old.'

One of the problems of the play was that when Bette made her appearance onstage, the audience applauded long and enthusiastically, breaking the mood, making it more than clear to the other actors and the playwright why they had bought their tickets and packed the theater.

Williams said, 'It filled the coffers, but it was a bit disruptive.' The only more disruptive occurrence during the performances was when Williams himself was in attendance, and he laughed a loud cackle, always at what, for the audience, was an inappropriate place. The audience might have been less annoyed if they had known that the cackling man who had slid way down in his chair was the play's author, Tennessee Williams.

Shelley Winters took over the Maxine Faulk

role from Bette on April 4, 1962, during the Broadway run.

★ ★ ★

Bette's next picture, *What Ever Happened to Baby Jane?*, not only revived her career after a decade of mostly forgettable films, but also changed its direction.

According to director Robert Aldrich, Bette hadn't liked his choice of Victor Buono, whom he had seen in an episode of the popular television series *The Untouchables*.

'Bette came to me and said that Mr. Buono was too big and fat and too revolting to appeal even to her Jane character. I held my ground, and she accepted my decision. She was always polite to Buono, but not warm, and though I think he sensed the way she felt, he never said anything about it to me. He was very young, and this represented a big career opportunity for him, so any displeasure on her part would have had to make him even more nervous.

'Bette was a real lady and not only a professional, but a very honorable person, a square-shooter. After her first scene or two with him, when we stopped shooting, she strode toward him in that way she had, and she said, in my presence, looking up at him, 'I confess that before we began, I did not care for Bob's choice of you, and I tried to persuade him not to use you. He was right, and I was wrong. I hope you will accept my apology, because you are absolutely marvelous.'

331

'Of course he was, but this recognition of his performance by Bette Davis made him very, very happy!'

'It was Miss Crawford who brought me *What Ever Happened to Baby Jane?*,' Bette said. 'She came backstage after a matinee of *Iguana* and told me about a book which had parts for both of us. Robert Aldrich had bought it and thought he could get backing if we agreed to be in it. He was in Italy, and he'd asked Miss Crawford to approach me.

'When Bob Aldrich and I met in New York, I only needed to know I was Baby Jane and that he was not 'involved' with Miss Crawford. I didn't want him favoring her with more close-ups.'

His laughter answered her second question. His assurance that he couldn't imagine anyone else being Jane sufficed. Then came the struggle for financing. 'They didn't want to put their money on two old bags,' Bette said. Finally Seven Arts furnished enough backing to allow the film to be made.

'Miss Crawford and I each gave up part of our salaries in return for a percentage of the profits in order to make the project possible. After *Baby Jane* opened, it made each of us rich, for a while.' The film opened on October 31, 1962, in New York and New Jersey, where it recouped its production costs in eleven days.

For *What Ever Happened to Baby Jane?* Bette did her own makeup. She didn't feel any makeup man would dare go as far as she would. 'It was important that the makeup show the desperation. Miss Crawford wanted to look as nice as she could. I wanted to look as terrible as *I* could. Miss Crawford was a glamourpuss. I was an actress.

'Ernest Haller had always been my favorite cameraman. I never told him what to do, but I put my trust in him to do what he knew how to do, to make me look my best. In this case, I put my trust in him to make me look my worst. He did. He was *very* successful.

'I did my best to look my worst,' Bette told me, 'but when I saw myself as Baby Jane, I went home and cried. I'd been so successful in making myself a horror, I frightened myself.

'The film did so well, that afterwards many people were surprised I didn't really look that way. Can you imagine?'

What Ever Happened to Baby Jane? (1962) The Hudson sisters, Jane (Bette Davis) and Blanche (Joan Crawford), once show business headliners, grow old together, but not compatibly, in a run-down Hollywood mansion. As a child, Jane was a vaudeville star and later a mediocre film actress, while Blanche was a Hollywood superstar. After an accident crippled Blanche, Jane, feeling responsible and not being able to support herself, devotes herself to taking care of her invalid sister. Jane, resenting her status as nurse and caretaker, evinces symptoms of insanity, serving Blanche a huge rat for dinner.

Learning that Blanche plans to sell the mansion and put her into a sanatorium, Jane tortures Blanche. All the while, Jane dreams of a show business comeback. She hires an unemployed pianist, Edwin Flagg (Victor Buono), to help prepare her act.

Their part-time cleaning lady, Elvira (Maidie Norman), notices a deterioration in Jane's already alarmingly eccentric behavior, and Jane fires her.

When Jane's treatment of Blanche becomes intolerable, Blanche tries to escape, but is stopped by her sister, who is going mad. A suspicious Elvira, returning to investigate, finds Blanche bound and gagged. In panic, Jane picks up a hammer and kills Elvira.

Edwin finds Blanche half-dead and rushes out of the house terrified. Fearing he will return with the police, Jane drives Blanche to Malibu. As she is dying, Blanche confesses that it is she who is responsible for the accident that left her crippled and that she has lied to Jane to hold her sister as a prisoner of her guilt, taking care of her.

Spectators watch, police arrive, and Jane happily imagines herself performing again, as she dances on the beach.

'The real challenge for me,' Bette said, 'was not only to *look* younger, but to *feel* younger. When I go to get ice cream, and dance on the beach, I had to find the little girl inside me.'

Bette loved to dance, always proud of having studied with Martha Graham, for whom she maintained a lifelong respect. She told me that she particularly loved Baby Jane's dance on the beach, 'which was created and performed according to everything I had learned from Miss Graham.

'I had to gain weight to dance around well. I couldn't do that with padding. It was easy to gain the weight. It wasn't so easy to lose it.

'While I have always stressed that I am *not* a Method actress,' Bette said, 'I could draw on my understanding of sibling rivalry from my relationship with my own sister. I felt my mother, Ruthie, my sister, Bobby, and I were Three Musketeers. It was only later that I understood that our common goal, my career, wasn't sufficient to satisfy Bobby.

'I really didn't think at the time how Bobby felt. She had her own needs and desires, and the problem was, there was nothing Bobby did better than I.'

For the clips from Jane's and Blanche's earlier Hollywood careers, actual films of Bette Davis and Joan Crawford from the period were used. For Bette, it was *Parachute Jumper* and *Ex-Lady*, both from 1933, and for Joan, *Sadie McKee*, from 1934.

'After *Baby Jane* opened,' Bette said 'I gave a cocktail party here [in New York] and had the chef at the Plaza Hotel make a paté in the shape of a giant rat. It was served on a huge platter.

Not knowing how successful *Baby Jane* was going to be and against the advice of everyone she knew (advising Bette *not* to do something was to encourage her to *do* it), Bette placed an ad in the September 21, 1962, *Variety*. She offered her services as an actress, stating that she was 'mobile still and more affable than rumor would have it.' She told Joe Franklin on his television show, 'I've gone from being 'most wanted' to 'help wanted.''

'I believed I would receive an Oscar for *Baby Jane*,' Bette told me. 'I was certain. I was disappointed.

'Anne Bancroft won for *The Miracle Worker*. Well, she was wonderful, but she'd played the part on stage, which is not the same test as playing a part for the first time. There should be two Oscars, the way they do with writers who win for doing original work and those who are adapting.'

When Bette and her daughter went to the 1963 Cannes Film Festival, Seven Arts provided a party escort for B.D. He was Jeremy Hyman, the twenty-nine-year-old British nephew of Seven Arts owner Elliott Hyman. 'It appeared to be love at first sight,' Bette said. She was unhappy because of the difference in their ages, especially because her daughter was only fifteen. 'He was almost twice her age.

'I had told my daughter about lust at first sight, and it was not to be confused with love at first sight. Marrying for sex is a bad reason.'

★   ★   ★

Dead Ringer was Ernest Haller's last Bette Davis film. He died shortly afterward. Their relationship had begun in 1932 with *The Rich Are Always with Us*, and included such Bette Davis classics as *Jezebel*, *Dark Victory*, *Mr. Skeffington*, and *What Ever Happened to Baby Jane?*

Because Bette plays identical twin sisters, as she did in *A Stolen Life*, Haller was called upon

336

to photograph scenes in which the two sisters appear together. He used a double, Connie Cezon, a Bette Davis imitator. After one take, another take of the same scene would be shot, with the two changing places, careful to duplicate each other's actions exactly. Everything on the set had to be fastened securely so that the two takes would match. Then, in the laboratory, the process was completed by splitting the screen imperceptibly so that the double would be replaced on both sides by a real Bette.

Paul Henreid, who became a director after he retired from acting and had directed Bette in *Alfred Hitchcock Presents*, was now her director again. His daughter, Monika, plays the suspicious maid. Giving her the part was Bette's idea.

Dead Ringer (1964)

Identical twin sisters Edith and Margaret Phillips (Bette Davis) do not like each other. Edith has never forgiven Margaret for marrying Frank, the man she loved. When Frank dies, leaving Margaret a fortune, she offers Edith financial help. Edith learns that Margaret lied about being pregnant in order to win Frank. She kills Margaret, disguising it as a suicide, and assumes her twin sister's identity.

Detective Sergeant Jim Hobbson (Karl Malden) is convinced that the dead woman is Edith, his fiancée. Margaret's lover, Tony Collins (Peter Lawford), guesses the truth and blackmails Edith, demanding her sister's jewelry. When he tries to pawn the jewels it is reported to Hobbson, who searches Margaret's apartment. Finding arsenic, he suspects that Frank was poisoned. An exhumation proves that Frank died of arsenic poisoning.

Edith, aware that Frank was murdered, confronts Tony, who tries to kill her. She is saved by Margaret's Great Dane, who kills Tony while defending her. She confesses to Hobbson that she is really Edith, but he doesn't believe her.

Edith, as Margaret, is found guilty of murdering Frank and sentenced to death. Before she is executed, she tells Hobbson that she really is Margaret, not the sister he loved.

Largely due to the success of *What Ever Happened to Baby Jane?*, *Dead Ringer* did well at the box office, but it did not lead to the kind of films for which Bette hoped. Her next film was *The Empty Canvas*, with Horst Buchholz and Catherine Spaak.

Horst Buchholz went to the Rome airport to meet Bette, who was arriving to star with him in *The Empty Canvas*. His wife, Myriam, suggested he bring Miss Davis some flowers. He went to a florist and selected a lovely bouquet. He was so excited, however, that he forgot to take the flowers, leaving them in his car.

As it turned out, Buchholz told me, he approached the star, who greeted him warmly. In European style, he embraced her, kissing the air next to her cheek. As he did so, her lips met his.

'I felt her tongue in my mouth,' Buchholz said, 'and I didn't know what to do with it.'

Buchholz said he never found out whether she was serious, or joking.

The *Empty Canvas* (1964)

Dino (Horst Buchholz) tries to forget that he has nothing to say as a painter by falling in love with Cecilia (Catherine Spaak), an amoral model. He begs her to marry him, but even his family's wealth doesn't impress or persuade her. She wants only to be his mistress until another lover comes along.

Tiring of Dino, Cecilia leaves, and he has a nervous breakdown. Nursed back to health by his loving mother (Bette Davis), he returns to painting, having learned that life need not be an empty canvas.

Just before Bette started work on her next film, *Where Love Has Gone*, B.D. and Jeremy Hyman announced their engagement. Reluctantly, Bette had given consent for her sixteen-year-old daughter to marry twenty-nine-year-old Jeremy Hyman. 'I agonized for a long time over giving my permission,' Bette said, 'but B.D. was a very mature sixteen and already knew exactly what she wanted to do with her life. One actress in the family was enough for her. And for me, too. Absolutely.' The marriage took place in Beverly Hills on January 4, 1964. After their honeymoon, B.D. and her husband moved to New York, where he was a Seven Arts executive.

The Harold Robbins novel *Where Love Has Gone* was adapted for the screen by John Michael Hayes, who had worked on Hitchcock's *Rear Window*, *To Catch a Thief*, and *The Man Who Knew Too Much*. Since leaving Hitchcock, he had specialized in Robbins-style novels, starting with Grace Metalious's *Peyton Place* in 1957.

Where Love Has Gone was inspired by a real event. In 1958, the teenage daughter of actress Lana Turner killed her mother's lover. A sensational trial followed.

Where Love Has Gone (1964)

World War II hero Luke Miller (Michael Conners) rejects an attractive offer by an outspoken wealthy dowager, Mrs. Gerald Hayden (Bette Davis). If he will marry her beautiful daughter, Valerie (Susan Hayward), after the war, she will appoint him to an executive post in her company with a large dowry for her daughter. Valerie is an impetuous sculptress whom a previous lover (DeForest Kelley) has publicly declared sexually insatiable. Luke is an architect who has postwar ambitions, which he prefers to achieve on his own. Valerie, however, is so impressed by Luke's independent attitude, she pursues him, and they marry before he returns to active duty.

Back from the war, Luke tries to get backing for his building projects, but fails because his mother-in-law secretly uses her influence with bankers to deny him loans. He finally accepts a vice presidency in Mrs. Hayden's company when Valerie becomes pregnant.

After the birth of their daughter, Danny (Joey Heatherton), Valerie's reputation as a sculptress rises while Luke sinks into alcoholism. Disillusioned with her ex-hero, Valerie turns to other men. Finding Valerie with a lover, Luke divorces her, and she is awarded custody of Danny.

As an adolescent, Danny becomes the focus of a sensational murder case. She is accused of killing Valerie's current lover when he attacked her mother. It is judged justifiable homicide, and Mrs. Hayden requests that she be appointed guardian of her granddaughter. Valerie counters this move by her hated mother, confessing that Danny was really trying to kill her. Then, she commits suicide.

Luke vows to start a new life in which he will be able to take care of Danny, shielding her from the malevolent control of her grandmother.

Where Love Has Gone paid for B.D.'s wedding reception expenses. Even though the marriage wasn't what Bette felt was right for her 'too-young' daughter, once she had consented, she went forward wholeheartedly, the only way she knew how to do anything, and well beyond what her income justified. Bette wanted to give her daughter a beautiful memory, and she was proud, feeling that she had been successful in that.

* * *

Robert Aldrich called *Hush ... Hush, Sweet Charlotte* a follow-up rather than a sequel. 'You couldn't exactly do a sequel to *Baby Jane*,' Aldrich said, 'so the idea was to use the same actresses who'd brought in big bucks in a similar story, same genre, but they got kind of carried away, the theory being if gore is good, more gore is better. Not true.

'Actually, nothing had happened on the set in *Baby Jane* between our stars, but there was a tension because everyone was always expecting it. I think that tension carried over into the picture, which benefited from it. The anticipated offscreen blowup never occurred because these were two professionals. If it had occurred, it would have been to the detriment of *Baby Jane*, but the winner in any knock-down drag-out would have been Bette because she was made that way, to thrive on conflict. Joan was much more vulnerable.'

Novelist Henry Farrell, who had written *What Ever Happened to Baby Jane?*, was encouraged by Robert Aldrich to write another Gothic vehicle for two older female stars. His response was a story set in the Tennessee Williams South that he called 'Whatever Happened to Cousin Charlotte?' Bette liked the script, but not its title, which she believed would make the picture seem like a sequel, and which might make people laugh inappropriately.

A number of actresses were considered as her co-star, but much to Bette's regret, the leading candidate remained Joan Crawford. Finally, Bette agreed to work with Joan again for more money and a different title. 'They had already composed a song for the film,' Bette said, 'and I liked it. It was sort of a lullaby that started off with, 'Hush, hush, sweet Charlotte,' and I suggested that might be a better title.'

Crawford accepted the role of Miriam opposite Bette's Charlotte, but on one condition: This time her name must come first in the titles.

Bette would agree to this only if she got more money, which she did. Her salary equaled that of Aldrich's for both producing and directing the picture.

Shooting began on location in Baton Rouge, Louisiana, on June 4. The distinguished cast included, besides Bette and Joan, Joseph Cotten, Agnes Moorehead, Mary Astor, and Victor Buono.

It was Bette's idea to cast her friend Mary Astor. 'She hadn't worked for a long time and was grateful for the part. Even though it was small, it was crucial. I couldn't believe how much older she looked. I don't think she ever worked again.'

From the very beginning, when no one met her at the Baton Rouge airport, Joan Crawford felt out of place. She believed that a star should look and act like a star at all times, so she tended to be aloof while Bette mingled freely with the cast and the crew. To go any distance on the location, she traveled by golf cart while Bette walked. In the evening, she would leave the set with her maid and chauffeur in a limousine while Bette left in a station wagon with her fellow cast members.

More seriously, Crawford was frequently ill, slowing down production or even forcing it to stop.

When the production unit returned to Los Angeles, she checked into a hospital. Finally, Robert Aldrich reluctantly had to replace her. 'I would have done anything I could to keep Joan,' Aldrich said. 'It would have helped her a great

343

deal at that point in her career. But my backers were nervous.

'Joan Crawford saw her part as playing second fiddle to Bette Davis, and whether that contributed to her not feeling well, I don't know. Bette was happy when we got Olivia [de Havilland] for the picture, and it meant we didn't have the tension on the set. Bette and Olivia were great friends.'

Olivia de Havilland was selected as the ideal replacement, but she had to be persuaded to play an unsympathetic part. Aldrich accomplished this by traveling to Switzerland and explaining to her the positive, as well as negative, aspects of the character of Miriam. His argument was very much like that of Hitchcock, who always held that a truly villainous character could never get close enough to his or her intended victim to do any harm if he or she *appeared* to be a villain.

When I talked with Olivia de Havilland, who had been living in Paris after her marriage to Pierre Galante, the editor of *Paris Match*, she spoke of Bette as 'a unique person and a good friend. She would always be there for you. Your secrets were safe with her, because she never gossiped. She said what she thought. Her energy could overwhelm you. It overwhelmed me.

'I always thought it would be fun if we could work together. Then, I was offered the chance to work with her on the film that became *Hush . . . Hush, Sweet Charlotte* when Joan Crawford withdrew. I knew Bette wanted badly to work, and *Jane* had been such a success that Bette was quite anxious. They had to find the replacement, and Bette wanted me.

'The problem was I wasn't as anxious to work as she was. I didn't need to. I wasn't thrilled with the script, and I definitely didn't like my part. I was reverse-typecast, being asked to be an unsympathetic villain. It wasn't what people expected of me. It wasn't really what I wanted to do.

'Bette wanted it so much, so I did it. I can't say I regretted it, because working with her was special, but I can't say it was a picture I am proud to put on my résumé. Given the choice, I wouldn't have deprived Joan Crawford of the honor!'

Hush . . . Hush, Sweet Charlotte (1964)
Fearing a sordid family secret will be uncovered when the Hollis mansion is torn down for a new highway, reclusive, neurotic Charlotte Hollis (Bette Davis) turns to her cousin, Miriam Deering (Olivia de Havilland), for help.

Miriam, however, is conspiring with Dr. Drew Bayliss (Joseph Cotten) to drive Charlotte insane in order to inherit the Hollis fortune. Not suspecting this, Charlotte discharges Velma (Agnes Moorehead) when the faithful house-keeper accuses Miriam of being a fortune hunter.

Velma's suspicions are taken seriously by insurance investigator Harry Willis (Cecil Kella-way), who has always wondered why Jewel Mayhew (Mary Astor) never collected for the insurance policy on her husband when he died. John Mayhew (Bruce Dern), Charlotte's married lover, had been murdered thirty-seven years earlier.

Miriam causes Charlotte to believe she has murdered Dr. Bayliss during one of her hallucinations, and then his bloody corpse seems to be pursuing her. Seeing Miriam and Dr. Bayliss alive together, she realizes what is happening, and kills them.

Jewel dies unexpectedly, confessing in a letter to Willis that she murdered and mutilated her unfaithful husband in a jealous rage, and afterward was blackmailed by Miriam.

As Charlotte is driven away, she smiles knowingly as the full reality of the events of her life at last becomes clear to her.

In 1965, Bette traveled to England to make *The Nanny* for Seven Arts — Hammer. Jimmy Sangster, the screenplay writer and producer, was an acknowledged master of the cinematic genre he described as 'Gothic horror.' He had been inspired to do this kind of film after he saw Alfred Hitchcock's *Psycho* and Henri-Georges Clouzot's *Diabolique* in one week. In London, he talked with me about how Bette Davis came to be the Nanny.

'I first met Bette in Los Angeles. It was for *The Nanny*, and originally Greer Garson was supposed to be in it. I went to Santa Fe and met with Greer, and she said she liked the script, and everything was fine. When I got back to London, we had a message from L.A. saying that Greer Garson didn't think the script would do her career much good. I didn't like to say she didn't have a career in those days. Then they, at Twentieth Century Fox, said, 'But would you like Bette Davis?' Well, of course, we *jumped* at the chance.

'She had director approval, so I went over to L.A. with the director, Seth Holt, and she met him, and she said, 'Fine.' I'll tell you something she said about him *after* the picture. She said, 'He's a mountain of evil, but he's a bloody good director.''

The experience was not a happy one for her. She contracted the flu and didn't always get along with Holt. In spite of this, Bette said afterward, 'I felt Seth Holt was one of the best English directors. He deserved to be better known.' Holt died at forty-eight, six years after he directed *The Nanny*.

The Nanny (1965)

Ten-year-old Joey Fane (William Dix) has spent the past two years in a school for disturbed children because he is believed to have drowned his little sister, Susy, in the bathtub. He has always maintained that the family's nanny (Bette Davis) killed Susy. Joey assiduously avoids Nanny.

Joey tells his Aunt Pen (Jill Bennett) that Nanny has just tried to drown him in the tub. Aunt Pen goes to investigate, and finds Nanny acting suspiciously. Pen has an attack, and calls out for her medication. As Pen gasps for breath, Nanny calmly relates how on the day Susy died, she received a call from a doctor about her own daughter, now grown, whom she had given up

347

for adoption as an infant. Nanny left Joey and Susy alone for a time to go to a London slum, where she had found her daughter dead after an abortion. In Nanny's absence, Susy had fallen into the tub of water and drowned. Eight-year-old Joey was blamed. Nanny rationalized that all of 'her children' needed her, so it was necessary for her to save herself for them.

Pen dies and Nanny knocks Joey unconscious. She carries him to the bathroom and puts him into the tub, but is unable go through with her intention to drown him.

Instead, she goes to her room and packs all her possessions, including framed photos of 'her children,' and puts them into her suitcase.

'Wasn't the little boy [William Dix] marvelous?' Bette exclaimed. 'He went on to Oxford and grew up to be a beautiful guy. Seth Holt directed him brilliantly with great sensitivity.'

Bette defended *The Nanny* against being termed a horror film, arguing that Shakespeare is often more gory. She hadn't considered *Baby Jane* a horror film, either.

Sangster thought Bette 'one of the most professional people I've ever worked with. Like all stars, she complained about things, but whatever she complained about was only about what she thought was right for the picture. She never complained about her trailer outside, or anything like that. If she thought something was wrong for the picture, she'd bitch about it, and sometimes she was right, and sometimes she was wrong. If she was wrong, you could talk her out of it. Everything was for the good of the movie.

'She was the most punctual person I've ever met. You know, on movie call sheets, they say so-and-so is wanted on the set at eight-thirty, and sometimes they're not needed till about ten, and they just hang around in their dressing rooms. If she was told she was wanted on the set at eight-thirty, she'd be there, sitting on the set, at eight-thirty.

'When she used to complain, she used to start everything with, 'I have starred in sixty-seven movies . . . ' And she *had* starred in sixty-seven movies, you know, so what can you say to somebody like that? She knows what she's talking about.'

10

Legend for Hire

'After I did *The Nanny*,' Jimmy Sangster told me, 'my wife at the time said, 'If you ever do another Bette Davis movie, I am leaving the country.' I said, 'Ha, ha, ha, ha, ha. I'm *never* going to do another Bette Davis movie.'

'Then, one day, the man who ran Hammer said to me there's a play on called *The Anniversary*, would I go and see it. So, I saw it, and he said, 'Would you like to do a script for it?' and I did, and he said, 'Well done. We're gonna get Bette Davis. Would you like to produce it?' I said, 'No way! No, no, no, no, no, no!' In the end, he made me an offer I *couldn't* refuse, and, this is absolutely true, the day that Bette arrived, my wife left the country.

'We had a house in France. It wasn't a big deal, but she went, and Bette was here about ten or twelve weeks. The day Bette left, my wife came home again. Bette's a very, very demanding lady. *Very* demanding.

'She was here on her own, and she wanted to go out. I remember once, we were at a club, Danny La Rue's Club, it was called. Danny La Rue was a gay entertainer. We were watching the

350

show, and then, suddenly, the Beatles, all four of them, come in and sit at a table on the other side of the club. And Bette says, 'Oh, I must get their autographs for my daughter. I must.' She rushes over, and she comes back to the table, and she is so angry!

' 'They gave me the autographs,' she said, 'but the little buggers didn't know who I was!'

'I tried to get Seth Holt for *The Anniversary*, but he was not available. So, I schlepped another director, Alvin Rakoff, over to L.A. to meet Bette, and she said, 'Fine.' We came back, and we'd been shooting a week, and she said, 'I'm sorry. I can't work with that man anymore.' So I had to fire the director and reshoot the whole first week.

'I got Roy Ward Baker, who'd known her from way back. He hadn't worked with her before, but he did know her. This upset the rest of the cast, because they liked Rakoff. They thought he was a very good director. They got along with him, and they didn't like seeing him fired.'

Baker had been an assistant director to Alfred Hitchcock on *The Lady Vanishes* and was the director of *A Night to Remember*, a notable film about the maiden, and last, voyage of the *Titanic*.

'The trouble with Alvin,' Sangster went on, 'was that he *was* a very good director, but he was a television director. Bette said to me one day, 'I've starred in sixty-seven movies,' though she had sixty-eight then, 'and I have never had to work for the camera. The camera always works for me.' Alvin, being a television director, he had

351

everything marked out and worked out, because you *had* to in those days. He was used to doing live television, and you had to have everything pinned down and worked out before you do it. She repeated, 'I can't work for the camera. The camera always works for me.'

'So he had to go, and it was not a happy experience, because the rest of the cast didn't like her much after that. They all liked Alvin, and they considered it was her fault, which of course it was, that he got sacked. It wasn't as good a picture as it should have been. If Seth Holt had done it, it would have been marvelous, but I couldn't get him. He was doing a picture with Zero Mostel, which never got shown.'

Bette had more pleasant memories of working on *The Anniversary*.

'You asked me to name a film I liked that wasn't discovered by my fans,' Bette said to me. 'Well, I loved *The Anniversary*. I think people saw it in England. In America, the company just threw it away.'

'Bette Davis was in London to star in a Hammer film,' Baker told me. 'She was playing the part of a one-eyed horror in *The Anniversary*, which had been adapted from a successful West End play. Bette couldn't get on with the director, so they stopped production and brought me in, and I started all over again.

'I didn't much like the idea of stepping in for another director, and I was hesitant about directing Bette. We had been friends for fifteen years, and I didn't want to have that friendship spoiled. I spoke with Bette on the phone, and she was very happy I was directing.

'The sets were so well planned, we were able to shoot in continuity, which is a great luxury and especially helpful for stage actors. Several of the actors had appeared in the play. They were obviously well prepared, but when we began shooting, they were terribly worried that I was going to upset the apple cart.

'In the play, either the mother is the centerpiece, and the others revolve around her, or the opposite. Onstage, Mona Washburne didn't play a domineering mother. But they were in a movie with Miss Bette Davis, and who do you think's going to be the star?

'When we all met for the first time, I could tell the actors were worried, waiting to see if their new director knew his business.

'Then, Bette appeared. She made her entrance exactly as if the cameras were on, and she was already on film. I'll never forget it.

'Bette stepped forward and in that unique voice, with that diction, she said, 'Good morning, Mr. Baker. Here we are. Please tell us what you want us to do.'

'With that, the entire note was set for the actors. They looked to me because she had set it that way, and she understood very well what she was doing. It was an act of generosity in my behalf.

'She was, I believe, the supreme movie star of her time, but she always had compassion. She drove herself the hardest of all.

'She was wonderful to me, and I know I wasn't the only one. Then, she didn't want thanks or even for you to mention it. Directing Bette Davis was a wonderful, unforgettable experience.

'It seemed an easy film to do, and it was considered successful. Hammer films had their audience awaiting. I thought afterwards perhaps I didn't get the humor properly into it. Perhaps I might have done something more. There were places that I thought afterwards might have been done with a lighter touch.'

The Anniversary (1968)

On the tenth anniversary of her despised husband's death, Mrs. Taggart (Bette Davis), a vitriolic one-eyed matriarch with three grown sons who hate her, holds a family reunion. Her eldest son, Henry (James Cossins), is a transvestite. Her middle son, Terry (Jack Hedley), who shot out her eye with an air gun, is determined to leave the country with his wife, Karen (Sheila Hancock), to escape his domineering mother. Her youngest son, Tom (Christian Roberts), is a dedicated womanizer who has brought with him his latest girlfriend, Shirley (Elaine Taylor), whom he calls his fiancée and who is pregnant.

All three arrive prepared to fight with their mother, which they do, until it becomes impossible to do anything but leave and wait for next year's reunion.

'Bette didn't normally live in a hotel in London,' Baker continued. 'She usually rented a house in the country. There was one, a big one, near Ascot that she went to, and she would take it over, with a couple of staff, and live there privately and quietly. I think we took her out to dinner once or twice. She wasn't a great one for restaurants.

'Years before, about 1953, when I had returned to Hollywood after being away for ten or eleven months, I was informed that I couldn't go back to the house I had rented because somebody else was living in it. The landlord had double-crossed me, thinking that he might as well take my money because he thought I would never come back to Hollywood. There was no apology and there was no regret. I tried a lawyer, but it was hopeless, so I just had to pop myself into a hotel for the first few days after we got there from the rail journey.

'Bette was appalled when she heard this story. She was really roused about the whole thing. How could anybody do such a thing? To a stranger and an Englishman, at that, because she was mad about England, always. She was a New Englander, and she considered that half her background was in England. So, she took a very strong attitude toward what had happened to us.

'She had rented a small house on the beach at Malibu, not really in the Malibu colony, but just alongside it. There was a string of houses, sort of wooden-built bungalows. They were rather nice, and they were right on the beach. So, she got on the telephone, and she discovered that the bungalow two doors away was empty. She told me to ring up straight away and take it, which I did. It was a great piece of nifty footwork on her part, and very kind of her to take the trouble. We'd only known each other for a few days. It wasn't as if we were lifelong friends.

'The friendship continued from there, and I continued in the house about six months. I then decided to rent another house, which was up in Beverly Hills, actually. But during that time, we were next-door neighbors, so we were in and out of each other's houses, and all that sort of thing.

'When I was in Hollywood, we used to go out to dinner occasionally, to Romanoff's. Very glamorous and very Hollywood, and the food was good. The four of us would have a dinner. It was my turn to invite them, Bette and Gary. So, I rang up and booked a table at Romanoff's and said my name. When we arrived, the manager came forward and greeted me, and I gave him my name. Then, he looked over my shoulder, and he saw Bette, and it was a totally different story. 'Oh, not *that* table.' I thought it was quite funny.

'Actually, she would much prefer the house, a really nice, quiet dinner at home with several friends. She wasn't reclusive in any sense, but she liked the idea of a home, you know; a private base where she could be herself, do what she wanted, and all that.

'She was really absolutely charming, and she was busy looking after her own children, who were very small at the time I first met her. Obviously, there were great gaps of time in my seeing her, because I was only in Hollywood for three years, but after that, whenever she came to England to make a film, which was some considerable time afterwards, she would always come and see us.

'At that time, during the middle 1960s, I had a house in the country, and she would come and stay for weekends, and all that sort of thing. It couldn't have been nicer, actually. But Margot had been put into a home. Bette was very, very scrupulous about the way that was handled, and the child was well looked after.

'We had a small boy at the time we met. He had his first birthday when we got to Los Angeles, on that particular trip. Bette, you must know, had no time for women. She was devoted to men. She loved men. But for some reason, she took quite a shine to my wife, and they got on extremely well. That continued for many years after, until right up to Bette's last visit to England.

'We were still quite young. We'd been married for about, I suppose, five or six years when we had our son. He was the only child we had. So, there was him, who was one, and there were B.D. and Michael, who were also very young. We had a nanny, so it was all very domestic on this railway trip.

'As I recall it, I developed a rather bad cold, and I seem to remember being packed off to another compartment, so that I didn't give the cold to the children. And, so, the two ladies got on extremely well, looking after their children, gossiping and all the rest of it. Gary wasn't with us because he'd elected to go by plane. He was there at the other end when we got there.

'Gary was an extremely nice man. Very, very

amusing. He was tall, dark, and handsome, you know. Later on, of course, he was very disappointed with his adventures in Hollywood, which didn't really ever come to much. He was, I think, really more interested in the Broadway theater than in movies. He was an '*ac-tor*,' very much like the old style of actor. Very serious about acting and particularly in the theater. That's where he'd had considerable success, and that's why he was asked to go to Hollywood and be in *All About Eve* and various other things, and of course, Zanuck put him under contract. As things developed, when we got to Hollywood, I made a picture with Marilyn Monroe (*Don't Bother to Knock*), which was a success.

'Bette was a great homemaker. Wherever she went, she reorganized the place and made it very comfortable, and elegant. She had extremely good taste in furnishing, you know; all the bits and bogs that make up a house. She was really good at it, and she and Gary settled there quite well. There were parties and evening drinks, and things like that.

'She was a good cook, too, a first-class housewife. She did it as long as the relationship was good. She would settle into that role extremely well. She always had one or two slaves about her, you know, to get her off the donkey work. Too bad she never could find a man she could settle down with for life.

'She wasn't a good picker. She picked rather badly, even Gary. He was nice enough, a very good actor, but he didn't really *like* Hollywood. After I'd done the picture with Marilyn, I was supposed to do a picture called *White Witch Doctor*, which, thank heaven, I didn't in the end make.

'The next thing I had to do was a picture called *Night Without Sleep*, an original story about a man called Eric Mall, who wrote the script and co-produced it. Gary was to play the part, very much a starring part for him. It was really a long piece of psychoanalysis, terribly static. The writer thought nothing of having a dialogue scene between two people sitting at a restaurant table for about three or four pages of dialogue. You should never do that. It was a published book, but it wasn't a story. It was an anecdote. Gary and I made of it what we could, but there really wasn't much to make of it. Bette and I drifted apart until we came together again to do *The Anniversary*.'

★   ★   ★

Connecting Rooms was shot in 1969, and then not widely distributed. Though she said she did it for the money, Bette was pleased to work with Sir Michael Redgrave, and he with her. Redgrave told me that she was 'a wonderfully creative actress. She had a wonderful sense of character, especially for her own, which was what she claimed. But she was good for the other characters, too, though with anything but her character, she tried not to be intrusive, not to offer much advice, especially unasked-for advice. I found her a great collaborator. She had a wonderful sense of humor, great energy, and she

359

genuinely cared about the work and the people doing it. I noticed that she particularly had great respect for even the smallest bit player.

'People told me she would try to upstage me. Well, of course, I thought. She *is* Miss Bette Davis. She deserves it. She had, as she used to say, paid her dues. She deserved it just for being Bette Davis at that point in her career. In England, she would have been Dame Bette.

'But to the contrary, at the end of the day, it was *my* part she was building, at the expense of hers.'

Bette said publicly that she did *Connecting Rooms* because of Michael Redgrave and wanting to act in England with an actor of his stature. It was part of the reason. The other reason was that Bette wanted to work, and indeed, she *needed* to work.

'I would have wanted to work,' she said, 'even if I'd been the richest woman in the world, which I certainly wasn't. I can't imagine a life of *just* eating lunch and shopping, and you can't just live your life through your children and grandchildren, even if you wanted to, because they go their own way.'

Months before she started working on this film, Bette found out that B.D. was pregnant. In June of 1969, her grandson Ashley Hyman was born.

Connecting Rooms (1970)

Wanda (Bette Davis), a middle-aged cellist who lives in a London boardinghouse, barely earns a living by playing in front of theaters. One of her

360

neighbors is a young songwriter (Alexis Kanner), who finds it amusing to flirt with her. Another neighbor is a newly arrived schoolmaster (Michael Redgrave) who has just lost his job. As Wanda and the schoolmaster become closer friends, the songwriter resents being replaced in her affections. When he finds out that the schoolmaster lost his position because of a suspected teacher-student homosexual relationship, he reveals it, but Wanda remains the schoolmaster's steadfast friend.

For the cello-playing scenes, they reverted to the *Deception* technique, having Bette's hands tied behind her back while a professional musician did the bowing and fingering. In this case, the cellist was Ian Fleming's half-sister, Amaryllis.

★   ★   ★

'I made *Bunny O'Hare* because of Bette,' Ernest Borgnine told me. 'She was my first reason. Ask me what my second was.'

I asked.

'My second was Bette, and my third, too. I wanted to work with Bette again. I told her, 'I hope I work with you again and I won't have to read the script.'

'Maybe I should have.'

Bunny O'Hare (1971)

Because widowed Bunny O'Hare (Bette Davis) has lost her home in a bank foreclosure, she decides to get revenge by robbing banks for a living. She enlists as her partner in crime a former bank robber, Bill Green (Ernest Borgnine), who is currently peddling used toilets. Disguising themselves as counterculture characters, they cruise around New Mexico on a motorcycle robbing banks. From the proceeds of their enterprise, Bunny is able to support her grown children (John Astin and Reva Rose).

A policeman (Jack Cassidy) becomes so obsessed with Bunny and Bill that he will do anything to capture them, even break the law himself. Finally, he is distracted by an attractive young criminologist (Joan Delaney), who helps him get over his obsession by allowing the aging faux-hippies to avoid imprisonment on a legal technicality.

Bunny and Bill decide to go straight together. While he purveys toilets to needy illegal immigrants, she dismisses her worthless children with a 'Fuck 'em.'

'*Bunny O'Hare* was exactly the opposite to the kind of picture I like to make,' Bette said. 'It was shot entirely on location, in Albuquerque, New Mexico. At Warners, they would have built it on a back lot, and it would have looked a hell of a lot more like Albuquerque than Albuquerque actually looked, at least the part we were in. And we wouldn't have been so uncomfortable. In those days, we had artists and technicians who could construct *anything* better in the studio than the real thing. I'm absolutely against location shooting. Absolutely.'

★ ★ ★

I first met Alberto Sordi with Federico Fellini when I was writing about the Italian film director. Sordi, early in his career, and early in Fellini's, had played leading roles in *The White Sheik* and *I Vitelloni*. At the time that Sordi appeared in *The Scientific Cardplayer* with Bette Davis, he was one of Italy's biggest stars and an esteemed director, himself. 'She, Miss Davis, called me Mr. Sordid,' he told me.

The Scientific Cardplayer (1972)
An eccentric millionairess (Bette Davis) who is addicted to cards takes a special pleasure in winning from players who cannot afford to gamble. Every year, she visits Rome with her secretary and ex-lover, George (Joseph Cotten), to play with Peppino (Alberto Sordi), the ragman, and Antonia (Silvana Mangano), a cleaning lady, who live in a slum near her villa with their five children.

She offers the couple one million lire to gamble with her and George in a card game called *scopone*, to which she is passionately devoted and at which Antonia is a champion.

Even though they desperately need the money, the couple has always understood that they must lose in order to please the millionairess, but this year Antonia is determined to win. In spite of Peppino's erratic playing, it appears for a while as if they will, but in the end, the millionairess wins.

They get revenge by presenting her with what may be a poisoned cake as she is leaving Rome.

'An actress I admired very much was Anna Magnani,' Bette told me. 'I wish I could have known her. She died in Rome while I was there.

'There were two things I admired greatly about her. The first was that she was a magnificent actress, one of the best ever. She had a great power and magnetism, and a passion for what she did.

'The other was what I heard about her feeding the cats of Rome. She would buy them food herself and she would also get doggie bags and kitty bags from restaurants. The bags began with her own leftovers, and extended to huge packages of what was left over each night at the restaurants she frequented.

'I wonder how the dogs and cats felt about spaghetti? In other words, were they affected only by their genes, or did their Italian environment affect them? Perhaps it depended on how hungry they were.

'We were total twins, Italian and American, Anna Magnani and I. I respect her. I worship her.'

★ ★ ★

In the early 1970s, Bette appeared in three television feature films, *Madame Sin* (1972), *The Judge and Jake Walker* (1972), and *Scream, Pretty Peggy* (1973), as well as being a guest on such popular TV programs as *The Dean Martin Show*. She returned to the stage, appearing as herself. The occasion was John Springer's *Great Ladies of the American Cinema* series, which featured a different star each night in New York's Town Hall. Bette opened the series. Other guests included Myrna Loy, Rosalind Russell, and Lana Turner. The star of the night would be interviewed by Springer, following film clips illustrating her work.

Knowing how Bette felt about 'Miss Crawford,' Springer asked her if she would object to Joan Crawford appearing on the same series. 'I thought about it,' Bette said. 'I knew it was good for him. So I said, 'All right. Ask Crawford. You can have her as long as it's a different night and we're not on the same stage at the same time. And I'll sit in the first row and knit.''

Director Curtis Harrington remembered an occasion in the early 1970s when he and his producer had lunch with Bette Davis at the Universal commissary. 'My producer asked Bette, he wasn't totally serious, if she would be interested in doing a sequel to *Baby Jane* with Joan Crawford.

''Yes,' Bette retorted. 'And I'll tell you about the first scene. It'll be a scene of *this* one,' pointing at herself, 'putting flowers on *that* one's grave.''

Joan Crawford said that she never understood why Bette seemed to hate her. 'I don't feel that way about her,' she told me, 'but she's not my favorite person.' The legendary feud between the two may have been just that — a legend. They both read so much about hating each other, they came to believe it themselves.

Bette's evening was so well received that the next year Springer produced for the stage *Bette*

Davis in Person and on Film, which would go on tour. When they were about to leave for Australia, Springer's wife, June, drove him to the airport and then accompanied him to the VIP lounge, where Bette was meeting him.

'The moment Bette saw me,' June told me, 'she said loudly and very clearly, 'NO WI-VES!'

'She thought *I* was going along to Australia. I said, 'I'm not going with you, Bette.'

'Then, she was happy.'

Bette had told me that while she was doing research for *Elizabeth and Essex*, she read that Queen Elizabeth did not encourage wives to stay at court. She preferred not having female competition.

'Bette Davis always tried to be fair,' Springer told me. 'When I had to go back to New York and leave the show, I had to get someone to take my place. Within two days, Bette had fired the person, but she didn't cancel the tour. She struck out on her own — Europe, the British Isles, Scandinavia.'

Even though he wasn't there, Bette gave him full credit in all of the advertising and promotion and paid him a royalty on every show.

★ ★ ★

In 1974, Bette, needing money as always, and concerned about her career, was overjoyed to be offered the lead in *Miss Moffat*, a stage musical version of *The Corn Is Green*. The words were by Emlyn Williams, whom she said she 'adored professionally and personally. A dear man.' The

366

music was by Albert Hague, with Joshua Logan the producer, co-author, and director.

Logan had offered the role first to Mary Martin, but she withdrew after initially agreeing. Then, he offered it to Bette, who was enthusiastic, especially when she learned the story was being updated. Instead of Wales, the setting was the American South, with Miss Moffat helping a young black boy. She said, 'That sounded a very good idea.'

After rehearsals and a tour, the show was scheduled to open on Broadway in fall of 1975. The company gathered in New York during early August 1974. Bette was finding the experience much more difficult that she had anticipated. Just before they left for Baltimore, Bette checked into Columbia Presbyterian Medical Center, complaining of backaches.

When she finally did arrive in Philadelphia, it became obvious to Logan that the sixty-six-year-old actress would not be able to cope with the stress and strain, physical as well as emotional, of a Broadway musical. 'She forgot her lines, missed her cues, and then got mad at the rest of the cast,' Logan told me. 'But the house was always packed, and nobody ever asked for his money back. The advance ticket sales for Broadway were phenomenal.

'Then, she started getting sick, or *claiming* to be sick. I wasn't sure which. But I think audiences would have come if she'd played it in a wheelchair, or even on a stretcher.

'Pretty soon, *I* was the one who was sick, so when she finally pulled out, I was almost relieved, but not really. I was terribly sorry for all those young actors who were counting on this show to make their careers. A lot of broken hearts, and it was terrible for the backers, who lost so much money. But there's no doubt it placed a heavy burden on Bette, too.'

Bette said, 'I thought *Miss Moffat* was going to rescue me from being 'Daughter of Baby Jane' for the rest my life. I'd forgotten how hard the live stage is. It's *all* you can think of when you're doing it. Then, they told me they believed the show would run for at least a year, and I panicked. I had taken on too much. But my sicknesses were real. *That* they were.'

Logan continued: 'It took me a long time to forgive 'the Wicked Witch of the West,' as I called her, but I don't believe in holding grudges. Like me, Bette Davis believes in living life completely, till you're dead. But she doesn't live for your convenience. She doesn't even live life for her own convenience. But live it she *does!*'

After this ordeal, Bette retreated to her Connecticut house for most of 1975. Her next film was about a house that devours its inhabitants.

Burnt Offerings (1976)

Ben (Oliver Reed) and wife Marian (Karen Black) rent an old summer house that soon takes over their lives and the life of their son, David (Lee Montgomery). The house seems to be getting newer as *they* age rapidly. They turn against each other, sometimes murderously.

Aunt Elizabeth (Bette Davis) tries to free them

from the evil influence of the house, but everything in the house goes wild, and she is killed. After a series of nightmares about childhood funeral processions and menacing hearse drivers, Ben dies, too, while a comatose Marian brings food to an unseen personage at the top of the steps. Finally, she becomes part of the house's evil presence.

'I never saw so much ketchup in my life,' Bette told me. 'That's what they used for the blood. I probably shouldn't have done the film, but I wanted to work, so I imagined the script better than it was. I never saw the film. I was afraid I would hate it. I don't like to say bad things when a lot of other people have put part of their lives into a film. It has been easier just to say, 'I didn't see it.' Of course, I saw it as we were doing it, but that definitely is not the same. You are too deep into what you are doing to stand back and observe it. Perhaps someday I'll see it and like it more than I expected to.'

In 1976, Bette made a television feature, *The Disappearance of Aimee*, about an incident in the life of Aimee Semple McPherson, played by Faye Dunaway. Bette had wanted to play the famous evangelist, but at this point, she had to settle for being her mother. In the cast was James Woods, whom she described as 'my dividend.'

'My only regret,' she said, 'is that I wasn't a younger woman when I met him.' He remained her friend for the rest of her life.

★ ★ ★

Return from Witch Mountain was a sequel to *Escape to Witch Mountain*, an enormously successful 1975 Disney film.

Return from Witch Mountain (1978)
Extraterrestrial brother and sister Tony and Tia (Ike Eisenmann and Kim Richards) are abducted from their space traveler guardian by two avaricious scientists, Victor Gannon (Christopher Lee) and his associate, Letha Wedge (Bette Davis), who attempt to harness the superpowers of the children to their evil projects for world control. The children are saved by three brave young people (Brad Savage, Jeffrey Jacquet, and Christian Juttner), who combine their energies to defeat the wicked scientists.

At his London apartment, Christopher Lee, who had recently completed his work on *Lord of the Rings*, recalled for me what it was like working with Bette.

'*Return from Witch Mountain* was a Disney movie, and I realized that I was going to be working in what was basically almost a children's film, about these two young kids who could levitate. When I was told it was an opportunity to work with her, of course I didn't worry unduly about the script or the story. I said, 'Yes,' because she's the finest actress I can recall in American or world cinema.

'I remember when I first met her, we were in the street somewhere in Los Angeles, and Anthony James, I think it was, was being levitated into the air. He was one of the three bad guys, two of us and him. She suddenly appeared. I hadn't realized how small she was. She said, 'Now, *there's* a familiar face.'

'During the course of the filming, we got on wonderfully well. She chain-smoked, and she coughed quite a lot. Nothing seemed to get her down. I mean, she was in her seventies, and making a picture for Disney, with *her* background, was hardly a step up the ladder, if you see what I mean. I'd never made a film at Disney, and I don't think she had, either. We had a nice crew, a good cast, and the director was an Englishman, John Hough. I'd worked with him before, so it was a very pleasant atmosphere.

'When we weren't actually rehearsing or working, all of which she took intensely seriously, just as I did, I would sit in her caravan [trailer], and she would tell me innumerable stories, mostly about her family, actually, about her grandchildren, B.D.'s two sons, of whom she was obviously extremely fond.

'She was a very strong woman. She would never settle for second best. She always gave a hundred percent to everything she did, irrespective of what it was. She was encouraging, amusing, and we had a lot of laughs. She would tell me stories about some of her previous films, of her leading men — and women.

'There were two she did not get on with, to put it mildly, Miriam Hopkins and Joan Crawford. You only had to say Crawford, and she would start to soar toward the ceiling. She really *could* levitate!

'They did not get on, you might say. I didn't

ask why. You just don't do that sort of thing. But I always knew how to get her going. It was kind of a game. All I had to do was mention Hopkins or Crawford, and she would start erupting.

'She told me that the actor that she most admired, and whom she revered, really, was George Arliss. How wonderful he was, how he started her career, and how much she respected and admired him.

'She was devoted to George Brent, and very, very fond of Paul Henreid. And they were the two people she would hold up as an example of what a real professional actor should do.

'She did tell me that Oscar was named after her husband's rear end. She did say that, and I firmly believed it.

'What I liked about her, of course, was that she was, a) never inhibited by another person's talent, and, b) she wasn't afraid to take anybody on. She said what she thought, and was very forthright in her opinions. If she didn't like someone, she said so.

'There was no conflict on *Witch Mountain*. She was very nice to the two children. She was marvelous with me. She was nice to the director. I never saw her lose her cool. Never. I never saw her put her foot down, but you were always very, very conscious of whom you were working with, of whom you were playing a scene with.

'She may have been in her seventies, but that didn't make any difference. She would be quite quiet until somebody said, 'Turn over.' I mean, you'd rehearse a scene, and then she gave it absolutely the full treatment.

'She was professional in every way. And she appreciated and understood and got on with people who felt the same way, of which I like to think I was one. I was not a great actor, but she was a great actress.

'She had a *wonderful* sense of humor, with this harsh, harsh, cackling laugh that she had, as you know, between drags on a cigarette. People ask me, 'Who was the greatest actress you ever worked with?' There's no question, and that's by a mile. I've worked with some very good ones. Bette played this part in our Disney movie as if she were doing an Academy Award film.

'Even after she'd had her stroke, she never lost this tremendous spirit. She certainly never lost her courage in spite of all the problems she had in her career, and in spite of the fact that her home life had not always been all that happy.

'She was never at a loss for a phrase of encouragement for the others. She gave her all, and I thought she was superb in *Elizabeth and Essex*. Mind you, I thought that Errol Flynn was very good, too, even though Bette wasn't as thrilled by him.

'There's no Errol Flynn around today. Nobody has that panache. Nobody has that dazzling smile. He didn't falsify it in any way, but they were wonderful together. Absolutely wonderful.'

Olivia de Havilland recalled being present at a 1970s screening of *The Private Lives of Elizabeth and Essex* attended by Bette.

'As Bette watched,' de Havilland told me, 'she leaned farther and farther forward in her seat,

373

obviously fascinated.

'When the film ended, I remember she said softly, 'Damn! He's good. No. He's not *good*. He's *marvelous!* I was wrong all the time.''

★ ★ ★

Death on the Nile was photographed by Jack Cardiff, who won an Oscar as cinematographer for *Black Narcissus* in 1947. He was nominated in 1956 for *War and Peace*, and again in 1960 as the director of *Sons and Lovers*. He began as a clapper boy on early Hitchcock films, was the camera operator on the first British three-strip Technicolor film (*Wings of the Morning*, 1937), and became a director while continuing as a cinematographer.

I first spoke with him at the black-tie gala in London celebrating the fiftieth anniversary of the British National Film Theatre just before Christmas in 2002. While being much honored for his film career, only recently had he found that his hobby, still photography, was of interest to the public.

For many years, he had been photographing the stars with whom he worked, especially the women, Marilyn Monroe among others. Marilyn was pleased to pose for him, 'but after promising to be there at lunchtime, she arrived at dinnertime, so I took pictures of her then.' Because *Death on the Nile* was a location shoot, he never had the opportunity to photograph Bette.

For Bette, one of the joys of working on *Death*

on the Nile was the knowledge that Cardiff was 'a real artist.'

'*Death on the Nile* was the only occasion I had to meet Bette Davis,' Cardiff told me. 'I liked her very much. She was very forthright, wasn't she? I remember that we got on very well together. Her part didn't run through the whole picture, but it was a very nice experience working with her.

'The thing was, she fitted well into the part, a good start, and she fitted in well with everyone. It wasn't as if there was any kind of difficulty, like she wouldn't agree to this or that. She was perfectly happy, and everything went well. This is very dull, what I'm telling you, I know, but the fact was it really was all positive.

'I *had* worked with people who didn't like the script and wanted to change things, and all that. She didn't want to change anything.

'She did say, and I was very flattered, that she was very pleased to be working with me, and that she had a high regard for my lighting. She never said, 'I hope you'll light me this way or that way.' She trusted me, in other words. I wish I could think of something more dramatic, but as I say, these were happy occasions.'

Death on the Nile (1978)

One of the guests (Lois Chiles) aboard a houseboat cruising down the Nile is murdered, and Belgian detective Hercule Poirot (Peter Ustinov) sets out to find the murderer from among eight prime suspects.

They are the victim's husband (Simon

MacCorkindale), her lawyer (George Kennedy), the husband's ex-fiancée (Mia Farrow), an American dowager (Bette Davis) and her traveling companion (Maggie Smith), a political radical (Jon Finch), the victim's former doctor (Jack Warden), and a popular novelist (Angela Lansbury).

Two of the guests are murdered before Poirot solves the case in his usual elegant manner.

'I arranged for Bette to do *Death on the Nile*,' Robby Lantz told me. 'Then, she called from the set of *The Dark Secret of Harvest Home* and said, 'The way this is going, I won't be able to be in Egypt in time. I don't know what to do.'

'I called Lew Wasserman, who was head of Universal and who had been Bette's agent before me, and told him. It was a Universal television miniseries Bette was doing, and he said, 'We'll arrange everything we can.'

'Bette said, 'If I work at night and leave by plane for London for costume fittings and get on the plane that night, I can report in Egypt.' And that's the way it was.'

When Lantz told Bette that her part in *Death on the Nile* was comparatively small, she didn't mind because, as she told me, 'I was so thrilled to be working with actresses like Maggie Smith, Angela Lansbury, and Mia Farrow. My respect for Miss Smith and Miss Lansbury, no words!' She had an especially warm feeling toward 'that beautiful, dear young actress of truly great talent, Mia Farrow. Her father directed me, you know.'

In 1978, Bette was anxious to see Liv Ullmann in her new film, *Autumn Sonata*, which was directed by Ingmar Bergman and costarred Ingrid Bergman.

She put on a headscarf and dark glasses, and went into a theater on Third Avenue in New York City. The girl in the box office stared.

'Bette called right away,' Liv Ullmann remembered. 'She told me I was wonderful, that I had my character down perfectly, and she added that I didn't need to wear glasses to help my character.'

'Even after they'd released it, Disney couldn't decide how to end *Watcher in the Woods*,' Bette told me. 'The first time they showed it to a preview audience, they forgot to run the final reel at all, and nobody seemed to mind. Eventually, they tried three different endings, but I haven't the foggiest as to which one they chose for posterity. Not the foggiest.'

The Watcher in the Woods (1980)
Composer Paul Curtis (David McCallum) rents a summer home in an English forest for his wife, Helen (Carroll Baker), and his two young daughters, Jan (Lynn-Holly Johnson) and Ellie (Kyle Richards). The old woman from whom they rent the house, Mrs. Aylwood (Bette Davis), lives alone in the caretaker's cottage.

Jan soon becomes convinced that they are being watched by someone or something unseen. Then, strange events point to Mrs. Aylwood and the disappearance of her daughter, Karen (Katherine Levy), who vanished in flames and smoke thirty years ago during the initiation rites of an occult secret society.

By reenacting the 'night of doom' ritual in the estate's chapel, Jan is able to rescue Karen from her thirty years of entrapment by demonic forces.

Bette was quite active in television during the 1970s and '80s, appearing with co-stars such as James Stewart, Robert Wagner, Jamie Lee Curtis, and Gena Rowlands. She won an Emmy for her performance as Rowlands's mother in *Strangers*, and afterward they became close friends. 'When I got my Emmy,' Bette told me, 'Gena was happier for me winning than for herself. What a friend! What an actress she is!'

★ ★ ★

In June 1983 in New York City, Bette was diagnosed with breast cancer and underwent a mastectomy. While recuperating at New York Hospital, she suffered a stroke, which left her with slurred speech and partially paralyzed. She began physical therapy to learn to walk again and to regain her speech. With a great effort, she walked and spoke, but was told she could never work again.

During these critical weeks, her assistant, Kathryn Sermak, was at her side, even staying nights in the hospital with her. Bette always gave her the greatest credit for her companionship and encouragement. B.D. also visited her mother, coming from her Pennsylvania farm.

After Bette was released from the hospital, she returned to the Lombardy in New York City, where she could live comfortably in the ambiance of an apartment with the services of a hotel and Sermak there to assist her.

As soon as she was able, Bette had a cocktail party for all of her doctors, everyone who had been attending her in the hospital and afterward. They could drink, even if she couldn't.

After the guests arrived, Bette thanked them for all their efforts and told them she was bidding them 'adieu, a permanent goodbye, as I am returning to California and have had enough of all of you.' There was laughter, but Bette was serious.

Bette went back to Los Angeles after nine weeks in the hospital. In her Hollywood apartment at Colonial House, she fell and broke her hip. In spite of this, she continued to struggle to regain her physical abilities, with the help of Sermak.

Bette was *determined* to work again. She wanted to, and she needed to. Medical costs, the past support of her mother and sister, the continuing support of her adopted daughter, Margot, unwise career decisions, and overpriced property purchased on impulse and sold poorly had left her with what she was concerned wouldn't be enough to live on in her old age. In her seventies, she didn't feel that she had quite reached old age. She was worried because she didn't know how long that old age would be. 'I am determined not only *not* to cost anyone any money when I die, but to leave something for everyone I care about. I could not bear to disappear without leaving gifts.'

While Bette was recuperating, she and Sermak began writing a book, in collaboration with Michael Herskowitz. They were not aware that B.D. was also writing a book.

Bette learned about her daughter's book in 1985, after she had recovered sufficiently to make a trip to the East Coast. Robby Lantz told her about it.

'A phone call came to me saying that there would be the publication of a hostile book by her daughter,' Lantz told me. 'I had no inkling that such a thing was in the works. I called Harold Schiff [Bette's lawyer], and he and I decided that it was not the subject for a telephone call. When a child of a very famous mother secretly has written a book, you know there's trouble. Secretly probably means that it's not a nice book. It didn't bode well.

'Bette was in her house in Connecticut. Harold and I drove there. I knew this would break her heart, but we had to tell her in person. We couldn't just let her find out in some worse way. But there was no good way.

'She was a pretty good actress, you know. She asked if we were sure that the book was hostile. She didn't let show how upset she was. I said, 'No, I'm not sure. I haven't read it. But Bette, if *you* don't know, and *Harold* doesn't know, and *I* don't know, there's only one interpretation.'

'The publication of that book, when Bette read it, was a death in the family, you know. It was a deep blow, but I, to this day, am convinced that she never cried.

'She loved her daughter. She was foolishly generous to the best of my knowledge, even at times when money was short. There is nothing she ever refused B.D.

'In my opinion and from my knowledge of Bette, and Harold and I were in agreement, the book was totally undeserved. Yes, Bette was difficult. Many mothers are difficult. But that's the wrong way for the daughter to act, secretively.'

My Mother's Keeper was published in 1985. In it, B.D. portrays her mother as a tyrannical matriarch who with her stepfather, Gary Merrill, made her childhood an ordeal. She was afraid of and disliked Merrill and was terrified by their violent quarrels. She especially resented her mother's trying to impose her own ambition on her. She felt that the gifts her mother lavished on her were given only to win her love, and she didn't want to be what she believed her mother seemed to want, a traveling companion. At the end of the book, B.D. offered reconciliation, but on her own terms.

Her daughter having addressed these comments to her, Bette responded with a letter to 'Dear Hyman' in *her* book, *This 'n That*, which included some uncomplimentary reviews of *My Mother's Keeper*. Then she disinherited B.D. and B.D.'s two sons, her grandchildren. She believed that Sermak had shown her the devotion of a daughter, a devotion that had come at a crucial moment in her life.

Even after the mastectomy, stroke, a broken hip, and last but not least, her daughter's book, Bette worked whenever possible, even when *impossible*. *This 'n That* was published in 1988 and became a best-seller, largely due to Bette's personal appearances on television, in spite of the way she looked. 'I'm throwing vanity to the winds,' she said. 'I was never a vain woman. Well, a little.'

Bette wanted the book to be successful, and she did enjoy the TV appearances, saying, 'It's wonderful to be wanted.'

She also played supporting roles in two television films, *Agatha Christie's 'Murder with Mirrors'* and *As Summers Die*, but not until 1987 did she appear in another theatrical film. It was *The Whales of August*, directed by Lindsay Anderson, with Lillian Gish, Vincent Price, and Ann Sothern. Bette said she didn't enjoy making the film, and she didn't like her co-star, Lillian Gish.

11

'Old Age Ain't No Place for Sissies'

Shortly after the completion of *The Whales of August*, Lillian Gish told me, 'I can't imagine why Bette Davis seemed to dislike me and made our scenes difficult, even beyond normal scene-stealing techniques. Worse yet, she was hostile. We had no personal rapport at all, and that makes for greater strain on everyone, especially when you're on location and trapped there together.

'I had heard that Bette was difficult, but I thought that was a good sign, because 'difficult' for me meant trying hard. I had always tried hard and that may have made some people think *I* was difficult.

'Early in my career, to prepare for a film, I went to insane asylums to study insanity and county hospitals to study death. We went to Waterloo Station, to do as Mr. [D.W.] Griffith advised us — to see emotion off-guard.

'But Bette just didn't seem to like me from the first moment. I didn't know why she was so mean to me.'

The Whales of August (1987)

The elderly Strong sisters are spending the summer, perhaps for the last time together, in their Maine cottage on the ocean. They went there every summer as girls, and then they went there with their husbands, who are both dead.

Libby (Bette Davis) is now blind. She is haughty and demanding, and the patience of her kindly, protective sister, Sarah (Lillian Gish), is being sorely tried. Sarah would like to turn the care of her difficult sister over to Libby's daughter. All that holds them together are the happy memories of their youth there.

They have several visitors, one of them Mr. Maranov (Vincent Price), an elderly Russian aristocrat who survives by being a houseguest. Another is an intrusive neighbor, Tisha Doughty (Ann Sothern), who has told a real estate agent that the cottage is for sale when it isn't. The third is Joshua, the handyman (Harry Carey, Jr.), who is eager to put in a picture window for Miss Sarah. This is opposed by Miss Libby, who, being blind, cannot see the view.

Libby insults the pathetic Maranov, who receives an apology from Sarah. The real estate salesman is summarily dismissed by Libby. Finally, Libby relents and agrees to the picture window that Sarah wants.

Though Libby cannot see, the sisters make peace as, arm in arm, they look out at the waters where the whales once came at the end of every summer, but come no more.

Bette described the last three decades of her life, and her career, as 'my macabre period.' Robby Lantz, who represented her during part of this time, told me about his first meeting with Bette:

'It all began fifteen years before her death, when her lawyer and devoted friend, Harold Schiff, called me and said, 'Bette Davis would like to meet you.' At the time, she lived in Connecticut in a house, and Harold and I drove out to see her.

'My first impression of her was very surprising, because she heard the car coming, and she stood in the doorway, playing by the light from the house. Even though she was very small, the walls gave, you know. That woman was tiny, but she was larger than life.

'She was very formal, very nice. She said, 'We'll have tea. I've asked to meet you because I've heard nice things about you, and I would like for you to represent me.'

'I said, 'Miss Davis, it's a huge honor.' She had only one rule about her work, that even if she would do a cameo, because they were often offered to her, she would only do it if she was billed above the title. She had a good reason for it. She sometimes needed money, and still she said, 'No. A Bette Davis movie *has* to be a Bette Davis movie.' She felt she owed it to her public.

'Then, she showed me the house. We walked up to the second floor of that house. And up the staircase, there was a metalwork railing, very shiny, and I said, 'How do you get somebody to keep this in such good shape out here in the country? We can't get help in New York.'

'She said, 'I do it myself.' That turned out to be typical of her. All of it. She did everything. You know, a little like Marlene [Dietrich], who also did her own housework.

'With that unmistakable voice of hers, when she called my house, she would always say, 'Is Mr. Lantz there?,' and my wife would say no if I wasn't. But she knew my wife, and Sherlee got so irritated with this refusal to acknowledge her that one evening, when Bette said, 'Tell Mr. Lantz that I called,' Sherlee said, 'Who may I say called?' Bette never did that again.

'She assumed that people were overwhelmed by her, and she *was* overwhelming. Her work today is remarkable, because she was often in terrible movies in which she was good.

'I stopped representing her before her final illness. She was then in Hollywood, and needed representation there, and I was in New York and that was too difficult.'

Actress Carol Kane, who had just moved into Colonial House apartments in Hollywood, was preparing to leave for Australia to make a film. Kane had known Bette Davis lived in that building, and this weighed in favor of her selecting it. In the laundry room she met Kathryn Sermak, and they chatted about Kane's upcoming trip.

When Kane returned to her apartment, she found an envelope under her door. Inside was a handwritten note on lovely paper from Bette Davis inviting her to have a drink at six P.M. and hear Bette's advice on Australia.

Bette gave her some valuable travel tips, and reminisced about Australia, which she had very much liked. Kane was thrilled by Bette's consideration and effort, and followed all of the suggestions.

★ ★ ★

In spite of the seemingly insurmountable difficulties a frail eighty-year-old star posed, Larry Cohen, writer and director of Bette's last picture, *Wicked Stepmother*, remembered her fondly.

'She was all right,' Cohen told me. 'I'd heard all kinds of things about her, but I never found them true at all. I enjoyed all the time I spent with her. I would have spent all the time just shooting nothing but her if I'd known she was going to get sick and only work a week.

'She had this dental problem before the picture started, even before we were casting and preparing. Her bridge had broken in her mouth, and she was having trouble keeping the dentures in place. I wondered, 'Why is she reading the lines the way she is?' Of course, she was in a panic because she was having this problem. And we started production.

'If we had had any inkling of this problem, we would probably have postponed it a couple of weeks. But she wouldn't admit it to anybody. Even after it happened, and the picture was closed down, she still wouldn't admit it.

'We closed down and waited for her. Then they told me that she'd lost so much weight, she was down to, like, seventy-five pounds. She lost about ten pounds, and she was already very thin.

'Her downfall and our downfall was her teeth. Anybody who has dentures could have had that problem. If only she had told me about it. She was desperate to save her career, and I think she needed the money.

'Then, in a *New York Times* interview, she said, 'I have dealt with many directors in my career, but with Larry Cohen, I finally met my Waterloo.' I sent a bunch of flowers to her, signed, 'From your Waterloo, Larry Cohen.' But she didn't call me back.

'When she died, I called Kathryn Sermak on the phone. I knew there was a tribute at Warner Brothers on a soundstage, but I didn't want to go without asking her. She said, 'I'd rather you didn't come.' I didn't go.

'So, I got a copy of *The Letter*, and I ran that instead of going to the tribute.

'Bette liked hanging out at my house in Coldwater Canyon. It's a big old Spanish house, built in 1929 by the Hearst family. She loved that.

'She'd get herself comfortable in the living room on the couch, and she'd burn a few holes in it with her cigarettes. I didn't care about burn holes. I could tell people Bette Davis did it.

'We had the casting sessions up there. The actors all came up, and she read with everyone. She was very gracious. She read with all the young actors who came.

'She used to call me up to tell me things. She wouldn't say, 'Hello, this is Bette.' She'd just launch right into the conversation. You'd say, 'Hello,' and she'd say, 'I don't think I should have my own hair. I don't want people to think I'm playing myself. I think I should have a red wig.'

'So I haven't said a word, and she's hung up the phone.

'She calls me up and she says. 'You must come over and see the wigs I've got.'

'I go over there, and she has a couple of these red wigs, and she comes out and models them for me, very coquettishly, parading around. She was extremely flirtatious for an old woman. So I said, 'We'll have to see how they look when we shoot the tests.' It was so harsh, it made every line and wrinkle in her face stand out. But she insisted on it.

''How much money do I owe you?' She gives me the bill. It's like $178. I said, 'How could you get these for that price?'

''Oh, they gave me a huge discount.''

'I said, 'That's very nice of you, Bette, to save me all that money, because I've been used to paying thousands of dollars on other pictures.' When I was ready to leave, I put two one-hundred bills on the mantel piece and left. I got home, and the phone rang, and it was Bette.

'She said, 'Now I feel like a kept woman.' And she hung up.'

'I noticed when I went up to the apartment, she had the script out on the table, and she had it all marked. She was sitting there with her glasses on, going through it, highlighting all of her lines, just like all the young actresses do today. She was very, very hardworking and professional.

'On the set one time, she paused for a moment, and the script girl gave her the line, and she was outraged. She said, 'I know all my lines, and I know everyone else's lines as well.' The script girl was then terrified.

'It was her birthday a few weeks before we started shooting, and I went to Ralph Lauren, where they had an antique jewelry counter. I bought Bette a charm bracelet as a birthday present. Now, every day she came to the set, she wore that bracelet, and not only did she wear it, but she'd raise up her arm and jiggle her wrist so I could see that she had the bracelet. That was nice.

'Every day at the conclusion of the shoot, she'd always come up for a kiss, and I'd bend over and she'd give me a kiss before she left. The assistants would come over to me and say, 'Miss Davis is finished for the day and wants to go home. She's waiting to say good-bye to you.'

'So, then I had to stop what I was doing and find her, and bend over, and she'd give me the kiss. And the last time we had anything to do with each other in person was when she kissed me good-bye that Friday. Saturday, she was scheduled to see the dailies, because she'd been pestering me constantly.

'One afternoon, she actually took me into one of the bedrooms of the house we were shooting, and closed the door, and she sat down on the bed and started to cry. She said, 'I must see the dailies. It's very important that I see them.' And she was crying. Well, she really got to me that way.

'I understand now why she was crying. She was so upset about these dentures, and how she would look on the screen, 'When she did see the dailies, she got terribly upset. Everything she feared was true.

'One time when we were shooting in a location house, the next-door neighbors were harassing us. They told their teenagers to play their stereo system very loud, because they didn't like us coming there and closing down the whole block, and putting our lights in front of their house and shooting late in the night. They weren't getting any money, whereas the people who were renting the house were getting thousands of dollars a day.

'So, Bette said to me, 'Do you want me to go next door and tell them to turn off the stereo?' She was willing to go over and do that. I said, 'I'm going to send my production assistant back with a $100 bill in his hand and see if *that* makes any difference.'

'A few minutes later, the stereo went off. But I thought it was amusing and very nice that Bette was willing to go over there and do it herself. What a scene that would've been!

'One time, Bette said, 'I would like to stay seated in this scene.' I said, 'No, Bette. I think you gotta play it standing up.' The other actor said, 'I think Bette is right.'

'Bette's eyes flashed like Jezebel or Elizabeth the Queen, and she turned on the man with that voice of hers and said, 'You keep out of this. *He's* directing the movie!'

I looked over at the actor, and all I saw was his feet leaving the doorway. So, she could disagree with me, but if somebody else came in and tried to dispute my authority, Bette came right to my defense. That was very sweet of her. She could attack me, but nobody else could.

'She would always grab my hand and dig her little nails into the top of my hand as she'd sit there. She said, 'I don't want you to be afraid of me, like so many directors.' I had written the script especially for her. After she read it, she called me up.

' 'Mr. Cohen? Bette Davis. I read your script last night, and you certainly gave me quite a few laughs. I think we should meet. Will you come to my house and have a drink?'

'I arranged to go over and meet her, and I brought my manager, a man in his seventies, kind of attractive, looked like Ray Milland, with hair. I thought Bette would like him, but she liked me better.

'She had the famous cushion on the sofa, 'Old Age Ain't No Place for Sissies.' I'll never forget that.

'She'd had plenty of awards, but nothing displayed in the apartment. She had nothing on the walls of the apartment that would indicate she was a movie star. There were no pictures of her with different co-stars, no pictures of her with Presidents of the United States as when you go to everybody else's house.

'There were no Oscars to be seen. Most stars have all kinds of memorabilia, but she had

392

nothing but a small drawing of George Arliss framed on the wall.

'And she had a picture of the daughter. No matter what the daughter had done to her, she still had her picture. She said to me, 'If you're a good parent, you can't expect your children to like you.'

'We talked about everything, old movies, Warner Brothers, current movies, and the script. She said she wanted to do the picture. She had Kathryn open a bottle of white wine, and she made a toast:

' 'Let's hope we like each other as much at the end as we do at the beginning.' That was her favorite toast. Now, I always make that toast when I start a picture.

'When I left, my friend said, '*This* woman isn't able to make a picture.'

'I said, 'Well, I think she can, because she's Bette Davis!' '

Wicked Stepmother (1989)

When a family comes back from a vacation, they find that their widowed father has married, and they have a stepmother, Miranda (Bette Davis), who is a witch. The daughter (Colleen Camp) wishes her stepmother could be as young and beautiful as their mother had been, and Miranda makes it happen. Their new stepmother (Barbara Carrera) is young, beautiful, sexy, and evil. Eventually, the family goes back to normal life, but not until after Miranda has caused a great deal of mischief and confusion.

When Bette realized she couldn't do the picture up to the standard she had set for herself, she called Cohen and resigned. 'She hung up before I could even try to talk her out of it,' Cohen said.

His solution was to transform Bette Davis into Barbara Carrera, something a witch might be able to do, thus salvaging most of Bette's footage. It also preserved Bette's name at the top of the credits above the title. M-G-M, however, was not impressed and delayed the film's theatrical release, finally issuing it on video only. Even so, *Wicked Stepmother* is counted as a theatrical feature, Bette's eighty-seventh and last. She also made thirteen television feature films and one miniseries.

★   ★   ★

As she grew older, Bette realized that certain aspects of her personality, such as her penchant for sarcasm, had, over the years, irritated and even deeply hurt people without her being aware of it. She believed that her career and particularly her personal relationships probably had been damaged by her abrasive manner, especially with husbands and lovers. She blamed a man she knew and loved when she was very young.

'My mother coddled and protected me. She encouraged me, but she didn't push me. I wanted to make all of Ruthie's struggles for us worthwhile. That was my positive reason. But it seems the negative is stronger than the positive.

That lay deeper within me, unspoken to others, unthought even by me. Ruthie told me about men, their lack of constancy, their fleeting passion, their infidelity. Men were not reliable, never to be depended on, love didn't last. They only wanted one thing, though she never made clear exactly what that was. After the initial thrill had passed, though no specific details were given, men would go looking for it elsewhere, taking it whenever and wherever they could find it, always looking for novelty. I believed her, not because of her words, but because I had my father's example before me. My own father had proven it, departing early from his marriage and leaving us behind. And even before he left us, he was clearly discontented.

'But I believed that for me it would be different, because I was special. When I discovered I wanted to be a famous actress, a great one, I wanted my father to be impressed by me as he never was. I wanted to reach him. I wanted him to come and see me and tell me how wonderful I was, how proud he was to be my father. And then I wanted him to tell people, 'Bette Davis is my daughter.' And if he didn't, I was certain others would tell him, and he would realize that he had been wrong. And he'd be sorry he hadn't loved me more. And he *would* love me more . . .

'I vividly remember wandering into my father's study, and standing in front of him — stark naked. I was about one year old. He didn't look up from his books. I said, 'Papa.' He still didn't look up. Then he *did* look up, and he shouted, 'Ruthie — get this child out of here while I'm studying.' As my mother was leading me out, I looked back and said 'Papa' again. 'Harlow!' my mother said, 'did you hear? Betty just said her first word!' My father just went back to his homework.

'All my life I've talked about the importance of my mother. And I've brushed aside my father, because he brushed *me* aside. Since my father walked out on Ruthie and Bobby and me, I've always said I didn't care, but . . . Oh, hell! I did. He was a brain. I tried so hard to win him, to get his attention, but he didn't seem to like children, especially his own. After he left us, we lived in seventy-five rooms, apartments, and houses in eight years.

'A home is a haven. Everyone should have a home which greets you when you arrive and says good-bye to you when you leave. I dreamed of my cottage. I dreamed of a wonderful man who would dwell with me forever in my — in *our* cottage. But I think my memories of my father, which I had shut out so that I was scarcely aware of them, intruded on my own relationships with men.

'The first man in my life, my father, left me, and that started the pattern. I was always afraid it might happen again, so I tested each man until he failed. My mother gave me the support I needed, but not the challenge. If you know you're certain to please, there isn't the same motivation. My father gave me that challenge. He was responsible for my being strong. I had to work, to compete, to struggle, because I had to show *him* what a mistake he'd made in leaving his seven-year-old daughter who worshipped him. And, indeed, I *did* show him, except he didn't see it.

'I think that everything I am, as a woman of a certain age, was present in that little girl I was, trying to get the attention of my father. He was not interested. Now, he's long dead, my career is largely over, and so is my own life, but I think I'm still trying to get his attention.

'My father never struck me. He didn't have to. He battered you with his wit, which was devastating. And you couldn't hit back. Wit, especially sarcasm, is a dangerous weapon. Bright people are too often sarcastic. My father was, and I grew up being quite sarcastic, like him.

'Sometimes the shortest distance between two points of view is a straight lie. I'm still direct, but one can carry directness too far, where one goes around being so bright and so honest that you hurt people. I learned wrong lessons from my father that probably hampered me as a woman. But he gave me a very good brain, and that helped me to hang on.

'In his whole life, Daddy loved only one creature that I know of — his dog, a vicious chow who bit everyone in sight. Daddy would roar with laughter when I went to visit him and he saw how terrified I was by the dog's purple tongue and its sharp, fierce teeth. I think he enjoyed it immensely when his dog bit people. The last time I went to see him, Daddy was alone with that dog. My father died at only fifty-two. I think he was too bright to enjoy being alive. His contempt for all of humanity included himself.

'Poor Daddy! Now I understand and can have sympathy for him. How isolated from the world he was! I can only guess at his unhappiness; I understand his loneliness. He left me his wife, his daughter, all of the responsibilities of a man — and a lifetime of trying to fill the legacy of his absence.'

12

The Final Years

'I went on making films because I was too *old* to retire!' Bette told me.

'Do you know when you are old? When you don't have your health.

'As you get older, the years blend together, and you remember them that way, squashed together. One change in you is you wouldn't buy a five-year diary, although I never had one anyway. It's important, as you grow older, to have some dates to look forward to and be excited about, three months ahead, maybe six months ahead. It means a lot to mark a big date for the future on your calendar. That's prom psychology, like looking forward to your high school prom. It's always being said that you should live one day at a time. That sounds like preachy nonsense when you're young. Then one day you catch yourself really doing it. As I said, I especially don't like it when the days begin to meld together. Then, worse, they melt together. I like it when each day is different from the other.'

★ ★ ★

John Springer hadn't seen Bette since her 1983 stroke. At the Foreign Press Awards just before the 1985 Oscars, he was with Paul Newman and Joanne Woodward, Clint Eastwood, and Sylvia Sidney. As he walked down the aisle, suddenly he heard Bette's voice loudly, clearly, sharply, saying, 'John.' He believed his face betrayed his shock at seeing her so affected by the stroke, painfully thin. She said, 'You aren't going to speak to me?'

He said, 'Bette, I didn't see you.'

'Yes, you did. You saw me but you preferred *not* to, because you are with your important friends.'

Springer tried to protest, but Bette had shifted her attention.

'And, *Miss* Sidney — I believe I'm sitting in your seat, but I'm very comfortable here, and I'm not going to move, so you'll just have to find another seat,' which was exactly what Sylvia Sidney did.

'Bette was an extremely good person acting badly,' Springer said. 'She was angry at herself for being sick and looking the way she did.'

* * *

Robby Lantz had escorted Bette to a reception at the White House during the weekend of the 1987 Kennedy Center Honors. He remembered Bette, who was one of the honorees, saying to him that she was concerned about how she would be received by President Reagan, because he was aware of her being a lifelong Democrat.

Reagan originally had been a Democrat himself, but Lantz didn't mention it.

Lantz reassured her that there would no problem, that she certainly would be received as a great star, as an honored guest at the White House, and that she would be treated with the utmost respect and courtesy.

As their moment came in the receiving line, it was exactly as Lantz had predicted. The President couldn't have been more gracious to Bette, as he was to everyone, especially the guests of honor. He mentioned their days working together on *Dark Victory.*

When Mrs. Reagan saw them, she called out, 'Robby!' Suddenly she went back in time to being Nancy Davis, young, hopeful aspiring actress. Lantz had known her back then, and had helped her in her career. 'I'll be with you as soon as I'm finished in the receiving line,' she said to Lantz.

'When she joined us,' Lantz remembered, 'it was with great enthusiasm. She was lovely to Bette, and she was very warm to me, because she remembered those long-ago days of her struggle in Hollywood, before she knew what the future held for her.'

Bette was a bit put out because she didn't get to go onstage for the Kennedy Center Award. Most of the others who have been so honored enjoyed that aspect of it, remaining seated in a box with the President of the United States, and not having to feel nervous about making a speech. Not Bette.

'Whoever heard of an award where you don't

get to go up onstage and say, 'Thank you?'' she said.

'All you're allowed to do is stand up in the box and take a bow. You're next to the President, and you're not allowed to say a word. I never had an award like that.'

★ ★ ★

'Your French publisher has me working very hard here,' was Bette's greeting to me, as we met to have tea in Paris at the Plaza Athénée. 'I've let him know what I think about that.'

Bette was in Paris for the French publication of her book, *This 'n That*, in 1988. Its title in French was *Ceci et Cela*. I was there for the French publication of my own book about Groucho and the Marx Brothers, *Hello, I Must Be Going*. I had shown her book to my French publisher, and he had purchased the French rights, had it translated, and brought her to Paris for book promotion.

'I'll tell you a secret,' she went on. 'I don't really mind it. I like working hard. It's good to have work to do, especially at my age. But I have complained to the publisher. I don't like being taken advantage of, and I've always believed in taking a position.'

I noticed that she was wearing two extremely large Cartier pins on her dress, different from her usually more conservative and modest style. She, noticing my glance, said, 'I hope you don't think it's too much.

'I couldn't choose between my two favorite

pieces, so I decided I'd wear them both. After all, I don't have so much time remaining to wear either one of them.'

She had enjoyed giving television and newspaper interviews and speaking with fans in Paris. 'It's wonderful to feel so welcome and wanted.' There was one newspaper article, however, that had very much disappointed her. 'It was the one I was looking forward to, and the one most people I knew would see because it would be in English, in the *International Herald Tribune*, and I knew I would have a sympathetic interviewer.'

The interviewer was Thomas Quinn Curtis, a featured reviewer and film and theater critic at the paper, an American who was a longtime resident of Paris. He had written many times about Bette, always with respect and appreciation, and he had made a special point of saying at the paper that he *had* to be the person who would be interviewing her.

It was a long meeting, because Curtis was anxious to spend as much time as possible with the legendary star, even though he could never use that much material in the space he had available. He certainly would not have been the one to bring the meeting to an end.

Bette was accustomed to interviewers 'who didn't seem to have any other life they were ever going to and were ready to move in.'

Eagerly, Bette waited for his piece on her, which she hoped would be published while she was still in Paris. She checked each day in the newspaper delivered to her hotel suite.

Then, there it was. At first, she was pleased, but as she read further she was shocked, horrified. What stood out for her was Curtis's reference to her 'spindly legs.' She said she had not read further. She asked me, 'Do you think I have spindly legs?'

I said I didn't. Bette was extremely thin after her battle with cancer, and the battle was ongoing. She found it difficult to eat, but her legs, though thin, had kept their shapeliness. She had always been proud of what she usually referred to as her 'gams.' She told me that those words had spoiled her trip to Paris.

Curtis, who felt he had written a work of extravagant praise about the actress he respected, was hurt because he never had any word from her after his piece appeared. He wondered if she might have missed seeing his story.

'It would seem that I've already been mortified enough for one lifetime,' Bette said to me. I understood that she was referring to *My Mother's Keeper*.

Bette had been told her daughter's book was terrible, that it would hurt her deeply, but she hoped those who had told her had exaggerated. 'They hadn't. It was more horrible than anything I could have imagined. No question about it.'

She didn't want anyone to recognize her buying the book in the bookstore. 'That would have been *too* mortifying. I sent someone to the store to buy the book for me. I wanted to be able to say to anyone who ever asked me that I hadn't read it.'

She said she couldn't bear the idea that the salesclerk might tell someone, and that the story of her buying the book might appear in a column that B.D. might read, and which might give her daughter satisfaction. 'She didn't send me a complimentary copy of her highly uncomplimentary book,' Bette told me. 'I suppose she was counting every book sold. Even in writing her book, she had to depend on her mother in order to be able to sell her book to a publisher, and then to anyone else.

'I had to know what it said. I read every searing word. I read it only once. I will not need to go back. I will remember every hate-filled sentence branded on my soul, as long as I live.

'She said I 'bellowed'!' B.D. had left no doubt as to her picture of her mother, the picture she wanted to share with the world.

It was, Bette said, more painful than anything she had endured in the hospital, worse than her mastectomy, more terrible torture than the strokes.

'How cruel, not to leave you a happy memory! It's like leaving you only broken bric-a-brac in your mind.

'After I read it once, I threw it into the garbage where it belonged.

'You can love someone who doesn't love you. You *can't* love someone who *hates* you, once you have learned that that person hates you, and has hated you over a long time while pretending not to, and fooling you.

'I never considered not reading it,' Bette said. 'Can you imagine? Everyone else would know

405

what it said, and I would be the only one in the dark.

'Above all, I had to know what *I* would say to B.D., who was my only natural child, my pride and joy, whom I had always adored from the moment I held her on the day of her birth.

'I thought about when we came face-to-face, or when I called her. I couldn't imagine what words I would speak to her. After I read what she had written about me, I no longer needed to think about what I would say to her — *ever*.

'She had gotten out of me what she would get out of me. I don't have so much money, but whatever I have, if I die soon enough to have some left, it will *not* go to her. So what she has from me now is my name and reputation to attack in that book. I don't know if she did what she did for money or just to hurt me. Probably both.

'But even for that, take note, she needed my name, Bette Davis. If she hadn't been the daughter of Bette Davis, I repeat, who would have wanted her book?

'She broke my heart, if that's what satisfied her.

'I've always had my pride, and my first reaction was I didn't want her to know that she had broken my heart, though she probably did know it. Ruthie and she were the two persons I loved most in my life. Ruthie was the first half, B.D. the second half. Ruthie always gave everything for me. Sometimes, her advice wasn't the right thing for me, but it was always what she believed was best, and it was the best she had to offer.

'With B.D., I gave her whatever I had to offer, all my love, my presence, because I wanted to be with her. I gave her whatever money could buy, or at least whatever *my* money could buy, her kitten, her pony.

'Finding out that my only natural child not only didn't love me but actually detested me was the most terrible thing that happened in my life. Absolutely.'

Bette never again spoke to her daughter.

★ ★ ★

I asked Bette what she thought of our French publisher.

'Eugéne's a very attractive man, she said. 'Very.'

He told me *his* version of their meeting.

Visiting Bette in the Paris hotel suite he had provided for her, he was greeted more warmly than he had expected. She kissed him, but it was not the kiss he had anticipated, brushing each cheek, kissing the air in the French manner, or even the Russian style, since he was Russian, three kisses rather than two.

'This was none of that,' he said. 'Bette Davis came up to me and pressed against me as she kissed me on the lips, *passionately*.'

'How did you feel about her doing that?'

'I was very surprised. I had provided a lovely suite, but . . .

'She had great *joie de vivre*, even at about

407

eighty, and you could see she was so sick. At the moment, I was very embarrassed. She didn't seem to be embarrassed at all, so I got over it.

'Later, looking back, I remember the moment as if it just happened, and now I rather cherish it.

'I hope she enjoyed herself. I have enjoyed the memory.'

In November 1988, the French publisher gave a party for Bette at the ultra-chic Parisian club owned by Régine. The invitation was for nine P.M.

When I arrived there, a little before nine, the place was dark. It seemed closed. I kept my taxi, thinking I might have come to the wrong place, though the driver assured me he couldn't be wrong 'It would be like not being able to find the Eiffel Tower,' he said.

While venturing out to examine the building more closely, I heard a voice calling my name. There was no mistaking *that* voice.

'Come here,' Bette said. She was in the back seat of a small limousine. 'What time is it? What does this mean? What's wrong with *your* publisher? How do you explain this? Where is he?'

I was suddenly responsible for the French publisher. Needless to say, I could not answer where my publisher was, only minutes before the party was officially scheduled to begin.

As we spoke, lights went on, the door opened, and emissaries of Régine rushed to greet Bette. I entered behind her, without fanfare.

From nine to ten, guests straggled in, and

408

continued appearing until after eleven, when the party really became crowded. The guests were elegantly attired, the ladies in black cocktail dresses, some in long dresses, with high heels, jewels, and elaborate accessories. This truly pleased Bette, who regarded it as their token of respect for her.

Before ten, the host arrived. Bette was accustomed to seeing him in extremely casual clothes, and commented to me that she was happy to see him looking so elegant for the occasion. He presided grandly, obviously proud of his guest of honor, as he greeted people.

Bette confronted him and asked in a sharply accusatory tone, 'Where were you? Why were you so late?'

It hadn't occurred to him that she would be the first to arrive. He didn't know about Bette's propensity for punctuality and her belief that 'the only way to be perfectly punctual is to be perfectly early.'

'You should apologize,' Bette told him.

He apologized, though I didn't think he felt it was necessary. He later told me that nobody in Paris would come to a nine o'clock party at nine o'clock.

Bette was instantly satisfied, and she went on to enjoy the occasion.

As she left very late, or rather very early in the morning, she said, 'It's too bad the party can't last.'

★   ★   ★

The last time I saw Bette Davis was at the gala of the Film Society of Lincoln Center in New York City at which she was their honoree. It was April 24, 1989 in Avery Fisher Hall. Joseph Mankiewicz, James Stewart, and Geraldine Fitzgerald were among the stars who appeared to speak for her.

Roy Furman, president of the Film Society, introduced her as someone who had 'all by herself defined what it is to be an actress for the screen, using her brains and instinct and experience to play the widest possible spectrum of roles, and to give each the indelible stamp of her personality.'

Furman remembered being surprised by Bette's nervousness. One of the great cinema stars of the century, she had been the subject of numerous tributes, so Furman couldn't help noticing that she was extremely apprehensive before her appearance. It was also interesting for him to note how much she appreciated the Film Society of Lincoln Center's tribute to her. He observed her fragile state as she sat in her wheelchair, waiting, and despite her firm insistence that she would walk onstage, Furman had arranged an alternate plan should the need arise for her to make her onstage entrance in the wheelchair.

Following the film clips and recognition of her career by the speakers, Bette was introduced. On cue, she astounded Furman by virtually springing out of the wheelchair, and walking to the microphone.

After a standing ovation, Bette paused and surveyed the festive, glittering hall with its black-tie audience. Then, she said:

'What a dump!'

'There was an explosion of laughter,' Furman recalled. 'It was an extraordinary ice-breaker.'

When Bette told the audience that had come there to pay tribute to her, 'It's about time,' there was more laughter.

She closed her speech with a line from *The Cabin in the Cotton*, which was, she said, her favorite line from all of her films:

'Ah'd love to kiss you, but Ah just washed mah hair.'

At the end of the evening, Bette seemed the happiest I had seen her since the days before illness and frailty, and her daughter's book had brought her down.

Though exceedingly thin, she was carefully coiffed and made-up, and fashionably attired — bravely, to use her words, 'soldiering on.' After the program, a genuine glow seemed to have replaced the pallor that had come with her illness. I told her that she had 'celebrity glow.' We had some years before talked about how celebrities seem to radiate a glow in public that reflects the energy of all those eyes focused on them, and her smile indicated that she remembered our conversations.

'I like to think of it as keeping one's aura,' she said. 'You can't let people down. A little of it may be adrenaline. Adrenaline is a woman's best makeup. I've always enjoyed honors, and I particularly like this kind of thing tonight, where I'm not in competition with other actors. But the real secret behind my glow tonight is makeup

411

— some blue eye shadow, some brown mascara, and a nice red lipstick, without a fancy name, just a nice bright red.'

At the Tavern on the Green party afterward, Bette was in a serious mood. She told me that seeing the clips from her films had meant a great deal to her. 'I've really been very successful in my life. I'm proud. I did what I set out to do, something worth doing.' She said the Film Society honor meant more to her that evening and she appreciated it more than she would have at an earlier time. 'I am glad it was saved in my honors bank.

'When someone first called me a living legend, I wasn't so enthusiastic. It implied I was faded, old, or worse yet, retired. Well, now I've adjusted, resigned myself. At first, it sounded to me like I was a building that had been landmarked. Tonight, I found it very satisfying to be a living legend — well, *almost* living.

'I'm not as out-of-date as I used to be. There's nothing as out-of-date as that which has *just* gone out-of-date, and I've been out-of-date a *very* long time.'

The last words she spoke to me were:

'I'm like a cat. Nine lives. Throw me into the air, and I land on my feet.

'I want to die with my high heels on, still in action.'

★   ★   ★

I was in Paris when I read that Bette Davis had just died there.

412

I had been reading that Bette was in Spain where the San Sebastian Film Festival was honoring her, and I knew that she would be enjoying the affectionate acclaim of fans, not only the Spaniards, but visitors from many countries. Her appearances were triumphant.

Then she became ill. At first it seemed to be flu, brought on by exhaustion from the trip, her insecurity because of her physical appearance, the effort of always being Bette Davis, and her abiding concern with never disappointing her public.

She had been accompanied to San Sebastian by Kathryn Sermak, who immediately arranged for 'Miss D.,' as she called her, to leave by chartered plane for Paris. The doctors in Spain had strongly advised against attempting the trip back to America.

Bette's greatest concern was that she be able to board the plane without using a wheelchair, though she was barely able to walk. She didn't want her fans there to have their last image of Bette Davis be of her in a wheelchair, and the press would be there taking photographs that would be seen everywhere.

Her force of will proved stronger than her illness. She did manage to board the plane without using a wheelchair. Though I didn't see a full-length picture of her, I imagined she was wearing her high heels, as she would have wished.

When she arrived on October 3 at the American Hospital in Neuilly, the French doctors initially offered some hope, but soon

413

they determined there was none.

It is the French policy for doctors, if the patient seems strong enough and able to cope with it, to tell the person when there is no more hope, in case there is something the patient has left undone.

The doctors told Sermak that Bette Davis would not be recovering, that there was nothing more they could do. They asked her if she knew how Madame Davis would feel if they told her the truth. Was she a person who would want to know? Would she be able to cope with what she heard — that her death was imminent, a matter of hours at worst, days at best?

Sermak knew that Bette did not want lies. Bette had said, 'I cannot tolerate not knowing in what condition I actually am. If there has to be pain, I will take it, but not knowing what is really the matter with me is intolerable.' Without any hesitancy, Sermak told the doctors to tell her the truth.

Bette's reaction was to ask for a telephone. She went into action with all of her remaining strength. There was no time to waste.

She had to call Harold Schiff, whom she trusted to handle her affairs after she was gone. She was anxious not to leave unfinished business, great or small, because she did not wish to burden anyone.

Then, she called California to speak with Lew Wasserman, who had meant so much in her career, to tell him that she would not be able to have lunch with him on the next Friday.

Bette died in Paris on Friday, October 6,

1989. She was eighty-one years old.

In her will, Bette specifically disinherited her daughter, B.D., who did not contest the will. Except for a few small bequests, Bette left everything to her companion, Kathryn Sermak, who had faithfully supported her through her illnesses and all she had endured in her last years, and to Michael Merrill, the son she and Gary had adopted, who had become a successful lawyer.

★ ★ ★

As I read the lengthy obituaries in the Paris newspapers, I remembered Bette talking with me, looking back on 'my life as Bette Davis,' as she put it.

'The reason most people look back on their youth as the best time of life,' she said, 'is because a blank page looks better than one that is filled not quite according to our youthful expectations and optimistic dreams. Personally, I'm proud of the way I've filled the pages of my life, anyway my professional life. I'm enjoying my life as Bette Davis now, since I probably won't be around to read about it when it appears in the obituaries.

'I see my life now as a voyage of discovery. My problem was I didn't know myself. I used to think it was because I didn't understand the others, but now I know it's because I didn't understand me.

'They said I was a monster, but if I became a monster, it was because I was in a monstrous

415

business. I couldn't ever afford to have my armor penetrated, because underneath, I was unprotected. Or so I thought. Now, as I approach the winter of my life, that winter which does not lead to spring, I realize that I've nothing to be ashamed of as a person.

'I've discovered that underneath the vulnerable person is the real armor. I've always wanted to like people, though it gets harder to trust. You don't want to be hurt. But unless you can trust, you aren't open to life, and when you aren't open to life, you are old, whatever age you are.

'One could live one's life differently if one knew how long one had to live. Some people might spend their last dollar on the holiday they'd always wanted. Money is heavenly when you're young. It can buy so much that you want. When you are old, money doesn't buy so much. Age is a leveler. But I'd want to be sure I had enough money to leave to take care of the people I care about who've grown used to depending on me. I'd also want to be sure I didn't die owing anyone any money. Once I owed my lawyer, Harold Schiff, forty thousand dollars. I'd put up my house for sale, and it wasn't selling. I was terrified something would happen to me before I could pay him back.

'If you ask me, is getting old worth it, the answer is yes, considering the alternative. 'Old age ain't no place for sissies.' You've seen the pillow in my home that says that.

'Old age is when you want things to stay the same because you've stopped hoping they're going to get better.

416

'One certainly can't get used to the idea of dying because, after all, it's so new. One has never done it before.

'I always thought something I could enjoy after my career slowed down was more leisurely travel. My plan was to go to the Savoy Hotel for as many days or weeks as I thought I could afford, maybe even a little more than I thought I could afford, a splurge, you know. A late-life splurge. I felt I'd earned that for myself, a selfish pleasure. At the Savoy Hotel in London.

'Many people say that staying in an expensive hotel is a waste of money because all you do is sleep there. I disagree mightily. I feel that the view from the river suite, looking out and looking in, colors your whole stay there.

'I stayed in one of the most beautiful suites I was ever in, a river suite, of course. That old gorgeous furniture. The drawing room. That view. And the gorgeous bed.

'But not alone. With *whom* you go is more important than *where* you go.

'I can't forget a line from *Watch on the Rhine*. I didn't realize it at the time, but it was to become the dominant theme of my life. My character, Sara, said:

''I don't like being alone at night. Now it's going to be for always — all the rest of my life.'

'It's terrible to believe, to know, that every night for all the rest of your life, you are going to get into bed alone. That's an enormous truth.

'I had a terrifying thought the other night. I realized that most of me is in the past. The days behind me are many, and the days ahead of me are few. It all went so fast. If I could just borrow one of those days or nights from the past and live it now.

'It's strange to look like an old lady on the outside, to see your own wrinkles, while you feel just as you did when you were a girl. To be a mother, a grandmother, and just to want to cry out for your own mother! Sometimes when I was the sole support of all of those people, I just wanted to cry out for my mother and have her hold me.

'I never thought about it before, but I wonder — did Ruthie ever feel that way when she was left with Bobby and me? A part of me never grew up, but now it's too late. Lamentable.

'The saddest moment in any woman's life is when she says goodbye to being a woman. I could not have survived that moment if I'd recognized it when it happened. It was only long afterwards during the Great Void that I knew it had already taken place.

'A woman can live without sex, but not without the hope of sex.

'I was Margo Channing when what I wanted to be was Jezebel. Now I'm what's left of Baby Jane. The worst thing is when you see it in other people's eyes. They see you on television in *Eve* or *Now, Voyager* or something, and then they see you in person. You're expected to look the same. There's such a terrible disbelief in their eyes.

'As a struggling young actress, I idolized Jane Cowl on the stage. Many years later, in *Payment on Demand*, I got to work with her. I can't forget

418

the lines her character spoke to me in the final scene:

'"When a woman grows old, loneliness is an island and time is an avalanche.'

'How prophetic! There's another line in that film I can't forget:

'"When you love a man and lose him, you may think it makes you an individual again — but it doesn't! It makes you a nothing!'

'A woman can't be on her own as easily as a man, even if she has all the money she needs, even if she made it herself. It simply isn't as comfortable for her sitting in a restaurant alone as it would be for a man. Everyone wants an extra man. People certainly don't want an extra woman at their dinner party. Even in a restaurant they put you at an out-of-view table. Men feel we can't exist without them. Well, we *can*. Sort of. But it isn't much fun.

'Men have it so much better in life. They can buy sex and still enjoy it. I could never do that, pay for love. And I'm sure nobody wants this old body for free. They say a woman can enjoy sex longer than a man. Tommyrot! How can she enjoy it if she can't *get* any? That's not very enjoyable, is it? Sex really isn't one of those things that's a whole lot of fun to do alone.

'But as far as sex is concerned in my life, I'm all zipped up.

'They say that a woman gets over her desire for sex, the way I was once told your skin stops breaking out at a certain age. Well, they're wrong. My wishes are the same as those of the romantic girl who thought nothing of saying no.

Funny thing — I spent most of my youth protecting my virginity, and now I'm a virgin again, and it doesn't need any protecting! But one's second virginity is even more frustrating.

'A good actress can always play more stupid, fatter, older than she is. It's only a problem going in the other direction. I had the advantage over other actresses because I was happy to play a woman in her sixties when I was in my thirties.

'Willie Wyler told me that Greer Garson hadn't wanted to do *Mrs. Miniver* because she had to play a mother to a grown son, Richard Ney. The hysterical part of the story was, when they finished the film, she married Ney!

'Personally, I've always been drawn to men younger than I. They aren't so set in their ways, and they still have their optimism and sense of adventure. But I couldn't act on it because society doesn't condone such a relationship. Older men can choose someone younger than their granddaughters, while no one believes a younger man can really love an older woman. She's laughed at behind her back. Why is it so forbidden, especially when women have a much longer sexual prime than men? Maybe someday this attitude will change, and it will be better for women. Alas, too late for me!

'As I've told you, Queen Elizabeth was sixty-five at the time I played her. Falling in love with Essex, she felt no differently from so many other women throughout the centuries, but she could dare to show her feelings, because she was a queen. Speaking to an Essex who had already been lost to her, she said, 'I could be young with you, but now I'm old. I know now how it will be without you.' That was when Elizabeth knew she was old, when she knew she would be alone . . .

'Do you know when I felt old? When I believed I'd never fall in love again. The greatest human need is to love and be loved.

'What I wanted most in life was love, but I was never good at getting love and I couldn't understand why. Looking back, it could have been because I wasn't lovable.

'What advice do I have for living? Leave your baggage. Get a bunch of flowers for your bare little apartment instead of waiting for the house you're going to build someday.

'Not everything turned out as I expected. Oh, if only life could be lived backwards, how much we'd appreciate youth. But perhaps the true great joy of youth is that we *don't* appreciate it. Not until we don't *have* it anymore. We just take it for granted, which is the greatest luxury.

'I was always afraid of being alone. I was less afraid of dying. And my worst fear came true. Perhaps my utter fear of it even helped to make it come true. I've been lonely *with* people for much of my life. Now I shall be exploring what it's like to be lonely alone.

'Everyone needs to be 'us' instead of 'me.' There's nothing in life worth having unless you have someone to share it with. Person-to-person — that's what life is all about.

'Perhaps my sense of self was *too* well developed. Perhaps my problem wasn't loneliness, but *only*-ness.

'Life is a Dark Victory. When confronted with

death, we're all engaged in the Dark Victory. What I've been able to do in these last years, even after illness and betrayal, I consider that *this* was my Bright Victory.

'Happiness should never be postponed. Life is the past, the present, and the perhaps . . . '

Filmography

The Bad Sister A Universal Picture. Carl Laemmle, Jr., production head. Directed by Hobart Henley. Screenplay by Raymond L. Schrock and Tom Reed, with additional dialogue by Edwin Knopf, based on *The Flirt* by Booth Tarkington. Photographed by Karl Freund. Edited by Ted Kent. Opened Globe Theatre, N.Y., March 29, 1931. 68 minutes.

Cast: Conrad Nagel, Sidney Fox, Bette Davis, Zasu Pitts, Slim Summerville, Charles Winninger, Emma Dunn, Humphrey Bogart, Bert Roach, David Durand.

Seed A Universal Picture. Carl Laemmle, Jr., production head. Produced and directed by John M. Stahl. Screenplay by Gladys Lehman, based on the novel by Charles G. Norris. Photographed by Jackson Rose. Edited by Arthur Tavares. Opened Rivoli Theatre, N.Y., May 14, 1931. 90 minutes.

Cast: John Boles, Genevieve Tobin, Lois Wilson, Raymond Hackett, Bette Davis, Frances Dade, Zasu Pitts, Richard Tucker, Jack Willis, Don Cox, Dick Winslow, Kenneth Seiling, Terry Cox, Helen Parrish, Dickie Moore.

Waterloo Bridge A Universal Picture. Carl Laemmle, Jr., production head. Directed by James Whale. Screenplay by Benn W. Levy, with continuity and additional dialogue by Tom Reed, based on the play by Robert E. Sherwood. Photographed by Arthur Edeson. Edited by James Whale. Remade by MGM in 1940 with Vivien Leigh and Robert Taylor, and in 1956 as *Gaby* with Leslie Caron and John Kerr. Opened RKO Mayfair Theatre, N.Y., September 4, 1931. 72 minutes.

Cast: Mae Clarke, Kent Douglas (Douglass Montgomery), Doris Lloyd, Ethel Griffies, Enid Bennett, Frederick Kerr, Bette Davis, Rita Carlisle.

Way Back Home An RKO Picture. Produced by Pandro S. Berman. Directed by William A. Seiter. Screenplay, *Other People's Business*, by Jane Murfin. Based on radio characters created by Phillips Lord. Photographed by J. Roy Hunt. Music (unbilled) by Max Steiner. Opened RKO Mayfair Theatre, N.Y., January 15, 1932. 81 minutes.

Cast: Phillips Lord, Effie Palmer, Mrs. Phillips Lord, Bennett Kilpack. Raymond Hunter, Frank Albertson, Bette Davis, Oscar Apfel, Stanley Fields, Dorothy Peterson, Frankie Darro.

The Menace A Columbia Picture. Produced by Sam Nelson. Directed by Roy William Neill. Screenplay by Dorothy Howell and Charles Logue, with additional dialogue by Roy

Chanslor, based on the novel *The Feathered Serpent* by Edgar Wallace. Photographed by L. William O'Connell. Edited by Gene Havlick. Opened Beacon Theatre, N.Y., January 29, 1932. 64 minutes.

Cast: H. B. Warner, Bette Davis, Walter Byron, Natalie Moorhead, William B. Davidson, Crauford Kent, Halliwell Hobbes, Charles Gerrard, Murray Kinnell.

Hell's House A Capitol Film Exchange release. Produced by Benjamin F. Zeidman. Directed by Howard Higgin. Screenplay by Paul Gangelin and B. Harrison Orkow, based on a story by Howard Higgin. Photographed by Allen S. Siegel. Edited by Edward Schroeder. Also released as *Juvenile Court*. Opened Strand Theatre, N.Y., January 30, 1932. 72 minutes.

Cast: Junior Durkin, Pat O'Brien, Bette Davis, Junior Coghlan, Charley Grapewin, Emma Dunn, James Marcus, Morgan Wallace, Wallis Clark, Hooper Atchley.

The Man Who Played God A Warner Brothers —Vitaphone Picture. Produced by D. F. Zanuck. Directed by John Adolfi. Screenplay by Julien Josephson and Maude T. Howell, adapted from a short story by Gouverneur Morris and the play *The Silent Voice* by Jules Eckert Goodman. Photographed by James Van Trees. Edited by William Holmes. Costumes by Orry-Kelly. Makeup by Perc Westmore. Piano solos by Salvatore Santaella. Remade by Warner Brothers in 1955 as *Sincerely Yours* with Walter Liberace.

Opened Warner Theatre, N.Y., February 10, 1932. 80 minutes.

Cast: George Arliss, Violet Heming, Ivan Simpson, Louise Closser Hale, Bette Davis, Donald Cook, Paul Porcasi, Oscar Apfel, William Janney, Grace Durkin, Dorothy Libaire, André Luget, Charles Evans, Murray Kinnell, Wade Boteler, Alexander Ikonniko, Ray Milland, Hedda Hopper.

So Big A Warner Brothers — Vitaphone Picture. Production supervisor, Lucien Hubbard. Directed by William A. Wellman. Screenplay by J. Grubb Alexander and Robert Lord, based on the novel by Edna Ferber. Photographed by Sid Hickox. Edited by William Holmes. Music by W. Franke Harling. Costumes by Orry-Kelly. First made by First National Pictures in 1925 with Colleen Moore, and by Warner Brothers in 1953 with Jane Wyman. Opened Strand Theatre, N.Y., April 29, 1932. 82 minutes.

Cast: Barbara Stanwyck, George Brent, Dickie Moore, Bette Davis, Guy Kibbee, Mae Madison, Hardie Albright, Robert Warwick, Arthur Stone, Earle Foxe, Alan Hale, Dorothy Peterson, Dawn O'Day (Anne Shirley), Dick Winslow, Elizabeth Patterson, Rita LeRoy (Rita La Roy), Blanche Friderici, Lionel Bellmore.

The Rich Are Always With Us A First National Picture, released by Warner Brothers. D. F. Zanuck in charge of production. Production supervisor, Raymond Griffith. Directed by Alfred E. Green. Screenplay by Austin Parker, based on the novel by E. Pettit. Photographed by Ernest Haller. Edited by George Marks. Music by W. Franke Harling. Costumes by Orry-Kelly. Opened Strand Theatre, N.Y., May 15, 1932. 73 minutes.

Cast: Ruth Chatterton, George Brent, Adrienne Dore, Bette Davis, John Miljan, Mae Madison, John Wray, Robert Warwick, Virginia Hammond, Walter Walker, Eula Gray, Edith Allen, Ethel Kenyon, Ruth Lee, Berton Churchill.

The Dark Horse A First National Picture, released by Warner Brothers. D. F. Zanuck in charge of production. Production supervisors, Raymond Griffith and Hal B. Wallis. Directed by Alfred E. Green. Screenplay by Joseph Jackson and Wilson Mizner, based on an original story by Melville Crossman (D. F. Zanuck), Joseph Jackson, and Courtenay Terrett. Photographed by Sol Polito. Art direction by Jack Okey. Edited by George Marks. Opened Winter Garden Theatre, N.Y., June 8, 1932. 75 minutes.

Cast: Warren William, Bette Davis, Guy Kibbee, Frank McHugh, Vivienne Osborne, Sam Hardy, Robert Warwick, Harry Holman, Charles Sellon, Robert Emmett O'Connor, Berton Churchill.

The Cabin in the Cotton A First National Picture, released by Warner Brothers. D. F. Zanuck in charge of production. Production supervisor, Hal Wallis. Directed by Michael

Curtiz. Screenplay by Paul Green, based on the novel by Harry Harrison Kroll. Photographed by Barney McGill. Edited by George Amy. Opened Strand Theatre, N.Y., September 29, 1932. 79 minutes.

Cast: Richard Barthelmess, Bette Davis, Dorothy Jordan, Henry B. Walthall, Berton Churchill, Walter Percival, William Le Maire, Hardie Albright, Edmund Breese, Tully Marshall, Clarence Muse, Russell Simpson, John Marston, Erville Alderson, Dorothy Peterson, Snow Flake, Harry Cording.

Three on a Match A First National Picture, released by Warner Brothers. D. F. Zanuck in charge of production. Production supervisor, Ray Griffith. Directed by Mervyn LeRoy. Screenplay by Lucien Hubbard, based on an original story by Kubec Glasmon and John Bright. Photographed by Sol Polito. Art direction by Robert Haas. Edited by Ray Curtiss. Sheila Terry sang 'My Diane.' Remade by Warner Brothers in 1938 as *Broadway Musketeers*. Opened Strand Theatre, N.Y., October 28, 1932. 63 minutes.

Cast: Joan Blondell, Warren William, Ann Dvorak, Bette Davis, Grant Mitchell, Lyle Talbot, Sheila Terry, Glenda Farrell, Clara Blandick, Buster Phelps, Humphrey Bogart, John Marston, Patricia Ellis, Hale Hamilton, Frankie Darro, Dawn O'Day (Anne Shirley), Virginia Davis, Dick Brandon, Allen Jenkins, Jack La Rue, Edward Arnold.

20,000 Years in Sing Sing A First National Picture, released by Warner Brothers. D. F. Zanuck in charge of production. Production supervisor, Raymond Griffith. Directed by Michael Curtiz. Screenplay by Wilson Mizner and Brown Holmes. Adaptation by Courtenay Terrett and Robert Lord, based on the book by Warden Lewis E. Lawes. Photographed by Barney McGill. Music by Bernhard Kaun. Edited by George Amy. Remade in 1940 by Warner Brothers as *Castle on the Hudson* with John Garfield and Ann Sheridan. Opened Strand Theatre, N.Y., January 9, 1933. 77 minutes.

Cast: Spencer Tracy, Bette Davis, Lyle Talbot, Arthur Byron, Sheila Terry, Edward McNamara, Warren Hymer, Louis Calhern, Spencer Charters, Sam Godfrey, Grant Mitchell, Nella Walker, Harold Huber, William Le Maire, Arthur Hoyt, George Pat Collins.

Parachute Jumper A Warner Brothers Picture. D. F. Zanuck in charge of production. Production supervisor, Raymond Griffith. Directed by Alfred E. Green. Screenplay by John Francis Larkin, based on the story *Some Call It Love* by Rian James. Photographed by James Van Trees. Art direction by Jack Okey. Edited by Ray Curtiss. Opened Strand Theatre, N.Y., January 25, 1933. 65 minutes.

Cast: Douglas Fairbanks, Jr., Leo Carrillo, Bette Davis, Frank McHugh, Claire Dodd, Sheila Terry, Harold Huber, Thomas E. Jackson, George Pat Collins, Pat O'Malley, Harold Healy, Ferdinand Munier, Walter C. Miller.

The Working Man A Warner Brothers — Vitaphone Picture. D. F. Zanuck in charge of production. Production supervisor, Lucien Hubbard. Directed by John Adolfi. Screenplay by Maude T. Howell and Charles Kenyon, based on the story 'The Adopted Father' by Edgar Franklin. Photographed by Sol Polito. Art direction by Jack Okey. Costumes by Orry-Kelly. Edited by Owen Marks. Opened Radio City Music Hall, N.Y., April 20, 1933. 73 minutes.

Cast: George Arliss, Bette Davis, Hardie Albright, Theodore Newton, Gordon Westcott, J. Farrell MacDonald, Charles Evans, Frederick Burton, Edward Van Sloan, Pat Wing, Claire McDowell, Harold Minjir, Douglass Dumbrille.

Ex-Lady A Warner Brothers — Vitaphone Picture. D. F. Zanuck in charge of production. Production supervisor, Lucien Hubbard. Directed by Robert Florey. Screenplay by David Boehm, based on an original story by Edith Fitzgerald and Robert Riskin. Photographed by Tony Gaudio. Edited by Harold McLernon. First made by Warner Brothers in 1931 as *Illicit*, with Barbara Stanwyck. Opened Strand Theatre, N.Y., May 14, 1933. 62 minutes.

Cast: Bette Davis, Gene Raymond, Frank McHugh, Monroe Owsley, Claire Dodd, Kay Strozzi, Ferdinand Gottschalk, Alphonse Ethier, Bodil Rosing.

Bureau of Missing Persons A First National Picture, released by Warner Brothers. Production supervisor, Henry Blanke. Directed by Roy Del

Ruth. Screenplay by Robert Presnell, based on the book *Missing Men* by Police Captain John H. Ayers and Carol Bird. Art direction by Robert Haas. Photographed by Barney McGill. Edited by James Gibbon. Opened Strand Theatre, N.Y., September 8, 1933. 75 minutes.

Cast: Bette Davis, Lewis Stone, Pat O'Brien, Glenda Farrell, Allen Jenkins, Ruth Donnelly, Hugh Herbert, Alan Dinehart, Marjorie Gateson, Tad Alexander, Noël Francis, Wallis Clark, Adrian Morris, Clay Clement, Henry Kolker, Harry Beresford, George Chandler.

Fashions of 1934 A First National Picture, released by Warner Brothers. Production supervisor, Henry Blanke. Directed by William Dieterle. Screenplay by F. Hugh Herbert, Gene Markey, Kathryn Scola, and Carl Erickson. Based on the story 'The Fashion Plate' by Harry Collins and Warren Duff. Photographed by William Rees. Art direction by Jack Okey and Willy Pogany. Costumes by Orry-Kelly. Songs by Sammy Fain and Irving Kahal. Choreography by Busby Berkeley. Edited by Jack Killifer. Opened Hollywood Theatre, N.Y., January 19, 1934. 77 minutes.

Cast: William Powell, Bette Davis, Frank McHugh, Verree Teasdale, Reginald Owen, Henry O'Neill, Philip Reed, Hugh Herbert, Gordon Westcott, Nella Walker, Dorothy Burgess, Etienne Girardot, William Burress, Spencer Charters, Jane Darwell, Arthur Treacher, Hobart Cavanaugh, Albert Conti.

The Big Shakedown A First National Picture, released by Warner Brothers. Production supervisor, Samuel Bischoff. Directed by John Francis Dillon. Screenplay by Niven Busch and Rian James, based on the story 'Cut Rate' by Samuel Engel. Photographed by Sid Hickox. Edited by James Gibbon. Opened Mayfair Theatre, N.Y., February 11, 1934. 64 minutes.

Cast: Charles Farrell, Bette Davis, Ricardo Cortez, Glenda Farrell, Allen Jenkins, Henry O'Neill, Philip Faversham, Robert Emmett O'Connor, John Wray, George Pat Collins, Adrian Morris, Dewey Robinson, Samuel S. Hinds, Matt Briggs, William B. Davidson, Earl Foxe, Frederick Burton.

Jimmy the Gent A Warner Brothers — Vitaphone Picture. Production supervisor, Robert Lord. Directed by Michael Curtiz. Screenplay by Bertram Milhauser, based on the story 'The Heir Chaser' by Laird Doyle and Ray Nazzaro. Art direction by Esdras Hartley. Photographed by Ira Morgan. Edited by Tommy Richards. Opened Strand Theatre, N.Y., March 25, 1934. 66 minutes.

Cast: James Cagney, Bette Davis, Alice White, Allen Jenkins, Arthur Hohl, Alan Dinehart, Philip Reed, Hobart Cavanaugh, Mayo Methot, Ralf Harolde, Joe Sawyer, Philip Faversham, Nora Lane, Howard Hickman, Jane Darwell, Joseph Crehan, Robert Warwick, Harold Entwhistle.

Fog Over Frisco A First National Picture released by Warner Brothers. Production supervisor, Henry Blanke. Directed by William Dieterle. Screenplay by Robert N. Lee and Eugene Solow, based on an original story by George Dyer, 'The Five Fragments.' Photographed by Tony Gaudio. Edited by Harold McLernon. Remade by Warner Brothers in 1942 as *Spy Ship*. Opened Strand Theatre, N.Y., June 6, 1934. 67 minutes.

Cast: Bette Davis, Donald Woods, Margaret Lindsay, Lyle Talbot, Art Byron, Hugh Herbert, Douglas Dumbrille, Robert Barrat, Henry O'Neill, Irving Pichel, Gordon Westcott, Charles C. Wilson, Alan Hale, Sr., William Davidson, Douglas Cosgrove, George Chandler, Harold Minjir, William Demarest.

Of Human Bondage An RKO Radio Picture. Produced by Pandro S. Berman. Directed by John Cromwell. Screenplay by Lester Cohen, based on the novel by W. Somerset Maugham. Photographed by Henry W. Gerrard. Art direction by Van Nest Polglase and Carroll Clark. Edited by William Morgan. Gowns by Walter Plunkett. Music by Max Steiner. Remade by Warner Brothers in 1946 with Eleanor Parker and Paul Henreid and by MGM in 1964 with Kim Novak and Laurence Harvey. Opened Radio City Music Hall, N.Y., June 28, 1934. 83 minutes.

Cast: Leslie Howard, Bette Davis, Frances Dee, Kay Johnson, Reginald Denny, Alan Hale,

Sr., Reginald Owen, Reginald Sheffield, Desmond Roberts.

Housewife A Warner Brothers — Vitaphone Picture. Production supervisor, Robert Lord. Directed by Alfred E. Green. Screenplay by Manuel Seff and Lillie Hayward, based on an original story by Robert Lord and Lillie Hayward. Art direction by Robert Haas. Costumes by Orry-Kelly. Music and lyrics by Mort Dixon and Allie Wrubel. Photographed by William Rees. Edited by James Gibbon. Made before *Of Human Bondage*, but released afterward. Opened Strand Theatre, N.Y., August 9, 1934. 69 minutes.

Cast: George Brent, Bette Davis, Ann Dvorak, John Halliday, Ruth Donnelly, Hobart Cavanaugh, Robert Barrat, Joseph Cawthorn, Phil Regan, Willard Robertson, Ronald Cosbey, Leila Bennett, William B. Davidson, John Hale.

Bordertown A Warner Brothers — Vitaphone Picture. Production supervisor, Robert Lord. Directed by Archie Mayo. Screenplay by Laird Doyle and Wallace Smith, adapted by Robert Lord, based on the novel by Carroll Graham. Photographed by Tony Gaudio. Art direction by Jack Okey. Edited by Thomas Richards. Music by Bernhard Kaun. Made before *Of Human Bondage*, but released afterward. Remade by Warner Brothers in 1941 as *They Drive by Night*, with Ida Lupino. Opened Strand Theatre, N.Y., January 23, 1935. 80 minutes.

Cast: Paul Muni, Bette Davis, Margaret

Lindsay, Gavin Gordon, Arthur Stone, Robert Barrat, Soledad Jiménez, Eugene Pallette, William B. Davidson, Hobart Cavanaugh, Henry O'Neill, Vivian Tobin, Oscar Apfel, Samuel S. Hinds, Chris Pin Martin, Frank Puglia, Jack Norton.

The Girl from 10th Avenue A First National Picture, released by Warner Brothers. Production supervisor, Henry Blanke. Directed by Alfred E. Green. Screenplay by Charles Kenyon, based on a play by Hubert Henry Davies. Photographed by James Van Trees. Costumes by Orry-Kelly. Edited by Owen Marks. Opened Capitol Theatre, N.Y., May 26, 1935. 69 minutes.

Cast: Bette Davis, Ian Hunter, Colin Clive, Alison Skipworth, John Eldredge, Philip Reed, Katherine Alexander, Helen Jerome Eddy, Gordon Elliott, Adrian Rosley, André Cheron, Edward McWade, Mary Treen, Heinie Conklin.

Front Page Woman A Warner Brothers — Vitaphone Picture. Production supervisor, Samuel Bischoff. Directed by Michael Curtiz. Screenplay by Roy Chanslor, Lillie Hayward, and Laird Doyle, based on the story *Women Are Bum Newspapermen* by Richard Macaulay. Photographed by Tony Gaudio. Art direction by John Hughes. Edited by Terry Morse. Music by Heinz Roemheld. Opened Strand Theatre, N.Y., July 11, 1935. 80 minutes.

Cast: Bette Davis, George Brent, June Martel, Dorothy Dare, Joseph Crehan, Winifred Shaw,

Roscoe Karns, Joseph King, J. Farrell Mac-Donald, J. Carroll Naish, Walter Walker, DeWitt Jennings, Huntley Gordon, Adrian Rosley, Georges Renevent, Grace Hale, Selmer Jackson, Gordon Westcott.

Special Agent A Claridge Picture, released by Warner Brothers. Produced by Samuel Bischoff in association with Martin Mooney. Directed by William Keighley. Screenplay by Laird Doyle and Abem Finkel, based on an idea by Martin Mooney. Art direction by Esdras Hartley. Photographed by Sid Hickox. Edited by Clarence Kolster. Remade by Warner Brothers as *Gambling on the High Seas* in 1940 with Jane Wyman. Opened Strand Theatre, N.Y., September 18, 1935. 76 minutes.

Cast: Bette Davis, George Brent, Ricardo Cortez, Jack La Rue, Henry O'Neill, Robert Strange, Joseph Crehan, J. Carroll Naish, Joseph Sawyer, William B. Davidson, Robert Barrat, Paul Guilfoyle, Irving Pichel, Douglas Wood, James Flavin, Lee Phelps, Louis Natheaux, Herbert Skinner, John Alexander.

Dangerous A Warner Brothers — Vitaphone Picture. Production supervisor, Harry Joe Brown. Directed by Alfred E. Green. Screenplay and original story by Laird Doyle. Photographed by Ernest Haller. Art direction by Hugo Reticker. Edited by Thomas Richards. Costumes by Orry-Kelly. Music by Bernhard Kaun. Remade by Warner Brothers in 1941 as *Singapore Woman* with Brenda Marshall.

Opened Rivoli Theatre, N.Y., December 25, 1935. 78 minutes.

Cast: Bette Davis, Franchot Tone, Margaret Lindsay, Alison Skipworth, John Eldredge, Dick Foran, Walter Walker, Richard Carle, George Irving, Pierre Watkin, Douglas Wood, William B. Davidson, Frank O'Connor, Edward Keane.

The Petrified Forest A Warner Brothers — Vitaphone Picture. Production supervisor, Henry Blanke. Directed by Archie Mayo. Screenplay by Charles Kenyon and Delmer Daves, based on the play by Robert E. Sherwood. Photographed by Sol Polito. Art Direction by John Hughes. Costumes by Orry-Kelly. Edited by Owen Marks. Music by Bernhard Kaun. Remade by Warner Brothers in 1945 as *Escape in the Desert.* Opened Radio City Music Hall, N.Y., February 6, 1936. 75 minutes.

Cast: Leslie Howard, Bette Davis, Genevieve Tobin, Dick Foran, Humphrey Bogart, Joseph Sawyer, Porter Hall, Charley Grapewin, Paul Harvey, Eddie Acuff, Adrian Morris, Nina Campana, Slim Thompson, John Alexander.

The Golden Arrow A First National Picture, released by Warner Brothers. Production supervisor, Samuel Bischoff. Directed by Alfred E. Green. Screenplay by Charles Kenyon, based on the play *Dream Princess* by Michael Arlen. Costumes by Orry-Kelly. Photographed by Arthur Edeson. Edited by Thomas Pratt. Music by W. Franke Harling and Heinz Roemheld.

Opened Strand Theatre, N.Y., May 23, 1936. 68 minutes.

Cast: Bette Davis, George Brent, Eugene Pallette, Dick Foran, Carol Hughes, Catherine Doucet, Craig Reynolds, Ivan Lebedeff, G. P. Huntley, Jr., Hobart Cavanaugh, Henry O'Neill, Eddie Acuff, Earl Foxe, E. E. Clive, Rafael Storm, Sara Edwards, Bess Flowers, Mary Treen, Selmer Jackson.

Satan Met a Lady A Warner Brothers — Vitaphone Picture. Production supervisor, Henry Blanke. Directed by William Dieterle. Screenplay by Brown Holmes, based on the novel *The Maltese Falcon* by Dashiell Hammett. Photographed by Arthur Edeson. Edited by Max Parker, reedited by Warren Low. First made by Warner Brothers in 1931 as *The Maltese Falcon*, with Ricardo Cortez. Remade in 1941 as *The Maltese Falcon* with Humphrey Bogart. Opened Strand Theatre, N.Y., July 22, 1936. 68 minutes.

Cast: Bette Davis, Warren William, Alison Skipworth, Arthur Treacher, Winifred Shaw, Marie Wilson, Porter Hall, Maynard Holmes, Olin Howlin, Charles Wilson, Joseph King, Barbara Blane, William B. Davidson.

Marked Woman A Warner Brothers — First National Picture. Produced by Hal Wallis in association with Lou Edelman. Directed by Lloyd Bacon. Screenplay by Robert Rossen and Abem Finkel, with additional dialogue by Seton I. Miller. Costumes by Orry-Kelly. Art direction by Max Parker. Photographed by George Barnes. Music by Bernhard Kaun and Heinz Roemheld. Songs by Harry Warren and Al Dubin. Edited by Jack Killifer. Opened Strand Theatre, N.Y., April 11, 1937. 96 minutes.

Cast: Bette Davis, Humphrey Bogart, Eduardo Ciannelli, Jane Bryan, Lola Lane, Isabel Jewell, Rosalind Marquis, Mayo Methot, Ben Welden, Henry O'Neill, Allen Jenkins, John Litel, Damian O'Flynn, Robert Strange, Raymond Hatton, William B. Davidson, Frank Faylen, Jack Norton, Kenneth Harlan, William Pawley.

Kid Galahad A Warner Brothers Picture. Executive producer, Hal B. Wallis, in association with Samuel Bischoff. Directed by Michael Curtiz. Screenplay by Seton I. Miller, based on the novel by Francis Wallace. Photographed by Tony Gaudio. Edited by George Amy. Art direction by Carl Jules Weyl. Costumes by Orry-Kelly. Songs by M. K. Jerome and Jack Scholl. Remade by Warner Brothers in 1941 as *The Wagons Roll at Night* and by Paramount in 1962 as a musical with Elvis Presley. Opened Strand Theatre, N.Y., May 26, 1937. 100 minutes.

Cast: Edward G. Robinson, Bette Davis, Humphrey Bogart, Wayne Morris, William Haade, Jane Bryan, Harry Carey, Soledad Jiménez, Veda Ann Borg, Ben Welden, Joseph Crehan, Harlan Tucker, Frank Faylen, Joyce Compton, Horace MacMahon.

That Certain Woman A Warner Brothers — First National Picture. Executive producer, Hal B. Wallis, in association with Robert Lord. Directed by Edmund Goulding. Screenplay by Edmund Goulding, based on his original screenplay *The Trespasser*. Art direction by Max Parker. Costumes by Orry-Kelly. Photographed by Ernest Haller. Music by Max Steiner. Edited by Jack Killifer. Opened Strand Theatre, N.Y., September 15, 1937. 91 minutes.

Cast: Bette Davis, Henry Fonda, Ian Hunter, Anita Louise, Donald Crisp, Katherine Alexander, Mary Phillips, Minor Watson, Ben Weldon, Sidney Toler, Charles Trowbridge, Norman Willis, Herbert Rawlinson, Rosalind Marquis, Frank Faylen, Willard Parker, Dwane Day, Hugh O'Connell, William Pawley.

It's Love I'm After A Warner Brothers Picture. Executive producer, Hal B. Wallis, in association with Harry Joe Brown. Directed by Archie Mayo. Screenplay by Casey Robinson, based on the story, 'Gentlemen After Midnight,' by Maurice Hanline. Art direction by Carl Jules Weyl. Costumes by Orry-Kelly. Music by Heinz Roemheld. Photographed by James Van Trees. Edited by Owen Marks. Opened Strand Theatre, N.Y., November 10, 1937. 90 minutes.

Cast: Leslie Howard, Bette Davis, Olivia de Havilland, Patric Knowles, Eric Blore, George Barbier, Spring Byington, Bonita Granville. E. E. Clive, Veda Ann Borg, Valerie Bergere, Georgia Caine, Sarah Edwards, Lionel Hellmore, Irving Bacon.

Jezebel A Warner Brothers Picture. Executive producer, Hal B. Wallis, in association with Henry Blanke. Directed by William Wyler. Screenplay by Clements Ripley, Abem Finkel, and John Huston, with Robert Bruckner, based on the play by Owen Davis, Sr. Photographed by Ernest Haller. Art direction by Robert Haas. Costumes by Orry-Kelly. Music by Max Steiner. Opened Radio City Music Hall, N.Y., March 10, 1938. 100 minutes.

Cast: Bette Davis, Henry Fonda, George Brent, Donald Crisp, Fay Bainter, Margaret Lindsay, Henry O'Neill, John Litel, Jordon Oliver, Spring Byington, Margaret Early, Richard Cromwell, Theresa Harris, Janet Shaw, Irving Pichel, Eddie Anderson.

The Sisters A Warner Brothers Picture. Produced by Hal B. Wallis, in association with David Lewis. Directed by Anatole Litvak. Screenplay by Milton Krims, based on the novel by Myron Brinig. Photographed by Tony Gaudio. Art direction by Carl Jules Weyl. Costumes by Orry-Kelly. Music by Max Steiner. Edited by Warren Low. Opened Strand Theatre, N.Y., October 14, 1938. 95 minutes.

Cast: Errol Flynn, Bette Davis, Anita Louise, Ian Hunter, Donald Crisp, Beulah Bondi, Jane Bryan, Alan Hale, Sr., Dick Foran, Henry Travers, Patric Knowles, Lee Patrick, Laura Hope Crews, Janet Shaw, Harry Davenport, Ruth Garland, John Warburton. Paul Harvey, Mayo Methot, Irving Bacon, Arthur Hoyt.

Dark Victory A Warner Brothers — First National Picture. Produced by Hal B. Wallis, in association with David Lewis. Directed by Edmund Goulding. Screenplay by Casey Robinson, based on the play by George Emerson Brewer, Jr., and Bertram Bloch. Photographed by Ernest Haller. Art direction by Robert Haas. Costumes by Orry-Kelly. Song 'Oh, Give Me Time for Tenderness' by Edmund Goulding and Elsie Janis. Music by Max Steiner. Edited by William Holmes. Remade by United Artists in 1963 as *Stolen Hours* with Susan Hayward. Opened Radio City Music Hall, N.Y., April 20, 1939. 105 minutes.

Cast: Bette Davis, George Brent, Geraldine Fitzgerald, Humphrey Bogart, Ronald Reagan. Henry Travers. Cora Witherspoon, Dorothy Peterson, Virginia Brissac, Charles Richman, Leonard Mudie, Fay Helm, Lottie Williams.

Juarez A Warner Brothers Picture. Produced by Hal B. Wallis, in association with Henry Blanke. Directed by William Dieterle. Screenplay by John Huston, Aeneas MacKenzie, and Wolfgang Reinhardt, based on the play *Juarez and Maximilian* by Franz Werfel and the book *The Phantom Crown* by Bertita Harding. Art direction by Anton Grot. Costumes by Orry-Kelly. Photographed by Tony Gaudio. Edited by Warren Low. Opened Hollywood Theatre, N.Y., April 24, 1939. 125 minutes.

Cast: Paul Muni, Bette Davis, Brian Aherne, Claude Rains, John Garfield, Donald Crisp, Joseph Calleia, Gale Sondergaard, Gilbert

Roland, Henry O'Neill, Harry Davenport, Louis Calhern, Walter Kingsford, Georgia Caine, Montagu Love, John Miljan, Vladimir Sokoloff, Irving Pichel, Pedro de Cordoba, Gilbert Emery, Monte Blue, Manuel Díaz, Hugh Sothern, Mickey Kuhn.

The Old Maid A Warner Brothers — First National Picture. Produced by Hal B. Wallis, in association with Henry Blanke. Directed by Edmund Goulding. Screenplay by Casey Robinson, based on the Pulitzer Prize-winning play by Zoë Akins, adapted from the novel by Edith Wharton. Photographed by Tony Gaudio. Art direction by Robert Haas. Costumes by Orry-Kelly. Music by Max Steiner. Edited by George Amy. Opened Strand Theatre, N.Y., August 16, 1939. 95 minutes.

Cast: Bette Davis, Miriam Hopkins, George Brent, Donald Crisp, Jane Bryan, Louise Fazenda, James Stephenson, Jerome Cowan, William Lundigan, Rand Brooks, Cecilia Loftus, Janet Shaw, DeWolf Hopper.

The Private Lives of Elizabeth and Essex A Warner Brothers Picture. Produced by Hal B. Wallis, in association with Robert Lord. Directed by Michael Curtiz. Screenplay by Norman Reilly Raine and Aeneas MacKenzie, based on the play *Elizabeth the Queen* by Maxwell Anderson. Art direction by Anton Grot. Costumes by Orry-Kelly. Photographed in Technicolor by Sol Polito and H. Howard Greene. Music by Erich Wolfgang Korngold. Edited by Owen Marks.

Opened Strand Theatre, N.Y., December 1, 1939. 105 minutes.

Cast: Bette Davis, Errol Flynn, Olivia de Havilland, Donald Crisp, Vincent Price, Alan Hale Sr., Henry Stephenson, Henry Daniell, James Stephenson, Leo G. Carroll, Nanette Fabares (Fabray), Rosella Towne, Maris Wrixon, Ralph Forbes, Robert Warwick, John Sutton, Guy Bellis, Doris Lloyd, Forrester Harvey.

All This, and Heaven Too A Warner Brothers — First National Picture. Produced by Jack L. Warner and Hal B. Wallis, in association with David Lewis. Directed by Anatole Litvak. Screenplay by Casey Robinson, based on a novel by Rachel Field. Art direction by Carl Jules Weyl. Costumes by Orry-Kelly. Photographed by Ernest Haller. Music by Max Steiner. Edited by Warren Low. Opened Radio City Music Hall, July 4, 1940. 140 minutes.

Cast: Bette Davis, Charles Boyer, Jeffrey Lynn, Barbara O'Neil, Virginia Weidler, Helen Westley, Walter Hampden, Henry Daniell, Harry Davenport, George Coulouris, Montagu Love, Janet Beecher, June Lockhart, Ann Todd, Richard Nichols, Fritz Leiber, Ian Keith, Sibyl Harris, Mary Anderson, Edward Fielding, Ann Gillis, Peggy Stewart, Victor Kilian, Mrs. Gardner Crane.

The Letter A Warner Brothers — First National Picture. Produced by Hal B. Wallis, in association with Robert Lord. Directed by William Wyler. Screenplay by Howard Koch,

444

based on the play by W. Somerset Maugham. Art direction by Carl Jules Weyl. Costumes by Orry-Kelly. Photographed by Tony Gaudio. Music by Max Steiner. Edited by George Amy. First made by Paramount in 1929 with Jeanne Eagels and in 1947 by Warner Brothers as *The Unfaithful* with Ann Sheridan. Opened Strand Theatre, N.Y., November 22, 1940. 95 minutes.

Cast: Bette Davis, Herbert Marshall, James Stephenson, Frieda Inescort, Gale Sondergaard, Bruce Lester (David Bruce), Elizabeth Earl, Cecil Kellaway, Doris Lloyd, Sen Yung, Willie Fung, Tetsu Komai, Roland Got, Otto Hahn, Pete Katchenaro, David Newell, Ottola Nesmith, Lillian Kemple-Cooper.

The Great Lie A Warner Brothers Picture. Produced by Hal B. Wallis, in association with Henry Blanke. Directed by Edmund Goulding. Screenplay by Lenore Coffee, based on the novel *January Heights* by Polan Banks. Art direction by Carl Jules Weyl. Costumes by Orry-Kelly. Photographed by Tony Gaudio. Music by Max Steiner. Edited by Ralph Dawson. World premiere, Premiere Theatre, Littleton, N.H., April 5, 1941. Opened Strand Theatre, N.Y., April 12, 1941. 102 minutes.

Cast: Bette Davis, George Brent, Mary Astor, Lucile Watson, Hattie McDaniel, Grant Mitchell, Jerome Cowan, Sam McDaniel, Thurston Hall, Russell Hicks, Charles Trowbridge, Virginia Brissac, Olin Howland, J. Farrell MacDonald, Doris Lloyd, Addison Richards, Georgia Caine, Alphonse Martell.

The Bride Came C.O.D. A Warner Brothers Picture. Produced by Hal B. Wallis, in association with William Cagney. Directed by William Keighley. Screenplay by Julius J. and Philip G. Epstein, based on a story by Kenneth Earl and M. M. Musselman. Art direction by Ted Smith. Costumes by Orry-Kelly. Photographed by Ernest Haller. Music by Max Steiner. Edited by Thomas Richards. Location scenes filmed at Death Valley. Opened Strand Theatre, N.Y., July 25, 1941. 90 minutes.

Cast: James Cagney, Bette Davis, Stuart Erwin, Jack Carson, George Tobias, Eugene Pallette, Harry Davenport, William Frawley, Edward Brophy, Harry Holman, Chick Chandler, Keith Douglas, Herbert Anderson, Creighton Hale, Frank Mayo, DeWolf Hopper, Jack Mower, William Newell.

The Little Foxes A Samuel Goldwyn Production, released by RKO Radio Pictures, Inc. Produced by Samuel Goldwyn. Directed by William Wyler. Screenplay by Lillian Hellman, based on her stage play, with additional scenes and dialogue by Arthur Kober, Dorothy Parker, and Alan Campbell. Art direction by Stephen Goosson. Costumes by Orry-Kelly. Photographed by Gregg Toland. Edited by Daniel Mandell. Music by Meredith Willson. Opened Radio City Music Hall, N.Y., August 21, 1941. 115 minutes.

Cast: Bette Davis, Herbert Marshall, Teresa Wright, Richard Carlson, Patricia Collinge, Dan Duryea, Charles Dingle, Carl Benton Reid,

Jessie Grayson, John Marriott, Russell Hicks, Lucien Littlefield, Virginia Brissac.

The Man Who Came to Dinner A Warner Brothers Picture. Produced by Hal B. Wallis, in association with Jerry Wald, Sam Harris, and Jack Saper. Directed by William Keighley. Screenplay by Julius J. and Philip G. Epstein, based on the play by George S. Kaufman and Moss Hart. Art direction by Robert Haas. Costumes by Orry-Kelly. Photographed by Tony Gaudio. Edited by Jack Killifer. Opened Strand Theatre, N.Y., January 1, 1942. 112 minutes.

Cast: Bette Davis, Ann Sheridan, Monty Woolley, Richard Travis, Jimmy Durante, Reginald Gardiner, Billie Burke, Elizabeth Fraser, Grant Mitchell, George Barbier, Mary Wickes, Russell Arms, Ruth Vivian, Edwin Stanley, Charles Drake, Nanette Vallon, John Ridgely.

In This Our Life A Warner Brothers Picture. Produced by Hal B. Wallis, in association with David Lewis. Directed by John Huston. Screenplay by Howard Koch, based on the Pulitzer Prize-winning novel by Ellen Glasgow. Art direction by Robert Haas. Costumes by Orry-Kelly. Photographed by Ernest Haller. Edited by William Holmes. Music by Max Steiner. Opened Strand Theatre, N.Y., May 8, 1942. 97 minutes.

Cast: Bette Davis, Olivia de Havilland, George Brent, Dennis Morgan, Charles Coburn, Frank Craven, Billie Burke, Hattie McDaniel, Lee Patrick, Mary Servoss, Ernest Anderson, William

B. Davidson, Edward Fielding, John Hamilton, William Forrest, Lee Phelps.

Now, Voyager A Warner Brothers Picture. Produced by Hal B. Wallis. Directed by Irving Rapper. Screenplay by Casey Robinson, based on the novel by Olive Higgins Prouty. Art direction by Robert Haas. Costumes by Orry-Kelly. Photographed by Sol Polito. Music by Max Steiner. Edited by Warren Low. Opened Hollywood Theatre, N.Y., October 22, 1942. 117 minutes.

Cast: Bette Davis, Paul Henreid, Claude Rains, Gladys Cooper, Bonita Granville, Ilka Chase, John Loder, Lee Patrick, Franklin Pangborn, Katherine Alexander, James Rennie, Mary Wickes, Janis Wilson, Frank Puglia, Michael Ames, Charles Drake, David Clyde.

Watch on the Rhine A Warner Brothers Picture. Produced by Hal B. Wallis. Directed by Herman Shumlin. Screenplay by Dashiell Hammett, with additional scenes and dialogue by Lillian Hellman, based on her play. Art direction by Carl Jules Weyl. Costumes by Orry-Kelly. Photographed by Merritt Gerstad and Hal Mohr. Music by Max Steiner. Edited by Rudi Fehr. Opened Rialto Theatre, N.Y., August 27, 1943. 114 minutes.

Cast: Bette Davis, Paul Lukas, Geraldine Fitzgerald, Lucile Watson, Beulah Bondi, George Coulouris, Donald Woods, Henry Daniell, Donald Buka, Eric Roberts, Janis Wilson, Mary Young, Kurt Katch, Erwin Kaiser, Clyde

Fillmore, Robert O. Davis, Frank Wilson, Clarence Muse, Anthony Caruso, Howard Hickman, Elvira Curci, Creighton Hale, Alan Hale, Jr.

Thank Your Lucky Stars A Warner Brothers Picture. J. L. Warner in charge of production. Produced by Mark Hellinger. Directed by David Butler. Screenplay by Norman Panama, Melvin Frank, and James V. Kern, based on a story by Everett Freeman and Arthur Schwartz. Art direction by Anton Grot and Leo Kuter. Costumes by Milo Anderson. Photographed by Arthur Edeson. Music and lyrics by Arthur Schwartz and Frank Loesser. Musical direction by Leo F. Forbstein. Dances created and staged by LeRoy Prinz. Edited by Irene Morra. Opened Strand Theatre, N.Y., October 1, 1943. 124 minutes.

Cast: Dennis Morgan, Joan Leslie, Edward Everett Horton, S. Z. Sakall, Richard Lane, Ruth Donnelly, Don Wilson, Henry Armetta, Joyce Reynolds, with guest stars Humphrey Bogart, Eddie Cantor, Bette Davis, Olivia de Havilland, Errol Flynn, John Garfield, Ida Lupino, Ann Sheridan, Dinah Shore, Alexis Smith, Jack Carson, Alan Hale, Sr., George Tobias, Hattie McDaniel, Willie Best, Spike Jones and His City Slickers.

Old Acquaintance A Warner Brothers Picture. J. L. Warner in charge of production. Produced by Henry Blanke. Directed by Vincent Sherman. Screenplay by John Van Druten and Lenore

Coffee, based on the play by John Van Druten. Art direction by John Hughes. Costumes by Orry-Kelly. Photographed by Sol Polito. Music by Franz Waxman. Edited by Terry Morse. Filmed before *Thank Your Lucky Stars*, but released afterward. Opened Hollywood Theatre, N.Y., November 27, 1943. 110 minutes.

Cast: Bette Davis, Miriam Hopkins, Gig Young, John Loder, Dolores Moran, Philip Reed, Roscoe Karns, Anne Revere, Esther Dale, Ann Codee, Joseph Crehan, Pierre Watkin, Marjorie Hoshelle, George Lessey, Ann Doran, Leona Maricle, Francine Rufo, Jimmie Conlin.

Mr. Skeffington A Warner Brothers Picture. J. L. Warner in charge of production. Produced and written by Julius J. and Philip G. Epstein, based on the novel by 'Elizabeth' (Mary Annette Beauchamp Russell). Art direction by Robert Haas. Costumes by Orry-Kelly. Photographed by Ernest Haller. Music by Franz Waxman. Edited by Ralph Dawson. Opened State Theatre, N.Y., May 25, 1944. 145 minutes.

Cast: Bette Davis, Claude Rains, Walter Abel, Richard Waring, George Coulouris, Marjorie Riordan, Robert Shayne, John Alexander, Jerome Cowan, Johnny Mitchell, Dorothy Peterson, Peter Whitney, Bill Kennedy, Tom Stevenson, Halliwell Hobbes, Bunny Sunshine, Gigi Perreau, Dolores Gray, Walter Kingsford, Molly Lamont, Richard Erdman.

Hollywood Canteen A Warner Brothers Picture. J. L. Warner in charge of production.

Produced by Alex Gottlieb. Directed by Delmer Daves. Screenplay and original story by Delmer Daves. Art direction by Leo Kuter. Costumes by Milo Anderson. Photographed by Bert Glennon. Edited by Christian Nyby. Musical direction by Ray Heindorf. Musical numbers created and directed by LeRoy Prinz. J. L. Warner contributed a large portion of the proceeds to the Canteen. Opened Strand Theatre, N.Y., December 15, 1944. 124 minutes.

Cast: Joan Leslie, Robert Hutton, Janis Paige, Dane Clark, Richard Erdman, James Flavin, Joan Winfield, Jonathan Hale, Rudolph Friml, Jr., Bill Manning, Larry Thompson, Mell Schubert, Walden Boyle, Steve Richards, with guest stars: the Andrews Sisters, Jack Benny, Joe E. Brown, Eddie Cantor, Kitty Carlisle, Jack Carson, Joan Crawford, Helmut Dantine, Bette Davis, Faye Emerson, Victor Francen, John Garfield, Sydney Greenstreet, Alan Hale, Sr., Paul Henried, Andrea King, Peter Lorre, Ida Lupino, Irene Manning, Nora Martin, Joan McCracken, Dolores Moran, Dennis Morgan, Eleanor Parker, William Prince, Joyce Reynolds, John Ridgely, Roy Rogers and Trigger, S. Z. Sakall, Alexis Smith, Zachary Scott, Barbara Stanwyck, Craig Stevens, Joseph Szigeti, Donald Woods, Jane Wyman, Jimmy Dorsey and His Band, Carmen Cavallaro and His Orchestra, Rosaria and Antonio, Sons of the Pioneers, Virginia Patton, Lynne Baggett, Betty Alexander, Julie Bishop, Robert Shayne, Johnny Mitchell, John Sheridan, Colleen Townsend, Angela Green,

Paul Brooke, Marianne O'Brien, Dorothy Malone, Bill Kennedy.

The Corn Is Green A Warner Brothers Picture. J. L. Warner in charge of production. Produced by Jack Chertok. Directed by Irving Rapper. Screenplay by Casey Robinson and Frank Cavett, based on the autobiographical play by Emlyn Williams. Art direction by Carl Jules Weyl. Costumes by Orry-Kelly. Photographed by Sol Polito. Music by Max Steiner. Edited by Frederick Richards. Opened Hollywood Theatre, N.Y., March 29, 1945. 115 minutes.

Cast: Bette Davis, John Dall, Joan Lorring, Nigel Bruce, Rhys Williams, Rosalind Ivan, Mildred Dunnock, Gwyneth Hughes, Billy Roy, Thomas Louden, Arthur Shields, Leslie Vincent, Robert Regent, Tony Ellis, Elliot Dare, Robert Cherry, Gene Ross.

A Stolen Life A Warner Brothers Picture. A B. D. Production. Directed by Curtis Bernhardt. Screenplay by Catherine Turney, adapted by Margaret Buell Wilder, based on the novel by Karel J. Benes, *Uloupeny Zivot.* Costumes by Orry-Kelly. Art direction by Robert Haas. Photographed by Sol Polito and Ernest Haller. Music by Max Steiner. Edited by Rudi Fehr. Remake of *A Stolen Life*, a 1939 Paramount film with Elisabeth Bergner. Opened Hollywood Theatre, N.Y., July 6, 1946. 109 minutes.

Cast: Bette Davis, Glenn Ford, Dane Clark, Walter Brennan, Charles Ruggles, Bruce

Bennett, Peggy Knudsen, Esther Dale, Clara Blandick, Joan Winfield.

Deception A Warner Brothers Picture. J. L. Warner in charge of production. Produced by Henry Blanke. Directed by Irving Rapper. Screenplay by John Collier and Joseph Than, based on a play titled *Monsieur Lambertheir*, then *Satan*, and finally *Jealousy* by Louis Verneuil. Art direction by Anton Grot. Costumes by Bernard Newman. Photographed by Ernest Haller. Musical score and the Hollenius Cello Concerto by Erich Wolfgang Korngold. Edited by Alan Crosland, Jr. Opened Hollywood Theatre, N.Y., October 18, 1946. 110 minutes.

Cast: Bette Davis, Paul Henreid, Claude Rains, John Abbott, Benson Fong, Richard Walsh, Suzi Crandall, Richard Erdman, Ross Ford, Russell Arms, Bess Flowers, Gino Corrado, Clifton Young, Cyril Delevanti, Jane Harker.

Winter Meeting A Warner Brothers Picture. J. L. Warner in charge of production. Produced by Henry Blanke. Directed by Bretaigne Windust. Screenplay by Catherine Turney, based on the novel by Ethel Vance. Art direction by Edward Carrere. Photographed by Ernest Haller. Music by Max Steiner. Edited by Owen Marks. Opened Warner Theatre, N.Y., April 7, 1948. 104 minutes.

Cast: Bette Davis, Janis Paige, James Davis, John Hoyt, Florence Bates, Walter Baldwin, Ransom Sherman, Hugh Charles, George Taylor,

453

Lois Austin, Robert Riordan, Mike Lally, Doug Carter, Harry McKee, Joe Minitello, Paul Maxey, Cedric Stevens.

June Bride A Warner Brothers Picture. J. L. Warner in charge of production. Produced by Henry Blanke. Directed by Bretaigne Windust. Screenplay by Ranald MacDougall, based on the play *Feature for June* by Eileen Tighe and Graeme Lorimer. Costumes by Edith Head. Art direction by Anton Grot. Photographed by Ted McCord. Music by David Buttolph. Edited by Owen Marks. Opened Strand Theatre, N.Y., October 29, 1948. 96 minutes.

Cast: Bette Davis, Robert Montgomery, Fay Bainter, Betty Lynn, Tom Tully, Barbara Bates, Jerome Cowan, Mary Wickes, James Burke, Raymond Roe, Marjorie Bennett, Ray Montgomery, George O'Hanlon, Sandra Gould, Esther Howard, Jessie Adams, Raymond Bond, Alice Kelley, Patricia Northrop, Debbie Reynolds.

Beyond the Forest A Warner Brothers Picture. J. L. Warner in charge of production. Produced by Henry Blanke. Directed by King Vidor. Screenplay by Lenore Coffee, based on the novel by Stuart Engstrand. Costumes by Edith Head. Art direction by Robert Haas. Photographed by Robert Burks. Music by Max Steiner. Edited by Rudi Fehr. Opened Strand Theatre, N.Y., October 21, 1949. 97 minutes.

Cast: Bette Davis, Joseph Cotten, David Brian, Ruth Roman, Minor Watson, Dona

Drake, Regis Toomey, Sarah Selby, Mary Servoss, Frances Charles, Harry Tyler, Ralph Littlefield, Creighton Hale, Joel Allen, Ann Doran.

All About Eve A Twentieth Century Fox Picture. Produced by Darryl F. Zanuck. Written and directed by Joseph L. Mankiewicz, based on 'The Wisdom of Eve' by Mary Orr. Costumes by Edith Head and Charles LeMaire. Art direction by Lyle Wheeler and George W. Davis. Photographed by Milton Krasner. Music by Alfred Newman. Edited by Barbara McLean. Opened Roxy Theatre, N.Y., October 13, 1950. Hollywood premiere, Grauman's Chinese Theatre, November 9, 1950. 138 minutes.

Cast: Bette Davis, Anne Baxter, George Sanders, Celeste Holm, Gary Merrill, Hugh Marlowe, Thelma Ritter, Marilyn Monroe, Gregory Ratoff, Barbara Bates, Walter Hampden, Randy Stuart, Craig Hill, Leland Harris, Claude Stroud, Eugene Borden, Steve Geray, Bess Flowers, Stanley Orr, Eddie Fisher.

Payment on Demand An RKO Radio Picture. Produced by Jack H. Skirball and Bruce Manning. Directed by Curtis Bernhardt. Screenplay *The Story of a Divorce* and original story by Bruce Manning and Curtis Bernhardt. Costumes by Edith Head. Art direction by Albert S. D'Agostino and Carroll Clark. Photographed by Leo Tover. Edited by Harry Marker. Music by Victor Young. Filmed before *All About Eve*, but released afterward. Opened Radio City Music

Hall, N.Y., February 15, 1951. 90 minutes.

Cast: Bette Davis, Barry Sullivan, Jane Cowl, Kent Taylor, Betty Lynn, John Sutton, Frances Dee, Peggie Castle, Otto Kruger, Walter Sande, Brett King, Richard Anderson, Natalie Schafer, Katherine Emery, Lisa Golm, Moroni Olsen.

Another Man's Poison An Eros Production. released by United Artists. Produced by Douglas Fairbanks, Jr., and Daniel M. Angel. Directed by Irving Rapper. Screenplay by Val Guest, based on the play *Deadlock* by Leslie Sands. Art direction by Cedric Dawe. Photographed by Robert Krasker. Music by Paul Sawtell. Edited by Gordon Hales. Opened Metropolitan Theatre, Brooklyn, N.Y., and saturated booking, Loew's Theatres, N.Y., January 6, 1952. 88 minutes.

Cast: Bette Davis, Gary Merrill, Emlyn Williams, Anthony Steel, Barbara Murray, Reginald Beckwith, Edna Morris.

Phone Call from a Stranger A Twentieth Century Fox Picture. Produced by Nunnally Johnson. Directed by Jean Negulesco. Screenplay by Nunnally Johnson, based on a story by Ida Alexa Ross Wylie. Costumes by Eloise Jenssen. Art direction by Lyle Wheeling and J. Russell Spencer. Photographed by Milton Krasner. Music by Franz Waxman. Edited by Hugh Fowler. Opened Roxy Theatre, N.Y., February 1, 1952. 96 minutes.

Cast: Shelley Winters, Gary Merrill, Michael Rennie, Keenan Wynn, Evelyn Varden, Warren

Stevens, Beatrice Straight, Ted Donaldson, Craig Stevens, Helen Westcott, Bette Davis, Sydney Perkins, Hugh Beaumont, Thomas Jackson, Harry Cheshire, Tom Powers, Freeman Lusk, George Eldredge, Nestor Paiva, Perdita Chandler, Genevieve Bell.

The Star A Bert E. Friedlob Production, released by Twentieth Century Fox. Produced by Bert E. Friedlob. Directed by Stuart Heisler. Screenplay and original story by Katherine Albert and Dale Eunson. Costumes by Orry-Kelly. Art direction by Boris Levin. Photographed by Ernest Laszlo. Music by Victor Young. Edited by Otto Ludwig. Opened Rivoli Theatre, N.Y., January 28, 1953.

Cast: Bette Davis, Sterling Hayden, Natalie Wood, Warner Anderson, Minor Watson, June Travis, Katherine Warren, Kay Riehl, Barbara Woodel, Fay Baker, Barbara Lawrence, David Alpert, Paul Frees.

The Virgin Queen A Twentieth Century Fox Picture. Produced by Charles Brackett. Directed by Henry Koster. Screenplay and original story 'Sir Walter Raleigh' by Harry Brown and Mildred Lord. Costumes by Mary Wills. Art direction by Lyle Wheeler and Leland Fuller. Photographed in Cinemascope by Charles G. Clarke. Music by Franz Waxman. Edited by Robert Simpson. Makeup by Perc Westmore. World premiere Strand Theatre, Portland, Maine, July 22, 1955. Opened Roxy Theatre, N.Y., August 5, 1955. 92 minutes.

Cast: Bette Davis, Richard Todd, Joan Collins, Jay Robinson, Herbert Marshall, Dan O'Herlihy, Robert Douglas, Romney Brent, Marjorie Hellen, Lisa Daniels, Lisa Davis, Barry Bernard, Robert Adler, Noel Drayton, Ian Murray, Margery Weston, Rod Taylor, Davis Thursby, Arthur Gould-Porter.

The Catered Affair A Metro-Goldwyn-Mayer Picture. Produced by Sam Zimbalist. Directed by Richard Brooks. Screenplay by Gore Vidal, based on the teleplay by Paddy Chayefsky. Art direction by Cedric Gibbons and Paul Groesse. Photographed by John Alton. Music by André Previn. Edited by Gene Ruggiero and Frank Santillo. Previewed at Fox Beverly Theatre, Beverly Hills, April 20, 1956. Opened Victoria Theatre, N.Y., June 14, 1956. 92 minutes.

Cast: Bette Davis, Debbie Reynolds, Ernest Borgnine, Barry Fitzgerald, Rod Taylor, Robert Simon, Madge Kennedy, Dorothy Stickney, Carol Veazie, Joan Camden, Ray Stricklyn, Jay Adler, Dan Tobin, Paul Denton, Augusta Merighi, Sammy Shack, Jack Kenny, Robert Stephenson, Mae Clarke.

Storm Center A Phoenix Production, released by Columbia Pictures. Produced by Julian Blaustein. Directed by Daniel Taradash. Screenplay, originally titled *This Time Tomorrow*, then *The Library*, by Daniel Taradash and Elick Moll. Art direction by Gary Odell. Photographed by Burnett Guffey. Music by George Dunning. Edited by William A. Lyon. Made before *The*

Catered Affair, but released afterward. Previewed at Columbia Studios, July 11, 1956. World premiere, Midtown Theatre, Philadelphia, Pa., July 31, 1956. Opened at the Normandie Theatre, N.Y., October 20, 1956. 86 minutes.

Cast: Bette Davis, Brian Keith, Kim Hunter, Paul Kelly, Kevin Coughlin, Joe Mantell, Sallie Brophy, Howard Wierum, Curtis Cooksey, Michael Raffetto, Edward Platt, Kathryn Grant, Howard Wendell, Burt Mustin, Edith Evanson.

John Paul Jones A Samuel Bronston Production, distributed by Warner Brothers. Produced by Samuel Bronston. Directed by John Farrow. Screenplay by John Farrow and Jesse Lasky, Jr., from the story *Nor'wester* by Clements Ripley. Costumes by Phyllis Dalton. Art direction by Franz Bachelin. Photographed in Technicolor by Michael Kelber. Music by Max Steiner. Edited by Eda Warren. Produced in Spain. Previewed at Warner Brothers Studio, June 2, 1959. Opened Rivoli Theatre, N.Y., June 16, 1959. 126 minutes.

Cast: Robert Stack, Marisa Pavan, Charles Coburn, Erin O'Brien, Tom Brannum, Bruce Cabot, Basil Sydney, Archie Duncan, Thomas Gomez, Judson Laure, Bob Cunningham, John Charles Farrow, Eric Pohlmann, Pepe Nieto, John Crawford, Patrick Villiers, Frank Latimore, Ford Rainey, Bruce Seaton.

Cameo appearances: MacDonald Carey, Jean Pierre Aumont, David Farrar, Peter Cushing, Susana Canales, Jorge Riviere, Bette Davis.

The Scapegoat A du Maurier — Guinness Production, released by Metro-Goldwyn-Mayer. Produced by Michael Balcon. Directed by Robert Hamer. Screenplay by Gore Vidal and Robert Hamer, based on the novel by Daphne du Maurier. Art direction by Elliot Scott. Photographed by Paul Beeson. Music by Bronislau Kaper. Edited by Jack Harris. Previewed at MGM Studio, July 16, 1959. Opened Guild Theatre, N.Y., August 6, 1959. 92 minutes.

Cast: Alec Guinness, Bette Davis, Nicole Maurey, Irene Worth, Pamela Brown, Annabel Bartlett, Geoffrey Keen, Noel Howlett, Peter Bull, Leslie French, Alan Webb, Maria Britneva, Eddie Byrne, Alexander Archdale, Peter Sallis.

Pocketful of Miracles A Franton Production, released by United Artists. Produced by Frank Capra in association with Glenn Ford and Joseph Sistrom. Directed by Frank Capra. Screenplay by Hal Kanter and Harry Tugend, based on the screenplay *Lady for a Day* by Robert Riskin and the story 'Madame la Gimp' by Damon Runyon. Costumes by Walter Plunkett and Edith Head. Art direction by Roland Anderson. Photographed in Eastman color and Panavision by Robert Bronner. Music by Walter Scharf. Edited by Frank P. Keller. Previewed at Grauman's Chinese Theatre, Hollywood, Calif., October 13, 1961. Simultaneous opening in 650 U.S. theaters, December 18, 1961. 136 minutes.

Cast: Glenn Ford, Bette Davis, Hope Lange,

Arthur O'Connell, Peter Falk, Thomas Mitchell, Edward Everett Horton, Mickey Shaughnessy, David Brian, Sheldon Leonard, Ann-Margret, Peter Mann, Barton MacLane, John Litel, Jerome Cowan, Jay Novello, Frank Ferguson, Willis Bouchey, Fritz Feld, Ellen Corby, Gavin Gordon, Benny Rubin, Jack Elam, Mike Mazurki, Hayden Rorke, Doodles Weaver, Paul E. Burns, George E. Stone, Snub Pollard.

What Ever Happened to Baby Jane? A Seven Arts Associates and Aldrich Production, released by Warner Brothers. Executive producer, Kenneth Hyman. Associate producer and director, Robert Aldrich. Screenplay by Lukas Heller, based on the novel by Henry Farrell. Costumes by Norma Koch. Art direction by William Glasgow. Photographed by Ernest Haller. Music by Frank De Vol. Edited by Michael Luciano. Previewed at Pantages Theatre, Hollywood, Calif., October 16, 1962. Simultaneous opening in 116 theaters in N.Y. and N.J., November 6, 1962. 132 minutes.

Cast: Bette Davis, Joan Crawford, Victor Buono, Marjorie Bennett, Maidie Norman, Dave Willock, Anna Lee, Julie Allred, Gina Gillespie, Ann Barton, Barbara Merrill.

Dead Ringer A Warner Brothers Picture. Produced by William H. Wright. Directed by Paul Henreid. Screenplay by Albert Beich and Oscar Millard, based on the story 'Dead Pigeon' by Rian James. Remake of *La Otra* with Dolores Del Rio, released in 1946. Costumes by Don

461

Feld. Art direction by Perry Ferguson. Photographed by Ernest Haller. Music by André Previn. Edited by Folmar Blangsted. Makeup by Gene Hibbs. Opened in 110 theaters in N.Y. area, February 19, 1964. 115 minutes.

Cast: Bette Davis, Karl Malden, Peter Lawford, Philip Carey, Jean Hagen, George Macready, Estelle Winwood, George Chandler, Mario Alcalde, Cyril Delevanti, Monika Henreid, Bert Remsen, Charles Watts, Ken Lynch.

The Empty Canvas A Joseph E. Levine — Carlo Ponti Production, released by Embassy Pictures. Produced by Carlo Ponti. Directed by Damiano Damiani. Screenplay by Tonino Guerra, Ugo Liberatore, and Damiano Damiani, based on the novel *La Noia* by Alberto Moravia. Art direction by Carlo Egidi. Photographed by Roberto Gerardi. Edited by Renzo Lucidi. Produced in Italy. U.S. premiere, El Rey Theater, Los Angeles, March 10, 1964. Opened N.Y., May 15, 1964. 118 minutes.

Cast: Bette Davis, Horst Buchholz, Catherine Spaak, Daniela Rocca, Lea Podovani, Isa Miranda, Leonida Repaci, George Wilson, Marcella Rovena, Daniela Calvino, Renato Moretti, Edoardo Nevola, Jole Mauro, Mario Lanfranchi.

Where Love Has Gone A Joseph E. Levine Production, released by Paramount. Produced by Joseph E. Levine. Directed by Edward Dmytryk. Screenplay by John Michael Hayes, based on the novel by Harold Robbins.

Costumes by Edith Head. Art direction by Walter Tyler. Photographed in Technicolor and Techniscope by Joseph MacDonald. Edited by Frank Bracht. Opened Capitol Theatre, N.Y., November 2, 1964. 114 minutes.

Cast: Susan Hayward, Bette Davis, Michael Connors, Joey Heatherton, Jane Greer, DeForest Kelley, George Macready, Anne Seymour, Willis Bouchey, Walter Reed, Ann Doran, Bartlett Robinson, Whit Bissell, Anthony Caruso, Jack Greening, Olga Sutcliffe, Howard Wendell, Colin Kenny.

Hush . . . Hush, Sweet Charlotte An Associates & Aldrich Company Production, released by Twentieth Century Fox. Produced and directed by Robert Aldrich. Screenplay by Henry Farrell and Lukas Heller, based on a story by Henry Farrell, 'What Ever Happened to Cousin Charlotte?' Costumes by Norma Koch. Art direction by William Glasgow. Photographed by Joseph Biroc. Musical score by Frank De Vol. Edited by Michael Luciano. Opened Village Theatre, Westwood, Calif., December 15, 1964, to qualify for the Academy Awards, then at the Capitol Theatre, N.Y., March 3, 1965. 134 minutes.

Cast: Bette Davis, Olivia de Havilland, Joseph Cotten, Agnes Moorehead, Cecil Kellaway, Victor Buono, Mary Astor, William Campbell, Wesley Addy, Bruce Dern, George Kennedy, Dave Willock, John Megna, Ellen Corby, Helen Kleeb, Marianne Stewart, Frank Ferguson, Mary Henderson, Lillian Randolph, Geraldine West,

William Walker, Idell James, Teddy Buckner and his All-Stars.

The Nanny A Seven Arts — Hammer Film Production, released by Twentieth Century Fox. Produced by Jimmy Sangster. Directed by Seth Holt. Screenplay by Jimmy Sangster, based on the novel by Evelyn Piper. Costumes by Rosemary Burroughs. Photographed by Harry Waxman. Edited by James Needs. Produced in England. Opened at the Normandie Theatre, N.Y., and neighborhood theaters, November 3, 1965. 93 minutes.

Cast: Bette Davis, Wendy Craig, Jill Bennett, James Villiers, William Dix, Pamela Franklin, Jack Watling, Maurice Denham, Alfred Burke, Nora Gordon, Sandra Power, Harry Fowler.

The Anniversary A Seven Arts — Hammer Production, released by Twentieth Century-Fox. Produced by Jimmy Sangster. Directed by Roy Ward Baker, who replaced Alvin Rakoff. Screenplay by Jimmy Sangster, based on the play by Bill MacIlwraith. Photographed in wide screen and Technicolor by Harry Waxman. Edited by Peter Wetherly. Produced in England. Previewed at Rialto Theatre, London, January 11, 1968. U.S. opening, neighborhood theaters, N.Y., March 20, 1968. 95 minutes.

Cast: Bette Davis, Sheila Hancock, Jack Hedley, James Cossins, Christian Roberts, Elaine Taylor, Timothy Bateson, Arnold Diamond.

Connecting Rooms An L.S.D. Production, released by Hemdale. Produced by Harry Field and Arthur Cooper. Directed by Franklin Gollings. Screenplay by Franklin Gollings, based on the play by Marion Hart. Produced in England in 1969, released May 1972. Not released in U.S. 103 minutes.

Cast: Bette Davis, Michael Redgrave, Alexis Kanner, Kay Walsh, Gabrielle Drake, Olga Georges-Picot, Leo Genn, Richard Wyler, Brian Wilde, John Woodnutt, Tony Hughes.

Lo Scopone Scientifico (The Scientific Card-player) A C.I.C. Production. Produced by Dino de Laurentiis. Directed by Luigi Comencini. Screenplay by Rodolfo Sonego. Art direction by Luigi Scaccianoce. Photographed in wide screen and Eastman color by Guiseppi Ruzzolini. Music by Piero Piccioni. Opened Roma Theatre, Rome, Italy, October 16, 1972. 113 minutes.

Cast: Alberto Sordi, Silvana Mangano, Joseph Cotten, Bette Davis, Domenico Modugno, Mario Carotenuto.

Bunny O'Hare An American International Pictures release. Executive producers, James H. Nicholson and Samuel Z. Arkoff. Produced and directed by Gerd Oswald. Co-producer, Norman T. Herman. Screenplay by Stanley Z. Cherry and Coslough Johnson, based on the story 'Bunny and Billy' by Stanley Z. Cherry. Photographed in wide screen and Movielab color by Loyal Griggs and John Stephens. Edited by Fred Feitshans, Jr. Shot on location near Albuquerque, N.M.

465

Previewed at Picwood Theatre, Los Angeles, June 24, 1971. Opened at neighborhood theaters, N.Y., October 18, 1971. 91 minutes.

Cast: Bette Davis, Ernest Borgnine, Jack Cassidy, Joan Delaney, Jay Robinson, John Astin, Reva Rose.

Burnt Offerings A PEA Films, Inc., production. Released by United Artists. Produced and directed by Dan Curtis. Screenplay by William F. Nolan and Dan Curtis. Based on the novel by Robert Marasco. Photographed in DeLuxe Color by Jacques Marquette and Stevan Lamer. Music by Robert Cobert. Edited by Dennis Verkler. Released 1976. 116 minutes.

Cast: Oliver Reed, Karen Black, Burgess Meredith, Bette Davis, Eileen Heckart, Lee Montgomery, Dub Taylor, Anthony James, Orin Cannon, James T. Myers, Todd Turquand, Joseph Riley.

Return from Witch Mountain A Walt Disney Production, released by Buena Vista Distributing Co. Produced by Ron Miller and Jerome Courtland. Directed by John Hough. Screenplay by Malcolm Marmorstein, based on characters created by Alexander Key. Photographed in Technicolor by Frank Phillips. Music by Lalo Schifrin. Edited by Bob Bring. Released 1978. 93 minutes.

Cast: Bette Davis, Christopher Lee, Ike Eisenmann, Kim Richards, Jack Soo, Anthony James, Dick Bakalyan, Ward Costello, Christian Juttner, Poindexter, Brad Savage, Jeffrey Jacquet.

Death on the Nile A John Brabourne — Richard Goodwin Production. Released by Paramount Pictures. Produced by John Brabourne and Richard Goodwin. Directed by John Guillermin. Screenplay by Anthony Shaffer. Based on the mystery by Agatha Christie. Photographed by Jack Cardiff in Camera Color. Music by Nino Rota. Edited by Malcolm Cooke. Released 1978. 140 minutes.

Cast: Peter Ustinov, Jane Birkin, Lois Chiles, Mia Farrow, Bette Davis, Maggie Smith, Jon Finch, Olivia Hussey, George Kennedy, Angela Lansbury, Simon MacCorkindale, David Niven, Jack Warden, Harry Andrews, I. S. Johar.

The Watcher in the Woods A Buena Vista Distribution Release of a Walt Disney Production. Produced by Ron Miller. Directed by John Hough. Screenplay by Brian Clemens, Harry Spalding, and Rosemary Ann Sisson. Based on the novel by Florence Engel Randall. Photographed in Technicolor by Alan Hume. Music composed and conducted by Stanley Myers. Edited by Geoffrey Foot. Released 1980. 100 minutes.

Cast: Bette Davis, Carroll Baker, David McCallum, Lynn-Holly Johnson, Kyle Richards, Ian Bannen, Richard Pasco, Frances Cuka, Benedict Taylor, Eleanor Summerfield, Georgina Hale, Katherine Levy.

The Whales of August An Alive Films Release of a Nelson Entertainment Film. Produced by Carolyn Pfeiffer and Mike Kaplan. Associate producer, Shep Gordon. Directed by Lindsay Anderson. Screenplay by David Berry, based on his play. Photographed in color by Mike Fash. Music by Alan Price. Art direction, K. C. Fox and Bob Fox. Production design by Jocelyn Herbert. Edited by Nicolas Gaster. Released 1987. 90 minutes.

Cast: Lillian Gish, Bette Davis, Vincent Price, Ann Sothern, Harry Carey, Jr., Frank Grimes, Frank Pitkin, Mike Bush, Margaret Ladd, Tisha Sterling, Mary Steenburgen.

Wicked Stepmother A Largo Production of a Larry Cohen Film for MGM. Executive producer, Larry Cohen. Produced by Robert Littman. Written for the screen and directed by Larry Cohen. Photographed by Bryan England. Music by Robert Folk. Edited by David Kern. Shot in 1988. Released as MGM VHS tape. 92 minutes.

Cast: Bette Davis, Colleen Camp, Lionel Stander, Barbara Carrera, David Rasche, Shawn Donahue, Tom Bosley, Richard Moll, Seymour Cassel, Evelyn Keyes, Laurene Landon.

Television Feature Films

Madame Sin An ITC Production. Executive producer, Robert Wagner. Produced by Julian Wintle and Lou Morheim. Directed by David Greene. Teleplay by David Greene and Barry Oringer. Created by Lou Morheim and Barry Oringer. Photographed by Tony Richmond. Art direction by Brian Eatwell. Music by Michael Gibbs. Edited by Peter Tanner. Pilot film for a proposed television series. Released as a feature in Europe, May 12, 1972. Released in U.S. as an 'ABC Movie of the Week,' January 15, 1972.

Cast: Bette Davis, Robert Wagner, Denholm Elliott, Gordon Jackson, Dudley Sutton, Catherine Schell, Paul Maxwell, Pik-sen Lin, David Healy, Alan Dobie, Roy Kinnear, Al Mancini, Frank Middlemass, Burt Kwouk.

The Judge and Jake Wyler Universal Television. Produced by Richard Levinson and William Link. Directed by David Lowell Rich. Teleplay by David Shaw, Richard Levinson, and William Link. Costumes by Burton Miller. Art direction by Alexander A. Mayer. Photographed by William Margulies. Edited by Budd Small. Music by Gil Melle. Shot as pilot film for proposed television series, with extra footage added for television feature length. Originally

469

written for male lead. Released as an 'NBC Movie of the Week,' December 2, 1972.

Cast: Bette Davis, Doug McClure, Eric Braeden, Joan Van Ark, Gary Conway, Lou Jacobi, James McEachin, Lisabeth Hush, Kent Smith, Barbara Rhoades, John Randolph, Milt Kamen, John Lupton, Rosanna Huffman, Eddie Quillan, Virginia Capers.

Scream, Pretty Peggy Universal Television. Produced by Lou Morheim. Directed by Gordon Hessler. Teleplay by Jimmy Sangster and Arthur Hoffe. Photographed by Leonard J. South. Art direction by Joseph M. Alves, Jr. Costumes by Burton Miller. Music by Robert Prince. Edited by Larry Strong. Released as an 'NBC Movie of the Week,' November 22, 1973.

Cast: Bette Davis, Ted Bessell, Sian Barbara Allen, Charles Drake, Allan Arbus, Tovah Feldshuh, Johnnie Collins III, Jessica Rains, Christiane Schmidtmer.

The Disappearance of Aimee Tomorrow Entertainment, Inc. Executive producer, Thomas W. Moore. Produced by Paul Leaf. Directed by Anthony Harvey. Teleplay by John McGreevey. Photographed by James Crabe. Art direction by Charles Rosen. Costume supervisor, Edith Head. Edited by Jerry Greenberg and Arline Garson. Released 1976.

Cast: Faye Dunaway, Bette Davis, James Sloyan, James Woods, John Lehne, Lelia Goldoni, Severn Darden, William Jordan, Sandy Ward, Barry Brown, Irby Smith.

The Dark Secret of Harvest Home Universal Television. Produced by Jack Laird. Directed by Leo Penn. Teleplay by Jack Guss and Charles E. Israel. Adapted by James M. Miller and Jennifer Miller from the novel *Harvest Home* by Thomas Tryon. Photographed by Charles Correll, Frank Phillips, and Jim Dickson. Art direction by Phil Barber. Music by Paul Chihara. Edited by Robert Watts and Robert F. Shugrue. Released as a five-hour mini-series, 1978.

Cast: Bette Davis, David Ackroyd, Rosanna Arquette, René Auberjonois, John Calvin, Norman Lloyd, Linda Marsh, Michael O'Keefe, Laurie Prange, Lina Raymond, Tracy Gold, Michael Durrell, and the voice of Donald Pleasence.

Strangers: The Story of a Mother and Daughter Chris-Rose Productions. Produced by Robert W. Christiansen and Rick Rosenberg. Directed by Milton Katselas. Teleplay by Michael DeGuzman. Photographed by James Crabe. Art direction by Spencer Deverill. Music by Fred Karlin. Edited by Millie Moore. 1979.

Cast: Bette Davis, Gena Rowlands, Ford Rainey, Donald Moffat, Whit Bissell, Royal Dano, Kate Riehl, Krishan Timberlake, Renee McDonell, Sally Kemp. (Bette Davis won an Emmy for best actress in a drama.)

White Mama Tomorrow Entertainment, Inc. Executive producer, Thomas W. Moore. Produced by Jean Moore Edwards. Directed by Jackie Cooper. Teleplay by Robert C. S. Downs.

Photographed by William K. Jurgensen. Art direction by Ned Parsons. Music by Peter Matz. Edited by Jerry Dronsky. 1980.

Cast: Bette Davis, Ernest Harden, Jr., Eileen Heckart, Virginia Capers, Anne Ramsey, Lurene Tuttle, Peg Shirley, Ernie Hudson, Dan Mason, Vincent Schiavelli, Cheryl Harvey, John Hancock, Eddie Quillan. (Bette Davis was nominated for an Emmy for best actress in a drama.)

Skyward Major H/Anson Productions. Executive producers, Ron Howard and Anson Williams. Produced by John A. Kuri. Directed by Ron Howard. Teleplay by Nancy Sackett, from a story by Anson Williams. Photographed by Robert Jessup. Aerial photography by John A. Kuri. Art direction by Jack Morley. Music by Lee Holdridge. Edited by Robert Kern, Jr. 1980.

Cast: Bette Davis, Howard Hesseman, Marion Ross, Clu Gulager, Ben Marley, Lisa Whelchel, Suzy Gilstrap, Jana Hall, Mark Wheeler, Jessie Lee Fulton, Rance Howard, Clint Howard, Cheryl Howard, Kate Finlayson.

Family Reunion Columbia Pictures Television. Produced by Lucy Jarvis. Directed by Fielder Cook. Teleplay by Allan Sloane. Based on a story by Allan Sloane and Joe Spartan from an article 'How America Lives' in *Ladies' Home Journal* by Joe Spartan. Production designer, Robert Gundlach. Music by Wladimir Selinsky. Edited by Eric Albertson. Four-hour mini-series, 1981.

Cast: Bette Davis, J. Ashley Hyman, David Huddleston, John Shea, Roy Dotrice, David

Rounds, Kathryn Walker, Roberts Blossom, Roberta Wallach, Jeff McCracken, Ann Lange, Beth Ehlers, Paul Rudd, Paul Hecht, Charles Brown.

A Piano for Mrs. Cimino A Roger Gimbel Production for EMI Television. Executive producers, Roger Gimble and Tony Converse. Produced by George Schaefer and Christopher N. Seitz. Directed by George Schaefer. Teleplay by John Gay, based on the book by Robert Oliphant. Photographed by Edward R. Brown. Art direction by Graeme Murray and Fred Price. Music by James Horner. Edited by Rita Roland. 1982.

Cast: Bette Davis, Keenan Wynn, Penny Fuller, Alexa Kenin, George Hearn, Christopher Guest, Graham Jarvis, Paul Roebling, LeRoy Schulz, Walter Marsh.

Little Gloria . . . Happy at Last Scherick Associates/London Film Productions. Executive producers, Edgar J. Scherick and Scott Rudin. Produced by David Nicksay and Justine Héroux. Directed by Waris Hussein. Teleplay by William Hanley, based on the book by Barbara Goldsmith. Photographed by Tony Imi. Production designer, Stuart Wurtzel. Music by Berthold Carrière. Edited by Malcom Cooke. 1982.

Cast: Martin Balsam, Bette Davis, Michael Gross, Lucy Gutteridge, John Hillerman, Barnard Hughes, Glynis Johns, Angela Lansbury, Rosalyn Landor, Joseph Maher, Christopher

Plummer, Maureen Stapleton, Leueen Willoughby, Jennifer Dundas. (Bette Davis was nominated for an Emmy Award for outstanding supporting actress in a drama.)

Right of Way Schaefer-Karpf Productions. Executive producer, Merrill H. Karpf. Produced by George Schaefer and Philip Parslow. Directed by George Schaefer. Teleplay by Richard Lees from his 1978 play produced at the Guthrie Theatre in Minneapolis. Photographed by Howard R. Schwartz. Production designer, John E. Chilberg II. Music by Brad Fiedel. Edited by Sidney M. Katz. Released as an HBO TV movie in 1983. Released to general TV in 1984.

Cast: Bette Davis, James Stewart, Melinda Dillon, Priscilla Morrill, John Harkins, Louis Schaefer, Jacque Lynn Colton, Charles Murphy, Edith Fields.

Agatha Christie's 'Murder with Mirrors' Hajeno Productions for Warner Brothers Television. Executive producer, George Eckstein. Produced by Neil Hartley. Directed by Dick Lowry. Teleplay by George Eckstein, based on Agatha Christie's novel. Photographed by Brian West. Art direction by Leigh Malone. Music by Richard Rodney Bennett. Edited by Richard Bracken. 1985.

Cast: Helen Hayes, Bette Davis, John Mills, Leo McKern, Liane Langland, John Laughlin, Dorothy Tutin, Anton Rodgers, Frances de la Tour, John Woodvine, James Coombes.

As Summers Die Chris/Rose Productions and Baldwin/Aldrich Productions. Executive producers, Frank Konigsberg and Larry Sanitsky. Produced by Robert W. Christiansen and Rick Rosenberg. Co-producers, Peter Baldwin and Richard Aldrich. Directed by Jean-Claude Tramont. Teleplay by Jeff Andrus and Ed Namzug, based on the novel by Winston Groom. Photography by Ernest Day. Art direction by Gene Randolph. Music by Michel Legrand. Edited by Michael Brown. 1986.

Cast: Scott Glenn, Jamie Lee Curtis, Bette Davis, John Randolph, Ron O'Neal, Beah Richards, Richard Venture, Paul Roebling, Penny Fuller, Bruce McGill, C. C. H. Pounder, John McIntire, Tammy Baldwin, Nadia Gray Brown.

We do hope that you have enjoyed reading this large print book.

Did you know that all of our titles are available for purchase?

We publish a wide range of high quality large print books including:
Romances, Mysteries, Classics
General Fiction
Non Fiction and Westerns

Special interest titles available in large print are:
The Little Oxford Dictionary
Music Book
Song Book
Hymn Book
Service Book

Also available from us courtesy of Oxford University Press:
Young Readers' Dictionary
(large print edition)
Young Readers' Thesaurus
(large print edition)

For further information or a free brochure, please contact us at:
Ulverscroft Large Print Books Ltd.,
The Green, Bradgate Road, Anstey,
Leicester, LE7 7FU, England.
Tel: (00 44) 0116 236 4325
Fax: (00 44) 0116 234 0205

Other titles published by
The House of Ulverscroft:

IT'S ONLY A MOVIE: ALFRED HITCHCOCK, A PERSONAL BIOGRAPHY

Charlotte Chandler

Alfred Hitchcock expressed his fantasies through films which became classics, such as *The 39 Steps*, *The Lady Vanishes*, *Rebecca*, *To Catch A Thief*, *North by Northwest*, *Psycho*, and *The Birds*. In *It's Only A Movie*, Charlotte Chandler shares the revealing insights she gained in her conversations with Hitchcock. He left Britain for America in 1939 and his cameo appearances in his films made him universally recognizable. But the more public his image became, the more private the man became. Chandler has interviewed many of the stars who appeared in his films, among them Cary Grant, Ingrid Bergman, James Stewart, Sir Laurence Olivier, Sir Michael Redgrave, Sir John Gielgud, James Mason, Grace Kelly and Anthony Perkins. *It's Only A Movie* is an affectionate look at the life of the master of suspense.

OUR BETTY

Liz Smith

Liz Smith is a familiar face to TV viewers.
Perhaps best recognized for her portrayal of
Nana in *The Royle Family*, she has appeared
in many TV series, including *The Vicar of
Dibley*, and films such as *Charlie and the
Chocolate Factory*. Our Betty is Liz's life
story, from her lonely childhood in
Scunthorpe with her beloved grandparents,
to her marriage and children; through divorce
and poverty, and working in dead-end jobs
for years. She was working at Hamleys toy
store when she received the phone call that
would change her life: director Mike Leigh
wanted her for an improvised film called
Bleak Moments. At fifty years old, Liz's
career had taken off . . .

NO ROOM FOR SECRETS

Joanna Lumley

Joanna Lumley uses the unique structure of a tour through her beloved home to tell you about her life: in the hall we learn about her childhood in India and the Far East; in the study her boarding school years in England; in the drawing room her passion for travel and love of books; in the kitchen we hear about her modelling career in the sixties and her opinions on dieting; in the bathroom her beauty regime (or lack of); in the attic her feelings about her life now. Personal letters and photographs inspire other memories, about the people she has met, the plays, films and TV series she has worked on, the experiences that have had most impact on her and the many places she has travelled to and called home.

THE BOOK WHAT I WROTE

Eddie Braben

This is the hilarious memoir of Britain's best-loved comedy writer, whose scripts for Morecambe and Wise catapulted the incomparable duo to stardom. Eddie has written his story — with all the timeless humour, warmth and affection for Eric and Ernie that made their classic sketches so hugely popular. It is as much a unique biography of the charismatic Eric and Ernie as it is the story of the man on whose jokes their success was made.

WHAT'S IT ALL ABOUT?

Cilla Black

Cilla Black is one of Britain's most treasured personalities. Generations have grown up with her music, TV shows and performances. Born Priscilla Maria Veronica White in Liverpool's heavily bombed, down-trodden Scotland Road in 1943, Cilla grew up as a tomboy in a staunchly Catholic household. But by the time she was twenty — caught up in the incredible youth explosion of the Sixties — she was a key player on the up-and-coming Mersey scene, managed by Brian Epstein, friends with the Beatles, and having hit after smash hit. Cilla has worked ceaselessly to stay at the top for forty years despite setbacks and personal tragedy. In this deeply personal autobiography she tells her unique story for the very first time.

VICTIM — THE SECRET TAPES OF MARILYN MONROE

Matthew Smith

Marilyn Monroe's death in August 1962, apparently a suicide, shocked the world. With fame, fortune, powerful friends and lovers, and the world at her feet, why would she have killed herself? Looking back at thousands of documents, some of them never published before, Matthew Smith argues strongly for a startling new version of events. His argument is based not only on these documents and on the complete forensic evidence, but also on the secret, confidential tapes Marilyn made for her psychiatrist in the weeks leading up to her death — tapes that portray a woman in charge of her life and looking forward to a busy, bright future. Here, from the transcripts of these tapes, are the most private thoughts of Marilyn Monroe.